READING
IN THE
SECONDARY
SCHOOL
CLASSROOM

READING IN THE SECONDARY SCHOOL CLASSROOM

Robert C. Aukerman

Professor of Education
University of Rhode Island

McGraw-Hill Book Company

New York   Kuala Lumpur   Panama
St. Louis   London   Rio de Janeiro
San Francisco   Mexico   Singapore
Düsseldorf   Montreal   Sydney
Johannesburg   New Delhi   Toronto

To our three sons: Robert, a university professor
                     Bill, a teacher and athlete
                     Jim, a state legislator

whose classroom experiences in secondary school
prompted me to undertake the writing of this book.

**Reading in the
Secondary School Classroom**

Library of Congress Catalog Card Number   78-37088

07-002483-9

2 3 4 5 6 7 8 9 0 K P K P 7 9 8 7 6 5 4 3 2

CONTENTS

PREFACE

This book is unique, as it has been written with the help of many secondary school teachers, principals, reading consultants, and students. Those who shared ideas for this book did so in the hope that their experiences might be helpful to others.

This project in reading was originated by Richard H. Goodman, presently Superintendent of Schools in Wellesley, Massachusetts. In the fall of 1965, Dr. Goodman, then Executive Secretary of the New England School Development Council (NESDEC), proposed that his organization convene a group of New England secondary school teachers, principals, and reading consultants for the purpose of formulating some guidelines that would help upgrade reading practices in secondary schools. Invitations were extended to school systems holding membership in NESDEC; from their nominations, fifteen teachers and fifteen principals were selected as the nucleus (later their number was increased to seventeen). The principals' group provided a separate dimension to the thinking of the teachers and supplied an administrative framework, which is reflected especially in Chapter 15.

Throughout 1966 and 1967, the teachers held periodic meetings in subject-matter groups and as a committee of the whole. Between meetings, dialogue among teachers was continued by correspondence.

This book, consequently, is the result of many hours of brainstorming, sharing of know-how, and intensive work sessions. Like the sessions themselves, what is presented here is not thought of as the "final word." On the contrary, the material given here is the distillation of practical classroom strategies which have proved worthwhile and which have distinguished the committee members as outstanding teachers in the secondary schools of New England. It is to be expected that in the future new and even better practices will be devised, and that they will be incorporated in future editions of this book.

Indicating what this book does *not* attempt to do may clarify what we are hoping to share with you. First: this is *not* a book on "remedial reading." Second: it is *not* a book on "how to teach reading." Third: it is *not* intended to make you a "reading specialist." Rather, the main objective of this book is the improvement of learning in the content areas. The book was designed for prospective teachers of content area subjects; it is a set of guidelines for teachers who are already working in secondary school subject-matter classrooms, and for students in teacher-training institutions who intend to become teachers of academic subjects in secondary schools.

The questions at the end of each chapter include exercises which provide practical projects for college students in professional methods courses. Most of the activities suggested may be done by the student on his own, with minimal direction from the professor. Many of the suggested activities are also successful as projects for in-service training sessions with secondary school content teachers.

Chapters 1 through 6 and 13 through 17 contain material that applies to all academic subjects in the secondary school: approaching reading as the common factor in classroom learning; teaching the survey technique; reading for main ideas; formulating reading assignments; assessing reading ability; determining the readability of textbooks; helping the college-bound student; helping the poorer student; utilizing the total resources of the school; and forming a professional bookshelf.

Chapters 7 through 12 are specific guidelines for each of the academic areas of instruction: social studies; English; sciences; mathematics; business, industrial arts, vocational education; and home economics. Those chapters provide the most comprehensive treatment in existence today of reading as the core of instruction in those content areas.

Inasmuch as most learning in junior and senior high schools is through the use of textbooks, reading is the common denominator of secondary school learning. Teachers should never feel that "textbook learning" per se is bad; and criticism of textbook learning has been directed not at the textbooks but at those teachers who have been merely assignment givers. This book is written, therefore, to help all who would aspire to teach more effectively in the secondary school content areas and who will be working with young people whose reading abilities range over a wide spectrum.

The following New England secondary school teachers and reading specialists have contributed countless hours working as members of the committee of the whole and on special subject-matter committees: Lillian Bailey, Hanover, New Hampshire; Charlotte Barrett, Warwick, Rhode Island; Fred Burnaby, Marblehead, Massachusetts; Richard Conley, Concord, Massachusetts; Charles Drake, Waltham, Massachusetts; Edith Dressel, Longmeadow, Massachusetts; Mary Ennis, Bloomfield, Connecticut; Tom Green, Masconomet, Massachusetts; Bernice Haigh, Plymouth-Carver Regional, Massachusetts; Edwin Leach, Cohasset, Massachusetts; Richmond Leach, Lexington, Massachusetts; Lee Blaney, Wayland, Massachusetts; Doryce Moosey, Worcester, Massachusetts; John Murray, Stoughton, Massachusetts; Dr. Olive Niles, Springfield, Massachusetts; Beverly Pearson, Branford, Connecticut; Mary Tormey, Needham, Massachusetts; and Frank Vara, Brattleboro, Vermont.

New England secondary school principals who responded to the invitation of the New England School Development Council to work on this project were: Erold Beach, Marblehead, Massachusetts; Benjamin Bernstein, Worcester, Massachusetts; Edgar Craver, Longmeadow, Massachusetts; Robert Diamond, Concord, Massachusetts; Julian Demeo, Plymouth-Carver Regional, Massachusetts; William Gallagher, Waltham, Massachusetts; Frank Guiliano, Cohasset, Massachusetts; Ernest Hatfield, Branford, Connecticut; Elson Herrick, Hanover, New Hampshire; Charles Johnson, Lexington, Massachusetts; Dan Pendergast, Warwick, Rhode Island; Wayne Porter, Bloomfield, Connecticut; John Shay, Springfield, Massachusetts; Corridon Trask, Masconomet Regional, Massachusetts; Harry Walen, Needham, Massachusetts; and Thomas Whalen, Stoughton, Massachusetts.

To the many classroom teachers and department chairmen who offered suggestions for making these guidelines practical and useful, NESDEC and the author express their appreciation.

As this book goes to press, its implementation throughout the schools of New England passes to the hands of Robert Ireland, Executive Secretary of the New England School Development Council. With his direction and with the help of the reading supervisors and principals who worked together on this project, local and regional conferences and workshops will be held in all six states of the Northeast. It is hoped that similar workshops and conferences will be generated in the other regions of America.

It is also anticipated that students of professional education in our colleges and universities will use this book as a textual guide to the teaching of secondary school social studies, English, mathematics, sciences, industrial arts, vocational education, business, diversified occupations, and home economics, where reading is the preponderant medium of learning.

Robert C. Aukerman

1. READING— THE COMMON DENOMINATOR OF LEARNING IN SECONDARY SCHOOL

Academic learning has for ages been dependent upon the learner's ability to cope with ideas and concepts transmitted through the medium of the printed page. For a long time after the invention of symbols as meaningful graphic representations of people, things, places, actions, and events, and the subsequent invention of alphabets to represent spoken sounds, the acquisition of academic knowledge has been reserved for those few who were permitted to unlock the code. These scribes and scholars were held in awe and, consequently, possessed power over the uneducated masses.

Today, all nations striving for full participation by all citizens in the democratic processes recognize the place of academic learning. Although lectures and oratory may be momentarily instructional or inspiring, it is through the written thoughts of mankind that skills, facts, beliefs, attitudes, concepts, and aspirations are transmitted from one generation to the next and from one island of culture to its neighbors.

The written poem, play, or short story remains long after any spoken version is over. History is provided by the written and printed daily record of man's achievements and failures. And mankind's accumulation of scientific and technical know-how is preserved by the written formula, computor program, or recipe, which then forms the basis for further research and discovery.

Although a great deal of learning can be achieved quickly through use of video media, the printed page still remains the prime means of input, storage, and retrieval of knowledge and culture.

The secondary school, subject-centered as it is, relies largely on the printed page for daily work in its academic classrooms. Lectures, demonstrations, discussions, and learning by doing are, of course, part of a good secondary school curriculum. The textbook, however, is the major source of information, the homework medium, and the base of academic operations. Indeed—and unfortunately—in many classrooms the secondary school textbook is the beginning and the end of learning.

Inasmuch as the secondary school textbook is and should be the prime medium of learning, attention must be paid to the fact that learning is dependent upon the learner's ability to read the textbook. There is absolutely no way to avoid the fact that *reading is the common denominator of academic learning in the secondary school classroom.*

THE "SPIRAL CONCEPT" OF READING

There would be no point to this book if it were true that all reading skills are learned in the elementary grades. In fact, of course, many students reach high school without having learned to read well. Moreover, there is a growing body of evidence that certain reading skills should be deferred until secondary school, and that certain others should be extended and strengthened in secondary school.

The development of reading skills is viewed as a spiral continuum, extending from the primary levels of the elementary school upward through the senior year of the secondary school. In this spiral, reading skills that are appropriate to the abilities and needs of the learner at each level serve as a foundation for learning advanced skills at the next level.

As the learner enters the junior high school, the demands of subject matter impose upon him the necessity of applying reading and study skills he has already mastered, of sharpening other reading skills which he has not previously used, and of learning new reading techniques appropriate to the nature of the various academic subjects. This kind of development calls for the attention of classroom subject-matter teachers who are willing to make a commitment to the "spiral concept" of reading. Such a commitment implies that the subject-matter teacher must be able to identify those most specific reading skills appropriate for his subject, and second, determine the abilities of the learners in his class. How able are the students to handle the subject-matter reading load?—which is to say, Where are they on the spiral continuum?

The "spiral concept" of reading may be new in the sense that it has only recently been discussed; but the need for some such concept has always existed. Despite this, it is generally conceded that the great majority of secondary school teachers have been little concerned with the reading skills of their students. This is not a condemnation of the teachers, but rather a condemnation of the training they have received. Colleges of education have been reluctant to require additional "methods" courses, and professors in the prospective teachers' major academic disciplines usually give no attention whatever to professional education training. As a result, the teacher of English, or social studies, or any other subject in the secondary school, frequently knows a great deal about the subject but very little about how the student should be helped to learn it. Recently, however, concern for the improvement of learning in the content areas has led to an active interest in reading and study skills in the secondary school. There is now an increased awareness that reading skills increase in difficulty—just as do, say, mathematics skills—and that many learners are not ready to be taught the higher critical reading skills before high school.

An understanding of the spiral concept of reading entails discarding the idea that all reading skills are taught in the elementary school, and emphasizing, instead, the idea that learning in the secondary school will be improved by attention to the reading techniques appropriate to each subject area.

The Primary Reading Program

In the first three grades of the elementary school, the reading skills program attempts to launch the beginning reader on a lifetime of successful reading. It is usually contended that success in reading is best encouraged by "instant" reading—by reading whole words rather than by learning the sounds of letters and long lists of isolated syllable sounds. Most basal readers in the primary grades, accordingly, provide what is known as the "whole-word" approach to reading. The immediate objective is to provide enough repetition of simple words so that the child will acquire a sight vocabulary sufficient to allow him to read many simple stories. At the same time that this sight vocabulary is being learned, the teacher holds sessions with the class, during which he calls special attention to certain elements of words. This is called the "development of word-recognition skills." Certain phonemic elements are stressed, and drill is provided to reinforce the learning of phonemic generalizations. A few rules of pronunciation and spelling are learned, and groups of words having common phonemic elements are studied.

Another approach to word recognition is through the contextual meaning in the phrase or sentence. Children are encouraged to make an educated guess what a word probably is. Shapes of words are sometimes used as clues to recognition. This "word analysis" approach also includes the study of roots, prefixes, suffixes, compound words, and cognates. Vocabulary development includes the acquisition of synonyms, opposites, and colorful or descriptive alternatives.

In controlled basal reader series, sentence structure becomes progressively more complicated, especially between the third grade and fourth grade. At the same time, words of three or more syllables are introduced, together with practice in syllabication.

The Intermediate Reading Program

It is in the intermediate grades that the primary reading skills are applied and expanded in content-area materials. Interpretation of subtle and abstract meanings and feelings calls for intellectual skills of a higher order. Figurative and picturesque language require more analysis of meaning than does simple, concrete language. Similarly, poetry presents greater problems of interpretation than do simple rhyme and rhythm.

All through those years, the child is given practice in such reading and study skills as locating information, outlining, and making and using a bibliography and a table of contents, etc. Considerable time is also spent on analysis of literary forms, authors' styles, and appreciation.

It might appear that everything has been accomplished during those first six years, and that the child should come to the secondary school with a complete repertoire of reading and study skills. Some of the more able children do, indeed, acquire such a battery of skills. The great majority of children, however, enter the secondary school just about ready to have those skills cultivated; and there are a number of slow learners who have not yet acquired sufficient reading skills to meet secondary school requirements.

READING IN SECONDARY SCHOOL

Applying Reading Skills in Secondary School Subjects

Students with wide ranges of abilities are grouped either homogeneously or heterogeneously in secondary school classrooms. There are many easy and simple reading strategies that can be used by the subject-matter teacher to help the student who has trouble with academic learning.

In a continuous-progress curriculum, it would be expected that phonics skills, techniques of word analysis, and other basic reading skills would be reviewed from time to time throughout the intermediate grades, and even in the junior high school, as the need appears. As the skills become part of the day-to-day work of classroom learning, less reteaching is necessary.

The secondary school classroom teacher may find it expedient to reteach a certain skill occasionally. In this book, each chapter on a specific subject area contains some suggestions which will be helpful in applying the spiral concept of reteaching.

Individual Differences in Reading Ability

Any discussion of secondary school learning must take into account the individual differences of the learners. Naturally, there are countless factors accounting for individual differences; but this book focuses on one factor specifically: reading. This is one of the variables that the classroom teacher can do something about.

Past experiences, home background, intelligence, vitality, self-image, and numerous other matters also should be the concern of the secondary school, but it is the student's reading ability which ultimately may be the key to his success or failure in school. Individual differences in reading ability are to be found in combination with all the other variables; low reading ability may be present even in students who score high on such factors as intelligence and background.

It is essential that the subject-matter teacher be aware of specific individual differences in reading abilities in order to work effectively with a secondary school class.

As we learn more and more about the vast range of individual differences found in secondary school populations, it becomes obvious that in any subject, in any grade, there will probably be students scattered along the entire continuum of reading abilities. One of the purposes of this book is to help the teacher of a content subject determine the range of abilities within his class. A second purpose is to give some practical suggestions about materials and techniques that can be used to help the learners in their reading tasks.

Reading scores are most often recorded on permanent records as "grade-level" scores. For example, a score of 6.4 means a performance on a reading test equal to that of the average child in the sixth grade, fourth month (December). Similarly, a score of 4.1 would indicate a performance equal to the performance of the average child beginning the fourth (September).

"Grade-level" scores are useful, but they have a disadvantage: they encourage teachers and administrators to think that all learners in a given grade should be "at grade level." We know, however, that this cannot be the case. Even in a homogeneously grouped class it is probably impossible for all students to be exactly at grade level. Some would doubtless be average ("at grade level"), some above average, and some below average. Grade-level-equivalent scores do, nevertheless, perform the valuable function of showing how far below or above average are the reading abilities of the individuals in a class. It is essential that subject-matter teachers have this information.

The range of individual differences in a secondary school varies greatly from community to community. Some schools report secondary school students with first-grade reading ability and, in the same grade, students with reading abilities beyond the twelfth-grade level. Some schools find it difficult to locate many students "at grade level," and others report that the majority of their students score above average. Knowing exactly what levels of reading ability are present in any classroom provides the classroom teacher with a foundation upon which to build.

The Readability of Textbook Materials

Some textbooks and supplementary materials are easy to read; some are difficult. An "average" textbook should be just right for an "average" class, but experience in the classroom will convince us that this is not necessarily so. One reason is that the average classroom includes students with a wide range of reading abilities. Another reason is that a textbook may have been designated "average" only by a salesman or an editor.

Most secondary school textbooks are written by teachers or professors who know nothing about reading ability or readability. The readability of such textbooks (we use the term "readability" to mean "level of difficulty") is seldom controlled by authors or editors; rarely is it even known to them. In fact, some authors and editors would have no idea how to measure the readability of a textbook. This leaves the control of difficulty largely up to chance—or, occasionally, to the good judgment of a secondary school teacher who may be an author or coauthor.

Because readability of textbooks is such an important factor in many students' success or failure in comprehending the material, one of the purposes of this book is to help the classroom teacher to determine the reading difficulty of the materials available in a particular subject area.

Reading-Study Techniques

It has been pointed out that not all students beginning secondary school are equipped with reading abilities adequate to handle the "average" textbook. There are techniques which can be used to help students with varying abilities in studying textual materials, and it should not be assumed that such techniques have been learned in the elementary grades. Some such techniques may have been learned, of course; but other techniques may be new to the students because they are actually learning skills appropriate to secondary school subject matter and are therefore now being used for the first time.

Giving assignments without providing training in the appropriate reading-study skills will produce frustration in many students. This often occurs, in fact; but it need not. In this book specific means of providing the learner with reading-study skills are suggested; the aim of these is to improve the learning of each individual significantly.

Using the Total Resources of the School

This book is based on the idea that no teacher should try to work entirely on his own. The total resources of the school exist for one purpose: to improve the learning of each individual student. Each classroom teacher is entitled to help from the ancillary services of the school—the guidance department, the reading specialist, and the coordinator of learning materials; the department head, the principal, and the psychologist. The more use the teacher makes of the resources available, the easier and more effective will his teaching be.

The Role of the Classroom Teacher

A number of years ago someone proposed the idea that "every teacher is a teacher of reading." The phrase has been repeated so often that many secondary school classroom teachers are justifiably concerned, or even rather frightened. But the idea has perhaps been misunderstood: what was said and what was meant are not precisely the same. The intent of the statement may be more clear if one starts with the notion that every academic classroom teacher is dealing with materials that must be read. It follows, then, that every teacher is a teacher of reading materials, and since every academic classroom teacher is working with students who must be able to read the materials assigned, every teacher is a teacher of students who are reading.

Now, this does imply that every secondary school teacher must teach students how to read if they cannot already do so. But to expect that of classroom teachers is to expect the impossible: the task of the classroom teacher is not to be a teacher of remedial reading but, rather, to plan a program through which all students will work most productively with reading materials.

What it boils down to is this: *Reading is the common denominator of learning in the secondary school classroom.*

Questions and Activities for Discussion and Growth

1. Take a tape recorder to a lecture and tape the entire presentation. At the same time, take notes in your usual style. Estimate the percentage of the lecture which escaped you while you were writing the notes. Check your estimate by replaying your tape.
2. Make a survey of a secondary school to determine to what extent textbooks are used as the major medium of instruction. Are most assignments made in textbooks? Are most tests based upon materials in the texts?
3. What is meant by the statement, "Reading is the common denominator of academic learning in the secondary school classroom"?

4. Check into the scope and sequence of subject matter in one academic area. What evidences can be found to illustrate the "spiral concept" in subject material?
5. Ask several secondary school content teachers if they teach reading in their classrooms. Note their answers. Do they seem to have some attitude in common?
6. What are the basic reading skills that the average student acquires in the elementary school?
7. List the "uncontrolled variables" that may account for individual differences in secondary school students.
8. List the three factors which probably are most closely related to academic achievement or academic failure.
9. What is the fallacy in speaking about "grade-level" scores and stating that the reading ability of all learners should be "at grade level"?
10. Defend or refute the statement, "Every teacher is a teacher of reading."

Selected References

Artley, A. Sterl: "A Study of the Relationships Existing Between Reading Comprehension in a Specific Subject-Matter Area," unpublished doctoral dissertation, The Pennsylvania State College, College Park, Pennsylvania, 1942.

Aukerman, Robert C.: "Differences in the Reading Status of Good and Poor Eleventh Grade Students," *Journal of Educational Research,* vol. 41, no. 7 (March, 1948), pp. 498–515.

Bond, Eve: "Reading and Ninth Grade Achievement," *Contributions to Education,* no. 756, Teachers College, Columbia University, 1938.

Hill, Walter: "Content Textbook: Help or Hindrance?" *Journal of Reading,* vol. X, no. 6 (March, 1967), pp. 408–413.

Michaels, Melvin: "Subject Reading Improvement: A Neglected Teacher Responsibility," *Journal of Reading,* vol. IX, no. 1 (September, 1965), pp. 16–20.

Olson, Arthur V.: "Attitude of High School Content Area Teachers Toward the Teaching of Reading," *Seventeenth Yearbook,* National Reading Conference, 1968, pp. 162–166.

Penty, Ruth C.: *Reading Ability and High School Dropouts,* Bureau of Publications, Teachers College, Columbia University, New York, 1956. (One of the first books to describe the relationship between reading failure and dropping out of high school.)

2. READING ABILITY

Among the many variable factors determining academic achievement in the secondary school, two that must be considered simultaneously are intelligence and reading ability. Measures of these two factors of ability are very valuable to the secondary school content teacher, and they require only a small amount of time to obtain.

UTILIZATION OF INTELLIGENCE QUOTIENTS

Raw scores on intelligence tests are translated into intelligence quotients (IQs), and it is IQs which are recorded. Unfortunately, IQs have been subject to gross misinterpretation and have been maligned as "unreliable," "racist," and "meaningless." It would be much more constructive to recognize, first, that IQs are not absolute or perfect measures of native intelligence (indeed, our way of measuring intelligence is quite primitive); but, second, that IQs are extremely useful *relative* measures when properly interpreted. Are not *all* measures of human performance relative? Sports records, for example, are relative: an athlete's performance is related to performances by other athletes. One person's performance on an intelligence test should, similarly, be related to the performance of others who take the same test.

The first step in the utilization of IQs, then, is to convert them into relative measures—*percentiles*—which indicate where each individual stands in relation to all others in his group. Since IQs are estimates, the percentiles derived from them are also approximations. But percentile approximations are good enough for our purposes. Such a loose attitude may outrage the specialist in measurements and statistics, but our concern here is to provide the busy classroom teacher with a workable, efficient method for understanding the abilities of a class of thirty young people.

The table of approximations below provides a base to work from. The following procedure is recommended: First, list the names of the students in each class in alphabetical order. Second, from the permanent records in the office, transcribe their IQs. Third, using the conversion table, place the corresponding percentile opposite each IQ.

Percentile rankings provide the only valid means of comparing individuals with each other and with established norms. They provide the only usable figures for developing a profile of abilities, and the only support for a teacher's expectations concerning an individual or group. (In the few schools that have been pressured into abolishing intelligence testing, there may be some other relative measure of general ability that will have to suffice.)

The second step in the utilization of IQs is to compare them with performance on tests of reading ability.

CONVERSION TABLE: IQs INTO PERCENTILES

IQ (approximate)	Percentile (approximate)	
130+	97th–99th	
125	95th	
120	90th	(Upper 10%)
115	80th	
110	75th	(Upper quartile)
105	60th	
100	50th	(Midpoint)
95	40th	
90	25th	(Lower quartile)
85	20th	
80	10th	(Lowest 10%)
75	6th	
70	3d	

DETERMINING READING ABILITY

The Relationship Between Reading Ability and Achievement

Over the past years, research studies by Eldon Bond,[1] Eva Bond,[2] Artley,[3] Shores,[4] Treacy,[5] Swenson,[6] Aukerman,[7] and others indicate that there is a distinct relationship between reading ability and academic achievement in secondary school content areas. There is also, of course, every reason to believe that intelligence, being a factor in general ability, is a factor in reading ability. Moreover, most group intelligence tests are largely reading tests. The existence of these interrelationships causes considerable problems for anyone who tries to factor out reading ability from intelligence tests, or intelligence from reading performance. For the secondary school content teacher, however, this is essentially an academic question. In the day-to-day operation of the classroom, both factors are operating, and the teacher must be able to deal with them easily. The teacher needs to find the reading ability of each student.

Reading Tests

It is seldom necessary for the secondary school classroom teacher to undertake a testing program in reading. It is very helpful, however, for each teacher to have some basic knowledge of the three types of reading tests so that the information given on permanent records may be interpreted adequately. The three types are (1) informal reading inventories, (2) diagnostic reading tests, and (3) reading achievement tests.

The informal reading inventory. An *informal reading inventory* (generally referred to as an IRI) is a quick way of placing an individual in a reading group. Although used most extensively in the elementary grades, it has a place in any secondary school located in an area where there is a rapid turnover of

[1] Eldon A. Bond, "Tenth Grade Abilities and Achievements," *Contributions to Education*, no. 813, Teachers College, Columbia University, New York, 1940.

[2] Eva Bond, "Reading and Ninth Grade Achievement," *Contributions to Education*, no. 756, Teachers College, Columbia University, New York, 1938.

[3] A. Sterl Artley, "A Study of Certain Relationships Existing Between General Reading Comprehension and Reading Comprehension in a Specific Subject-matter Area," unpublished Ph.D. dissertation, Pennsylvania State College, 1942.

[4] James Harlan Shores, "Skills Related to the Ability to Read History and Science," *Journal of Educational Research*, vol. XXXVI, (April, 1943), pp. 584–593.

[5] J. P. Treacy, "Relationship of Reading Skills to the Ability to Solve Arithmetic Problems," *Journal of Educational Research*, vol. XXXVIII (October, 1944) pp. 86–96.

[6] Esther J. Swenson, "A Study of the Relationships Among Various Types of Reading Scores on General and Science Materials," *Journal of Educational Research*, vol. XXXVI (October, 1942), pp. 81–90.

[7] Robert C. Aukerman, "Differences in the Reading Status of Good and Poor Eleventh Grade Students," *Journal of Educational Research*, vol. XLI (March, 1948), pp. 498–515.

students. Proximity to a military installation, port, or center of seasonal activity where migrant workers come and go usually produces conditions where students arrive with few or no permanent records. In such a situation, the classroom teacher needs a means for placing a new student quickly. The IRI provides a four- to six-minute estimate of reading ability.

The IRI is individually administered. It is usually a "general" estimate of reading ability; in addition, it has some of the features of a diagnostic test. The purpose for which the classroom teacher would use the IRI makes it unnecessary for him to bother with all the diagnostic qualities a reading specialist would attend to.

The classroom teacher may want to refer a new student with no record of reading ability to the reading specialist for a quick informal reading inventory.

Diagnostic reading tests. The *diagnostic* reading test is an instrument that should be administered only by a reading specialist. It provides the specialist with a complete profile of an individual's reading habits, abilities, and disabilities. It is an individually administered test that takes a considerable amount of time both to administer and to interpret. It is used by the reading specialist for remediation of specific reading handicaps; for referral of an individual who exhibits other disabilities contributing to academic failure or personal maladjustment; or for both purposes.

Reading achievement tests. All *reading achievement tests* have three things in common: they test vocabulary and comprehension; they provide grade-level scores; and they are administered to an entire group at one time.

Some reading achievement tests are "general" in content, whereas others are "specific" for social studies, literature, science, etc. Specific tests, however, are seldom used; and, unless it is definitely indicated otherwise, all reading scores on permanent records will have been obtained on a test of "general" reading ability.

The vocabulary section of a reading achievement test is merely a small sampling, seldom consisting of more than 100 words, usually presented in the order of increasing difficulty.

Comprehension is often tested with sentences and short paragraphs of increasing difficulty. Each sentence and paragraph is followed by questions of fact, inference, or cause and effect.

There are currently available a score of general and specific reading tests at the secondary school level. Some are on the brink of obsolescence; for others, content has been revised and up-to-date national norms have been developed. They are listed here for convenience, as it is likely that grade

equivalents in reading appearing on a student's permanent records will have
been obtained from his performance on one of them:

American School Reading Tests
   Willis E. Pratt and Stanley W. Lore
   Bobbs-Merrill

Burnett Reading Series: Survey Test
   Richard W. Burnett
   Scholastic Testing Service
   1967—Grades 7–9 (Advanced)
   1968—Grades 10–12 (Senior)

California Reading Test
   Tiegs and Clark
   California Test Bureau
   Grades 7–9 and 9–12

California Survey Series (part of the longer California Achievement Tests)
   Survey of Reading Achievement
   Grades 7–9 and 9–12, 1963 norms.

Canadian English Achievement Test, Part 1: Reading Comprehension
   Dept. Ed. Res., Ontario College of Education, U. of Toronto
   Grades 8–9

Reading Comprehension: Cooperative English Tests
   Clarence Derrick, David Harris, & Biron Walker
   Co-op Test Division, 1960
   Grades 9–12 and 13–14

Davis Reading Test
   Frederick B. Davis and Charlotte Croon
   Psych Corp., 1962
   Grades 8–11

Gates-MacGinitie Reading Test
   Arthur I. Gates and Walter H. MacGinitie
   Teachers College Press, 1965
   Grades 7–9

High School Reading Test: National Achievement Tests
   Robert K. Speer and Samuel Smith
   Psychometric Affiliates, 1952
   Grades 7–12

Iowa Silent Reading Tests
   H. A. Greene, A. N. Jorgensen, and V. H. Kelley.
   Harcourt Brace Jovanovich, 1943
   Grades 9–14   (Advanced)

Kelley-Greene Reading Comprehension Test
   V. H. Kelley and H. A. Greene
   Harcourt Brace Jovanovich, 1955
   Grades 9–13

Metropolitan Achievement Tests: Reading
   Walter N. Durost, Harold H. Bixler, Gertrude H. Hildreth,
   Kenneth W. Lund and J. Wayne Wrightstone
   Harcourt Brace Jovanovich, Inc., 1962
   Grades 7–9

Nelson-Denny Reading Test: Vocabulary-Comprehension-Rate
   M. J. Nelson, E. C. Denny, and James I. Brown
   Houghton Mifflin, 1960
   Grades 9–16

SRA Reading Record
   Guy T. Buswell
   Science Research Associates, 1959
   Grades 6–12

Sequential Tests of Educational Progress (STEP)
   Cooperative Test Division
   Level 3: Grades 7–9; Level 2: Grades 10–12; Level 1: Grades 13–14

Stanford Achievement Test
   Truman L. Kelley,   Richard Madden,
   Eric F. Gardner, & Herbert C. Rudman
   Harcourt Brace Jovanovich, 1966
   Grades 9–12, also Grades 7–9

Tests of Academic Progress
   Henry P. Smith
   Houghton Mifflin, 1964–1965
   Grades 9, 10, 11, 12

Traxler High School Reading Test, Grades 10–12 (1967)
Traxler Silent Reading Test, Grades 7–10 (1942)
   Arthur E. Traxler
   Bobbs-Merrill

Tests of Natural Sciences: Vocabulary and Interpretation of Reading Materials
(also Social Studies)
   Co-Op Inter-American Tests
   American Council on Education
   Guidance Testing Associates, 1950
   Grades 8–13

VanWagenen Analytical Reading Scales
   VanWagenen Psychoeducational Labs., 1954
   Grades 7–9, 10–11, 9–11

Interpretation of Reading Test Scores

Grade-level equivalents derived from performance on reading achievement tests are often recorded in years and months. Thus, a rating of 9.4 means that the student's performance was equal to that of the average student in the fourth month (December) of the ninth grade. Although it is common practice to report in such detail in elementary schools, there is little or no point in doing so in the secondary school. A grade-placement score is quite sufficient for comparative purposes.

All comparisons of reading test scores are relative, and, as with IQs, a comparison of a grade-level score with any other score must wait until the score is translated into a percentile. This is done by referring to the examiner's manual that accompanies a reading test: it should contain a table for converting scores into percentiles. The percentile rating indicates where a student stands in comparison to all who take the test. If his score on a reading test places him in the 15th percentile, this means that 85 percent of those in his grade did better than he did. It also means that he is 70 percent below the *average* student in his grade on that test; that he is near the bottom of his group; and that he is a retarded reader.

It is the responsibility of the reading consultant to provide the classroom teacher with a test manual for converting grade-level designations into percentiles. An example of a conversion table for tenth-grade reading scores is shown below.

The data sheet on page 16 is provided as an example. The IQs and scores shown for Nelson-Denny Reading Test are all arbitrarily contrived for illustrative purposes. The percentile rankings are derived from the conversion tables.

A Class Profile of Reading Abilities and Intelligence

The data sheet provides the information necessary for constructing a profile of the reading abilities and intelligence rankings of a class. The comparison of those two variables is possible only because both measures have been converted into percentiles.

The accompanying graph was derived by plotting the percentile data from the table, and shows the relative position of each member of the class.

CONVERSION TABLE: RAW SCORES
IN READING INTO PERCENTILES*

Raw Score (Approximate)	Percentile (Approximate)
135 +	96th–99th
120	90th
112	85th
108	80th
105	75th
100	70th
93	60th
85	50th
80	40th
70	25th
65	20th
52	10th
45	6th
37	3rd

*M. J. Nelson and E. C. Denny, *The Nelson-Denny Reading Test*, Houghton Mifflin Company, Boston.

DATA SHEET FOR THE NELSON-DENNY
READING TEST

Pupil	Sex	Intelligence		Reading	
		IQ	Percentile	Score	Percentile
1	M	99	49	85	50
2	M	101	51	90	55
3	M	99	49	83	45
4	F	101	52	80	40
5	M	89	24	52	10
6	F	118	88	112	85
7	M	105	60	94	62
8	F	95	40	77	35
9	F	128	96	108	80
10	M	120	90	104	74
11	M	90	25	50	8
12	M	97	44	80	40
13	F	124	94	130	97
14	M	131	98	141	99
15	F	99	49	90	55
16	F	86	21	35	2
17	F	102	54	93	61
18	M	88	23	65	20
19	M	102	57	98	65
20	M	81	12	30	1
21	F	96	42	83	45
22	M	98	47	86	49
23	M	103	56	92	60
24	F	118	87	107	79
25	F	100	50	82	44

It is immediately obvious that there are three distinct divisions of ability: those whose scores fall into the upper righthand quadrant are highly intelligent and have a correspondingly high reading ability; those in the lower lefthand quadrant are low in both measures; and those clustering near the intersection of the two axes are average on both measures.

Whether or not reading tests are also partial measures of intelligence is irrelevant. Similarly, the charge that some intelligence tests are highly verbal measures is of little consequence. What is important is that the percentile rankings of any student on both intelligence and reading ability make it possible to approximate his position relative to the rest of the class and to established national norms. Approximations are more than adequate for the purpose of determining a student's relative position.

The factors that caused students 5, 11, 16, 18, and 20 to be at the bottom of the heap cannot be identified from these data, of course; the fact staring

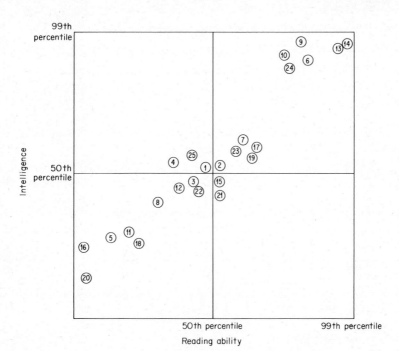

Scattergram showing class profile when percentile data on reading ability and intelligence are plotted.

us in the face is their relative position. In the academic classrooms, where reading is the common denominator of learning, they are likely to be non-achievers.

CONCLUSION

A graphic profile of a class provides the teacher with invaluable information:

1. It indicates the need for specific groupings within the class.
2. It can identify an individual who has intellectual potential but lacks corresponding reading ability. Such a student should be referred for special help in reading.
3. It identifies individuals who are low on both measures and who cannot successfully handle the usual textbook reading assignment.
4. It identifies students who are gifted in both intelligence and reading ability and whose retention in an average class structure would be a waste of human resources.
5. It contains visual data that the supervisor or principal may use in regrouping classes within a subject-matter area.

The determination of reading ability and its relationship to the intellectual potential of each student is the most important prerequisite for improving instruction and learning in the academic classroom.

Questions and Activities for Discussion and Growth

1. Your principal mentions that one of your students has an IQ of 90 and states that this "is only 10 percent below average." How would you refute this idea?

2. You have been asked to work on a project that proposes to take all the students who are "below grade level" in reading and "bring them up to grade level" by means of special reading instruction. What is your reaction?

3. You are on a committee, one member of which insists that "intelligence tests should be thrown out because they are culture-centered and do not relate to minority groups." What case can you develop for keeping intelligence tests?

4. With the help of a specialist in testing or a school counsellor, obtain a nonverbal intelligence test and compare its content with that of the usual general intelligence test.

5. Prepare a case for the use of nonverbal intelligence tests as measures for comparison with reading ability.

6. Suppose a student has a grade-level-equivalent reading score of 9.3. Under what conditions would that represent "average" ability?

7. Under what conditions would the grade-level-equivalent score of 9.3 indicate that the student is an underachiever?

8. Under what conditions would a grade-level-equivalent score of 4.5 indicate that a tenth-grade student is *not* a suitable candidate for remedial reading?

9. List IQs and reading scores for one secondary school class. Use the table for converting IQs into percentiles and the table (from the specific reading test) for converting reading scores into percentiles. Use the data for graphing a profile of the class. What groupings would you recommend?

10. Use the data obtained in question 9 to develop some behavioral objectives for one class in a secondary school content area. Would the data indicate the same behavioral objectives for all content areas?

Selected References

Buros, Oscar K. (ed.): *Reading Tests and Reviews,* The Gryphon Press, Highland Park, N.J., 1968. (This is, essentially, a regrouping of the data and reviews of reading tests, scattered through previous editions of the *Mental Measurements Yearbooks,* that have distinguished Buros. It is, consequently, the most valuable reference of its kind in existence.)

Pescosolido, John, and Charles Gervase: *Reading Expectancy and Readability,* Kendall/Hunt Publishing Co., Dubuque, Iowa, 1971. (An excellent handbook which gives a simplified treatment of several reading-expectancy formulas and an easily understood presentation of the major readability formulas—Dale-Chall, Spache, etc.)

Strang, Ruth: *The Diagnostic Teaching of Reading,* McGraw-Hill Book Company, New York, 1964.

Traxler, Arthur E.: "Standardized Tests—What They Are, How They Are Used—and Misused," *NEA Journal,* vol. 48 (November, 1959), pp. 18–20.

3. ASSESSING THE READABILITY OF TEXTBOOKS

In Chapter 2, we discussed intelligence and reading ability as significant factors in academic achievement. The difficulty of secondary school textbook reading materials is an equally important factor.

"Readability" is the term used to cover the various aspects of written materials which together determine the reading *difficulty* of a printed page. "Readability" equals "difficulty" (with the result that books which are very difficult to read are described as being of "high readability," and books which are easy to read are described as being of "low readability").

Some textbooks are easy to read; some are difficult. Those at the extremes of simplicity and difficulty are probably easy to identify, but others are not. For many years, teachers have been wishing for some method of measuring the difficulty of a textbook—a method more accurate than the "educated guess." Secondary school teachers are well aware of the problem of "readability" of textbooks, but few know how to measure readability.

THE DEVELOPMENT OF MEASURES OF READABILITY

Interest in measuring the difficulty of written materials dates back many centuries. There was a time when the degree of complexity of writing was thought to be the measure of its quality; the more complex, the higher the quality. Anyone who examines some of the philosophic writings in German will discover the extremes to which complexity can be carried. Sentences containing a dozen or more subordinate and sub-subordinate clauses and running more than a page in length were common in the literature of nineteenth-century German philosophy. We should be thankful that such writing is out of fashion today; but although present-day communication has been streamlined, many textbooks continue to be written in a style that is difficult for many high school students. To cope with this situation, researchers have devised measures of difficulty and have set those measures up in formulas known as "readability formulas." In the past fifty years, more than fifty readability formulas have been developed. Clearly, the originators of these formulas must have had differing views of what constitutes readability. Moreover, some authors have committed themselves to the development of all-inclusive, complex formulas; others have provided very simple measures of selected factors of readability. Some readability formulas are applicable to books at the elementary school level, while others apply more specifically to secondary school texts. Some are very specific: for example, those that have been developed for periodical articles and for foreign language materials.

FACTORS IN READABILITY

A "readability formula" may be defined as *an objective method of measuring several components of writing which, when considered in relationship to each other, result in a quantitative estimate of the reading difficulty of the sample.*

The several components may be:

Length of sentences
Types of sentences—simple, compound, complex
Complexity of sentences
  Subordinate clauses
  Order of clauses—direct or inverted
  Extent of use of modifiers
Vocabulary
  Simple or complicated (or unfamiliar)
  Obsolete (archaic)
  Colloquial
  Scientific, technical, specific
  Allusive (e.g., to mythology)

Ambiguous (containing double meanings)
Related to past or contemporary events
Polysyllabic
Abstractions, abstract concepts
Sophisticated usage of parts of speech: verbals (gerunds), participles, infinitives

Length of Sentences

A few long sentences interspersed with shorter sentences may not cause difficulty for the average junior or senior high school reader. But a textbook that persists in confronting the reader with a succession of long sentences has a built-in factor of reading difficulty affecting a large number of students. Several researchers have found that as many as 50 percent of the high school students they examined cannot read the textbooks in their classes. In a large number of cases, this is due to the length of sentences in those texts.

Psychologists provide an explanation for this. Reading a long sentence calls for the input of a number of concepts in sequence. Many individuals have not developed a visual memory adequate to arrange several concepts into an organized whole and hold them so. In fact, some people cannot even separate the several individual concepts which an author may present in one long sentence.

The solution to this would be to find a textbook written in short sentences, each containing only one or two concepts.

Types and Complexity of Sentences

Simple sentences, per se, cause little if any difficulty. A compound sentence consisting of two simple sentences joined by a conjunction usually is no more difficult for the average reader than if it were two sentences separated by a period. But for the below-average learner, compound sentences do introduce an element of difficulty—that is, the necessity of holding two related concepts in mind. The individual with a low IQ, a learning disability involving sequencing and memory, or both, will find compound sentences a major problem.

Teachers dealing with students who have such problems should attempt to find reading materials for them that have a minimum of compound sentences.

The complex sentence is the culprit. Although it is not meant to cause difficulty, it does increase the demands upon the reader to a point where it becomes a very important element of difficulty.

The purpose of a complex sentence is to place concepts and subconcepts in their proper relationship to each other. The individual with an average or above-average IQ will probably have little if any difficulty in seeing the organizational pattern and the structure of thought presented in most complex sentences. But again, the individual with a low IQ, learning disabilities, or both, will probably be completely lost. (This is to be expected, since there is a close correlation between ability to see relationships and total intellectual performance.) As a consequence, textbooks which consist of sentences with subordinate clauses should be considered highly complex and rated as having a level of readability that is above average for high school students, even if none of the other factors of readability are measured. It should also be noted that sentences technically classified as "simple" or "compound" may contain elements, such as inverted order or numerous modifiers, which make them too difficult for many students. This kind of complexity is also to be avoided when a text of low readability is sought.

Vocabulary

The number of words in a textbook may be so great that it alone poses a formidable problem to poorer students. To hand a poor reader a history text weighing 2 pounds and containing 700 or more pages is simply to encourage failure and dropping out. A student who finds it difficult to manage one page of a history text is psychologically defeated by the prospect of 700 pages. But small quantities of success can be achieved if assignments are made in a book with fewer pages and fewer words. And this kind of day-to-day success in a smaller book encourages the student and improves his self-image. Success— not failure—is the goal of good secondary schools; and subject-matter teachers help reach this goal by selecting texts of low vocabulary load for their poorer readers.

The number of words is, of course, only a gross measure of the vocabulary load. It is the other characteristics of vocabulary which actually constitute the contribution of vocabulary to reading difficulty.

Complicated or unfamiliar vocabulary. Unfamiliar words are "reader stoppers." Even though a word may be known to a student as part of his spoken vocabulary, it will raise the level of readability if it is a new word to him in print. Some authors embellish their writing with seldom-used words, a practice which may be natural for an author but is discouraging to a high school reader. Such a disparity between author and reader often results when the author is a college professor with little or no knowledge of the vocabulary ability of secondary school students. A number of readability formulas include a count of unknown and unfamiliar words.

Obsolete vocabulary. Obsolete and archaic words also fall into this category. They are unknown to most high school students today and unless explained can ruin comprehension. Moreover, although with an explanation they may enhance comprehension for above-average and gifted students, at the same time they are an added annoyance to the below-average student. If the obsolete and archaic are the essence of a selection, the choice of that selection should be reserved only for those students who can handle them successfully. There is naturally always a generation gap between the authors of secondary school textbooks and their young readers. Words familiar to an author when he was in high school may be quite obsolete to the young people of today. (A few examples that come to mind are *tin Lizzie, nosegay, spyglass, speakeasy, hooch,* and *arctics.*)

Colloquial vocabulary. Colloquialisms and dialect present the same inherent difficulties, although they may be accepted more readily. The speech of certain geographic areas has been made well known through radio and television, but it is quite another matter when confronted on the printed page. For example, the poor reader who has not adequately learned to use phonetic analysis of new words will have extreme difficulty with the dialect found in Mark Twain's writings.

One way to reduce the difficulty caused by dialect or colloquial speech is for the teacher or some well-prepared student to read some of the material aloud. This will provide the "set" necessary for the silent reading that will follow. The entire selection need not be read aloud—only enough to indicate the nature of the speech patterns and to express enjoyment in reading them. This is time well spent in warmup for reading.

Scientific, technical, and specific vocabulary. Every subject-matter area in the secondary school employs certain words to convey meanings specific to it. These words may be terms used exclusively with scientific and technical meanings, or they may be general words given specific meanings in context.

A few examples will illustrate this point. In social studies, the word *plunder* is used in several ways: to *plunder* a village in war; to *plunder* our natural resources; to *plunder* the public treasury. In each case, the connotation is the same: *nothing is left. Plunder* is a general word used almost exclusively in social studies, and only occasionally in literature.

In science, the word *hydrogen* is a specific technical word which must be learned with its scientific definition. If it should appear in a social studies text or in a literary selection, it will carry the same precise meaning as in science. *Hydrogen* is part of a large scientific vocabulary that constitutes part of the readability load of science texts.

It is not so much the use of specific, scientific, and technical words that increases difficulty, but how those words are introduced and defined. Some writers are sensitive to the difficulty such words create, and they provide immediate parenthetical definitions in context. For example, from a text in business: "There were quite a few 'hedge funds' (speculative funds usually operated in behalf of a group of wealthy partners and not available to the public)." There would be no point in expecting a student to look up *hedge funds* in a dictionary, so the term is defined at once. One difficulty with such a definition, however, is that the explanation itself may be complicated by the presence of further difficult terms. The example given has at least two difficult words: *speculative* and *behalf*. Here is another example, from a selection on health education: "The foundation on which any exercise program should be built is aerobic ('with oxygen') exercises."

Another way of providing a definition is to include a straightforward explanation as part of the text, thus: "Some children suffer from *otitis media*, an infection in the middle ear that can cause fluid to build up, causing deafness or illness."

From a description of bullfighting in Spain: "Many men have died in what the Spanish call *la fiesta brava*, the 'festival of courage'."

Unfortunately, not many secondary school textbook writers are aware of the need for contextual definitions. As a result, scientific, technical, and specific vocabulary greatly complicate the materials in which they appear and raise their readability level beyond the ability of a large percentage of students.

Allusive, ambiguous, and referential vocabulary. Literature is full of allusions to mythology and the classics, to famous people and events, to legends, and to other elements of our cultural heritage. The secondary school reader constantly confronted with words which have no immediate, current meaning is subject to frustration and failure.

Psychologists use the term "readiness" to indicate a state of mind which is a necessary preliminary for learning. One factor in readiness is past experience. The student who has had little or no experience with the gods and godesses of ancient Greece and Rome, the mythological heroes of the Norsemen, the plays of Shakespeare, or the slogans of past political campaigns will have no readiness at all for allusions like "the sword of Damocles," "the muses," "terpsichorean activities," and "gerrymandering."

Reading involving vocabulary with hidden meanings needs some preliminary work by the teacher. The teacher will give his class assurance by recognizing that certain words will cause trouble and by providing carefully worded mimeographed explanations of their meanings when he assigns the passages where they appear. Help of this sort is appreciated by even those students in the upper-level groups and classes. It reinforces the concept that the teacher is interested in their success.

One word of caution, however: Vocabulary which can be figured out from the context should not be explained beforehand, since the students should be required to apply their skill in extracting meaning from contextual clues wherever possible. It is only in situations like those described above that help must be given.

Polysyllabic vocabulary. How often polysyllabic words are used is the greatest single factor in determining level of readability. Consequently, most measures of readability include a count of words of more than two syllables and weight this factor within the readability formula. Words of three, four, five, and more syllables are classified as "difficult" chiefly because understanding them depends upon the reader's skill in structural analysis, and structural analysis depends upon the ability to syllabicate—a skill which poor readers seldom have learned.

Syllabication is taught to beginning readers as a part of the process of "hearing" the vowel sounds in a word. The general rule is: "How many vowel sounds do you hear? Therefore, how many syllables does the word have?" If the student has not learned this skill before he enters secondary school, he will have trouble with polysyllabic words. The more polysyllabic words there are in the text, the higher is its level of readability.

Abstract Concepts

Most readability formulas do not include a measure of abstraction. This is unfortunate, for there is a direct relationship between abstraction and diffi-culty of comprehension. Moreover, individuals with a low IQ should deal mainly with concrete concepts; abstract concepts are best handled by students with high IQs.

Any measure of abstraction would be highly subjective, depending upon the background and experience of the individual who does the judging. To one individual, a word may be clear and concrete; to another, it may be highly allusive or abstract. Consider the following selection:

HUMANITARIANISM

In the early march of modern industry abuses have arisen. Children, women, have broken their health because they have been forced by need into work they ought not to have undertaken. Men have risked unnecessary hazards of accident, have chanced their health in miserable surroundings—martyrs to the progress of industry—to earn a living. Individually, employers were caught in the mesh of competition where they could not afford to ease the lot of their employees. The ruthlessness of a single factory or mine owner could hold back whatever voluntary improvements his competitors might wish to introduce. Only a rule equally applicable to all would work. And such rules could come only from government.

SOURCE: From AMERICAN GOVERNMENT IN TODAY'S WORLD, third edition, by Robert Rienow, copyright © 1966 by D. C. Heath and Company, Boston, Mass., pp. 471–472.

The preceding paragraph contains 114 words. The following words are judged to be abstract in the manner in which they are used:

march	chanced	improvements
industry	martyrs	surroundings
abuses	mesh	health
broken	ease	living
need	lot	competition
hazards	ruthlessness	

The incidence of abstraction amounts to 15 percent if one counts single words; but if the seventeen abstract concepts are compared with the total of fifty concepts in the paragraph, the incidence of abstraction is actually 34 percent.

Any secondary school reading material that is 34 percent abstract would probably be a total loss to more than half of the high school population. Even well-trained adult readers find material that is one-third abstract extremely difficult to follow.

The rule for designating a concept as "abstract" is to ask the question, "Is this a specific and definite thing or circumstance?" If one cannot answer questions such as "how much?" "what kind?" and "in what way?" it is a good indication that one is dealing with an abstract concept. In assessing the degree of abstraction of secondary school textual materials, the teacher should attempt to make the evaluation from the level of the students who will be reading the materials.

Sophisticated Syntax: Verbals (Gerunds), Participles, and Infinitives

Any grammatical element that introduces a departure from the direct simple sentence may be considered as contributing to increased reading difficulty. This is usually true of verbals (or gerunds), participles, and infinitives.

Verbals (gerunds) are verbs made into nouns by using "-ing" as a suffix. A common example is *Seeing is believing:*

see + ing
feel + ing
belief + ing = believing

Participles are adjectives which have become "partly" verbs. A participle qualifies a noun (like an adjective), yet it acts like a verb.

Infinitives used as the subject of a sentence cause some difficulty. For example: *To see is to believe.*

The teacher must use judgment in assessing the amount of difficulty such verbals contribute to a particular group of students. Ordinarily they occur so seldom that they are no problem. Certain writers, however, tend to use them

The Umbrella

GUY DE MAUPASSANT

Mme. Oreille was a very economical woman; she thoroughly knew the value of a half-penny, and possessed a whole store-house of strict principles with regard to the multiplication of money, so that her cook found the greatest difficulty in making what the servants call their "market-penny," while her husband was hardly allowed any pocket-money at all. They were, however, very comfortably off, and had no children. It really pained Mme. Oreille to see any money spent; it was like tearing at her heartstrings when she had to take any of those nice crown-pieces out of her pocket; and whenever she had to spend anything, no matter how necessary it was, she slept badly the next night.

Oreille was continually saying to his wife: "You really might be more liberal, as we have no children and never spend our income."

"You don't know what may happen," she used to reply. "It is better to have too much than too little."

She was a little woman of about forty, very active, rather hasty, wrinkled, very neat and tidy, and with a very short temper. Her husband very often used to complain of all the privations she made him endure; some of them were particularly painful to him, as they touched his vanity.

He was one of the upper clerks in the War Office, and only stayed there in obedience to his wife's wish, so as to increase their income, which they did not nearly spend.

For two years he had always come to the office with the same old patched umbrella, to the great amusement of his fellow-clerks. At last he got tired of their jokes, and insisted upon his wife buying him a new one. She bought one for eight francs and a half, one of those cheap things which large houses sell as an advertisement. When the others in the office saw the article, which was being sold in Paris by the thousand, they began their jokes again, and Oreille had a dreadful time of it with them. They even made a song about it, which he heard from morning till night all over the immense building.

Oreille was very angry, and peremptorily told his wife to get him a new one, a good silk one, for twenty francs, and to bring him the bill, so that he might see that it was all right.

She bought him one for eighteen francs, and said, getting red with anger as she gave it to her husband:

"This will last you for five years at least."

Oreille felt quite triumphant, and obtained a small ovation at the office with his new acquisition. . . .

SOURCE: From OURSELVES AND OTHERS, by Harold H. Wagenheim, Elizabeth Voris, and Matthew Dolkey. Holt, Rinehart and Winston, Inc., New York, © 1963. Reprinted by permission. (The underlining is added here for illustrative purposes.)

extensively. For that reason, subject-matter teachers should be alert to the incidence of verbals.

EXAMPLES OF PROBLEMS OF READABILITY

Fortunately, not all the factors creating difficulty are likely to be concentrated in any one selection of secondary school content reading. In fact, certain types of problems seem to be more prevalent than others. For example, the literary style of some writers of fiction creates a real handicap, as the accompanying excerpt from "The Umbrella," by Guy de Maupassant, shows. It illustrates the difficulty produced by long sentences, abstractions, and strange and obsolete terminology. The first sentence (underlined for reference here) consists of 58 words; its compound-complex structure consists of three independent clauses and two dependent clauses. This sentence could easily be made into a complete paragraph, thus:

> Mme. Oreille was a very economical woman. She thoroughly knew the value of a half-penny. She possessed a whole storehouse of strict principles with regard to the multiplication of money. Consequently, her cook found the greatest difficulty in making what the servants call their "market-penny." Her husband was hardly allowed any pocket money at all.

Even when restructured into smaller units, the sentence contains several difficult phrases: *storehouse of strict principles, multiplication of money,* and *market-penny.* There is little opportunity within the paragraph for the student to obtain the meaning of those terms from their context. Students reading such a passage should be encouraged to make educated guesses and verify them by an appeal to context.

In the second underlined sentence, which consists of 51 words, we have the phrase "tearing at her heartstrings"—a term likely to be strange to today's generation, with whom this type of figurative language has gone out of style. The context will supply some clues for students who have the ability to perceive relationships, but students who cannot cope with figures of speech like this will need to be told the meaning. As soon as they grasp the concept, they might be encouraged to translate it into contemporary idiom, for students are likely to feel more comfortable when the teacher accepts their expressions as valid vehicles for thought.

The third underlined sentence, although it consists of only 28 words, still must be considered a long sentence. It too contains unusual terms that present obstacles to the reader: *privations* and *touched his vanity.* The fourth underlined sentence, containing 38 words, includes an entirely strange word—*peremptorily*—which should be dealt with honestly. The teacher might present it in some such way as this: Having written it on the chalkboard, he could say to the class,

> "*Peremptorily* is a strange word that you will encounter in this short story. Look for it in the second paragraph in the righthand column. It has something to do with the man's being angry.
>
> "It is a good word; but we do not use it much now, for it is difficult to pronounce and is difficult to spell.
>
> "I am going to look it up in the dictionary for you. (At which point he would turn to a marked place in dictionary.) The definition reads: 'Positively, stubbornly, dictatorially.'
>
> "As you read that part of the story, decide which of those meanings fits best."

By doing this for the class before the selection is read, the teacher is dealing honestly with a strange word, providing a model for use of the dictionary and application of dictionary meanings, and giving his students the assurance that he does not expect them to look up such words on their own.

However, if the teacher is giving practice on dictionary skills, *peremptorily* might be a good exercise. The teacher should, in either case, introduce the word first, indicating that it is a strange but useful word, and why it is not used much today. The teacher might introduce directed dictionary practice thus:

> "When you look it up in the dictionary, you will find that its Latin derivation is not very helpful. You will find several definitions. As you read that part of the story, decide which of those meanings fits best."

When a new word is encountered and there is little or no clue to its meaning in the context, comprehension will be greatly improved if the word is discussed during the assignment of the reading selection. This holds true in any of the academic content areas. This simple, direct, and honest way of removing such roadblocks elicits a positive response from secondary school students.

Difficult reading materials are not confined to the literature of past centuries. The example on page 30, from a contemporary secondary school text in American literature, attests to this fact.

MEASURING READABILITY

It is unlikely that the ordinary secondary school classroom teacher will wish to undertake detailed assessments of the readability of textbooks. Such a project would involve the use of readability formulas, and none of these include all the contributors to difficulty. A more practical approach to the measurement of readability would be a *comparison* of texts with the objective of rating some as being of "high difficulty," or "high readability," some as

NONFICTION

Nonfiction prose—this indifferently named activity carries under its banner centuries of words, hardly more easily computed than the sum of the grains of sand on the earth. Great imaginative philosophies that have changed the world, minute records and large interpretations of man's existence in history: you would hardly want to call this merely "prose," but rather to designate each under its own title of philosophy or history. Original ideas, our deepest memories, our most inspired efforts to understand and to describe nature, to formulate discovery and principle—some would say that truth itself lies in the humble grave of "prose." It is no wonder that, in *Le Bourgeois Gentilhomme*, Molière's upstart gentleman made people laugh when he discovered he had been speaking prose all his life. In a way, prose is the mystery we all take for granted.

Sometimes prose writers feel the need to defend the imaginative and artistic roots of their work. "I am not a critic," declared Claude-Edmonde Magny, a French lady who wrote literary criticism, "I am a writer." By this she meant to stress the element of composition and inspiration, of literary achievement over and beyond the ability to present reasonable ideas. Prose communicates by way of language, nuance, tone; its persuasiveness may often be due more to the skillful ordering of these elements than to the strength of ideas. Yet it is hard to think of any important thinker who is a bad writer, although the great American philosopher John Dewey was sometimes nominated for the post. Curiosities, awkwardness of style, and even an alarming wordiness may justify themselves as the mark of certain notable minds in action.

The essay—that is, the short piece of prose—and the longer prose books by men of a literary imagination have been the special glory of English literature. Lamb and Ruskin, Macaulay and DeQuincey, Samuel Johnson and the American Ralph Waldo Emerson—the very names call to mind those grave sets, bound in red or brown leather, that stood with such unquestioning assurance on the shelves of homes that may otherwise have been quite modest. The contents made heavy demands on the reader. They asked his most careful attention to ideas and summoned him to follow argu-

NONFICTION   357

SOURCE: From ADVENTURES IN MODERN LITERATURE, by Robert Freier, Elizabeth Hardwick, Arnold Lazarus, and Robert Lowell, © 1970 by Harcourt Brace Jovanovich, Inc., and printed with their permission. P. 357.

"medium," and some as "low." The following method provides an educated guess that is quite adequate:

1. Select several representative 500-word samples from each text. If possible, choose samples from the same broad topics.
2. Count the number of actual words in each sample. Try to get them as close as possible.
3. Count the number of sentences in each sample.
4. For each sample, divide the number of words by the number of sentences, to obtain the average sentence length.
5. Tally the number of subordinate clauses in each sample.
6. For each sample, tally the number of words of three or more syllables.
7. For each sample, tally the number of words that are found on the list of "impedilexae" for that particular subject area.
8. For each sample, complete a "readability résumé," using the form given on page 42.
9. Compare the readability résumés of all the samples, designating each sample as being of "high," "medium," or "low" readability.

"Impedilexae" is a term coined to designate words that create reading problems in specific content areas—i.e., that impede reading.

IMPEDILEXAE IN SOCIAL STUDIES

The words on this list are only a sampling: the list does not include all the difficult vocabulary in social studies. It does, however, provide a common means for comparing the difficulty of various social studies texts as far as vocabulary is concerned.

All roots and derivatives of words listed here should also be counted as impedilexae.

abandoned	amendment	bourgeoisie	commercial
abolish	ancient	boycott	commodities
abolitionist	annexation		community
absolute	appeasement	**capitalism**	communication
abundance	achitecture	caravans	comparative
acceleration	aristocratic	carpetbaggers	compelled
achievements	armistice	centuries	compensation
adaptability	assassination	ceremonies	comprehensive
admission	assistance	characteristics	compromise
adventurous	assurances	chronological	concerned
administrative	authority	circumstances	concentration
adversaries	automation	civilian	concessions
agitation	autonomous	civilization	conquered
aggression		clash	conquests
agricultural	**barbarians**	classical	conservation
aliens	barriers	coexistence	conservative
allegiance	besieged	collective	consolidation
alliance	blockade	colonization	constitution
alluvial	boundaries	commerce	consumer

contemporary
continental
contrasted
contribution
corruption
crisis
crusade
cultivation
cultural
currency

decentralize
decisive
defeated
defending
deflation
democracy
denounced
density
dependencies
depreciation
depression
desperate
determined
dictatorship
diminishing
diplomacy
diplomatic
disarmament
discrimination
disputed
domesticated
dominate
dominions

economic
economically
elevation
emancipate
embargo
empire
enacted
endanger
engineering
enormous
enriched
enslaved
enterprise
entrepreneur
environmental
equilibrium

erosion
escarpment
established
evacuation
exchange
execution
existence
expedition
exploitation
exploration
extensive

federal
fertile
fertility
figurehead
finances
fiscal
flourished
founding
fractional
fragments
freedom
frontier
functional
fusion

genius
geographical
glacial
glaciation
global
grazing
guaranteed

hemisphere
humanitarian
humanity

ignorance
ill-fated
immediate
immigrants
inflation
impeached
imperialism
implements
impressed
inaugural
indemnity
indentured

independence
influences
inhabitants
initiative
injunction
irrigation
inscription
interdependent
interference
intermediate
investment
isolation
isthmus
internal
intolerable
insufficient
insurrection
invasion
investment

judicial
jurisdiction

latitude
legally
legislative
legislature
longitude

majority
manufacturing
manuscripts
marginal
martyr
massacre
meandering
menace
metropolitan
migratory
militarists
minority
mistress
monarchy
monetary
mongoloid
monotonous
mountainous
mutual

nationalism
natural
neutrality

nullify
numerous

obligation
obtained
occurring
offensive
opponents
oppression
overpopulation
overthrown

parliamentary
peasantry
peninsula
persecution
philanthropy
philosophers
pillaged
pioneer
plateau
plight
plunder
political
Polynesians
popularity
population
populous
possessions
postglacial
potential
poverty
powerful
precipitation
prevailed
preservation
principles
privileges
proclaim
proclamation
production
productivity
proprietary
proprietorship
prosperous
protection

rationing
rebellion
recession
recently

reconstruction	rural	struggle	thrived
recovery		subsistence	tillage
referendum	**scribes**	suburban	toleration
reform	secession	succession	topographical
regime	seclusion	suffrage	totalitarian
regional	secured	summoned	traditional
regulation	security	suppression	tributary
rehabilitation	sedition	surrender	tropical
reigned	segregated	superstitious	tyranny
repeal	selective		
republic	settlement	**tactics**	**unanimous**
representative	sharecroppers	technological	unconstitutional
requirements	solidarity	temperance	underdeveloped
resistance	speculation	temperate	unification
resources	sphere	temperature	urban
retaliation	splendor	tenements	
reverence	spoils	tension	**vegetation**
revival	status	territories	vocational
revolutionary	strategic	territorial	volcanic
rivalry	strengthened	threatened	voyage

IMPEDILEXAE IN ENGLISH

The words on this list are a sampling, and do not include all the difficult vocabulary in the field of English. But the list does provide a valid basis for comparison of the vocabulary loads of the various literary anthologies. All roots or derivatives of these words should also be counted as impedilexae.

abashed	antithesis	aversion	bravado
abated	apparition	avert	bridled
abeyance	apprehension	avocation	brigantine
abject	approbation		brusque
absurdly	aquisition	**baleful**	buoyant
acclimate	arbitrary	befoul	burgeon
accouterment	ardent	beguile	burgher
acquiescent	ardor	beholden	burnish
acumen	articulate	belligerent	
admonition	artifice	bemused	**cadaverous**
adventitious	askance	beneficent	caprice
adversely	assail	benevalent	carnage
aesthetic	assiduous	benign	carnivorous
affliction	assimilate	bereft	cataract
affront	assuage	beseech	celibacy
alacrity	asunder	bestial	chastened
altercation	atrocity	bittern	chateau
ambiguous	audacious	bizarre	chivalry
anathema	audience	blasphemy	chronicle
animated	austere	blatant	circumstantial
animosity	autocratic	boisterous	clemency
anonymity	avarice	brash	cloistered

colossal
comely
commendable
commensurate
commiserate
compassionate
complaisant
complementary
concede
condone
conflagration
congeniality
conjure
conservative
consignment
consummate
contemplation
contemptuous
contingent
contrary
contrive
converge
cordial
countenance
cranny
credulity
crux
culminate
curmudgeon
cynical
cynicism

dazedly
debonair
decadent
decorum
deduction
deference
defile
deft
deliberately
delineation
demagogue
demeanor
demented
demonic
demur
denizen
denunciation
deploy

deprecate
depredation
derisive
desecrate
despicable
despondent
despotism
destitute
detached
detest
dexterity
diabolical
diadem
diffidence
dilemma
dilettante
diminutive
direful
disconcerted
disconsolate
disenfranchise
disheveled
disquietude
dissipated
distended
distraught
docile
dogged
dotage
droll
dubious

eccentric
eccentricity
ecstatic
eddied
edifice
edifying
eerie
effete
effrontery
ejaculation
emaciated
embodiment
enmity
epitaph
equanimity
equestrian
erratic
erudite

eulogize
excruciating
exemplary
expedient
expeditious
extenuating
exuberant

façade
falsetto
fastidious
fatuously
ferret
festooned
filial
firmament
fledgling
fluently
fondle
foray
foreshadowing
founder
foundling
fraught
frivolous
frugality
furtive

gable
galvanized
gangling
gangrenous
garrulous
gendarmes
genteel
gingerly
girth
gloaming
gnarled
gradation
grapple
gravity
grimace
grizzled
groveling
gullibility

habiliment
haggard
harangue
heinous

horrible
hostages
humiliating
hypocrite

illusion
impalpable
impeccable
imperative
imperceptible
impervious
impious
importune
impotent
impropriety
improvise
impunity
inauspicious
incantation
incongruous
incorrigible
incredulity
indemnity
indentured
indigent
indigenous
indomitable
indulgence
indulgent
inequitable
inexplicably
infallibly
infamous
infernal
ingenious
inherent
inimitable
iniquity
innately
innocuous
inquisition
insatiate
inscrutable
insinuate
intangible
intercede
intermediary
intimidation
intrinsic
intuitive

inundation
inverterate
ironical
irretrievable
itinerant

jaundiced
jocular
jostled

knave
knighthood

labyrinth
laceration
laconic
lamentation
landlubber
languid
leering
lethargy
lenient
levity
lewd
lintel
listless
litigant
livid
loquacious
ludicrous
lugubrious
luminescent

magnanimity
magpies
malcontent
malevolent
malicious
meagre
mediocrity
meditative
mercenary
metaphysical
meticulous
mimicry
miniscule
miserable
molested
mortification
mourned
multitudinous

munificence
muttered

naiveté
nocturnal
noxious

obliquely
oblivious
obtuse
omen
ominous
omnipotent
omnipresence
onerous
oracle
ordination
orgy
ostensibly
ostentation
ostracized

palliate
pallid
panderer
paradox
paragon
parsimonious
patriarchal
patronage
peradventure
perambulation
peremptorily
perfidious
perfunctory
peripheral
perseverance
perspicacious
petulant
phlegmatic
phosphorescence
picturesque
piety
pinion
placidly
plague
poignant
portentous
precipice
precipitate
precocious

predestination
predominate
premature
premonition
preposterous
presentiment
presumptuous
pretension
prodigious
prodigy
profane
profligate
profuse
proletarian
prolific
promontory
promulgation
pronouncement
propensity
proselyte
provocative
proximity
prudence
pundit
purloin

quadruped
quaff
quagmire
quell
quietude

raiment
rancor
ravenous
realization
recalcitrant
reconnoiter
regime
reiteration
reminiscence
remonstrance
remuneration
renegade
replete
repugnant
requisite
resilience
resonance
respite
reticent

retinue
retracted
reverberation
reverie
rudiment
rue
ruefully

sacrilegious
sadistic
sagacity
salient
sallow
sardonic
sceptic
scrutiny
semblance
sensuous
simultaneous
solace
sordid
spasmodic
stealthy
stigma
stipulate
stoical
stultify
subjugate
sublime
suffice
sullen
supercilious
superfluous
supernumerary
supplication
surfeit
surplice
surreptitious
swaggered
swarthy

tableau
taut
taciturn
temperance
tenacious
terrestrial
thrashed
throes
timorous
topography

tractable	uncanny	variegated	vulnerable
transcendent	undulation	venerable	
translucent	unobtrusive	verbose	**waif**
travail	unorthodox	verdant	wherewithal
tremulous	unprecedented	vernal	wont
troubador	unpretentious	vestiges	
trudge	urgency	vicious	**yearling**
turpitude	utilitarian	vilify	yeoman
tutelage		visage	
	vagrant	voluptuous	
ubiquitous	valet	vortex	**zenith**

IMPEDILEXAE IN SCIENCE

The words on this list are only a sampling: they do not include all the difficult vocabulary in the sciences. To these common terms might be added the specific technical vocabulary of each of the sciences. The list as it stands does, however, provide a valid basis for comparison of the vocabulary load of the various textbooks in each science.

All roots and derivatives of words listed here should also be counted as impedilexae.

aberration	biodegradable	constant	**electrolysis**
absorb		constituents	electrolyte
abundance	**calorie**	contraction	electromagnet
acceleration	capacitor	convection	electron
acetate	capacity	converted	elements
agents	capillary	convex	emission
alkaline	carbonate	coolant	emit
alloy	catalyst	copper	emulsion
alluvial	centrifugal	crystallization	environmental
aluminum	centripetal	cylinder	essential
amplitude	characteristics	cylindrical	equation
anemometer	chromosphere		equinox
applications	coefficient	**deceleration**	equivalent
artesian	collision	decompose	erosion
assumptions	combustible	decomposition	evaporation
astronomical	compensate	dehydrated	existence
atmosphere	component	density	expansion
atomic	compound	desalination	experiment
attitude	compressed	detergent	
attraction	compression	diffusion	
aurora	comprise	digestion	**factors**
axis	concave	dilute	filament
	condensation	diodes	filtration
bacteria	conduction	disintegrate	fission
barometer	conductor	dissolve	flotation
beaker	concentrate	distillation	fluorescent
behavior	conservation	distinguish	fluid

formation
formula
fractionation
frequency
friction
fusion

gamma
galaxy
gaseous
glacial
gravitational
gravity

halogen
heaviness
heredity
homogeneous
humidity
hydrocarbon
hydrogenation
hypothesis

ignite
immerse
impenetrable
impurities
incidence
induction
inertia
insoluble
insulate
interference
inverse
ionization
isotope

kinetic

liberated
liquid
longitudinal

magnetic
magnitude
malleable
material
matter
megaton
metallic
meteorite
mineral
molecular
momentum

negative
nitrate
nitrogen
nonmetallic
nuclear
nucleus
nutrients

organism
oxidation
oxidize
oxygen

parallel
particles
pendulum
periodic
phenomena

phosphates
phosphorescence
phylum (phyla)
pollutants
porous
positive
potential
precipitation
predict
pressure
principle
process
propellant
properties
proportion
proteins
protons
pulverize

qualitative
quantity
quasar

radiation
radioactive
radioscope
reaction
reflection
refraction
relationship
replacement
repulsion
residual
resistance
reverberation

saturated
sedimentary
seismograph
solids
solubility
solution
spectrograph
spectroscope
spectrum
spherical
spontaneous
stalactite
stalagmite
structure
substance

temperature
theory
thermodynamic
thermoplastics
transformed
transition
translucent
transmission
transparent
turbine

unite

valence
vaporize
vaporization
varies
velocity
vibration
volatile
volume

IMPEDILEXAE IN MATHEMATICS

This list is only a sampling: it does not include all the difficult vocabulary in mathematics. But the list does provide a basis for comparing the difficulty of various mathematics books as far as vocabulary is concerned.

All roots and derivatives of words listed here should also be counted as impedilexae.

absolute
additive
adjacent

alternate
altitude
approximately

approximation
assigning
associated

associative
assumption

binary
bisect

cancellation
characteristics
circumference
coefficient
coincide
combination
commutative
computing
conceptual
conclusions
conditional
congruent
connecting
consecutive
constant
coordinates
corresponding
cumulative

decimal
definition
demonstrated
denominator
derivation
determine
deviation
diagonal
diagram
difference
displacement
distributive

divisible

eliminated
equally
equation
equidistant
equilateral
equivalent
estimate
exclusive
exponential
expression

factor
formula
fractional
frequency

geometrical
graphically

horizontal

identical
illustrated
imaginary
inconsistent
indicate
inequality
infinite
intercept
intersect
inverse
irrational

isosceles

linear

measurement
midpoint
multiple
multiplication
mutually

negative
nonassociative
noncommutative
numerical

obtuse
operations
origins

parallel
parallelogram
parentheses
pentagon
perpendicular
polygon
polynomial
prime
principle
probability
projection
properties
proportion
proportional

quadratic
quadrilateral

rational
reciprocal
rectangle
relationship
replacement
represent
representation

segment
significant
simplify
simultaneous
solution
substitution
successive
supplementary
surface
symbol
symmetry

terminate
theorem
transform
trapezoid

unsolvable
unspecified

variable
variation
velocity
vertical

IMPEDILEXAE IN BUSINESS, INDUSTRIAL ARTS, AND VOCATIONAL EDUCATION

The words on this list are merely a sampling; they do not include the entire difficult vocabulary in the fields of business, industrial arts, and vocational education. But the list does provide a valid basis for comparison of the difficulty of the various textbooks in these fields as far as vocabulary is concerned.

All roots and derivatives of words listed here should also be counted as impedilexae.

abrasive
absenteeism
accessories
accommodations
accomplished

accordance
accounting
accumulated
adjustment
advantageous

advertising
alignment
allowance
alloys
alternating

alternator
analysis
anneal
appreciable
appropriate

approximate
arrangement
assembly
assistance
assortments
attainment
automated
automatic
automotive
authorized

babbitt
balancing
bargaining
budgetary
budgeting
burnish
business

capacities
capitalism
carburetor
carburetion
career
census
certainty
characteristics
charitable
classification
clearance
collective
combination
combustion
commercial
commission
communication
comparative
compensation
competition
composite
comprehensive
compression
compulsory
computorized
concessions
confirmation
connecting
consignment
consolidate
consumer
consumption

contending
contour
contractual
contribution
controller
conveniently
conventional
cooperative
coordinated
corporation
corrugated
countersink
courteous
coverage

damages
dealership
deficit
deliberately
demonstrator
departmental
dependability
depreciation
destination
detecting
determining
diagonal
diagram
dimensions
disadvantage
discount
discrepancy
discretionary
discrimination
displacement
distribution

economy
efficiency
electrical
electromagnetic
electronic
eliminating
employee
enlargement
enterprise
equipment
established
evaluation
excessive
exclusiveness

executing
executive
expansion
expenditures
expense

facilities
financial
financing
fluorescent
fluctuations
functional

geometric
governmental

handcraft
hazardous
hostelry
husbandman
hydraulic
hydroelectric
hydrostatic

identification
illumination
impulse
incentives
inclination
incorporate
indebtedness
independent
indicative
indorsement
induction
inefficient
inexperienced
ingredient
installments
insurance
institutional
integrity
interdependence
interviewing
inventory
invoice
isometric

judicious
justified

laminate
liability

lithography
lubrication

maintenance
malleable
managerial
management
manufacturer
margin
markdown
markup
measurements
mechanical
mechanism
mechanization
mechanized
media
memorandum
merchandise
merchandising
minimize
minimum
miscellaneous
misunderstanding
misrepresent

neglected
negligent
neighborhood
nuclear

occupational
occupations
operating
operational
optimum
optional
organizational
orientation
oscilloscope
overage

parallel
penetrating
percentage
performance
perpetual
personality
personnel
perspective
placement

policy
polyurethane
potential
preferences
preliminary
procedures
processing
production
profit
profitability
projection
promotion
promotional
proposal
proprietorship

qualifications
quality

reasonable
receiving
reciprocal

reconsider
regulate
remuneration
repetitive
replacement
representation
representative
reproduction
reputable
requirements
requisition
residential
residual
resistance
resourceful
responsibility
restraints
resurfacing
revolutions
revolving
routine

salesmanship
schematic
seasonally
sensitivity
servicing
shortage
specialized
specialty
specifications
standardized
statement
structural
suburban
suggestive
summary
supervision
suspension
synchronize

tabulation
technical

techniques
tempering
thermoplastic
thicknesses
tolerances
transaction
transferable
transformers
transmission
transportation
turnover

ultimate
unconditionally
unethical
unprofitable

value
valuation
veneer
verification

workmanship

IMPEDILEXAE IN HOME ECONOMICS

The words on this list are a sampling and do not include all the difficult vocabulary in home economics. The list does, however, provide a basis for comparing the difficulty of various home economics books as far as vocabulary is concerned.

All roots and derivatives of words listed here should also be counted as impedilexae.

acceptance
accessories
accommodation
achievement
activities
adjustment
adolescence
adulthood
affluent
aggression
allowances
alternate
ambivalent
amortization
analyze
antisocial
anxieties
appearance
appliances
appropriate
approval
approving

arrangement
aspiration
attitudes
attractive
authoritarian
automatic
awkward

balanced
behavior
biodegradable
budgeting

calories
capabilities
careers
centerpiece
characteristics
circumstances
classifying
combination
communicable
communication

communities
companionship
compatibility
compensation
competencies
complement
compromising
conditions
conflict
consequences
contagious
contaminated
contrast
convenience
conversation
cooperative
coordination
courtship

decisions
desertion
desirable

detergents
development
different
disorganization

economics
efficiency
embarrassing
emergencies
embroidery
emotional
encouragement
environment
essential
establishing
establishment
eugenics
equipment
expectations
expenditures
experiences
explosion

extravagant
extrovert

facilities
fashionable
fashioning
femininity
friction
frustration

guarantee
guidance

harmonize
heredity
homogenized
horizontal
housekeeping
household

identical
imagination
impulse
inadequacy
inadequate
inconspicuous
inconvenience
independence
individualistic
inferiority
ingredients
inheritance
initiative
installment

institutions
introvert
investigation
investment
involvement

judgment

livable

maintenance
management
marital
masculinity
maternal
matriarchal
maturation
measurements
mechanism
merchandise
metropolitan
minerals
misunderstanding
mobility
motivation

neighborhood
nonessentials
nonpollutant
nutrients
nutrition

occupation
opportunities
organism
outgoing

parental
patriarchal
perishable
perpendicular
personal
personality
phosphates
physiological
pollutants
popularity
population
possessive
possibilities
practical
preferences
premarital
prenatal
preparation
productive
projection
proteins
psychological
punishment

qualities

rationalization
recommended
refreshments
refrigerator
regression
requirements
resourceful
resources

responsibilities
retardation
rivalry
role

sacrifice
scheduling
security
self-confidence
sensitivities
serious
sibling
simplifies
socialization
standards
sterility
sterilization
·suggestion
supervise

techniques
temperament
tensions
textured
traditions
transition
transmitting

uncomfortable
utilities

vegetables
vigorous
vitamins

Two selections from secondary school texts in American History are presented on pages 43 and 44 to illustrate how readability may be assessed and compared. They are on the same topic—the "Open Door" policy and the Boxer Rebellion.

A readability rating would indicate that one is low in difficulty and the other is average. Close inspection discloses that the Steinberg account includes ten names of Chinese provinces and such unusual terms as *wrung*, *wrested*, and *lion's share*, but these are not reflected in the weighted readability level. The teacher who is comparing the readability of textbooks should be sensitive to such usage, for it exerts a very real influence on the difficulty of the material.

For illustrative purposes, four selections on the same topic were rated and are presented in the accompanying table.

READABILITY RÉSUMÉ FORM

Title of textbook _____

Author(s) _____

Publisher _____City _____Copyright year _____

Subject-matter area _____Grade _____

Topic _____Pages _____

Evaluation made by _____Date _____
　　　　　　　　　　(Your name)

For each sample, record the following:
Number of words　　　　　　　　Number of
in selection _____　sentences _____

Number of words divided by number of sentences = _____ Average sentence length

Number of subordinate clauses = _____ $\times$ 3 = _____
　(Multiply number of subordinate clauses times three)

Number of words of three or more syllables　　　 = _____
Number of words on the
　list of impedilexae = _____ $\times$ 5 = _____

　　　　　　　　　　　　　(add)
　　　　　　"Weighted readability" total = _____

READABILITY RATINGS

	Book A	Book B	Book C	Book D
Average sentence length	19	23	21	17
Number of subordinate clauses $\times$ 3	$11 \times 3 = 33$	$20 \times 3 = 60$	$20 \times 3 = 60$	$8 \times 3 = 24$
Words of three or more syllables	42	53	60	49
Impedilexae $\times$ 5	$10 \times 5 = 50$	$23 \times 5 = 115$	$24 \times 5 = 120$	$19 \times 5 = 95$
Weighted readability level	144 (Low)	251 (High)	261 (High)	185 (Medium)

"Spheres of Influence" in China. A war between China and Japan in 1894-1895 showed China to be a weak nation. Japan and the stronger European nations soon forced their way into China and took over large regions for their own use—regions containing valuable harbors, railroads, mines, and raw materials of all kinds. Each country thus set up a "sphere of influence" in which it could make its own trade regulations, and from which it could get some control of China's internal trade.

The "Open-Door" Policy. In 1899, seeing that our trade with China was threatened, John Hay, our Secretary of State, wrote a note to the larger European powers. In it he asked each power to agree that it would not interfere with trade passing to or from Chinese ports, nor close its own "sphere of influence" to the trade of any other nation by raising railroad rates, harbor dues, and the like. This policy of allowing all nations to trade with China on an equal basis became known as the "open-door" policy.

The Boxer Rebellion. The taking over of whole sections of China by Europeans made some Chinese angry. An organization of Chinese called the Righteous Fists of Harmony—or more simply, the "Boxers"

1. What did China do with the money we returned after the Boxer Rebellion's damage claims were settled?

—began an open rebellion against all foreigners. The Boxers endangered the lives of all non-Chinese and of native Chinese who had adopted European ways or religious beliefs. Attacks were made on ambassadors and on missionaries, on merchants and their families. Houses and places of business were pillaged and burned.

In order to protect the lives and property of their citizens, the United States, Japan, Russia, Great Britain, France, and Germany sent troops to China. Within a short time these troops had put down the Boxers. China was required to pay an outrageous sum of money to each nation whose citizens had lost lives and property in the uprising. The United States received over $24,000,000, but this amount was more than was necessary to meet damages. Consequently the balance was returned to China. China in turn used some of the returned money to send young men to study in American colleges and universities.

SOURCE: Harold H. Eibling, Fred M. King, and James Harlow, History of Our United States, Laidlaw Bros., River Forest, Illinois, © 1964, pp. 491–492. Reprinted by permission.

Readability comparisons are designated "weighted readability levels" rather than being given as grade levels. Grade-level designations are frequently given by publishers and authors of readability formulas; but they have purposely been avoided here. There is no point in designating a text as being of "tenth-grade readability" when, as often occurs, a large number of tenth-graders cannot read it. Moreover, some teachers will accept a grade-level designation as a signal that *all* students in that grade should be given that text to read.

The comparative measures "difficult," "medium," and "low" (or, "high readability," "medium readability," and "low readability") should aid the teacher in matching materials appropriately to the reading abilities in each class. An hour or two spent on this project will reward both students and teacher with success.

We become involved in Chinese affairs. The Philippine rebellion had not been under way long when, in 1900, a secret society in China started an organized attack upon foreigners. The "Boxers" or "Righteous Patriotic Fists," as they were called, had been driven to this action by the steady invasion of China by imperialist powers. In 1894, Japan attacked China and proceeded to annex the Liaotung peninsula (within striking distance of the capital city of Peking) and Formosa. She also forced China to give up her control of Korea. Concerned about a possible danger to their Chinese trade, Russia, Germany, and France stopped Japan from retaining her conquests, except Formosa. Four years later (1898) they, along with Great Britain, decided to take Chinese bases for themselves. Russia wrung from the Emperor a "leasehold" of the Liaotung peninsula (including Port Arthur) and with it trading concessions in Manchuria. A few years later she began to eye Korea. Germany acquired a similar ninety-nine year lease of Kiaochow and trading concessions in the province of Shantung. France wrested a like lease of Kwangchow and economic rights in the mainland provinces of Kwangsi and Yünnan. She thus improved her Indo-China boundaries. To Great Britain fell the lion's share. Not only did she gain political control of the Yangtze Valley (China's most populous region), but she also gained boundary concessions along her Burmese and Indian borders.

In retaliation against these moves the Boxers went about massacring Europeans in the major cities and threatening their legations in Peking. They were suppressed quickly by an international military expedition, including United States marines. In 1901, the Chinese government accepted the allied terms of peace: payment of a huge indemnity; the promise to safeguard foreigners and their interests within China; and permission to be granted to the foreign powers to maintain armed forces in China for self-protection. The United States returned her share of the indemnity received for the Boxer Uprising. This money China applied to founding scholarships to enable Chinese nationals to study in the United States.

The "Open Door" policy. The most important outcome of the Boxer Uprising was a statement by John Hay, McKinley's Secretary of State, reaffirming what is known as the "Open Door" policy. It asked all the powers which had been grabbing parts of China to declare that the trade and shipping of every country would be treated alike in the twenty-two parts where they were in control. Furthermore, it requested that the territorial independence of China be preserved. The powers grudgingly accepted. But later events showed that Hay's doctrine was ignored. The powers went about dividing their Chinese spoils among themselves.

SOURCE: Samuel Steinberg, **The United States, Story of a Free People,** Allyn and Bacon, Inc., Boston, © 1954, 1958, 1963, pp. 421–422. Reprinted by permission.

CONCLUSION: MATCHING READABILITY TO READING ABILITY

The ultimate purpose of readability measures and reading-ability percentiles is to achieve a match: students with high reading ability should be given reading materials of high readability; students with low reading abilities should be given materials of low readability; average students should be given materials of medium readability.

Such a situation seems ideal, but really it is not too much to expect when one contemplates the tens of thousands of excellent books that are available today. The accuracy of the match is limited only by the teacher's time and energy—naturally, it would take years for any one teacher to complete the task alone. A huge project of this type should be eligible for government research grants and computer time. The results of such a project should be a computer readout giving the readability of all secondary school textbooks and supplementary materials, and the consistency of reading difficulty throughout each text. The latter is especially important for anthologies of literature, some of which vary from the most simple to the most complex selections within the same volume.

It is disappointing that readability scores are not yet available, but one encouraging fact remains: since all measures are only estimates, the match does not need to be perfect. With this in mind, the classroom teacher should make readability measurements for a few texts and supplementary books, ranking them in order of difficulty. With a slight adjustment here and there, the teacher may provide more difficult materials to students with better reading ability, while students with inferior reading ability will be given books on their reading levels. The books of medium difficulty will be given to students with average reading ability.

The objective of assessing readability of materials and matching those materials to the reading abilities of the students in a class is to provide for the optimum learning of each individual according to his abilities. Success in learning is the result. Failure to do this produces failure for a large segment of secondary school students.

The classroom teacher, then, determines whether success or failure is to be the lot of each individual student in the class.

Questions and Activities for Discussion and Growth

1. Select a secondary school textbook in each of these major content areas: social studies, English, science, mathematics, home economics, and business. Write to the publishers of the texts to ascertain the grade level for which the book is usually sold. Ask the publishers for an explanation of the means by which they determined the reading difficulty of the text.
2. Select three secondary textbooks in one subject area. Look through them carefully from cover to cover. Make an "educated guess" of the relative difficulty of each. Give the books to a colleague (or another student) and ask for his estimate of which is most difficult to read and which easiest. Do your estimates agree?
3. Using the "readability résumé" form, make a tabulation of measures on a 500-word sample from each of three textbooks. Compare your weighted readability totals. How do your results compare with your estimates in question 2?

4. Select a 1,000-word sample from a literary classic commonly used in high school. Make a listing of all difficult words: words with three or more syllables, and strange, obsolete, and colloquial words. Calculate the percentage of difficult words. How does this amount of difficulty contribute to the reading problem in English?

5. Study the same classic in comic-book format. Is the percentage of difficult words any less than the percentage for the original version?

6. Examine a popular secondary school science text to determine how the authors have handled the specific science vocabulary.

7. Examine a social studies text to determine whether or not the authors have provided contextual clues to the meanings of new vocabulary as it is encountered. How would you use that text if you wanted to help students learn vocabulary in context rather than by using the dictionary?

8. Select four textbooks in one of the content areas and conduct readability résumés similar to those made in this chapter. Rank the books according to their relative difficulty.

9. Select a 500-word sample from a secondary school textbook. Rewrite the entire selection, simplifying the material to the very lowest readability possible. How much meaning is "lost" in your version? Explain and defend your answer.

10. Select a difficult 500-word selection in a high school textbook in your major field. Make a complete lesson plan (including statements, questions and probable answers, examples, visuals, and everything else you would need to use) to help the students in reading that material for full comprehension.

Selected References

Aukerman, Robert C.: "Readability of Secondary School Literature Textbooks: A First Report," *English Journal,* vol. 54, no. 6 (September, 1965), pp. 533–540.

Klare, George R.: *The Measurement of Readability,* Iowa State University Press, Ames, Iowa, 1963. (This is the review and summary of readability research over the past fifty years.)

Lee, Wayne D.: "What Does Research in Readability Tell the Classroom Teacher?" *Journal of Reading,* vol. VIII, no. 2 (November, 1964), pp. 141–144.

McCullough, Constance: "What Does Research in Reading Reveal About Practices in Teaching Reading?" *English Journal,* vol. 58, no. 5 (May, 1969). (Concerns sentence structure as it affects readability.)

Pescosolido, John, and Charles Gervase: *Reading Expectancy and Readability,* Kendall/Hunt Publishing Co., Dubuque, Iowa, 1971. (This excellent little handbook provides a simplified treatment of a number of reading-expectancy formulas and an easily understood presentation of the major readability formulas—Dale-Chall, Spache, etc.)

Wall, Sinclair: "Readability—A Neglected Criterion in Secondary Textbook Selection," *Journal of the Reading Specialist,* vol. 9, no. 1 (October, 1969), pp. 12–16.

4. THE SURVEY TECHNIQUE

From past experience, it would seem that content in the secondary school is almost synonomous with fact finding. If this is true, any student who is to be successful in a subject-matter area must devise ways of reading for facts. In some instances, what will be required is rote memorization, which in itself is not reading. In other cases, students should learn a method of placing facts in perspective within the larger framework of the unit.

It has been stated that reading is the common denominator of all content learning. This is true largely because of the universal pattern of textbook writing and design. All textbooks in all academic areas of the secondary school (with the exception of literature) follow the same highly structured pattern:

Chapter title
  Introduction
  Heading for first main topic
    Subheadings
  Heading for second main topic
    Subheadings

Heading for nth main topic
   Subheadings
Summary
Review questions and exercises

This format is frequently embellished with numerals; boldface type; color overlays; visuals, such as pictures, maps, graphs, and charts; lists; vocabulary; glossaries; and marginal notes.

Because the great majority of secondary school classes in the content areas use such structured textbooks, good teachers have discovered that spending a portion of a class period in surveying a chapter (or some section of the textbook) is one sure way of helping students with the reading of that material.

If the teacher would only remember that *no one else is teaching the students how to read and study* in his subject-matter area, he would consistently utilize the reading skill known as the "survey technique." This technique may be used with secondary school classes having a wide range of reading abilities. Moreover, it may be used in instructing whole classes, with the textbook as the medium of instruction, even though there may be many students in a class who actually cannot read the textbook on their own.

The survey technique is an adaptation of the essential part of what has been called the "SQ3R" technique of reading and studying textbooks: "survey, question, read, recite, and review." The SQ3R method was introduced to the field of education through two publications by Francis P. Robinson.[1] Robinson's SQ3R method has undergone a number of adaptations, but the "survey" part has been retained in all the variations and is essential to all of them.

STEPS IN THE SURVEY

Step 1: Analysis of the Chapter Title

The first step in the survey technique is consideration of the chapter title.

Most of us who have had experience with secondary school students are aware of their habit of completely ignoring the titles of the chapters. But those who have written a book or assisted in writing one are aware of how much time and mental effort an author spends in selecting chapter titles that will provide insight into the contents of the chapter. Titles are clues to content and to meaning. Consequently, analyzing a chapter title provides a readiness for what is to follow as effectively as a stage setting provides readiness to enter the dramatic world of a play.

[1] Francis P. Robinson, *Effective Study,* rev. ed., Harper & Row, Publishers, Incorporated, New York, 1961; and Francis P. Robinson, *Effective Reading,* Harper & Row, Publishers, Incorporated, New York, 1962.

Analysis of a chapter heading by the whole class allows an exchange of educated guesses by various members of the class. This is a verbal thinking activity; it does not depend upon reading ability. All members of the class can participate equally well, whether they are good or poor readers. Only their past experiences and their abilities to relate past experiences to their survey account for their individual interpretations of the meaning conveyed by the title.

Some titles are straightforward; others are subtle and elusive; some are provocative; others are unimaginative. In all cases, however, they are intended as signals to the reader. They provide what psychologists call the "mind set" of the learner.

The unit headings and chapter tiltes of the junior high school geography text *The World Around Us*[2] provide examples of imaginative and motivational cues to thinking:

Unit Three: Hot, Dry, and Dangerous
Chapter Titles in Unit Three:
  Lands of Desert Nations
  Productive Deserts of the Americas
  The Mysterious Kalahari
  The Big Walkout

Other unit titles that are both imaginative and descriptive are "Warm, Moist Lands"; "Green and Busy Lands"; and "Lands of Four Seasons."

Once the title has been discussed and has provided the "set," the class should move to the second step in the survey.

Step 2: Analysis of Subtitles

The second step in the survey is the inspection and discussion of the subtitles (headings) within the chapter. In most well-organized textual material, the subtitles provide the author's outline, or clues to it. They show the main subsections into which a topic has been divided. Occasionally they are more than just headings, providing sentences or sentence-type statements which convey meanings by themselves. Sometimes the subtitles are numbered and lettered according to the outline devised by the author. Usually they are distinguished typographically, and they can therefore be spotted easily even by the poorest readers in the class.

If the teacher or one of the students reads the subtitles aloud, that will put all the students, including the poor readers, on an equal basis for discussing them.

Robinson suggested that each heading be turned into a question. "Changing a heading into a question should be a conscious effort to orient oneself

[2] Zoe A. Thrallis, Edward L. Biller, and William M. Hartley, *The World Around Us*, Harcourt Brace Jovanovich, New York, 1965.

actively toward the material to be read."[3] The habit of turning the subtitles into questions is a good one for secondary school students to develop. The objective of the question is to give the reader something for which he must find an answer.

The headings or subtitles within a chapter usually bear some structural relationship to each other. Good editing of a textbook ensures this fact; poor editing is evidenced by inconsistent and unrelated subtitles. The better the subtitles, the easier the book will be to use: good subtitles give a disabled reader some sense of accomplishment, and the gifted reader quickly organizes them into a frame of reference for reading and remembering.

Here is an example of well-structured subtitles in a secondary school geography textbook.[4] The chapter title is "Pacific Coastal United States"; under the section headed "Agriculture" the following subtitles are found:

> The Imperial Valley
> The Santa Ana and San Gabriel Valleys
> The Central Valley
> The Santa Clara and Salinas Valleys
> The Willamette Valley
> The Puget Sound Lowland
> Farmlands of Alaska
> Sugar and Pineapple State

Discussion of these subtitles would emphasize the factual nature of the material. It is obvious that the material will be informational, and perhaps comparative. Of course the survey of these subtitles would depend upon the philosophy and objectives of the teacher, but he might direct the student to concentrate on the similarities and differences among the eight regions; their products, the variety of climates, or any other factual aspect.

After the framework of the chapter has been exposed through discussion of the chapter title and subheadings, the survey moves to step three.

Step 3: Analysis of Visuals

The students are now asked to scan the pages of the chapter for visuals such as charts, graphs, pictures, maps, sketches, cartoons, and diagrams.

The extent to which such valuable visual aids to learning are ignored in many secondary school classes is almost unbelievable. It is even more discouraging when one contemplates the days and weeks of effort on the part of the author, the editor, the designer, the compositor, and the printer in planning and producing just the right visual aids in just the right spots.

[3]Robinson, *Effective Reading*, p. 34.
[4]Edward R. Kolevzon and John A. Heine, *Our World and Its People*, Allyn and Bacon, Inc., Boston, 1964.

FIG. 17-6. TWO WAYS OF LOOKING AT GROSS NATIONAL PRODUCT (1965 FIGURES IN BILLIONS OF DOLLARS)*

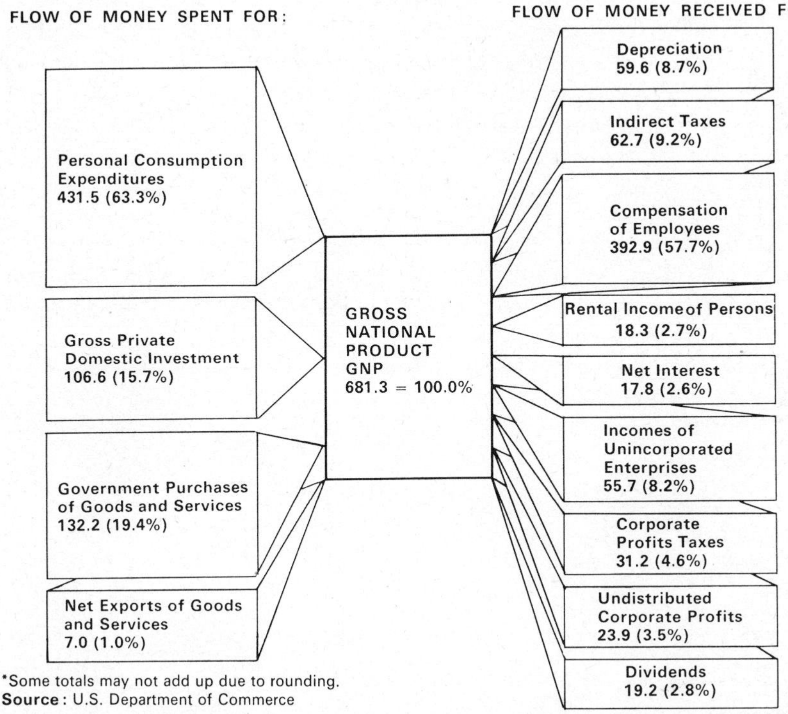

FLOW OF MONEY SPENT FOR:

FLOW OF MONEY RECEIVED FOR:

Personal Consumption Expenditures
431.5 (63.3%)

Gross Private Domestic Investment
106.6 (15.7%)

Government Purchases of Goods and Services
132.2 (19.4%)

Net Exports of Goods and Services
7.0 (1.0%)

GROSS NATIONAL PRODUCT GNP
681.3 = 100.0%

Depreciation
59.6 (8.7%)

Indirect Taxes
62.7 (9.2%)

Compensation of Employees
392.9 (57.7%)

Rental Income of Persons
18.3 (2.7%)

Net Interest
17.8 (2.6%)

Incomes of Unincorporated Enterprises
55.7 (8.2%)

Corporate Profits Taxes
31.2 (4.6%)

Undistributed Corporate Profits
23.9 (3.5%)

Dividends
19.2 (2.8%)

*Some totals may not add up due to rounding.
Source: U.S. Department of Commerce

SOURCE: From Leonard S. Silk and Phillip Saunders, The World of Economics, McGraw-Hill, Webster Division, St. Louis, © 1969. Reprinted by permission of McGraw-Hill, Inc. The original source is the U. S. Department of Commerce.

Some teachers do not utilize the visuals at any time during the study of a chapter, perhaps hoping that they will find time to direct the attention of their students to them "later." This is a poor procedure; the experience of many good teachers has been that it is most effective to explore visuals as an essential part of the survey technique.

Visuals, such as the one from the economics textbook showing gross national product (reproduced above), are included in textbooks to enrich understanding. Psychologically, they utilize the visual modality of learning, providing concrete visualization in place of what otherwise would be abstract. However, as in the case of the economics illustration, they do require reading ability. They should, as has been noted, be read and discussed as part of the survey.

Charts, graphs, maps, sketches, and diagrams often convey clues to the meanings of new vocabulary. A geography book that speaks of an "escarpment" and at the same time provides a diagrammatic sketch or a picture of an escarpment is providing the learner with a concrete visualization of what otherwise would remain an abstract term. This is true again and again in textbooks; they are planned that way. Visuals are very expensive additions to texts, and should be utilized for all they are worth.

Step 4: The Introductory Paragraph

The fourth step in the survey technique is to have the class read the introductory paragraph of the chapter. In classes where there is a high incidence of poor readers, it is wise for the teacher to read the paragraph aloud while the students follow in their texts.

The purpose of the introductory paragraph in most information-type textbooks is to provide the student with a statement defining the topic and including various essential aspects of it, some of which may be indicated by these questions:

Who?
What?
Where?
When?
Why?
How?
How much?
How many?

The following is an unusually short and terse introductory paragraph to a chapter in a high school physical science text.

Lenses serve us in many ways. In our eyes they make it possible for us to see the world around us. In our cameras they make it possible for us to keep a picture record of the past. In motion picture projectors lenses make it possible for hundreds of people to see the same pictures at once. You will also see in this chapter how lenses help us extend our sight into the invisible worlds of the extremely small and the extremely far away.

SOURCE: Richard Brinckerhoff, Burnett Cross, Fletcher Watson, and Paul F. Brandwein, The Physical World, Harcourt Brace Jovanovich, New York, 1958, p. 291.

The title of Chapter 26 in the physics text, together with this short introductory paragraph, provides the entire class with the following concept: "Lenses are used in cameras, our eyes, and motion picture projectors, and for helping us see things that are very small or very far away."

The conclusion could be that lenses are very important to man for seeing and finding out. The "set" for reading this chapter is the idea that lenses are important to everyone. The first three words in the paragraph are the key: "Lenses serve us . . . ". Surveying this paragraph with the whole class is a two-minute project which firms up the concept of the chapter and provides a valid reason for studying the material.

Step 5: The Concluding Paragraph

The teacher—or some student who has practiced for the occasion—should then read the concluding paragraph in the chapter while the students in the class follow in their own texts. Below is an excellent concluding statement.

WHAT THIS CHAPTER IS ABOUT

Just as the costs of government on the national level have increased markedly in the past few decades, so have those of State and local governments. State tax collections now total approximately $18,-000,000,000 each year, local tax collections come to about the same amount, and together these units collect another $15,-000,000,000 from nontax sources.

Taxes are charges imposed by a legislative body upon persons or property to raise money for public purposes. The canons of sound taxation center around the four concepts of equality, certainty, convenience, and economy.

The United States Constitution, each State constitution, State laws, and city and county charters impose a wide variety of limits on State and local taxing powers.

The principal State and local tax sources include the property tax, the general and selective sales tax, the individual and corporation income tax. the inheritance or estate tax, and various business taxes and license taxes.

Nontax revenues come especially from federal grants-in-aid, government-operated businesses, and such other sources as court fines and the sale of public lands.

Borrowing, which is subject to strict limitation in most States, is only in a sense a nontax source of revenue.

Each State now has a budget system for the planned and more or less effective control of State finances. There are three fairly distinct types of budget systems: the legislative budget, board or commission budget, and the executive budget.

The budget-making process involves six steps: preparation of estimates, review of estimates, consolidation and presentation of the budget, consideration and adoption of the budget, execution of the budget, and a post audit.

Population growth, inflation, and increasing demands for public services are chiefly responsible for the recent and rapid rise in State and local governmental spending. Education, highways, welfare, and public health programs take the bulk of the $60,000,000,000 these units now spend each year.

Chapter 31. STATE FINANCE

SOURCE: Frank A. Magruder, Magruder's American Government, revised by William A. McClenaghan, Allyn and Bacon, Inc., Boston, © 1961 by Mary Magruder Smith, p. 553. Reprinted by permission.

The concluding paragraph should serve as a summary of the main points in the chapter, or state the conclusions to be drawn from the chapter, or do both. The concluding section should later be emphasized again as a summary of the chapter or unit.

A note of caution should be sounded, however: *The first and final paragraphs of a chapter should be read as part of the survey only if they provide an overall statement of the main ideas of the chapter.* Consequently, the teacher must read those paragraphs beforehand and decide if they do indeed add this dimension to the survey.

Step 6: Deriving the Main Idea

The object of reading the introductory and final paragraphs is to summarize the main idea of the chapter. If the paragraphs do not provide such a summary, they certainly should not be included as part of the survey, as has just been noted. Instead, the teacher must lead a class discussion which will produce an educated guess as to the main idea of the chapter. This should be dictated by the various members of the class, with suggested revisions decided upon by all, and copied by the teacher onto a chalkboard (or onto large lined paper, using a felt pen). This derivation of the main idea of the chapter is the final step of the survey. The main idea should be stated concisely and carefully printed large enough for all to see and read. It should usually be no more than one well-formed compound-complex sentence. Such a sentence, since it has been developed by the entire class, should cause no difficulty to anyone in the class, regardless of reading ability.

TIMING THE SURVEY TECHNIQUE

The survey technique is an investment of time. Each teacher will have to try the technique to determine the amount of time it is best to invest. It is suggested that a subject-matter teacher set aside one-half hour of class time for a first attempt at the survey technique. The teacher will also have to invest at least one hour of homework in preview and in marking marginal notes in his own copy of the textbook.

Three or four minutes should be enough time allotted to brainstorming on the meaning implied by the chapter title. The subtitles—depending upon the length and complexity of the chapter—will probably require two minutes each. However, no more than ten minutes altogether should be spent on them. Visuals may take another six to ten minutes. Reading the introductory paragraph and the concluding paragraph (with some discussion and feedback) should take no more than eight minutes. A concluding summary of the content of the chapter (Who? What? When? Where? Why? How? How much? How many?) should not exceed five minutes.

PLANNING THE READING SURVEY

A teacher cannot expect a survey to "just happen." In fact, very little good learning "just happens." To ensure that an effective survey lesson takes place, there must be careful and thorough planning. This may be done in several ways, always keeping in mind that the object of the survey is to provide a frame of reference for subsequent reading of the chapter or section of the textbook. *The survey is the preview to reading.*

Method 1: Marking the Teacher's Copy of the Textbook

The most simple and direct method of planning a survey is by marking your own copy of the textbook. A transparent water-based felt marking pen is good for marking. You may wish to use two or three pens of different colors: one for the main heading, one for subheadings, and one to indicate visuals. For writing marginal notes, use a ballpoint pen of a color contrasting with the typeface of the text. Colored pencils may also be used; but remember that too many different colored pencils and pens will be confusing. The survey should be simplified as much as possible. Simplification requires planning.

The example on pages 56–57, from a science text, has been marked as it would be in planning for a full survey—headings, subheadings, italics, boldface, and visuals are all pointed out.

The survey technique is most easy to plan for textbook material in the social studies, science, home economics, vocational training, diversified occupations, business practices, health, and driver education—that is, in any area where the text is likely to be organized in a traditional outline form. It is usually more difficult and therefore less applicable in mathematics, literature, art, music, and physical education, although a partial survey may be helpful for chapters of texts in those areas as well.

Occasionally a textbook appears with a built-in survey provided by the author or authors and editor. The example on page 58, from a textbook in American history, illustrates how useful this can be.

Method 2: Making Transparencies for an Overhead Projector

A second method of planning the survey lesson is to make transparencies of the pages of the chapter direct from the textbook. The audiovisual department of the school system will aid the classroom teacher in producing the transparencies. Some processes will not reproduce color and consequently are of no use when colored headings, subheadings, and visuals are part of a text—as is the case with most modern textbooks. Be sure to use a process capable of reproducing everything on the page.

The transparencies should be projected by an overhead projector onto a large screen in a semi-darkened room, while the students in the room keep their own texts open for reference. As the survey progresses, the teacher or a team of students coached for the demonstration should mark on a transpar-

INTRODUCTION

The Ways of Science

question → ## A. What Is Science?

definition #1
bold-face
sub-heads
Science is organized knowledge. Like scientists, most people are curious about the living and nonliving things in our universe. Scientists work to *understand* our surroundings, called the *pronunciation* ings, called the (environment) (en-*vy*-ron-ment), so that they can try to (control) and make (predictions) about them.

Many different fields are included in the study of science. For example, *Vocabulary in boldface* (biology) is the study of living things, (chemistry) is the study of the composition of matter and the changes it undergoes, and (physics) is the study of the forces that affect various substances around us. (Astronomy) the study of the bodies in space, and (ge-

(ology) the study of the earth, are also major fields of scientific study.

The above fields of science are (classifications) made by man so that he may organize his search for knowledge. There are many relationships between the branches of science. For example, it is impossible for a person to be a good biologist without having some knowledge of chemistry and physics. It is for this reason that we shall study science in its entirety, not subdivided into branches.

Science is the continuous search *definition #2* **for knowledge.** *Dr. James Conant,* *← famous name* (1893-   ), an American scientist and former president of Harvard University, defined science as *obser-* *← his definition in italics* *vations followed by experimentation which leads to further observations and then further experimentation.* What do you think this means? *← question*

_____ LANGUAGE OF SCIENCE _____

see also
page 17 and
page 18
Vocabulary

environment—that which makes up our surroundings.
hypothesis (hy-*pahth*-eh-sis)—a scientific guess to explain a problem.
controlled experiment—an experiment in which only one factor at a time is allowed to change.

inferences—individual findings drawn from data.
natural laws—happenings in nature which can always be observed.
theory—an explanation of natural happenings which fits all of the observed evidence.

1

ency overlay the headings, subheadings, italicized and boldface items, and visuals with a transparency marker. The students, of course, should not mark their texts unless they own them and do not expect to sell them for secondhand use.

Method 3: Making Facsimiles of Text Pages

An even more effective, but more expensive, method of planning the survey is to use a drycopying machine (such as a Xerox copier) to reproduce those parts of each page which should be emphasized in the survey. This takes considerable planning, but the results are extraordinarily good. The repro-

photo helps explain definition Visuals

Fig. A-1. Scientists are specialized to carry on work in different fields. This researcher is experimenting with a radioactive form of carbon.

The scientist usually begins by observing something and then asking questions about it. You should try to improve your powers of observation and curiosity. One famous physicist said that as a young boy whenever he returned home from school his mother would ask, "Did you ask any good questions in school today?" Let us test our powers of observation.

STUDENT ACTIVITY *demonstration of science experiment*

Your teacher will light a candle and place it on the demonstration desk. On a sheet of paper write all the different things you observe about the candle. It is important that you organize the facts you collect, called data (day-ta), and record exactly what you see. How many different things do you observe? List your classmates' observations along with your own. How many do you have now?

transfer of knowledge

Fig. A-2. Scientists apply relationships from various fields. This physicist is using color patterns (background) to study the breaking process in a plastic sample. Different patterns give clues to how plastics break and how they can be strengthened.

2 INTRODUCTION TO SCIENCE

duced passages are then cut apart, and the parts essential to the survey are pasted on 8½- x 11-Inch sheets of paper in exactly the same position as they had in the text; all other material is eliminated. The resulting pages will contain only headings, subheadings, boldface and italics, introductory and concluding statements, and whatever visuals will reproduce adequately; these make up a set of pages which contain the skeleton of the chapter—the parts that consititute the survey. The pages are then recopied and collated, and each student is given a set for the survey. (The sets may be kept from one semester to the next.) The survey is then conducted as described previously.

The United States Enters World War One

BEFORE YOU BEGIN THE CHAPTER

Know What to Look For

1. A submarine is a ship that is designed and built to operate under water. The first submarine was a leather covered rowboat which was built by a Dutch scientist in 1620. Americans used a small, one-man submarine named the "Turtle" in the Revolutionary War. The "Turtle" rammed into a British warship in New York harbor but failed to sink it. Robert Fulton, the inventor of the steamboat, made improvements in submarines in the early 1800's.

During the early 1900's, Germany succeeded in building large submarines which were powered by diesel engines. At about the same time, a new weapon was invented for use in the submarine. This weapon was a torpedo that steered itself toward the enemy's ship. In this chapter, you will read how the submarine played an important part in causing the United States to enter World War One.

2. Read the title of the chapter. Then look through the chapter and read each heading. From the headings, what topics do you expect to read about as you study this chapter?

3. Look at the pictures in the chapter and read each caption. What is happening in the first chapter picture? Study the map on page 476. Which color shows the Allies? Which color shows the Central Powers? Note also the time line at the beginning of the chapter. What

years are included in this chapter? Compare this chapter time line to the unit time line on page 453.

4. Read the last part of the chapter called Summing Up. What actions caused the United States to enter World War One? What is the topic of the next chapter?

Know These Important Terms
Allies   Central Powers

Know the Main Idea
Here is the MAIN IDEA of this chapter.
When World War One broke out in Europe, the United States tried to remain neutral. Germany's sinking of American ships, however, forced the United States to enter the war.

Keep this MAIN IDEA in mind as you study the chapter. Ask yourself the following questions as you read. They will help you remember the MAIN IDEA.

1. Name the nations that made up the Allies. The Central Powers.

2. Which side did most Americans favor even though the American government was neutral?

3. Name the British passenger ship that was sunk by German submarines.

THE YEARS OF THIS CHAPTER ARE 1914 TO 1917

1865   1914   1917   1921

THE CHAPTER LESSON BEGINS HERE

The United States Tried to
Stay Out of World War One

World War One broke out in Europe in 1914. The two main groups of nations in

World War One were called the **Allies** and the **Central Powers**. Great Britain, France,

SOURCE: From BUILDING THE UNITED STATES, by Jerome R. Reich, Arvarh E. Strickland, and Edward L. Biller, © 1971 by Harcourt Brace Jovanovich, Inc., and printed with their permission. Pp. 472–473.

This method is expensive in both money and time. But if the school is fortunate enough to have teacher aides and money for drycopying, it should be done, for the results are more than worth the time, effort, and money. The set of facsimile pages provides each student with a foolproof survey which he has available as his plan for reading the chapter.

A much less expensive version of this method is to type mimeograph stencils of the chapter title, subheadings, italicized and boldface materials, introductory and final paragraphs, and titles of the visuals. Such copy can be reproduced cheaply. Material duplicated like this can be used either with overhead transparencies or with the textbook.

THE SQ3R STRATEGY

So far we have been discussing the *survey* part of Robinson's SQ3R technique. A survey is adequate for most subject-matter teachers who wish to improve learning by conducting an overview with their students; but after a teacher feels comfortable in the use of the survey technique, he may want to try the other segments of SQ3R. They are: "question, read, recite, and review."[5]

Questions evolve naturally as part of the survey; or the teacher may use the questions usually found at the end of a chapter. Robinson, as has been noted, suggested that all headings be converted into questions: this is a third source of questions. Questions provide the "set" for reading by verbalizing the concepts and facts that the student will expect to find in the chapter. The usual form of the questions that a class will develop as they proceed through the survey is, "What do we expect to find in the chapter on this topic? On this subheading? On this concept? On this method?"

The reading itself may be conceived of as the process of finding answers to such questions. This process will be easier for some students than for others. The more intelligent students will be able to find the obvious answers rapidly. The perfectionists will search for details. The poorer students will do well if they discover a few truths that they can relate in their own words. And it is a fact of life that some of the students in the class should not be expected to go beyond the survey done by the class as a whole. They are the young people who cannot read and who cannot and do not learn by means of the usual subject-centered textbook. Secondary school teachers should relinquish the illusion that such students should read textbooks.

The next step of Robinson's SQ3R approach is recitation, which is construed as a do-it-yourself ritual occurring as soon as possible after the first reading of the material. It is an introspective self-examination. The teacher should recommend that during the recitation phase each student should rephrase the concepts in his own words. Students who can do this successfully can be assured that they have understood what they have read.

[5]Robinson, *Effective Study.*

Review is the last step in the SQ3R approach. The student should use as guides for review the questions in the textbook or those developed by the class during the survey. The psychological principle of reinforcement is utilized in review.

"Survey, question, read, recite, and review" is a process that should be tried by all secondary school students. The reaction invariably is, "It takes too long"; but this is a relative value judgment. SQ3R may indeed take more time than some high school students are accustomed to spending on a textbook assignment. By the same token, it may yield results far better than those ordinarily achieved by those same students.

A teacher may try to insist that the SQ3R routine be followed daily, but the decision to follow this routine really remains with the learners—not the teacher. The skillful teacher acts merely as a coach, to demonstrate this superior method of reading a textbook. The *survey*, then, is actually the main part of SQ3R that the teacher may utilize as a teaching tool with the entire class to preview and prepare for reading. The rest of the procedure is followed by each individual student largely on his own, and the individual differences of the learners determine how each reads the material. Some are more knowledgeable than others, some more interested and motivated than others. All, however, can be aided in their reading by the survey and the other steps in SQ3R.

SUMMARY

The *five steps of the survey technique recommended in this chapter* are analyses of the following:

1. Unit and chapter headings
2. Subheadings
3. Visuals
4. Introductory and concluding paragraphs
And, working from these,
5. Development of the main idea

It should be evident that participation by the entire class in these five steps provides a high degree of success for all students, compared with the almost certain failure and discouragement awaiting those with low reading ability when they are forced into a chapter with unknown material and unfamiliar vocabulary.

The original survey technique suggested by Robinson as part of the SQ3R approach was designed as an individual do-it-yourself method which would take only a minute or so. Robinson envisioned the survey as simply a scanning of headings and titles and not as a learning situation for the class as a whole. The survey technique described and recommended here is a more thorough learning situation, directed by the teacher. It ensures some degree of success for *all* students. It provides for participation by the whole class. It aids in the development of the main idea of the chapter, which in itself is essential to comprehension. It supplies concrete explanations for otherwise abstract vocabulary. It is an intense, verbally oriented teaching-learning situation in which all students, regardless of ability, can share the textbook as the common medium of learning.

The survey technique orients every student to the contents of the textbook, regardless of whether he can read it independently or not. The textbook thus becomes the framework for each subject-matter lesson, since each student, regardless of reading ability, has a preview of the contents of the lesson and has identified with the main idea by relating his past experience to it. Each student feels some degree of success and self-satisfaction when the survey technique is used as an introduction to a chapter. No one goes into the chapter "cold." All are warmed up, albeit to varying degrees.

The survey provides the "set" for reading the chapter. The quantity and quality of learning that follow in subsequent daily lessons are directly dependent upon the skillful use of the survey technique. Success in moderating the survey session can be ensured only through careful planning by the teacher. Students are quick to detect this. The use of the survey in introducing a chapter will gain for the teacher the reputation of being well-organized and knowing what he is doing.

The survey technique provides each student with a guide he himself has had a part in developing. It involves each student immediately and provides each with a criterion for further evaluation of the chapter's content.

Using the survey technique is an immediate step toward improving reading in the secondary school classroom.

Questions and Activities for Discussion and Growth

1. Obtain one textbook from each of the academic departments of your high school. Note the elements common to the format of the chapters in these texts.
2. Obtain one textbook from each of the departments in a junior high school. Compare the format of the chapters in the junior high school texts with those from the senior high school. What is your conclusion?
3. Why did Robinson suggest that the chapter headings and subheadings be rephrased as questions? What is to be gained by doing that?
4. After a complete SQ3R procedure has been conducted, what remains to be done?
5. Why is the survey technique not usually appropriate for most literature textbooks? When might it be advantageous to use the survey in the English classroom?

6. Write out questions to ask at each step of the survey lesson. Each question should be related to *reading* rather than to subject-matter content. (This is difficult to do. After a few attempts, you will become more skillful.)
7. Type an outline of a chapter in a high school textbook in your major academic area. Include in the outline all major headings, subheadings, sub-subheadings, italicized items, numbered items, and captions for visuals.
8. Select from a high school content-area textbook a chapter which does not provide subheadings. Insert at proper points the headings which will provide guidelines for a survey of that chapter.
9. Plan additional enrichment reading for each subheading in a chapter of a high school textbook; this is for the better students who need only to skim the chapter.
10. Using the same chapter material as in question 9, plan the nontextual reading which you would provide for slow readers. Insert your suggestions in your own copy of the textbook under each main heading and each subheading. Why is planning like this an absolute necessity for success in your subject matter classroom?

Selected References

Donald, Sister Mary: "The SQ3R in Grade Seven," *Journal of Reading*, vol. 11, no. 1 (October, 1968), pp. 33–35.

Robinson, Francis P.: *Effective Reading*, Harper & Row, Publishers, Incorporated, New York, 1962. (This 94-page paperback is *the* handbook on Robinson's SQ3R method of surveying.)

5 READING SKILLS FOR SECONDARY SCHOOL CONTENT SUBJECTS

The nature of secondary school content materials demands amplification of the specialized reading skills that were introduced in the last years of the student's elementary school experience. As Herber appropriately points out, secondary teachers should *not assume* that students come to their classes equipped with those skills.[1] Herber accuses the teacher who ignores this fact of being guilty of "assumptive teaching."

Six skills constitute the battery of proficiencies necessary for effective reading in the content areas. They are:

1. Reading for main ideas
2. Knowledge of advanced and specialized vocabulary
3. Utilization of contextual clues to meaning
4. Proficiency in structural analysis
5. Ability to adjust reading rate and technique to purpose
6. Skill in analytical and critical reading

[1]Harold L. Herber, *Teaching Reading in Content Areas*, Prentice-Hall, Inc., Englewood Cliffs, N.J., 1970.

READING FOR MAIN IDEAS

A survey of secondary school programs of study would lead to the conclusion that much time is required for reading for information. Consequently, secondary school students need to develop a recognizable and consistent method for finding main ideas and supporting details.

Little has been written on techniques for finding main ideas. Apparently teachers have assumed that this skill somehow develops as it is needed. Yet, when several groups of social studies teachers, totalling more than four hundred, were asked to describe how one knows when he has extracted the main idea from a section of a textbook, or how one would teach students to pick out main ideas, not one teacher had any identifiable sequential scheme for this basic skill. This should not be taken as evidence, however, that it is impossible to teach such a reading skill. On the contrary, it should convince us that the time is long past when secondary teachers should have developed and learned such a skill and passed it on to their students.

Patterns for Finding Main Ideas

For years, secondary school students have been introduced to the idea that every paragraph has one concept and a "key" sentence; but an analysis of secondary school textbooks reveals that the matter is not quite so simple. Most authors of secondary school texts are neither English majors nor reading specialists. They are subject-matter specialists and secondary school teachers or administrators. Their writing, consequently, tends to stray from careful literary style; it is more concerned with presenting facts and information. Paragraphs in this kind of writing may be classified by their structure as follows:

1. Main idea + examples (or details)
2. Examples (or details) + main idea at end
3. Main idea + examples + main idea restated
4. Examples (or details) + main idea + examples
5. Main idea (part 1) + details + main idea (part 2) + details
6. Main idea (part 1) + details + *but* + main idea (part 2) + details + *on the other hand* + main idea (part 3) + details
7. Details, with main idea implied or obscured

Let us examine these seven categories one by one.

1. Main idea + examples (or details). Teachers at the Needham (Massachusetts) High School have suggested that paragraphs of this sort be diagrammed thus:

Main idea
  Detail 1
    Detail 2
      Detail 3
        Detail 4

A hypothetical example, from the field of economics, will serve to illustrate the point:

[Main idea]
It is easy to start a business slump such as that of the years 1970–1971, but it is much
                              [Detail 1]
more difficult to end one. The President ordered the Federal Reserve Board to raise the
                              [Detail 2]
discount rate. This was done in an effort to "cool" inflation and slow down the economy.
[Detail 3]
This action made money more expensive to borrow, and consequently many companies curtailed expansion of facilities or found themselves unable to continue in business.
[Detail 4]
When the rate for borrowing money was lowered, it was too late, for many people had been put out of work and a large number of manufacturers were being very cautious in their spending. A feeling of despair and gloomy predictions for the future snowballed **into what some called a recession and some economists recognized as a depression.**

This simple method of presenting a main idea with supporting facts, details, or both is also common in science texts, as the following example (from a physics text) indicates:

THE ENERGY STATES

                [Main idea]
Matter exists in three states or phases: solid, liquid, and gas. Each state represents a
    [Detail 1]   [Detail 2]
different energy level. To change from one state, or energy level, to a state of greater energy requires that heat must be paid into the substance in order to make the change.
                              [Detail 3]
Furthermore, the change from one state to another is not gradual; it occurs at a definite temperature and involves a definite amount of heat.

SOURCE: Elements of Physics, revised by Paul J. Boylan, © 1959, 1962, by Allyn and Bacon, Inc., Boston, p. 237.

---

2. Examples (or details) + main idea at end. Sometimes the key sentence is found at the end of a paragraph, with all the other sentences leading into it. In that position, it acts as a summary. Students should be taught that authors occasionally use this style, which may be visualized thus:

    Detail 1
      Detail 2
        Detail 3
          Detail 4
Key sentence

The selection at the top of page 66, from a text on problems of democracy, illustrates this format.

[Detail 1]
A president must be very confident that he can secure Senate confirmation or else he will not submit a treaty to that body. No president will send a treaty to the Senate
[Detail 2]   [Detail 3]
if he possibly can avoid doing so. The fear that treaties are likely to be rejected prevents desirable treaties from being undertaken.

[Detail 4]
Because of the fear that the two-thirds rule would make a probable rejection by the Senate, President Theodore Roosevelt entirely abandoned the submission in 1904
[Key sentence]
of nine treaties of arbitration. Thus, the two-thirds rule is an unfortunate factor in destroying the teamwork between the Executive and Legislature, which is so essential for effective dealing with foreign nations.

SOURCE: Horace Kidger, **Problems Facing American Democracy,** Ginn and Company, Boston, 1950, p. 678. Copyright © 1950 by Ginn and Company.

3. Main idea + examples + main idea (restated). In a long and detailed paragraph the main idea may be expressed twice, at the beginning and at the end (in the latter position it summarizes in different words). The diagram for such a paragraph would be:

>   Key sentence
>   Detail 1
>   Detail 2
>   Detail 3
>   Detail 4
>   Etc.
>   Main idea (restated)

For example:

[Key sentence]   [Detail 1]
The Indians were caught in the middle of this contest. Most of them did not like the English, who moved into their land in such alarming numbers and with such permanent
[Detail 2]
plans. The English cleared the land of trees in order to build farms. In so doing they
[Detail 3]
drove out the wildlife upon which the Indians depended for a living. Moreover, the
[Detail 4]
English settlers had no particular liking for the Indians, whom they regarded as
[Detail 5]
savages. The French, on the other hand, had enjoyed friendly relations with the
[Detail 6]
Indians since the time of their early explorers. They came to trade with the Indians; not to drive them from their land. Perhaps, then, it was only natural that the French
[Main idea restated]
and Indians should team up in any attempt to drive out the invading English.

SOURCE: Harold H. Eibling, Fred M. King, and James Harlow, **History of Our United States,** Laidlaw Brothers, River Forest, Illinois, 1968, p. 93.

Well-written textbooks often include a visual as a restatement of the main idea, as in this example, from a biology text:

[Key sentence]
A mold plant is a common many-celled plant that produces asexual spores. As the
[Detail 1]   [Detail 2]
plant develops, it sends up stalks. At their ends are spore-bearing structures. Inside
[Detail 3] ,
or upon these structures many tough-walled spores are formed. When sufficiently

[Detail 4]   [Detail 5]
mature, they are released. They float about in the air. Whenever one settles upon a
[Detail 6]
favorable spot, it develops into another mold plant.

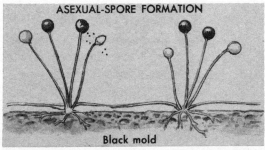

ASEXUAL-SPORE FORMATION

Black mold

SOURCE: Francis D. Curtis and John Urban, Biology: The Living World, Ginn and Company, Boston, 1958, pp. 516–517. Copyright © 1958 by Ginn and Company.

4. Details + main idea + details. A fourth method of presenting the main idea is by placing it in the middle of a paragraph. Such organization lends itself well to a controversial subject—that is, one with two sides. Also, it may be used to break the monotony of a long list of details or points: for example, advantages could be separated from disadvantages, with the main idea placed in the middle. The diagram of such a structure would look like this:

    Detail 1
      Detail 2
        Detail 3
    Key sentence (main idea)
      Detail 4
        Detail 5
          Detail 6

Such construction could lead to verification of the main idea showing that all the other sentences are examples of it. However, inserting the main idea in the middle increases reading difficulty. The poorly motivated student, moreover, may quit before he reaches the middle and consequently miss the main idea entirely. This construction, therefore, is more appropriate for the better readers. Here is an example, from a geometry text, of the main idea surrounded by details:

[Detail 1]
You have already become familiar with some properties of geometric figures; for example, you have learned that in every triangle the sum of the angles is 180 degrees.
[Detail 2]
It is likely that this property was brought to your attention by a series of experiments
[Detail 3]
or measurements. Arriving at a conclusion after a number of observations is called
[Detail 4]
"inductive reasoning." This is a very important and helpful way of learning. In this
[Main idea]
course, however, we shall be more concerned with "deductive" or "if-then" reasoning.
[Detail 5]
It is possible that your course in algebra last year made you aware of this type of
[Detail 6]
thinking. For example, the solution of equations is dependent upon the "if-then" pattern. In fact, "if-then" thinking is found in all forms of mathematics, and our
[Detail 7]
geometry illustrates, to a certain degree, how any mathematical system is developed.

SOURCE: Arthur W. Weeks and Jackson B. Adkins, A Course in Geometry, Plain and Solid. Ginn and Company, Boston, 1961, p. 3. Copyright © 1961 by Ginn and Company.

---

5. Main idea (part 1) + details + main idea (part 2) + details. When the main idea is to express two opposing viewpoints, it may be considered a compound main idea. It calls for changes in thought by the reader, signalled by terms such as *although, but, on the other hand, however, on the contrary,* and *nevertheless.* The construction of such a sentence may usually be outlined to show two distinct ideas actually making up "part 1" and "part 2" of the compound main idea. The diagram would be:

Main idea (part 1)
   Detail 1
      Detail 2
         Detail 3
Main idea (part 2) (Introduced by *but, on the other hand, however, etc.*)
   Detail 4
      Detail 5
         Detail 6

The following excerpt provides an example:

[Main idea, part 1]
These young Germans had lived through a most unusual period of history. Their early
[Detail 1]
education had been in the Nazi schools of the Hitler dictatorship. In their teens they
[Detail 2]
had seen their country divided by the Russian Iron Curtain. Western Germany became
[Detail 3]
a democracy; Eastern Germany was ruled by the Russian Communist dictatorship.
[Detail 4]
These German youth talked about political ideas. They were disturbed that an Ameri-
[Detail 5]
can soldier could not explain clearly what his country stood for.
　　　　　　　[Main idea, part 2]　　　　　　　　　　　　　　　　　[Detail 6]
　　But they were not the only ones who were disturbed. General Omar Bradley was
the commanding officer of the American Zone in Germany at that time. He once
　　　　　　　　　　　　　　[Detail 7]
stated that this inability of the American soldier to explain the philosophy and origin
of our system of government was one of the weakest spots in the education of our
youth.

SOURCE: Stanley Dimond and Elmer Pflieger, Our American Government, J. B. Lippincott Company,
Philadelphia, 1963, p. 4.

**6. Main idea (part 1) + details + *but* + main idea (part 2) + details +
on the other hand + main idea (part 3) + details.** A main idea in three parts
is often one in which similarities and contrasts are being emphasized. The
concepts are related but separated for emphasis and clarity, as is illustrated
in the following paragraph:

[Main idea, part 1]
Missionaries went from New England to Hawaii in the early years of the last century.
[Details]
They were sent to begin their "labors in the vineyard of the Lord." Their history-making
　　　　　　　　　　　　　　　　　　　　　　　　[Main idea, part 2]
voyage was made on the brig *Thaddeus* in the spring of 1820. *But* their work was
　　　　　　　　　　　　　　　　　　　　　　　　[Details]
criticized by some because of jealousies or conflicts of interest. Hundreds of whaling
vessels were arriving at about the same time, and the motley group of sailors found
that the missionaries' strict taboos were restricting their pleasures when they were
in port. The missionaries also managed to keep competing religious groups out of the
[Main idea, part 3]
Islands for many years. *On the other hand*, the Hawaiian people today revere the
　　　　　　　　　　　　　　　[Details]
dedication and work of the first missionaries. They recognize that it was the missionaries who taught the natives to read and write, cultivate new crops, and protect
themselves against diseases. Moreover, the missionaries brought a new religion of
love and peace rather than fear and superstition.

In all the examples given so far, it is assumed that each paragraph contains a main idea. Occasionally this is not true of a paragraph or a main section of a textbook; but the fact that stating a main idea is an almost universal pattern of writing paragraphs makes it necessary to teach students how to find main ideas and organize the supporting data. By so doing, the teacher greatly increases the reading efficiency of the students and, consequently, their achievement in the subject area.

Students should practice reading with two main patterns in mind: first, topic sentence with accompanying examples; second, topic sentence with details. If they approach paragraphs with these patterns in mind, they will be provided with a "set"—that is, with expectations of what they will encounter and a mental image against which to check content and comprehension. For example, if the reader has missed the main idea, he will be alerted to the fact when he comes to the examples, and will know he can find the main idea by going back. But the rare paragraph which does not state a main idea explicitly presents a problem for students and teachers.

7. Details, with main idea implied or obscured. Only occasionally does one encounter a paragraph in which the formulation of the main idea is left to the reader. In such cases, the reader must employ a process of deduction in order to develop the main idea from the facts that are given. Although such a process calls for rather sophisticated thinking, it sometimes is required of all students—when this occurs, the classroom teacher must help students over this stumbling block to comprehension of the text.

An example may be helpful (this paragraph was contrived as an illustration):

When a car is brought into the garage for a tune-up, the driver usually has some idea what is wrong with it, and he tells the mechanic about its performance and troubles. Many mechanics are not factory-trained. They have learned merely by "hanging around cars." Some are school dropouts who cannot even read the manuals provided for them. In order to use an engine diagnosis machine a mechanic must go to a training course. Some drivers pretend to know all about automobiles, and some mechanics tend to use the same solution for any and all troubles. Some mechanics try hit-and-miss techniques for curing troubles, hoping that something will work to get the car back into running condition. Many cars today are so complicated that the average garage cannot repair them. Just recently one company has installed a computorized brake system that is controlled by a real tiny computor. Some states require periodic inspection of cars, to get "junkers" off the road and reduce accidents. Insurance companies favor this.

In the paragraph above, a number of details and facts are stated, but the reader is left with a very fuzzy idea of what the main idea is and what the relationships within the paragraph are.

None of the explicit statements is actually the main idea. Rather, the main idea is implied: "It is extremely difficult to diagnose engine problems unless one is highly trained and has sophisticated equipment." The readability of the paragraph is further complicated by the fact that the first sentence sounds like a main idea.

When dealing with such a conglomeration of poorly related fragments of information, a wise teacher may tell the students what the author meant. A *very* wise teacher will notice that such a paragraph is mixed up and will recommend that the students skip it—all will probably concur in this suggestion.

Teachers and students will find such examples of unreadable material from time to time in secondary school texts; they are evidence that authors are not reading specialists, and that editors are not yet sufficiently concerned with the readability of secondary materials. This leaves the task of dealing with such content in the hands of the classroom teacher, who should realize that the situation must be resolved in an honest manner.

Four Developmental Steps in Reading for Main Ideas

The Bloomfield (Connecticut) Secondary School faculty has investigated means to teach reading for main ideas in the social studies. They have concluded teaching this skill is like teaching any skill—it is a developmental process. Consequently, they suggest that secondary school students be introduced to an easy approach first. The simple concept to be presented first is that *the main idea is the "big" idea that contains the facts.* They recommend introducing this idea by using a very easy paragraph, from which the students can pick out the facts and then select the "big" idea.

The second step in developing this skill is to practice picking out main ideas from a list. The ideas should be very simple at this stage.

The presentation of "scrambled" sentences is recommended as the third step. The students are to place these sentences in sequence, putting the sentence containing the main idea first.

For the fourth step, it is suggested that the teacher provide simple paragraphs in which the main idea is not expressed. Each such paragraph is followed by four or five statements, from which the student is to choose the one which most adequately expresses the main idea.

When the students have mastered these four steps, they are ready to work on picking out main ideas in their text. Be sure the students *have* mastered the steps and really understand the various ways main ideas may be presented: many students start with the concept that the main idea is always in the first sentence and then rely on that as their only technique.

Self-Checks on Reading for Main Ideas and Supporting Details

One way a student may check on the adequacy of his reading for the main idea is to answer the question, "What do all these sentences have in common?"

Another good check is to answer the question, "How do all these facts relate to one another?" These checks will lead the reader to a formulation of his own statement of the main idea. Only when he can restate the main idea should one consider that he has really understood the material. Paragraphs in which the main idea is not stated present a special problem, as has been noted. To deal with such a paragraph, the reader must search for clues to the main idea—for example, he may find significant repetitions of words or meanings. What he will ultimately do is state the main idea (in his own words) for the first time, so the check is essentially the same.

Supporting details are also most useful in providing a family of related concepts to use as a check on comprehension of the main idea. Unfortunately, the untrained reader finds it difficult, if not impossible, to recognize which details are "important" and which are not important. Consequently, he will often attempt to memorize all details, with the result that he will know many details but be unable to formulate a main idea. On the other hand, details may be so cleverly arranged by the author or by the editor they provide clues to the main idea. A listing using numerals (1, 2, 3, etc.), ordinals (first, second, third, etc.), or letters (a, b, c, etc.) is a signal that details are being elaborated or that examples reinforcing a previously stated main idea are being given. Somewhat less direct, but equally effective, is the enumeration "first," followed by such terms as next, then, and finally. A similar technique, which students should learn to recognize, is the use of one reason, another reason, and yet a third reason, etc.

Since cognition is based upon the anticipation of certain characteristics within the writing, the presence of clues such as these will be exploited by the skillful and trained reader. It requires very little help from the competent teacher to alert students to these aids in finding main ideas.

Students often need assurance that they are picking out main ideas correctly. A self-administered quick check would call for answers to the following questions: Who? What? When? Where? Why? How? How much? How many? This self-check is a comprehensive one. Not all main ideas are surrounded by all of these elements, but most of the questions on this self-check must be satisfied if the main idea is to be comprehended.

The following paragraph, from an American history text, illustrates this type of self-check:

Sherman Takes Atlanta. At the beginning of Grant's Wilderness Campaign in early May, General William T. Sherman, under Grant's orders, led a second great Union army of 100,000 men out of Chattanooga into an invasion of Georgia. Greatly outnumbered, the Confederate army of General Joseph E. Johnston was forced to withdraw. A master of skillful retreat, Johnston left destroyed bridges and railroad tracks behind him and avoided open warfare, fighting only when he had the advantage of a fortified line. Nevertheless, every backward step he took brought Sherman's pursuing army near to Atlanta—an important railroad, manufacturing, and supply center. Impatient with Johnston's defensive tactics, Jefferson Davis replaced him with John B. Hood. Hood struck hard at Sherman but in the end was forced to evacuate the city. Sherman entered Atlanta on September 2, 1864.

SOURCE: Jack Allen and John L. Betts, History: USA, American Book Company, New York, 1967, p. 304.

Who? *General Sherman*
What? *captured Atlanta*
When? *September 2, 1864*
Why? *His Union army outnumbered the Confederates*
How many? *100,000 men*
Where? *through Georgia to Atlanta*

This is a quick, foolproof check on comprehension as well as on ability to pick out main ideas.

Classroom Techniques for Developing the Ability to Find Main Ideas

The responsibility for helping secondary school students read for main ideas falls upon the classroom teacher in each subject area. Indeed, if students cannot and do not pick out main ideas, very little learning, if any, can be expected to result from their reading assignments. Fortunately, helping students toward this reading skill is very easy.

Here is the most simple technique. Use a black felt pen and strips of manila drawing paper or thin tagboard about 24 inches long and wide enough to hold one sentence printed in lowercase letters 1 inch high and capital letters 2½ inches high. Students in class can be conscripted to print the sentences on the paper strips. The only other equipment needed is a package of the kind of plastic adhesive material (sold at teachers' conventions and in stationery stores under brand names like "Plasti-tak," "Stick-tak," etc.) which adheres to any hard surface. (The backs of the sentence strips may also be flocked, so that they will adhere to a large flannelboard.) These stips are then arranged and rearranged on a surface visible to the whole class, to demonstrate or develop paragraph structure, from which the main idea will change.

Transparencies and an overhead projector may also be used, but this entails considerably more time, effort, and equipment—and the results are no more effective. In fact, unless the instructor is a skillful operator of transparencies, the results may be unimpressive to the class (for today's students are accustomed to the professional presentations of animated visuals on television.)

A considerably less effective method is to have students make posters illustrating the structure of paragraphs. This method is not recommended in this day of dynamic presentations, since a poster is static once it is made.

Chapter 25 Review

OUTLINING THE MAIN IDEA

In Chapter 25, you read how Americans turned to the federal government to help promote their general welfare as they faced the many new problems of an urban-industrial nation. The following outline will help you trace this main idea.

A. The federal government aided the growth of business and industry in the United States.

    1. Before the Civil War, when the United States was an agricultural-commercial nation, the federal government had a limited role.

    2. As the United States developed into an urban-industrial nation, the federal government began to play an increasingly important role.

        a. The federal government aided the development of railroads, highways, and airways.

        b. The federal government improved the nation's banking system by setting up the Federal Reserve System. The Federal Reserve Board helps to prevent the "boom and bust" cycle in the nation's business system.

        c. Generally, tariffs protected American industry, but later tariff policies helped to promote world trade.

B. The federal government began to regulate business.

    1. The Interstate Commerce Commission (I.C.C.) was organized to regulate freight rates on the railroads. Its powers were soon extended to cover the trucking industry and oil pipe lines.

    2. The Federal Communications Commission (F.C.C.) was formed to regulate radio broadcasting and, later, television networks.

    3. The federal government found it necessary to control the growth of monopolies and trusts, which began to develop during the late 1800's.

        a. The Sherman Anti-trust Act (1890) and the Clayton Anti-trust Act (1914) tried to end monopolies.

        b. The government also forbids individual companies to get together and agree to fix prices.

        c. The government has favored the free private enterprise system of business.

C. The federal government helped both to promote and to control organized labor.

    1. Labor unions were formed to help American workers to obtain higher wages and better working conditions.

        a. The Knights of Labor, one of the first labor unions, died out after the Haymarket riot, in 1886.

        b. The American Federation of Labor (A.F. of L.) organized the skilled workers of the nation.

        c. The Congress of Industrial Organization (C.I.O.) unionized all the workers in each of the mass-production industries.

        d. The A.F. of L. and the C.I.O. joined to form one large union organization— the A.F.L.-C.I.O.—but later split apart.

    2. The federal government helped the labor unions to gain more members by passing the National Labor Relations Act, or Wagner Act, of 1935.

    3. The federal government also began to control the power of the labor unions by the Taft-Hartley Act of 1947.

D. The federal government began to help America's farmers and to conserve the nation's natural resources.

    1. As America became an urban-industrial nation, farmers were faced with the problem of crop surpluses and low farm prices.

    2. The federal government, through a series of laws, tried to control farm production but at the same time increase farm income.

    3. Shiploads of food sent to foreign countries since World War II have helped to reduce American farm crop surpluses.

    4. The federal government has helped to conserve the natural resources of the nation.

        a. President Theodore Roosevelt was the first American President to interest the nation in conservation.

662

SOURCE: From AMERICA: ITS PEOPLE AND VALUES, by Leonard C. Wood and Ralph H. Gabriel, © 1971 by Harcourt Brace Jovanovich, Inc., and printed with their permission. P. 622.

Unit 118. Ignition System

The electric system of an internal-combustion engine is either a magneto or a battery type. The magneto system is used on most of the small two- and four-stroke cycle gas engines. The battery system is used on all automobile engines and some larger outboard motors. There are many similar devices used in both systems.

Review of Basic Electrical Principles

1. A current of electricity is a flow of electrons through a wire.

2. There must be a complete circuit to have a flow of electricity.

3. When electricity flows through a wire, a magnetic field of force is created around it. This magnetic field travels in a circular pattern forming a magnetic cylinder the full length of the wire.

4. If several loops of wire are shaped in the form of the coil, the magnetic effect is greatly increased.

5. Voltage can be induced in windings by magnetism. If the magnetic lines of force of one coil cut a second coil, voltage is induced whenever the lines of force build up or collapse. In other words, with two coils the electric energy can be transferred from one circuit to the other through a magnetic coupling. This transfer of energy is called *mutual induction.* Mutual induction is used in the ignition coil of both the magneto system and the battery system.

Magneto Ignition System

The magneto ignition system of a small gas engine consists of the following:

1. The *rotor* is a strong permanent magnet attached to the crankshaft that revolves inside the armature (Fig. 118–1A).

2. The *armature* consists of lamination of metals with the coil wound around part of the armature (Fig. 118–1A).

3. The *condenser* is a safety valve in a primary circuit (Fig. 118–1B and C).

4. The *coil* consists of a few heavy windings of wire over which many windings of finer wire are wound (Fig. 118–1A, B, and C).

5. The *breaker points* open and close to make and break the primary circuit (Fig. 118–1A, B, and C).

6. The *spark plug* produces the spark to ignite the fuel. This is part of the secondary circuit (Fig. 118–1A, B, and C).

Notice that there are two circuits—the primary circuit and the secondary circuit. The *primary circuit* consists of the primary windings on the coil, the breaker points, and the condenser (Fig. 118–2). The secondary circuit consists of the secondary, or fine, windings on the coil and the spark plug (Fig. 118–3).

Operation of the Magneto Ignition System

As the rotor revolves inside the laminations of the armature, it causes a magnetic flux that cuts the coil of the armature. In this process the moving magnetic flux builds up a voltage in the primary circuit.

At the beginning of the process, the breaker points are closed, and the current flows freely through the primary circuit. At just the right time, when the primary current is high, the breaker points are opened by a cam. The opening of the breaker points causes the magnetic field in the primary circuit to collapse. This action in turn causes a current flow in the secondary circuit.

The amount of current flow is determined by the proportion between the number of turns on the secondary circuit and the number of

350

SOURCE: Chris H. Groneman and John L. Feirer, General Shop, 4th ed., McGraw-Hill, New York, © 1969, p. 350. Reprinted by permission.

The least effective method, it should be noted, is use of the chalkboard. This wastes the teacher's and the class's time (because it is constantly necessary to erase and rewrite) and is indefensible when other techniques are equally simple and significantly more effective.

Note in rare instances the author or editor of a textbook will provide explicit identification of the main idea. In the example shown on page 74, the main idea of the entire chapter has been outlined in package form:

KNOWLEDGE OF ADVANCED AND SPECIALIZED VOCABULARY

Each academic discipline conveys its message through specialized vocabulary. One kind of vocabulary, as has been noted in Chapter 3, is technical terms used exclusively for a particular subject; the other kind, common terms which have been given a specialized meaning.

The need for a working knowledge of specialized vocabulary is nowhere more apparent than in areas that teachers traditionally consider the refuge of the nonreader—auto mechanics and shop. The page from a general shop textbook shown on page 75 illustrates this fact. Every sentence contains technical vocabulary—and this book is used with classes of students who are considered notoriously poor readers. Note these examples of technical vocabulary: *internal combustion, magneto, four-stroke cycle, current, circuit, magnetic field, cylinder, voltage, induced, mutual induction, armature, lamination, ignite, magnetic flux, proportion.*

Identifying Specialized Vocabulary

When common words are used with new meanings in the specialized context of an academic discipline, they also must be understood in their technical setting. A few examples from each content area are given in the following lists: all of them have been taken from secondary school textbooks.

SOCIAL STUDIES—SOME GENERAL WORDS USED WITH SPECIAL MEANING

thriving	settlements	mistress	oppression
struggle	enslaved	conquered	empire
militarists	philosophers	tactics	barriers
domesticated	genius	geographical	interference
expansion	tyranny	democracy	clash
compelled	succession	preservation	dominions

SCIENCE—SOME GENERAL WORDS USED WITH SPECIAL MEANING

compressed	capacity	mixture	agents
compound	filament	attraction	equivalent
applications	repulsion	fluorescent	emulsion
immerse	transparent	nonmetallic	filtration
condensation	parallel	friction	saturated
humidity	resistance	compensate	dehydrated

MATHEMATICS—SOME GENERAL WORDS USED WITH SPECIAL MEANING

rational	inverse	inconsistent	eliminated
solution	approximation	intercept	determine
coincide	difference	variation	circumference
graphically	connecting	velocity	computing
infinite	inequality	multiple	parentheses
projection	approximately	conceptual	probability

BUSINESS, INDUSTRIAL ARTS, AND VOCATIONAL TRAINING—SOME GENERAL WORDS USED WITH SPECIAL MEANING

collective	independent	bargaining	authorized
reputable	comprehensive	residential	contending
executing	accumulated	miscellaneous	verification
analysis	commercial	installment	automated
excessive	connecting	resurfacing	lubrication
automatic	arrangements	diagram	processing

HOME ECONOMICS—SOME GENERAL WORDS USED WITH SPECIAL MEANING

parental	suggestion	desirable	standards
encouragement	approval	fashionable	communicable
requirements	contagious	contaminated	utilities
simplifies	budgeting	household	livable
refreshments	centerpiece	harmonize	vegetables
accessories	essential	appliances	guarantee

Literature presents a special case of "technical" vocabulary. Words are the tools, the materials, the technique of the literary artist. He has only words to work with. He must use common words in uncommon ways, and uncommon words in common ways. The vocabulary of literature is both its appeal and, for the poor reader, its drawback. Indeed, even among good readers, "literary" writing annoys some as much as it delights others. Consider the following terms:

LITERATURE—SOME WORDS USED WITH SPECIAL MEANING, AND SOME UNCOMMON WORDS

miserable	swaggered	shrieked	vicious
renegade	solemnly	horrible	ironically
bridled	audience	colossal	girth
eddied	dulling	magpies	realization
prudence	muttered	sufficed	sodden
retrieved	scamp	thrashed	decadent

Methods for Helping Students Understand Specialized Vocabulary

The task of the reader is to understand the explicit and implicit meanings of words. Whether or not he adopts the words for his own use is of secondary concern.

Words are windows that open to meanings. There are several ways to see through those windows.

Definition. In textbooks, definitions may be provided in a glossary at the end of the book, in a special glossary section in each chapter, or within the text itself (often as an appositive within a line of text). In any case, authors and editors will provide definitions specific to the subject being discussed, thus ensuring that the particularized meaning they have in mind will be attached to each specialized word. This is by far preferable to the classroom exercise in which students are directed to "look it up in your dictionaries." We should face facts: the great majority of secondary school students do not even own a dictionary, and those few who do are often unenthusiastic about using it.

Similarity and contrast. A psychological principle applies here: "Things that go together are best learned together." Grouping synonyms or antonyms together increases the probability that vocabulary will be understood. The lower the student's intelligence is, the more limited his experience has been; and the more deprived his cultural background may be, the less benefit will be derived from dwelling on nuances of meaning. For students handicapped by such problems, concrete illustration is needed. The more the teacher can replace abstractions with concrete illustrations, the more cognitive learning will result. Similarity and contrast are two of the best means for accomplishing this.

Experiences. Jean Piaget, the great Swiss psychologist, has said, "I only know that which I can experience." Words are words—nothing more, until meaning is brought to them by the sensory experience of the individual who hears or reads them. The individual who has had no sensory experience of, say, *Spanish moss* can never really *know* what those words mean. (Indeed, he may have a completely erroneous idea, based upon his previous knowledge of the word *Spanish* and his previous experience of moss.) Gaps in experience can create problems of understanding in textbooks. For example, a tenth-grade geography book states: "The Dutch built polders." The student memorizes this. The teacher asks, "What did the Dutch build?" The student answers, "Polders." The student receives a perfect score in comprehension. But cognitive learning is completely absent unless the student can have experiences which let him realize what a polder *is*—for example, if he can see the Dutch constructing a polder, either in an illustration in the text or on a transparency or film.

Vocabulary is dependent entirely upon the experiences of the student for the meaning it conveys.

UTILIZATION OF CONTEXTUAL CLUES TO MEANING

This skill is started in the kindergarten and first grade, when the teacher reads open-ended sentences and asks the children to think of words that would complete them. The skill of contextual analysis is supposed to be further developed all through the elementary grades; but more often than not, it is left to atrophy. It should be revived by the secondary school content teacher. Opportunity presents itself whenever the meaning of a word can be gleaned from its neighbors in a sentence.

Unfortunately, contextual analysis demands mental exertion—an exercise that is unknown to many secondary school students—but it can be made enjoyable; especially if it replaces the deadly "dictionary practice."

In the following excerpt, the definitions of the terms *state* and *adjustment* are implied in the context.

In the time of our great-grandparents, marriage was considered a *state*, and people actually talked about the "married state." This implied that relationships and social roles of man and wife were fixed by custom. Today, with the emergence of the individualistic family pattern, we think of marriage not as a state but as an *adjustment*. This is so because custom no longer rigidly defines the roles of men and women. Every marriage presents the man and wife with the problem of working out together their relationships and roles.

SOURCE: Paul H. Landis, *Your Marriage and Family Living*, McGraw-Hill Book Company, Webster Division, St. Louis, 1954, p. 216.

The question to be answered when encouraging a student to use contextual clues is, "What do you think the word means as it is used in the sentence?" This can be amplified: "Make an educated guess." "What could it mean?" "Could it mean anything else and make sense in the sentence?"

PROFICIENCY IN STRUCTURAL ANALYSIS

Structural analysis is one of the reading skills taught in the primary grades; it starts with the study of simple derivatives. Plurals, for example, and words expressing past tense are analyzed; and pupils learn simple generalizations: that the addition of -*s* makes plural and adding -*ed* makes a past tense. They also deal with other suffixes (-*ing* and -*ly*, for example) and with compound words (such as *baseball* and *mailman*).

When the student moves into secondary school, the skill of analyzing the structure of words must be retaught as he encounters more complicated reading material. In the secondary school, analysis of derived forms demands more sophistication. Derivations are frequently formed by adding English suffixes (such as -tion, -ists, -ism, -ity, -ary, -ment, -tious, -ship, -ate, -ability, -sive, -tal, -ally, -ized) or prefixes. A second source of derivation is foreign roots: this, in fact, is one of the chief characteristics of our language. We are still adopting and adapting foreign words. But if a student has no background in any foreign language, it little profits him to hear that a particular word "comes from the Latin" or from "Old French" or whatever. This is merely substituting one meaningless element for another.

A few basic foreign roots may be helpful to students with high-average or superior abilities. Similarly, a few suffixes and prefixes may serve as guides, but there is so much inconsistency involved here that this must be of limited usefulness. One example will serve to illustrate this point. The prefix pre- often denotes before (as in prenatal, predestined, precaution, etc.). But the language is full of words—such as present and predicament—where the pre is not actually a prefix. And as a matter of fact the prefix pre- is probably more consistent than any of the others. There are several manuals and work- books that will aid a teacher who wants to work with roots and affixes, and the school's reading specialist will be able to supply several samples. In general, the classroom teacher will concentrate attention on the structure of individual words, to reveal the meaning of each word specifically, rather than using generalized guides.

Structural analysis is also used for purposes of pronunciation, the idea being that if a student can break a word into syllables, he may be able to pronounce it—and that if he can pronounce it, he may recognize it as a word he knows.

Skill in the use of structural analysis in all academic areas must be retaught by the content teachers—who else?

ABILITY TO ADJUST READING RATE AND TECHNIQUE TO PURPOSE

Generations of secondary school students have been adjured by well-meaning teachers to "read every word so you will be sure to get the meaning." Research in reading techniques belies such advice. There is absolutely no need to read everything as though one were perusing a legal contract. Mature readers do not read that way. They adjust their rate of reading to the materials and purpose, just as a mature motorist adjusts his speed to road and weather conditions and to his purpose. "Sunday drivers" are different from "Monday morning drivers" because their purposes are different. This also applies to readers.

Secondary school students should be disabused of the notion that they must "read every word carefully," and at the same time they should be shown how to use the techniques of mature readers.

Purpose: To Find a Fact within a Body of Reading Material

The fact may be a date, an amount of money, a proper name, a place, a quantity, a quality, a title, a designation, a relationship, a difference or similarity, a listing or ranking, a formula, a quotation, an action, an achievement, a motion, etc.

Technique: Scanning. One scans to find an answer. Scanning is a form of mature reading that employs the psychological principle of the "set." The reader is cued by a visual image that directs his selection of visual input. For example, because the reader determines to search for the name of an individual, his mind rejects all visual stimuli except capital letters. Similarly, the cue may be a dollar sign, quotation marks, or numerals.

Many teachers reprimand students for "looking up answers" to the questions at the end of chapters. Such nonsense reveals a lack of understanding of scanning as one of the efficient techniques of mature readers. It is a skill that should be encouraged, not discouraged.

Purpose: To Get the Gist of an Article, Report, News Item, or Selection

Technique: Skimming. If all one wants to know is the general idea, or gist, of the material, he should skim it much as one might skim a picture, picking out details here and there and fitting them into a general impression.

Skimming involves the psychological principle of transference. As one skims a piece of writing, he transfers his previous knowledge to the situation and builds a new arrangement upon a pattern he already knows. He approaches reading material with his past experiences categorized for quick retrieval. For example, he may analyze the heading, the introduction, or both, and immediately notice that the material falls into one of his categories of past experience. He skims the article, passing over much detail, to get the main idea and the colorations—which are then constructed in the same image as the other mental pictures he has placed in that category.

One example will be sufficient. Suppose we have a newspaper article evidently about hippies and a reader who has stored in his mind a stereotype (a "category") of hippies that includes long hair, beards, costumes, nomadic living, love, demonstrations, and so on. As he skims the article, the aspects of this category provide the structure for his reading. Now suppose that the gist of the article is that hippies volunteered to wash birds caught in a massive oil slick caused by a disabled ocean tanker. As the reader skims, he gets a succession of details something like this: "Disabled ocean tanker—massive oil slick—covered feathers of sea birds—cannot fly—face certain death—hippies volunteer to wash birds . . . " But by this point he will be realizing that the experiences he has categorized for retrieval are not applicable, and will begin to switch to a different area of his own experience for structuring his reading. By skimming, the reader has discovered that the article is not about hippies *qua* hippies, but about a marine crisis, and will have arrayed for retrieval his experiences concerning sea birds, destruction of environment, pollution, navigation, the petroleum industry, and so on. Skimming has enabled the reader to determine the nature of the article and to decide on his purpose and technique for reading it in more detail.

Skimming, then, involves essentially a continual dipping into one's own storehouse of knowledge and experience and rearranging the elements thus retrieved into a pattern of mental images consistent with the rather skeletal facts he will have gathered from the material being skimmed. The success of skimming, consequently, depends on the wealth of previous input. The mind that has not received an abundance of sensory experiences holds little that may be retrieved and transferred.

Purpose: To Enrich One's Own Specialized Knowledge

Technique: Adjust reading speed to type of material. We read best in the fields in which we are most interested and knowledgeable. (It is no secret that many students considered "nonreaders" in academic areas are actually avid readers of materials in which they are interested, like hot rod magazines and movie magazines.) Students who are knowledgeable and interested in a certain field may be encouraged to read the material of that field as quickly as they can. In general, materials in a field in which the reader is at home should be read rapidly. Mature readers do not read every word concerning a topic they are familiar with. They skim for landmarks that assure them of the familiarity of the material; all they should pause over is the new and different, which will enrich or modify the concepts they already have.

In contrast to this fast reading of familiar material is the need for slower reading of strange material.

The classroom teacher may help students develop a sensitivity to what reading speed is appropriate to any material by proposing these questions:

1. What do I already know about the subject? (The principle of individual differences assumes that all students have different concepts and a different amount of information and experience with any topic.)
2. What do we know if we pool the combined knowledge of the entire class?
3. Do I have to read every word? Why or why not?
4. How fast can I read this material and still feel comfortable?

Adjusting speed of reading to content and purpose is an individual decision, but the opportunity to do it should be presented by the classroom teacher. The teacher of American history, for example, should recognize that much of the material has been covered before, and that of this some has been learned and much was irrelevant when encountered in previous reading and will remain irrelevant regardless of how many times it is encountered. The teacher will obtain greater cooperation when these facts are admitted. The commitment to reading and the responsibility for deciding the pace, then, is transferred from teacher to learner—where it belongs.

SKILL IN ANALYTICAL AND CRITICAL READING

One of the skills most appropriate for development in the secondary school is the ability to read critically and analytically, since meanings and shades of meaning create the nuances that are the hallmarks of good writing and good scholarship.

It is true that most secondary school textbooks are the antithesis of good literature; most are also the antithesis of good learning principles. Their very content and format tend to encourage rote memorization and blind repetition of "facts," a practice basic to the continuance of anti-intellectualism, prejudice, and totalitarianism. But the secondary school should be the training ground for the citizens of a democracy. There, young people should be provided with the ability to understand one of the bases of democracy—the free media of communications. They should be taught how to "read between the lines" and how to evaluate and criticize what they read.

Reading of sterile textbooks must be supplemented (not supplanted) by reading of more relevant materials—some of which will zero in on controversial issues. The highest behavioral objectives in a school in a democracy must be *thinking* and the *ability to deal rationally with issues.* To do this requires training and practice in analytical and critical reading.

A vast amount of material is now available on both sides of such issues as crime in the cities, pollution, war, poverty, welfare, taxation, the military-industrial complex, politics, labor, home construction, safety, abortion reform, black power, racism, foreign aid, environmental destruction, the quality of life, love, peace, health, science, the generation gap, the aged, and credibility. Teachers have no excuse for bypassing these issues—which are rich resources for learning how to read critically and analytically.

Assuming, now, that secondary school teachers are convinced that this skill must become part of the behavioral objectives in social studies, science, literature, home economics, business, industrial arts, vocational education, and home economics, what general strategies may be employed to develop it in those subject-matter fields?

There are eleven basic elements in the process of developing analytical and critical reading ability. These are summarized in the outline which follows.

1. The teacher must provide the materials, just as he provides materials for his shop, laboratory, or studio. This requires some doing. But "seek, and ye shall find." The director of the learning materials center (formerly, the librarian) is the most valuable ally in this search.

2. List the controversial issues currently relevant in the local community, the state, the nation, and the world.
3. Excerpt those that fall within the realm of your specific content area. (Specific suggestions are presented in Chapters 7 through 12.)
4. Develop subheadings within each topic.
   a. Subtopics.
   b. The affirmative attitude—the negative attitude.
      (1) Writers who are "pro."
      (2) Writers who are "con."
      (3) Organizations, pressure groups, lobbyists.
   c. Value judgments involved.
      (1) Moral.
      (2) Economic.
      (3) Political.
      (4) Social.
      (5) Religious.
   d. Vested interests involved.
5. Set up a system for classifying the materials that are discovered.
   a. Vertical file (for clippings).
   b. Library pamphlet file boxes (of heavy cardboard).
   c. Metal "Princeton" file containers (for heavier pamphlets and booklets).
6. Ask the learning materials center to set aside a special section where the collected books, pamphlets, clippings, simulation games, films, filmstrips, tapes, etc. on each topic can be centralized.
7. Determine the readability of each of the reading materials ("high," "medium," or "low"). Eventually, as the resources increase, it may be wise to separate the reading materials into three levels of difficulty.
8. Set up student committees (of no more than three members each) to act as research teams to discover new articles, pamphlets, books, editorials, etc. weekly. Their task also is to designate exactly which heading and subheading the material is to be filed under.
9. Select volunteers to act as file clerks.
10. Using the school's letterhead, write to legislators and to executive secretaries at national headquarters of involved organizations such as labor unions, pressure groups, religious denominations, and civic organizations, asking to be placed on their permanent mailing lists. (The letter should indicate that their *free* materials will be used in your class, otherwise some groups will make a charge to defray costs of printing.)
11. The culminating step is the development of an environment that permits and encourages inquiry. Young people should be urged to react to these questions:
    a. Does the author have the same background as I have?
    b. In what ways is the author different from me?
    c. Can I fully put myself in his place? Do I really understand him as a person?
       (1) Is he a leader of a group? What does that group expect him, as their leader, to say or write?
       (2) What would I say or write if I were he?
    d. What *can't* he say and still be leader?
    e. How does he cover up some things and not say others?
    f. How does he let us "read between the lines"?
    g. Does he contradict himself?
    h. Is he keeping up to date, or not?

i. How does the opposition deal with this writer? Emotionally? Logically? By attacking him slanderously? By name-calling? By ignoring him?

j. What is the other side to this issue?

k. What is a rational solution to this issue?

Acquisition of the skill of analytical and critical reading is demonstrated by the simulation technique—not by deadly "reports" or essays. Simulation, which involves role playing, has largely supplanted the more artificial debate technique. The individual who plays a role in a controversial discussion must not only know his facts but assume the role of the defender or opposer of an idea. He must become the defender or opposer as an actor becomes the individual he is portraying. Most important of all is the fact that, to become someone else for the purpose of expounding and defending (or opposing) a position on a controversial issue, the student must read extensively and in depth (within his own capabilities), and must employ the techniques described here for analytical and critical reading.

This should be one of the prime behavioral objectives of the schools in a democracy.

Questions and Activities for Discussion and Growth

1. Select one paragraph from a secondary school textbook in your major subject area as an example of type 1 of paragraph structure (see page 64). Xerox the paragraph, cut it apart into sentences, and arrange it to show the structure. (You may want to Xerox the pattern for each member of the class you are teaching.)

2. From the textbook used in the preceding exercise, select a paragraph of type 2. Arrange it so that the examples are listed in order of appearance, with the main idea at the end.

3. Select a paragraph in which the main idea is stated first, followed by examples, and restated at the end. Arrange this as a diagram.

4. Select a paragraph in which the details, examples, or both surround the main idea—with the main idea in the middle.

5. Select a paragraph in which the main idea is stated in two parts, with each part followed by details (type 5). Arrange the parts so the structure is visible.

6. Select a paragraph in which a three-part idea is stated in the form of contrasting statements (type 6). Arrange it for visual presentation.

7. Select a paragraph in which the details are given but the main idea is only implied. Arrange the details and print the main idea in colored ink.

8. Copy a good paragraph from a secondary school text and write Who? What? When? Where? How? Why? How many? How much? over the words or phrases which give this information.

9. Using the paragraph prepared in question 8, teach a lesson to a secondary school class. Mimeograph the paragraph (original version) for distribution to all the students in the class. Ask them to prepare the paragraph as you did, writing Who? What? Where? etc. in the appropriate spots.

10. Mimeograph a paragraph from a textbook and distribute it to a secondary school class. Ask them to write four plausible statements, only one of which correctly states the main idea. Discuss with the class the similarities and differences in the ways they interpreted the main idea.

Selected References

Gainsburg, Joseph C.: *Advanced Skills in Reading*, The Macmillan Company, New York, 1964. (Chapter 2 of Book 3 is excellent supplementary reading for the teacher who is planning lessons on reading for main ideas.)

6.
PLANNING READING ASSIGNMENTS IN SECONDARY SCHOOL SUBJECTS

There are many ways to introduce a chapter or a section of a textbook. One of the most common has been merely to "assign" it for study for tomorrow. There are advantages in making a chapter assignment. Such an assignment requires no preparation on the part of the teacher, it takes very little time, and it can be made at the very end of the class period, even after the bell has rung. "Assignment giving" is an obvious benefit to the teacher who wants to put little or no effort into the process. But since little effort goes into "assigning" a chapter, is there reason to expect that any notable learning will result? In fact, do not both students *and* teacher suffer from poorly conceived assignments?

The dictionary defines an assignment as an "allotment." We have all experienced the end-of-class allotment: "Just a minute, class! Your assignment for next time is pages 391 to 402." Of course, the assignment given after the bell rings is not good. At best, it can only be hoped that enough students will have heard the assignment to pass the word around in the hall or over the phone after school. But even when an assignment based upon an allotment of pages, exercises, or problems is given before the bell rings, it violates many principles of learning, so that little real learning can be expected. A better definition of the reading assignment might be this: *The reading assignment is that essential part of content-area learning in which teacher and students discuss (1) What is to be read? (2) With what materials? (3) Why? (4) How? (5) How long is the assigned material? and (6) When is it to be read?*

COMPONENTS OF THE READING ASSIGNMENT

What Is to Be Read?

A good textbook is sequential in organization and format; therefore, reading assignments, as parts of this sequence, do not exist in isolation. An essential principle of learning is that *all learning is based upon past experience*. The reading assignment may be the outgrowth of a class discussion, or it may be based upon the segments of a larger unit of work. In any event, it is a specific portion of the whole concept and has little relevance by itself.

The assignment must be specific. It must be more than just an allotment of pages. It must deal with a topic, a concept, an idea, a philosophy, a movement, a process, a genre. Many minutes before the pages to be read are indicated, the teacher must prepare the class for the assignment. The first part of the reading assignment deals with *what*, not *which pages*. A psychological "set" must be developed by the teacher and students as an introduction to the assignment.

Readiness may be accomplished in many ways; for example, by a field trip, or demonstration; through a presentation given by means of a recording, filmstrip, videotape, or motion picture; by posters; through a talk by an expert, an experiment, or a dramatization; by means of a mock-up; by a class discussion. In any case, it takes planning by the teacher, preferably with the help of the students.

Out of this kind of preparation will emerge a need to investigate the available means for finding out—the delineation of the materials to be read.

What Materials Are Available?

It is not enough merely to indicate a specific topic or certain pages to be read. The teacher and students must know that sufficient and appropriate materials are available to ensure some degree of success for each learner in completing the assignment. Vague assignments, such as "Tomorrow, try to see if you can find out something about computorized gardening," are violations of principles of learning. An assignment like this reveals that the teacher is not sure whether or not any materials exist on the subject. There is no direction as to how much should be read, or where the information may be found. It does provide for individual initiative, but the great majority of a class would not even undertake such an assignment, and for several very valid reasons. First, many secondary school students are bus students, and when they arrive home they are far from library resources. Second, most students do not have encyclopedias or other reference works in their homes. Third, most students do not have parents, neighbors, or acquaintances who are authorities on academic subjects. Fourth, if the assignment does not grow out of the intrinsic interests of the students (and few do), it cannot be expected that they will make special efforts of research. Fifth, and perhaps most important, is the fact that such a vague assignment cannot be successfully undertaken by the majority of the class because there is no indication of whether, and where, the relevant materials are to be found. Every reading assignment, therefore, must provide the materials for its completion. The learners have a right to expect the teacher to discuss two questions with them: What materials are available? Where may they be found?

Why This Assignment?

Every reading assignment has an objective. It may be to cover a quota of pages; it may be to acquire certain facts or skills; or it may be to cover part of the sequential development of a theme or concept.

The answers to the question Why? will indicate several things about the learning that is anticipated in any class. First, is the reading a natural outgrowth of a sequence of learning experiences which provide a foundation for the next step in learning? Second, does the reading clearly have some inherent value? Third, will its completion provide the learner with some knowledge, skill, attitude, or facts of potential value to him? Fourth, what are the extrinsic rewards for reading the material?

If the learner is to develop a productive and fulfilling self-concept, it is absolutely necessary that he have some assurance of success in reading. Any reading assignment that ignores this basic need or contains elements of failure is self-defeating and should never be given. If the student understands how an assignment fits into the sequence of learning and of what value it will be to him, he is most likely to handle it successfully. Students respond to honesty in the presentation of the *raison d'être* for a reading assignment. Before the student begins the task, he should be in possession of reasonable answers to the questions noted above, which from his personal point of view would take on some such phrasing as the following:

Why does the teacher want me to do this reading?
How does it fit into the larger unit of learning?
How will it help me? Now? Later?
What's in it for me?
What if I don't do the reading?

Such questions should be "learner-centered," for it is a principle of learning that the learner must identify with each learning task and approach it from the standpoint of how it relates specifically to him.

How May This Reading Assignment Be Done?

This question implies that there may be more than one way to accomplish a reading assignment. Indeed, there must be several alternatives which provide for individual differences in ability and interest.

No single overall reading assignment should be given to a class without alternative means for accomplishing it successfully. The ways and means differ greatly from one subject to another, but some characteristics are common to most content areas—the basic textbook assignment, of course, is one of these. Even the basic textbook, however, should be used on several levels; on which level a student reads depends on his own ability and past experiences. Some students may be able only to read the headings and look at the visuals. At the opposite end of the continuum of ability there may be students who already know most of the textual material and will be able to verify that by a quick survey of the chapter; these students will be ready to move from the textbook to more satisfying reading or other activities.

In addition to the textbook, there are many other materials available for completing a subject-matter assignment. These are generally available in the multimedia center; such materials include filmstrips, programmed workbooks, laboratory manuals, overhead-projector transparencies, tapes, supplementary books, recordings, motion pictures, games, and computer-assisted (learning-machine) programs.

If the assignment includes a bibliography of outside readings, it should be perfectly clear how many are to be read, for what purpose, and whether or not they should be skimmed for answers or read for critical thinking. The student should also know how he should take notes on his outside reading and how he will use such notes.

How a student undertakes a reading assignment must depend on the type of materials to be studied and the objectives of the lesson.

How Long Is the Reading Assignment?

The common textbook assignment is closed-ended and usually bounded by pages: "Read pages 114 through 118." This sort of thing is ineffective. But many an open-ended assignment—such as "See if you can find out anything about computerized gardening"—is just as ineffective. Both these examples leave much to be desired. The former is so highly structured that it allows for no differences in motivation. The latter is such a laissez-faire approach that nothing is defined at all, and consequently the teacher must be ready and willing to accept it if no commitment at all ensues.

Students are conditioned to the idea that a reading assignment has a beginning and an end. Some defined amount should, therefore, be indicated as the minimum to be read. If the teacher is working on the assumption that there should be room for individual differences in interest, motivation, and time available, the students should know this. If there is provision for open-ended "enrichment" work, the students should know that they can achieve extrinsic rewards, such as higher grades, for doing it; at the same time, they should know that completion of the minimum amount of reading will (all other things being equal) result in a specific "average" grade.

Like any task, reading in a content area demands a certain amount of time, and time is a limited resource.[1] The amount of time that a teacher asks a student to invest in a particular reading must be reasonable and in keeping with the importance of the task.

When Is the Reading to Be Completed?

Short-term reading assignments are, by their nature, related to specific day-to-day material covered in the subject-matter classroom. Consequently, such assignments should be short and to the point; the materials needed should be easily attainable; and an assignment should fall the day when it is most relevant to what is being taken up in class.

Long-term reading assignments naturally call for expenditures of time and effort over longer periods, and should be reserved for materials that cannot and should not be read overnight. To "give" a long-term reading assignment is not enough: short-term goals should be built into it—that is, certain achievements should be called for at intervals, ensuring a continuous effort as part of the developmental process inherent in the goal of the assignment.

Just as reading assignments should be reasonable in length, so also should they have reasonable terminal dates. The length, difficulty, importance, relevance, and terminal date of an assignment are all related.

PLANNING AND PREPARATION FOR THE READING ASSIGNMENT

Although the ideal reading assignment appears to grow from a discussion or needs which emerge during a lesson, good reading assignments, like all learning, do not just happen; they are *planned*.

To be sure, there is the occasional inspired outgrowth of a lively discussion that leads to a spur-of-the-moment assignment with special relevance and immediate motivation. This is as it should be, and when it happens, it calls forth the rich resources which distinguish the master teacher from his lesser colleagues. It is more realistic, however, for a teacher to invest many hours of time in planning and preparing good reading assignments.

[1] James A. Grob, "Reading Rate and Study-Time Demands on Secondary Students," *Journal of Reading,* vol. 13, no. 4 (January, 1970), pp. 285–288.

Good planning involves a tabulation of the materials available: How many? What kind? How difficult? How accessible? No assignment can be completed successfully if the appropriate reading materials are not available. This is a responsibility which the teacher cannot shift to someone else, although other personnel may of course help him locate, acquire, and prepare relevant materials. In preparation for the ideal reading assignment, the teacher should make an annotated list of materials and have it available to the students. The specific behavioral objectives determine the nature of the reading materials that will appear on such a list. The materials become the *what* that results from a determination of *why*. The methods and materials must be appropriate to the objective.

It is practical to recognize the fact that method is more often dictated by *available* materials than formed with reference to an unlimited amount of appropriate materials.

A reading assignment is successful only to the extent to which it enlists a commitment from the learner. Commitment can be achieved only if there is open communication between the learner and the teacher. The educational theorist suggests, as the ideal, planning by both teacher and students. No doubt this is ideal; yet the realities of everyday classroom teaching often make such an ideal impossible to realize. This does not mean, however, that the teacher becomes simply an assignment-giver. On the contrary, communication with the students will provide common understanding of objectives, materials, methods, expectations, limitations, and rewards. In this manner the reading assignment is "learner-centered" even though it is prepared by the teacher. Only when lines of communication are open can this be achieved.

GIVING THE READING ASSIGNMENT

There appear to be at least twelve features of value in the process of "giving" the reading assignment. The assignment should, for example, contain the elements discussed so far (What? Why?, etc.). We may envision the assignment, practically speaking, as a segment of the learning process prepared by the teacher. The following twelve suggestions will help make it successful:

1. Students should keep notebooks, or the teacher should provide mimeographed reading-assignment sheets (the latter alternative is preferable).
2. The objectives should be clear, reasonable, specific, and pertinent. The objectives of the teacher and those of the students are not necessarily the same, but both should be understood by everyone. This is accomplished through dialogue. It is unreasonable to expect students to become involved in a learning project if its objectives are not their own.
3. List the specific intrinsic and extrinsic outcomes of an assignment. Students may view these as "rewards." In any event, they are to be predetermined through discussion by teacher and students.

4. Provide an adequate allotment of time for completion of the reading.
5. It is wise to provide and duplicate the following data so that each student may refer to it: length, materials, form of written work, limitations, ways and means, skills to be used, vocabulary, due date.
6. Review reading skills necessary for completion of the assignment. This is especially pertinent when the assignment calls for skimming, scanning, or selecting main ideas. The survey technique should be part of every textbook chapter assignment.
7. Refer to certain vocabulary in context.
8. Provide students with a duplicated list of readings available, indicating where they may be located.
9. Provide sufficient alternatives and adequate readings to allow choices based upon differences in interest and motivation; ability, skills, intelligence, experience; time available; and degree of commitment.
10. Indicate what will be done with the completed reading assignment. Students want to know that they are not just doing busywork.
11. Provide guidelines in the form of directions, questions, or both, giving assurance that the reading will be done as a cognitive process.
12. Be sure that there is complete understanding before the students are launched on their own.

The length of time spent in "giving" the reading assignment varies according to the nature of the materials and how new they are to the students. If there are many different materials involved, it may take one whole class period. On the other hand, if the reading is merely an extension or refinement of a skill already learned, it may take only a few minutes of demonstration and emphasis on transfer of training. A reasonable amount of time should be allotted, since this should never be a hurried project. It should be the culmination of a class period and the outcome of a lesson, and therefore anticipated as the next sequential step in learning. When done in this way, the giving of the reading assignment is the hallmark of a well-organized and gifted teacher.

CONCLUSION: THE IDEAL READING ASSIGNMENT

The ideal reading assignment has a purpose. It indicates why the student is to do it. It is related to the general needs and objectives of the students and is relevant both to the developmental learning of the class and to the needs of each student.

In a homogeneously grouped class there may be provision for individual interests of students, but in a heterogeneously grouped class, there must be provision not only for differences in interest but also for differences in ability and commitment, and the teacher must adjust his expectations concerning the assignment to the students' individual differences.

The best assignment comes as an outgrowth of the day's lesson. It should be developed in cooperation with the class, although it has been planned by the teacher. It must relate to the work that precedes it and be part of a larger unit of learning.

It must be specific regarding what is to be done, how much is to be done, how long a time can reasonably be spent on doing it, and when the work is due.

The reading must relate to the self-concepts and interests of the learners. It should include elements of potential and actual inherent value, as well as extrinsic rewards.

The teacher must provide access to the reading materials for accomplishing the assignment. This is done in cooperation with the learning-materials specialist (see Chapter 15).

"Most of the real teaching takes place during the assignment."[2] The following Reading Assignment Planning Form may be helpful in making the assignment truly a teaching device.

READING ASSIGNMENT PLANNING FORM

1. What is to be done?

List the "readiness" activities:

Field trip to _____

Demonstration of _____

Experiment by _____

Recording of _____

Videotape, filmstrip, or film on _____

Posters or mock-up of_____

Prepared by _____

Talk or discussion on_____

Given by _____

Dramatization of _____

Done by _____

The outcome of these activities is to be a *decision:* To do *what?*

---

[2] This comment is credited to Dr. Olive Niles, a member of the NESDEC Committee on Reading in the Secondary School Classroom.

2. **With what reading materials? Where are they to be found?**

Textbook, pages _____

   For slow readers: _____

   For average readers: _____

   For good readers: _____

   For those with special reading skills: _____

3. **Why this reading assignment? Objectives?**

Objective: _____

Intrinsic values: _____

Extrinsic values: _____

4. **How may the reading be done?**

Alternative 1 _____

Alternative 2 _____

Alternative 3 _____

Alternative 4 _____

Is the survey technique to be used with this assignment? _____

   Scanning? _____

   Skimming? _____

   "Speed-reading"? _____

Special vocabulary: _____

5. **How long is the reading?**

Minimum length _____

Average length _____

Maximum length _____

6. When is it to be completed?

Date for part 1 (if any) _____

Date for part 2 (if any) _____

Final date(s)_____

7. Dialogue on the completed reading.

What use is to be made in class of the completed assignments?

_____

_____

Is discussion anticipated? Comments:

_____

_____

_____

8. Results of the reading.
Transition to other reading, discussion, or activity.

_____

_____

_____

9. What additional activities and materials would be needed to improve this reading assignment when it is given to another class?

_____

_____

_____

Questions and Activities for Discussion and Growth

1. Plan and conduct a demonstration of two methods of giving reading assignments: (1) the "after-the-bell-rings" assignment and (2) the planned reading assignment. Discuss what outcomes a teacher could anticipate from each.

2. Using a secondary school content area textbook, plan the directions to be given in introducing a new chapter to a class under the heading: "What is to be done?"

3. Use the same textbook as in 2 above as a guide for developing a list of reading materials and their location for use in the chapter chosen in 2 above.

4. Select a chapter in a secondary school content area textbook and work out specific answers to the four questions under section 3, "Why this reading assignment?"

5. Select a chapter in a secondary school content area textbook and make four alternatives for section 4, "How may the reading be done?" Be sure to devise these for students with varying degrees of reading ability.

6. Using the materials you have developed under 2 and 3 above, make educated guesses on the times you should allot to each part.

7. Use the same chapter as you have used in 2 and 3 above. Develop a vocabulary list, with accompanying sentences in which the words are used in context.

8. Develop questions for guidelines for reading a specific chapter of secondary school material.

9. Plan follow-up activities for enrichment for the better readers who will skim the chapter and be ready for more materials.

10. Develop several specific extrinsic "rewards" which would be relevant to the particular students for whom you have planned the reading assignment. Indicate why you believe each is relevant to young people today.

Selected References

Grob, James A.: "Reading Rate and Study-Time Demands on Secondary Students," *Journal of Reading,* vol. 13, no. 4 (January, 1970), pp. 285–288ff. (Provides charts indicating time necessary to read certain English and social studies assignments at various reading rates.)

Kollaritsch, Jane: "Organizing Reading for Detailed Learning in a Limited Time," *Journal of Reading,* vol. 13, no. 1 (October, 1969), pp. 29–32.

Struck, John W.: "How To Provide Better Assignments for Improved Instruction," *Industrial Arts and Vocational Education,* vol. LI (November, 1962), pp. 24–25.

Williams, M., and S. Black: "Assignments: Key to Achievement," *Journal of Reading,* vol. 11, no. 2 (November, 1968), pp. 129–133.

7.
READING IN THE SOCIAL STUDIES CLASSROOM

Bringing young people and books together in the social studies classroom requires far greater know-how than the simple giving out of assignments which was considered to be enough a few years ago. Textbook writers and publishers in the social studies spend years of work and millions of dollars to provide textbooks and supplementary enrichment materials at many levels of comprehension. The secondary school social studies teacher who is unaware of this vast wealth of materials and is satisfied with simply handing out assignments in one textbook is, indeed, an obsolete teacher. However, the overwhelming majority of secondary school social studies classrooms are and will continue to be oriented to a single textbook; therefore, we must investigate strategies for handling textbook reading, and delineate the behavioral objectives of reading in the social studies.

BEHAVIORAL OBJECTIVES IN THE SOCIAL STUDIES

The social studies have been called the "core of the curriculum." They are the areas most likely to be different in the schools of a democratic society than in the schools of a dictatorship or totalitarian state. In a democracy, the social studies are meant to train young citizens to think, to weigh alternatives, to distinguish fact from propaganda, and to make choices. Choice is based upon alternatives; weighing alternatives is a process that should be based upon facts.

One of the essential behavioral objectives of reading in the social studies is the acquisition of a body of relevant facts. Social studies textbooks do present facts; but since it is impossible to present all the facts, the texts are selective—and therein lies their weakness. It is not surprising that they have been accused of omission, prejudice, biased presentation, and even slander.

The facts presented by textbooks (which need, as has been noted, to be supplemented by other sources) are only one step toward the goal of producing an informed, reflective citizen fully capable of making rational decisions. The second behavioral objective for social studies reading, then, is the ability to think using facts as the building blocks. The result should be a coherent whole rather than a collection of unrelated facts.

Finally, the third prime behavioral objective of reading in the social studies is to train citizens in analytical and critical skills so that they may be competent to take part in formulating decisions.

READING SOCIAL STUDIES TEXTBOOKS

Although some would prefer it otherwise, most social studies classrooms are "textbook-centered" and oriented toward facts. This, in itself, is not entirely bad; only when unrelated facts become the total product does a social studies classroom fail to reach the behavioral objectives for which it exists.

Organizational Patterns

The organizational pattern of a social studies textbook reflects the philosophy of the authors. One valuable aid to reading comprehension is a preview of the organizational pattern. In most social studies texts, the pattern will be one of several alternatives: (1) chronological, (2) topical, (3) by social organizations, (4) by movements, (5) regional, (6) theoretical. Let us examine these organizational patterns. (Since history is the social studies area common to all secondary schools, most of the examples given here are drawn from history textbooks, usually eleventh-grade American history. The techniques suggested for dealing with the specific examples given may, of course, be applied equally well to other branches of the social studies in which classes are based on a textbook: economics, government, sociology, geography, world civilization, area studies, American problems, and contemporary affairs.)

Chronological organization. It has been traditional to present history as a running story, divided into periods identified by generally accepted titles—for example, "The Golden Age of Athens," "The Renaissance in Italy," "The Reconstruction Period." Chronological, or sequential, history is sometimes introduced into other areas of the social studies, when topics are presented as periods in time: "The Industrial Revolution," "The Growth of Big Business and Industry," "The Labor Movement," "The Rise of Socialism," "Colonialism and Exploitation," "The New Deal."

If a social studies textbook is organized chronologically, awareness of this is one of the first steps in helping the students prepare to read it.

Topical organization. Of course, periods of history are themselves topical. But a topic can cut across chronology, as do the following: "The Congress," "The Supreme Court," "Benevolent Despots," "The Middle East," "The Orient," "Welfare." A great deal of material in the social studies is presented in a framework of topics; and many textbooks in economics, government, sociology, geography, and contemporary affairs are organized topically.

Arrangement by social organizations. Although the social studies deal with the social organizations which men have developed, destroyed, and restructured through the ages, few textbooks have ventured to deal with the social organizations beyond "safely" mentioning them in purely factual terms. Unfortunately—or perhaps fortunately—this makes the study of social organizations largely a matter of outside reading. Most social studies textbooks deal "safely" with the potentially controversial organizations, presenting only unarguable facts about them: "The CIO," "The Democratic Party," "The Jesuits," "The British Empire," "The Police," "The National Association of Manufacturers"— all are handled in this way. The reason for this failure to grapple with the issues raised by the imperfections of social organizations is usually a fear of criticism and loss of sales.

The task of the teacher—and the students—is to be aware of the inadequacies of the textbook and to move on to less superficial reading and more enlightened discussion. Only through a serious examination of social organizations can one really understand topics in the social studies.

Organization by movements. "Movements" are usually a matter of organizations, but some social studies texts treat movements in isolation from the organizations involved. This is a poor plan. The reader cannot comprehend a movement isolated in this fashion. He can only memorize and repeat the facts presented.

For example, "The Labor Movement," is often presented by means of statistics on membership, names of leaders, and legislation resulting from pressure by labor (with name of act, date, and other uninspiring details). Other movements are presented similarly, with no evaluation and inadequate information on the organizations involved. Every "movement" is a cause-and-effect situation — a challenge to the *status quo*. Protecting the *status quo* is an in-group organization; and challenging it is an out-group organization. When an out-group wins, it becomes an in-group, and eventually it will have to defend its status against challenges from new out-groups. This is the story of mankind and the essence of the social studies. It is difficult to understand why few social studies texts deal with movements fron this viewpoint. Indeed, when movements are taken up at all, it is almost always in an inadequate fashion. Fortunately, the social studies student will find some of his most fascinating reading in supplementary materials on movements.

Regional organization. Regional studies are relatively new in the social studies, and few textbook writers have ventured to produce books organized regionally for use in secondary schools. This is primarily due to textbook publishers, whose chief purpose is to sell books and make a profit. The market for regional-studies texts is not yet sufficient to encourage this type of approach.

In geography, however, the regional framework is of course most common. Here it tends to become simply a factual presentation, mastery of which calls only for memorization. This is not "reading" in its true sense, but the facts gained may be the foundation for subsequent reading of enrichment materials on the regions studied.

Theoretical organization. This is a sophisticated way to arrange a textbook. Economics textbooks tend to imitate the content and theory of college texts; and their organization is consequently often theoretical. Economic theory is presented in such abstract segments as "wealth," "balance of trade," "labor," "imputed income," "land," and "cheap money."

Secondary school social studies texts that are structured in this way are extremely difficult for even college-bound students to read. They are quite inappropriate for nonacademic students.

Frame of Reference

It is essential to comprehension of secondary school social studies texts that the reader understand the particular frame of reference of the authors, for what is "truth" to one person may be "distortion" to another. Let us take history as an example.

History has often been called "the story of the past and the study of the future." This may be an oversimplification; perhaps it is more accurate to say that history is the seeking of truth within a frame of reference.

To name a few frames of reference which have been used by historians suggests the various ways in which history may be written: the "frontier theory," utilitarian philosophy, social history, geographic foundations, the "heartland theory," "great personalities." The ultimate purpose of history appears to be a better understanding of man. How one should go about reading a history text depends upon the viewpoint, training, experience, and competence of the author—these elements may work for or against the student. Moreover, the common assumption that the student approximates the reader the historian had in mind is often gratuitous and unwarranted.

Analytical and Critical Reading

The student not only must become familiar with organizational patterns mentioned above, but also must utilize analytical and critical reading skills—he must be alert to inconsistency, distortion, and fallacious reasoning, for any or all of these may creep into an account presented by a particular author. And the student must, furthermore, become aware of his own biases and those of his teacher.

Perhaps the most logical first step is to recognize the *themes* being presented. The sooner the student discovers general and specific themes, the easier it will be for him to read. Let us again take history as an example. In Bragdon and McCutchen's *History of a Free People*, the following themes appear:[1]

1. Economic opportunity
2. Wide participation in politics
3. Belief in reform (rather than revolution)
4. Mobile population
5. High status and freedom of women
6. Belief in education, and widespread educational opportunity
7. Concern for the welfare of others
8. Toleration of differences
9. Respect for the rights and abilities of others
10. World-wide responsibility

As a part of students' training in critical reading it will be well to test these themes against the reality of the students' own lives and American life in general. For instance, one theme is women's high status and high degree of freedom. Is this in comparison with other countries? If so, it may be true that American women have a better position than women of some other countries (such as China), but the comparison may not hold true as regards others (such as India, where the Prime Minister is a woman). On the other hand, perhaps the position of American women is being compared with that of American men; in this case, the validity of the theme is doubtful, for women are not enjoying

[1] Henry W. Bragdon and Samuel P. McCutchen, *History of a Free People,* 5th ed., The Macmillan Company, New York, 1964.

opportunities comparable to those for men. Although there are women senators, doctors, and college presidents (of women's colleges), opportunities for such positions are not commensurate with the number of women in the country—or even with the number of women who work outside the home. Similarly, themes 3, 5, 8, and 9 require closer scrutiny by students and teachers.

Steps for developing the ability to read critically are described in Chapter 5.

The "Spiral Concept" in the Social Studies

The spiral concept has two aspects in the social studies. First, much material and many concepts and facts are being retaught—it is hoped, at a higher level of cognition. Second, reading skills only touched upon in grades 4, 5, and 6 lend themselves to further development and elaboration in junior and senior high school. These reading skills have already been discussed, in Chapter 5. We can now see how they apply in social studies.

Surveying the chapter is an essential skill and must be utilized at every level in every social studies classroom. The textbooks are all designed so this may be done. Indeed, since their structure is important, it would be gross negligence not to conduct the survey as described in Chapter 4.

Reading for main ideas is a skill that must be utilized over and over in the social studies; and the ability to find and use main ideas is what most significantly differentiates good from poor achievers in this area.

Attention to advanced and specialized vocabulary in the social studies is the responsibility of the classroom teacher. It cannot be assumed that the student has sufficient skill in contextual or structural analysis to be able to figure out new words on his own. Those skills need to be retaught. (See also Chapter 5.)

Other Reading Skills in the Social Studies

Other elements of social studies reading that are essential to understanding are listed below; some of these have already been noted in our discussion of the more general skills of analysis and criticism.

> Interpretation of charts, maps, and graphs
> Locating, reading, collecting, and organizing data for reports
> Recognizing half-truths
> Detection and analysis of propaganda
> Distinguishing between fact and opinion
> Suspending judgment while gathering information
> Drawing conclusions

INQUIRY AND DECISION MAKING IN THE SOCIAL STUDIES

The latest trends in the teaching of secondary social studies include a definite effort to apply some of the basic principles of learning. Although any of several specialized terms for this may be used by the experts, we may describe the major thrust simply as the encouragement of decision making by the student. This decision making is contrasted with fact finding, which for generations was too often the end product of social studies instruction.

Decision making is based upon knowledge of facts, but it elicits thinking skills other than simple recall of facts. The student must be able to go through these steps in problem solving: observation, reading for information, recording information, analyzing and evaluating the information (critical reading), and deciding (that is, coming to some conclusion regarding the information). The linked processes of fact finding and decision making are known as the "inquiry approach." In this approach, the psychological processes of divergent and convergent thinking and the logical processes of deductive and inductive reasoning are involved.

Three factors determine the level at which each student operates: intelligence, experience, and reading ability. The responsibility of the social studies teacher, if the inquiry approach is to be successful, is threefold: (1) to provide reading materials appropriate to the students' reading abilities and relevant to their interests, (2) to plan assignments that incorporate the steps necessary for inquiry and problem solving, (3) to allow time for the process to function.

THE READING ASSIGNMENT IN THE SOCIAL STUDIES

In the preparation of a reading assignment, the elements listed below may be condensed, combined, modified, or rearranged. For example, discussing what the students already know could be the opening element for one unit or chapter. For another it may be more appropriate to discuss the topic at a personal level as the introduction to the reading material. A word, especially, about the elements listed under item 3: Learning to ask a question before reading is often very difficult, even for the best students; but asking the right questions sets the direction of reading and consequently is a most important thinking skill, one which ensures cognitive learning instead of memorization of facts.

Directed study (here, of history specifically) includes the following activities, which provide many alternatives:

1. Preparation for reading the assignment
   (a) Review what has gone before.
   (b) Relate this to what is coming.
   (c) Preview what is coming.
   (d) Discuss what the students know.
   (e) Relate this to what is coming.
   (f) Elicit questions related to content.
   (g) If their questions are not adequate, then provide a question to answer.

2. Vocabulary and development of concepts
   (a) Discuss concepts that need clarification.
   (b) Present vocabulary in context (not in isolation).
   (c) Relate general and specific word meanings to context.
3. The purpose of reading
   (a) Read to answer a question.
   (b) Tailor the question to the group.
   (c) When necessary, fit the question to an individual.
   (d) Pose problems when appropriate.
   (e) Read for more than one solution.
4. Discussion after reading
   (a) Use the purposes of the reading as a point of departure.
   (b) Challenge the students to probe below the surface facts.
   (c) Seek inferences.
   (d) Draw tentative conclusions.
   (e) Elicit alternative solutions.
5. Aftermath
   (a) When facts or interpretations are contested, follow through with more reading.
   (b) Skim for the gist.
   (c) Scan for specific information.
   (d) On occasion, read aloud from the text.
   (e) Follow up with readings from other sources.

The following excerpt on page 107, from Bragdon and McCutchen, has been used to develop three different lessons, for each of which five approaches are given.

SAMPLE LESSON 1—FOR AN ABOVE-AVERAGE GROUP

Behavioral objectives. Reading for implied relationships; evaluating statements; and seeking weaknesses in reasoning. This is, of course, "critical reading."

Approach 1

Before we start to study the next passage, who can put it into context for us? (The passage is taken from Chapter 20, "Protest Movements," which follows "The Opening of the Great West" and precedes "Parties and Politics.")

At what age in life is a person likely to be inclined to protest? (Can you see any relation between this period of time in the life of our country and adolescence in the life of a person?)

What kind of person is most likely to protest? (What forms does protest take today? Are they significant?)

Approach 2

What does *prohibition* mean? In general? In particular? What is a *reformer*? A *do-gooder*? A *dedicated* person? A *starry-eyed visionary*? A *hard-headed realist*? What is a *radical*? What do *Abolitionist* and *suffrage* mean? What is *the other half*? What does it mean to live on *the other side of the tracks*?

Reformers and Radicals

Several reform movements which started in the Jacksonian period continued throughout the nineteenth century. Prohibition supporters formed a political party and from 1872 on put up a presidential candidate who never gained more than a handful of votes. More effective than the Prohibition Party in promoting temperance was the Women's Christian Union, a national organization which waged a ceaseless campaign against the evils of liquor and the saloon.

Women's Rights.   The W.C.T.U. revealed again what the Sanitary Commission had shown during the War Between the States—that women were learning the technique of large-scale organization. The conditions of life in industrial cities offered women new job opportunities. These opportunities appeared not only in factories and stores, but also in offices as the invention of the typewriter and telephone created a need for thousands of stenographers and switchboard operators. Added to the independence gained from earning their own living was the fact that girls had the same public school education as boys. Women gained more chance for higher education with the opening of women's colleges such as Vassar, Smith, Wellesley, and Bryn Mawr, and the advantage of coeducation in state universities.

It is no wonder that women continued to demand the right to vote, and received support from the other sex. Wendell Phillips, the former Abolitionist, argued their case as follows:

> One of two things is true: either a woman is like a man—if she is, then a ballot based upon brains belongs to her as well as to him; or she is different, and then man does not know how to vote for her as well as she does herself.

Both the Knights of Labor and the American Federation of Labor supported women's suffrage. By 1900 eighteen states had given women the right to vote in school board elections: four—Colorado, Wyoming, Utah, and Idaho—had granted them full voting rights.

Slums and Settlement Houses.   While older reform movements continued, new ones appeared to deal with problems created by the rise of the city. One of the most horrible aspects of urban life was the slum, where human beings were packed together so closely that they sometimes averaged five to a room, where lack of sanitation bred disease, and where children had no playground but the street. In 1890 public attention was focused on this evil by a book called *How the Other Half Lives.* This was written by Jacob Riis, a Danish American, who as police reporter on a New York newspaper had seen a connection between slum conditions and crime. Riis's description of the misery of the slums stimulated demands for legislation to enforce minimum standards of human decency and to create public playgrounds for children. Meanwhile, other reformers tried to improve the lot of slum dwellers.

Settlement houses, inspired by Toynbee Hall in the slums of London, England, were established in the poorer districts of our cities. Although settlement houses attempted to brighten the lives of *all* slum dwellers, they were especially interested in children, on the principle that "a fence at the top of a precipice is better than an ambulance at the bottom." They provided playgrounds, boys' clubs, and vocational instruction. To the settlement houses flocked young college graduates, glad to enlist in a war against human suffering.

SOURCE: Bragdon and McCutchen, History of a Free People, The Macmillan Company, New York 1964. Reprinted with permission.

Approach 3

What question(s) occur to you when you read the title "Reformers and Radicals"? (How are they the same? How are they different? What do they have to do with protest movements? Is either term complimentary? Derogatory?)

Do you think reformers and radicals play an important part in society? Are they a necessary evil?

Does the following passage have logical integrity? Identify a fallacy or defend the logic. "One of two things is true: either a woman is like a man—if she is, then a ballot based on brains belongs to her as well as to him; or she is different, and then man does not know how to vote for her as well as she does herself."

Are the authors (Bragdon and McCutchen) aware of any fallacy in the statement? What were the credentials of the man making this statement? (Wendell Phillips, described as a former Abolitionist). Is he qualified to comment here as an authority on this subject (the rights of women)? Since history deals with documents and authorities, students of history must learn what these are. There are at least four kinds of "false authorities": (1) those taken from past contexts and cited in relation to a contemporary situation for which there is no exact historical parallel; (2) those whose reputation has been made in a field other than that concerning which they are being cited; (3) those who are not qualified to speak as authorities at all; and (4) ideas or concepts cited as an authority.

Approach 4

Consider this statement: "An ounce of prevention is worth a pound of cure." Is the statement valid? What analogy is implied? Can you think of another proverb which makes the same statement?

Consider this: "Although settlement houses attempted to brighten the lives of all slum dwellers, they were especially interested in children, on the principle that 'a fence at the top of a precipice is better than an ambulance at the bottom.'"

Is this a legitimate reason for being interested in children? Is this analogy a statement of the policy of settlement houses; or is it the authors' interpretation; or is there some other possibility—and, if so, what? Is the settlement house the only answer or the only way to deal with the problem of slums? What does contemporary society do about this problem?

Approach 5

Consider the statement on settlement houses (see above, approach 4). Would some of you read this aloud? (After reading, solicit reactions to the content of the passage.) What is the significance of the term all, emphasized in this selection? Who now attempts to "brighten the lives of all slum dwellers"? Is this a patronizing approach? How would you feel if people felt the need to "brighten" your life? Would you tell them to mind their own business?

What is the gist of the entire selection "Reformers and Radicals"?

What would you (the class) consider appropriate follow-up activities for this chapter on protest and this selection on reformers and radicals? (Here are possibilities: reading other sources; identifying and interviewing prominent local reformers, radicals, and founders or members of protest movements; writing letters to some who are more prominent, and remote; writing a protest play; reading a protest book; seeing a protest play.)

SAMPLE LESSON 2—FOR AN AVERAGE GROUP

Behavioral objective. To read through the written material more rapidly without sacrificing comprehension. In order to do this the student must use contextual aids.

Approach 1

Before we start to study this selection, we should recall that it comes from a chapter on the protest movement. People involved in this movement objected to what was going on in the cities (this took place around the turn of the century, and before).

Can anyone think of such movements going on today?

How are *reformers* and *radicals* different?

Approach 2

What do the terms *reformer* and *radical* mean?

Literally, *reform* means *to make over* or *shape again*; and the *-er* on the end of the word *reformer* means what? (Etc.)

Approach 3

Our purpose in studying this selection is to practice our skill in surveying an assignment —to see if we can get the gist of a passage before we become involved in the details. The best way to do this is to follow the structure of the text. For example, let's look at some of the subheadings.

"Women's Rights." What does this have to do with the section title? What does it have to do with the protest movement? What rights do women have? Did they have the right to vote at this period of history?

"Slums and Settlement Houses." Can you see a connection between this subheading and the one we just discussed?

"How the Other Half Lives." What does this title have to do with the selection? With the section heading? Could *the other half* refer to a group of people in the city about whom some might be protesting, and for whom they would seek help?

In New York City today, who might *the other half* be?

Approach 4

An analogy is quoted: "A fence at the top of a precipice is better than an ambulance at the bottom." What does this have to do with working with children? Is the statement realistic?

Was the purpose of the assignment achieved? (That is, to survey the passage without getting bogged down in a welter of details.)

Approach 5

After getting the general picture, and perhaps discussing the gist of the selection, a careful reading is in order. But a flow of ideas is to be encouraged before any reading is attempted. Brainstorming, free association, discussion of words with many meanings— these are possible warmups for this group. In counterpoint to women's rights there are men's rights, children's rights, animals' rights, civil rights, and so on.

Follow-up may include brief reports (some oral) on related readings and related events (radio, movies, and television are possible sources).

SAMPLE LESSON 3—FOR A BELOW-AVERAGE GROUP

Behavioral objective. To pick out main ideas. In each of the five approaches suggested here, the teacher should be helping the class to fill in an outline on the main idea of protest. It will be helpful to establish a familiarity with the subject by discussing contemporary protest. The following questions about contemporary protest will stimulate discussion and also provide models for reading for answers—a good way to find main ideas.

> *Who?* Who has been a protester that we know about?
> *What?* What did he protest about?
> *When?* When did he protest?
> *Why?* Why did he protest?
> *Where?* Where did he protest?
> *How?* How did he protest?

Approach 1

In this chapter on the protest movement we have seen how farmers, laborers, and reformers attempted to resist the power of organized business. The power of railroads, trusts, and monopolies gave rise to organization of some workers into labor unions. People then had an organized and powerful way of protesting the abuses of power by business and industry. Eventually, there was to be a protest against the abuse of power by the labor unions themselves. Protest is always against some concentration of power.

What do you suppose you would protest about if you were a slave? If you were a woman who could not vote? If you lived in one room with five of your family? If the landlord raised your rent and didn't fix your leaky ceiling?

Do people have a right to protest? What about? How? Why?

What are people protesting about today? Who are some of the protesters today? Where are they protesting? Why are they protesting? How are they protesting?

Approach 2

What does *reform* mean? *Re-* in *return* means . . . ? *Re-* in *replay* means . . . ? *Reform school* is different from prison. Would an individual who wants to "shape again" (a *reformer*), be more willing or less willing to help you than would a radical?

Prohibition is another word that may be new to some of you. You have seen signs that said: "The use of firecrackers is now *prohibited* by law." "The sale of cigarettes to minors is *prohibited*." What is the general meaning of *prohibition*? *Prohibition* (with a capital P) meant that something specific was forbidden; we will see what it was as we read the textbook.

After the selection has been read: Some of you disagreed about the meaning of *Prohibition*. Who can read the explanation in the text? We didn't discuss what an *Abolitionist* is; were you able to figure out by the way it was used in the text? Not really —there wasn't enough information. Some may have remembered the explanation from the chapter on the Civil War. We could look it up in the dictionary; but you can't always stop to look up a new word. There is another way. Look at the word *Abolitionist*. That *-ist* often can be found at the end of a word, like *scientist*. And *-tion* is a familiar noun ending that is added to a verb. In this case the root is *abolish*. People who want to ban the bomb want to *abolish* it. In the time of the Civil War some people felt strongly against slavery and they wanted to *abolish* it. They were called *Abolitionists*. Do you now have an idea of the meaning of the term?

Approach 3

Let us decide our purpose in studying "Reformers and Radicals" now. Does anyone have a suggestion? Girls can imagine working at home, doing what they are told and not being able to make even one suggestion about a better or easier way to do the housework. Boys can imagine not having any free time or money because they cannot get part-time jobs that pay much.

Now suppose, all of a sudden, you are the one in charge. What would you do? How would you go about running things? Should women have a say in how things are done? Should people always remain poor? What would you do to help people who are *really* poor?

How would you help? Now, read to find out if the reformers and radicals did what you would have done.

Approach 4

Now that you have read about what the reformers did, what do you think of their actions?

Is that the way you would have helped women get their rights? Would you have done what they did in the slums? What do you think of the way settlement houses approached the problems? What else might have been done? Is the situation in the slums the same today? What is being done now? What else can be done?

Approach 5

As a follow-up to this study, there are a number of projects we could do. For instance, we could plan a model city where protest would not be necessary; we could list everything that we could think of that people might protest against; we could find out what the students in our school now protest against, and see if they have a legitimate gripe and what form their protest has taken.

ASSESSING READING ABILITY IN THE SOCIAL STUDIES

Vocabulary is the essential feature of social studies reading materials, for the specialized terms used in history, economics, government, and the other content areas carry the key concepts of those fields. One of the ways to identify a secondary school student who will probably have trouble reading social studies material is to administer the following short diagnosis test, which has been devised specially for the social studies.

Ordinarily there will be no need to reproduce this test, since it is to be given individually to each student. The student can read directly from this book. One or two minutes is enough time to determine whether or not he will probably have trouble reading social studies material.

Three alternative forms of the test are provided, so students will not be able to memorize the content as they hear it read aloud by other students.

PROGNOSTIC TEST OF READING DISABILITY
IN SECONDARY SCHOOL SOCIAL STUDIES[2]

Directions:
Cover the two forms not being used (a 5-inch by 7-inch card or a sheet of paper will do).

Ask the student to pronounce the words, reading from left to right. He should read each word and move on to the next at his normal rate of reading. Observe his facial expression as he reads. Note hesitation, repetition, uncertainty, regression, and mispronunciations (including incorrect stress and accent); and note the student who is not able to move along smoothly at a minimum rate of one word every two seconds. When these things occur, the student is likely to have trouble in social studies because he lacks adequate proficiency in sight vocabulary.

Alternative Form A

monarchy	diplomacy	constitution	superstition
barbarians	environment	contribution	communication
mongoloid	Polynesians	plunder	migratory
adaptability	fusion	characteristics	postglacial
circumstances	fertility	civilization	irrigation
inscription	ancient	implements	cultural
conquests	ceremonies	reverence	monotonous
abundance	aristocratic	architecture	engineering
scribes	inhabitants	caravans	fertile
thriving	settlements	mistress	oppression

Alternative Form B

militarists	philosophers	tactics	barriers
domesticated	genius	geographical	interference
expansion	tyranny	democracy	clash
compelled	succession	preservation	dominions
achievements	strengthened	privileges	ignorance
martyr	influences	centuries	decisive
representative	surrender	fragments	popularity
abandoned	thrived	overthrown	resistance
numerous	opponents	ill-fated	independent
exploitation	enormous	magnificent	splendor

Alternative Form C

founding	compensation	proclamation	conquest
dependencies	reconstruction	annexation	intervention
insurrection	colonization	monopoly	majority
minority	nationalism	parliamentary	decentralize
consolidation	unification	automation	expansion
repeal	technological	temporary	concentration
suffrage	philanthropy	imperialism	alliance
crisis	diplomacy	assassination	neutrality
finances	obligations	disarmament	dictatorship
totalitarian	depression	prosperity	suppression

[2]Copyright 1971 by Robert C. Aukerman.

ASSESSING THE READABILITY OF SOCIAL STUDIES TEXTS

The elements of readability have been described in Chapter 3. The social studies lend themselves admirably to an application of the general concept of readability—that is, that difficult textbooks are appropriate for good readers, "average" texts are suitable for "average" readers, and texts of low difficulty are all that poor readers can handle.

A few examples from social studies texts will illustrate the extremes of readability which exist. All of the following selections are on the same subject, the dropping of the atomic bomb on Hiroshima. The first example is from a text written for secondary school students in low-ability sections.

President Truman warned the Japanese to surrender or face the consequences. When he received no answer to his warning, he authorized the use of the atomic bomb. In August of 1945 an American plane dropped one of these bombs on the city of Hiroshima. The main part of the city was wiped out. The world was astounded and horrified.

Two days later an atomic bomb was dropped on Nagasaki, with the same devastating results. The Japanese leaders, realizing that it was hopeless to continue, asked for peace. A surrender document was signed on the battleship *Missouri* on September 2, and American forces soon occupied Japan.

The war was over, but there was little rejoicing. It had been a horrible war. Millions of lives had been sacrificed; much of the earth's surface had been ruined. The war debts would never be paid. Use of the atomic bomb had shown that any future war would be even more horrible and devastating.

SOURCE: Harold H. Eibling, Fred M. King, and James Harlow, History of Our United States, Laidlaw Brothers, River Forest, Illinois, 1966, pp. 548–549.

For ease in reading, the authors have generally written short sentences; there is, however, no control of vocabulary, with the result that a number of difficult and abstract terms are included. Such terms as *consequences, authorized, astounded, horrified, devastating, realizing, document, rejoicing,* and *sacrificed* are beyond the everyday verbal usage of students with low ability. Moreover, students with low reading ability do not have the word-analysis skills necessary to "figure out" such terms. All are three- and four-syllable words, which means that they require skill in syllabication. Pronouncing them requires a knowledge of phonetic analysis. Few of these terms, if any, will have been mastered previously by students in low-ability groups.

The conclusion must be that each paragraph in this very short account of the atomic bomb contains enough unknown vocabulary to make it *unusable* with poor readers.

Here is a second, equally short, account of the same topic.

The Atomic Bombing of Japan. With the end of the war in Europe, Allied air attacks on Japan increased. Then, at 8:15 A.M. on August 6, an American B-29 changed the course of history by dropping an atomic bomb on the Japanese city of Hiroshima. Nearly 100,000 people were killed outright or died later from aftereffects, and many square miles of the city were destroyed. This one bomb had a destructive power equivalent to a raid by two thousand B-29's, or to 20,000 tons of dynamite. The atomic bomb was the result of four years of top-secret research by American scientists working with leading scientists of other nations. Among the leaders of this international group were Leo Szilard, Enrico Fermi, Harold Urey, and J. Robert Oppenheimer. Basic research and development were done at the University of Chicago; Oak Ridge, Tennessee; Los Alamos, New Mexico; and Hanford, Washington.

Two days after the bomb was dropped the Soviet Union attacked Japanese forces in Manchuria. The Russians had promised America and Great Britain that they would enter the Japanese war three months after the war in Europe ceased. The next day, August 9, an atomic bomb was dropped on Nagasaki. Five days later Japan stopped fighting, and on September 2 General MacArthur accepted the formal surrender of Japan aboard the *U.S.S. Missouri* in Tokyo Bay.

SOURCE: Walter Johnson, THE UNITED STATES SINCE 1865. Copyright © 1965 by Ginn and Company, Boston. Pp. 394–395. Reprinted by permission.

Although this passage is as factual as the previous example, it does not contain as many roadblocks to comprehension. The textbook in which it appears, moreover, includes a special section, "The Human Side of History," which gives a first-person account of the bombing by a young Japanese boy. A picture of destroyed Nagasaki also appears. The result is that the text provides alternatives. Good students can read the factual account and the first-person report and will also examine the picture. Average students can read the first-person report. Poor students can react to the picture of total destruction. All will gain some understanding of that fateful day in history.

Our third example (by Harlow and Noyes) is also factual, but it illustrates more difficult reading material that would be enjoyed by better students. It is embellished with "picturesque" description. This passage is reproduced on page 115. The following are a few phrases from it. The teacher would want to discuss the meaning of such descriptive phrases, in order to give the class a better understanding of this kind of writing:

"... succeed in turning the fantastic energy ... into a fearful weapon ..."
"... reeling under devastating American air and naval bombardments."
"Her cities were ablaze from fire bombs."
"... brought the Japanese to their knees ..."
"... Americans could not rest easy ..."
"... resistance had been brave and dogged ..."
"... live under its fearful shadow."

By that time, Japan was reeling under devastating American air and naval bombardments. She was cut off from her sources of food and raw materials. Her cities were ablaze from fire bombs. Still, her army stubbornly refused to admit defeat. President Truman decided to use the bomb to bring the war to a quick end. Accordingly, on August 6, 1945, a single B-29 bomber dropped the first atomic bomb ever used in combat on the Japanese city of Hiroshima. In a matter of minutes, the bomb wiped out the entire city and killed or injured over 160,000 human beings. Two days later, Russian forces, by pre-arrangement, poured into Manchuria and Korea. Then, the next day, a second atomic bomb was dropped on the port of Nagasaki, and the death and destruction of Hiroshima were repeated. The Japanese then asked for peace. On September 2, 1945, the formal surrender was signed aboard the battleship *Missouri*, anchored in Tokyo Bay. The Japanese had lasted just four months longer than the Germans.

Although the atomic bomb had brought the Japanese to their knees and ended the war, many Americans could not rest easy over what we had done to Hiroshima and Nagasaki. They argued that other means of defeating the Japanese might have been used. But our government claimed that the use of the atomic bomb had been a military neces-

THE ATOMIC BOMB. This deadly column over Nagasaki convinced the Japanese they should surrender, while the world gasped at the power that had been released.

sity, for the Japanese still had a million men in China and perhaps as many more on the home islands ready for a last stand. Their resistance had been brave and dogged all through the Pacific war, and the invasion of Honshu which was scheduled for early 1946 would have cost hundreds of thousands of casualties. Thus the atom bomb ended the war quickly and undoubtedly saved countless lives, both American *and* Japanese. However, the world now had to live under its fearful shadow.

SOURCE: Ralph V. Harlow and Herman N. Noyes, Story of America, Holt, Rinehart, and Winston, Inc., New York, 1961, pp. 721–722. Copyright © 1961 by Holt, Rinehart, and Winston, Inc., Reprinted by permission.

Here is a fourth description of the same event, presented in simple terms. No value judgments are implied, but none are expected; this is a purely factual account.

End of the war. On August 6, 1945, an American bombing plane dropped a single atomic bomb on the Japanese city of Hiroshima. The bomb destroyed nearly all of the city. Three days later, the United States dropped an atomic bomb on the Japanese city of Nagasaki.

The Japanese were now convinced that they could not win the war in the Pacific. On August 14, 1945, President Truman announced that Japan had surrendered. On September 2, 1945, representatives of the Japanese emperor came aboard the American battleship *Missouri* in Tokyo Bay. In the presence of General MacArthur, the Japanese signed the treaty of surrender. World War II was ended.

SOURCE: From AMERICA: ITS PEOPLE AND VALUES, by Leonard C. Wood and Ralph H. Gabriel, © 1971 by Harcourt Brace Jovanovich, Inc., and reprinted with their permission. P. 726.

Similarly, the following account is in the style of a news bulletin:

Then on August 6, 1945, an American bomber dropped the first atomic bomb ever used in warfare on the city of Hiroshima. Three days later, the second atomic bomb was dropped on the city of Nagasaki. The bombs destroyed the greater part of both cities and killed one-third of the populations. Faced with annihilation, Japan surrendered. On September 2, less than four months after Germany's surrender, Japanese delegates signed the terms of defeat aboard the "Missouri," Admiral Halsey's flagship. Again the Allies celebrated a victory, this time V-J Day (Victory over Japan).

SOURCE: Samuel Steinberg, THE UNITED STATES, STORY OF A FREE PEOPLE, Allyn and Bacon, Inc., Boston, © 1954, 1958, 1963. P. 570.

It should be quite obvious by now that there is considerable variation in readability and depth in social studies texts. The examples we have been discussing also illustrate the fact that authors and editors of social studies texts are not generally knowledgeable in the field of reading.

One of the major roadblocks to reading comprehension in social studies texts is the way they introduce abstract concepts. Terms, movements, and causes that had deep significance to past generations often are written about as if they had the same significance to today's generation of young people.

The following examples, taken from Bragdon and McCutchen's Chapter 20, "The Protest Movement," will illustrate the problem:

High building costs were passed on to the consumer in the form of higher freight and passenger rates. More common than overcharging for construction was "*stock watering*." Getting its name from the scheme of inducing cattle to drink heavily just before being weighed for market, this was the practice of increasing the number of shares of a company without adding to its assets.

Competing lines often managed to keep rates up artificially by the practice known as *pooling*, whereby companies made agreements to fix rates and divide the profits according to a prearranged formula.

Denouncing what they called 'the Crime of '73,' silver miners demanded a policy of *Free Silver*, meaning that the government should coin all silver brought to the mint.

Wherever industrialism appeared, it drove some people toward extreme solutions of the problems it created—especially toward *Socialism*. Something seemed wrong with a system which produced both idle rich living in palaces and unemployed paupers living in slums.

A small but vocal group wanted to use the power of organized labor to overthrow the capitalist system and establish socialism. Even more radical were *Anarchists* who preached, "All property is theft; all government is tyranny," and tried to create class hatred by bomb-throwing and assassination.

Unions faced strong opposition from employers. Workers were often required to take an *'Iron-clad Oath'* that they would not join a union.

If discharged for union activity, a man often could not get employment elsewhere because employers combined to keep *Black Lists* of all 'troublemakers'.

Fewer and fewer businessmen, he said, would monopolize all wealth, while the mass of people would be pushed into the ranks of the *Proletariate* (people without property).

There are several alternatives open to the teacher using materials which present such difficulties. First, it is incumbent upon the teacher to realize that a large percent of the students cannot read materials that are inherently high in readability. If such materials have been adopted for use by the school, the teacher must obtain alternative textual material or supplementary material for the poorer readers.

Second, if the text provides only the baldest factual information, as many do, the teacher may use it as a skeleton. Embellishment will come from the reading of enrichment materials. Unfortunately, some teachers stop at the presentation of the facts, depending upon memorization and rote answers to objective questions of fact as "proof of learning." Factual memorization without cognitive learning should have no place in a secondary school social studies classroom today.

The third alternative is to select a text that has reasonably low readability coupled with a high level of concept development. Such a text will tell the story clearly and simply; in addition, it will provide information which allows the students to visualize human situations with which they can identify. Such a text calls for reading as a thinking process involving the past experiences of the reader. The text provides a background of reality, rather than merely cold facts. Reality, identification, and involvement lead to true knowledge: this is what is meant by "cognitive learning," and it is the objective of reading in the social studies.

READING FOR INFORMATION AND ENRICHMENT IN THE SOCIAL STUDIES

When one recognizes that a comprehensive secondary school contains students whose reading ability ranges from a low primary level up through the college level, one is forced to recognize the need for materials compatible with this range of abilities. The matter is complicated by the fact that it is necessary to have informational and enrichment materials at each reading level in each of the social studies: history, government, economics, sociology, geography, international affairs, intergroup relations, and so on. Thus, it is expedient to select some rather broad classifications, with the expectation that if they are chosen wisely and handled adequately, they will provide for the reading needs of all the students.

As an example, let us select twelve broad classifications for American history:

Exploration
The colonial period
The frontier
The federal period
The Civil War
Expansion through the West and Southwest
The growth of big business
World War I
The 1920's
The Great Depression and the New Deal
World War II
Facing the present and the future

For each of these twelve categories, we would select and use three types of material:

Historical novels
Biographies
Factual material

Thus we will have thirty-six categories of reading materials.

In addition, the least that should be done is to provide materials in each of the thirty-six categories at levels of readability appropriate for students whose reading ability ranges over about ten grade levels. If we can successfully group the students into "poor," "fair," and "good" readers, we can then obtain materials in each of the thirty-six categories at each of three levels of readability: "easy," "fair," and "difficult." Actually, then, we would have to identify easy, fair, and difficult novels, biographies, and factual materials in each of the twelve units.

The same procedure can, of course, be followed for world history (or Western civilization), civics (government), economics, problems of democracy, sociology, geography, and whatever other social studies courses may be offered.

A Team Approach to Finding Enrichment Materials

Chapter 14 will expand the idea that no teacher should try to work entirely on his own. A team approach to selecting and evaluating supplementary reading materials in the social studies will make these tasks less formidable. In fact, for a team these jobs are not a major undertaking, since so many excellent materials are available. There may be a few difficulties to be surmounted, but they are insignificant when compared with the fine results such an organization of material will accomplish. There are also some prerequisites for the team approach. First, of course, there must be teachers committed to the idea of providing assignments that students can and will read. Second, there must be teachers willing to invest a little time in working with others in the department to build a master plan for resource materials. Third, there must be a media-center specialist (librarian) who is enthusiastic about the idea and supports it wholeheartedly, both as it is being planned and in its day-to-day operation. Fourth, it is of utmost importance that the reading consultant helps select books, in order to ensure a balanced collection at each of the three levels of readability.

The team should select reading materials at interest levels appropriate for young people in secondary school, written at three levels of readability—difficult, average, and easy—for the major topics in each of the social studies. Within the framework suggested above, a few guidelines will be suggested. Obviously, these suggestions are not all-inclusive; they are merely to serve as models to start from. Since hundreds of new novels, biographies, and factual books are published each year in a subject like American history, a "master plan" or "master list" can never be complete. It must always be open-ended, but it should be built within the guidelines of the master plan.

A Guide to Enrichment Materials in the Social Studies

The books suggested here are not the only good books available in the field. They are books which are proven favorites of adolescents. Any social studies resource center or library which makes them readily available to students will find need for multiple copies almost immediately; any teacher who uses them as suggested will find American history sparkling with life and reality; and any student who has been shackled to a text in American history—no matter how well written—will find himself liberated when brought together (through books that he can enjoy) with biography, historical novels, travel, adventure, and humor.

Biography is the most vivid way to bring the social studies to life, for the social studies are, in reality, the story of people and their relationships with each other. People who achieved greatness, who led lives of adventure and sacrifice, who displayed leadership and courage, who were heroes in their day—these people provide a heroic image for today's young people. Historical biography has become increasingly popular for several reasons. First, a number of important biographical movies have been made. Second, paperbacks have made historical biography more readily available. Third, within the past twenty years a number of excellent historical biographies have been written especially for the young teenager; these have been written at about the fourth-grade reading level, yet they deal with men and women who are studied in junior and senior high school.

Historical biography and historical novels immediately immerse the adolescent reader in the life and events of an era. The reader identifies not only with the characters—reacting to their personalities, motives, and maneuvering—but also to the specific "feel" of the times. The clothes, the noises and smells, the beauty or ugliness, the loneliness or crowdedness, the fears, hates, loves, lethargy, speed, uneasiness, futility, panic, or smugness—all are felt as the reader vicariously lives in another age.

How different is such personal involvement from the reaction to dull facts presented in a textbook.

Compare the effect on a teen-age reader of the following two excerpts—one made up in the style of a typical American history text, and one from a still-popular historical novel.

Slaves Become Freedmen With Problems. Reconstruction in the "New South" was made more complicated by the freedom given almost overnight to 3½ million slaves. Those people, suddenly without homes, with no skills and no knowledge of business transactions, with no experience in self-determination, political life, or living in society, had to face the future in a white man's society. Many, of course, were not able to handle their new freedom. Some continued to live where they had lived as slaves. Some camped alongside the roads, waiting for the government that had freed them to provide for their future. Many believed they had been promised "forty acres and a mule," but this turned out to be a false rumor started by Northern agitators. Negro settlements of shacks began to appear near towns and cities, and these places became centers of constant trouble and fear both for those who had to live in them and for the white communities nearby.

In this wild and fearful time, Scarlett was frightened—frightened but determined, and she still made her rounds alone, with Frank's pistol tucked in the upholstery of the buggy. She silently cursed the legislature for bringing this worst disaster upon them all. What good had it done, this fine brave stand, this gesture which everyone called gallant. It had just made matters so much worse.

As she drew near the path that led down through the bare trees to the creek bottom where the Shantytown settlement was, she clucked the horse to quicken his speed. She always felt uneasy driving past this dirty, sordid cluster of discarded army tents and slab cabins. It had the worst reputation of any spot in or near Atlanta, for here lived in filth outcast negroes, black prostitutes, and a scattering of poor whites of the lowest order. It was rumored to be the refuge of negro and white criminals and was the first place Yankee soldiers searched when they wanted a man. Shootings and cuttings went on there with such regularity that the authorities seldom troubled to investigate and generally left Shantytowners to settle their own dark affairs. Back in the woods there was a still that manufactured a cheap quality of corn whisky and, by night, the cabins in the creek bottoms resounded with drunken yells and curses.

SOURCE: Margaret Mitchell Marsh, GONE WITH THE WIND, pp. 777–778. The Macmillan Company, New York. Copyrighted by Stephens Mitchell 1964. Reprinted by permission.

Both excerpts concern the condition of black freedmen in the South immediately following the close of the Civil War. One is strictly factual. The other is just as factual, but a feeling of repulsion, uneasiness, and squalor is conveyed. It is the latter which calls forth self-involvement.

It is naturally impossible to list in the space available here all of the excellent books available at all readability levels in all units in all of the social studies. As has been mentioned, the selections listed are used as examples. They will serve two purposes: first, to indicate the extent of the task; second, to show that good materials do exist and that therefore the task is not a difficult one if it is undertaken as a team effort. Let us examine some of the available materials.

There probably are more materials available on the early American frontier period (the trans-Appalachian movement) and the Western and Southwestern frontier of the nineteenth century than on any other aspect of American history. This is entirely understandable, for these periods encompass a great deal of time—the late 1700s and all of the 1800s—and within that time the present nature of America was being formed. The pioneers exemplify the traits which are equated with "the American character": bravery; individual conquest over evil; honesty; courage; ingenuity; respect for the individual; homespun philosophy; hard work; faith in the future; and independence interwoven with neighborly sharing. Those are characteristics with which American youth can identify; they form threads of value woven into all the biographies and novels suggested here.

In the years before the American Revolution, into the Appalachians, the Cumberlands, and the Ohio valley trekked a group of sturdy, strong-willed people whose descendents remain there today. Interesting novels and biographies tell of their struggles with Indians, nature, and themselves. Among the most authentic are those written by Rebecca Caudill, who is herself a child of the Cumberlands. (Indeed, the name "Caudill" in eastern Kentucky is, and has been for generations, synonymous with life in the Cumberlands.) They should be available in the secondary school, for they portray the ancestors of a people whose lives command the special attention of the federal government today. Four of Rebecca Caudill's books are: *Tree of Freedom, House of the Fifers, Barrie and Daughter,* and *Far-Off Land.*

A historical novel that portrays conditions which have a counterpart in life today is a rare find. Such a gem is Wayne Doughty's *Crimson Moccasins,* published by Harper, which portrays a conflict and a struggle to overcome prejudice in the life of a boy raised as an Indian on the Ohio frontier. The disclosure to the boy that he actually is the son of white parents forces him (and the reader) to reassess his and other people's prejudices.

Books by Merritt P. Allen (Longmans, Green) are excellent on frontier life. Some popular ones are *The Wilderness Way, The Mud Hen, Make Way for the Brave,* and *Battle Lanterns.*

Probably the all-time favorite is Joseph A. Altersheler, whose books (published by Appleton-Century-Crofts) have been read and reread by adolescents for several decades. These books are appealing because they are in series and because they are written at a level of readability that most junior high school youngsters can handle. The French and Indian War series contains six (in historical sequence); the Young Trailer series, eight; the Texan series, three; the Civil War series, eight; the Great West series, two; and the World War series, three.

Equal in popularity with young teen-agers are Katherine Gray's two books on the days of the covered wagons, *Rolling Wheels* and its sequel, *Hills of Gold.* They are magnificent for young readers.

Considerably more difficult and more challenging, because of their length, are the old-time favorites by Emerson Hough. They were written at the turn of the century and have since achieved what most historical novelists consider the summit—adaptation into motion pictures. They are: *The Covered Wagon, Fifty-Four Forty or Fight, Magnificent Adventure,* and *North of '36.*

Conrad Richter's books also have special interest as epics of life in the American Southwest: *Sea of Grass, The Trees, The Lady, The Fields, The Town,* and *The Light in the Forest.*

Willa Cather's fiction, written for adults, has great appeal to the better readers among teenagers: *My Antonia, O, Pioneers, Death Comes for the Archbishop.* The geographic and historic settings of Cather's novels are superb for the social studies.

Across Five Aprils, the now-famous Civil War story by Irene Hunt (published by Follett) is one of the best for average or somewhat below-average readers.

Florence Means has also written novels on the Southwest for young people. Three of her best are: *Tangled Waters, A Bowlful of Stars,* and *The Rains Will Come.* The last is a portrayal of the Hopi Indians in the 1880s.

My True Love Waits, by Leona Weber, is one of the best novels of covered-wagon days in the West, especially for girls.

Young junior high schoolers enjoy Laura Ingalls Wilder's books, which actually are written in sequence, telling the story of the author's own family as they moved from the Midwest onto the prairie and then farther west. *Little Town on the Prairie* contains the element of realism characteristic of all her books.

Alice Cook Fuller provides an interesting story of the effect of the gold rush upon one family in her book *Gold for the Grahams.*

The life of Norwegian settlers in the Dakotas in the mid-1800s is the setting for O. E. Rolvaag's books, two of which are *Giants of the Earth* and *Jack Schaefer.* Katheryn Forbes McLean's best seller, *Mama's Bank Account,* which was made into a film and brought to television as a series called "I Remember Mama," has to do with Norwegian immigrants in San Francisco early in this century.

It is difficult to pinpoint the frontier, or any era, and thus to categorize books belonging exclusively in one historical category or another. As the frontier was moving westward, other events were also taking place. Historical books are also difficult to classify because a number of writers have not limited their investigation and writing to any one era or topic. The following books, therefore, are not grouped by era.

There are a number of series of historical novels for young adults. Librarians and authors of books for young people in secondary school use the category "Books for Young Adults," and many of the books they place in this category have become classics.

For example, Stephen Meader, a most versatile writer, has produced excellent junior novels spanning two centuries of American history, starting with *River of Wolves,* whose setting is the French and Indian War. *Away at Sea* and *Buccaneer* are set in the times of the early New England slave trade. *Clear for Action* is set in the War of 1812. *Jonathan Goes West* is set about 1845, *Longshanks* tells of Lincoln in Mississippi in the days before the Civil War, and *Everglades Adventure* is set after the Civil War. Meader has written at least two books about the great sailing ships: *Voyage of the Javelin* and *Whaler Round the Horn* (to Hawaii). His *Sabre Pilot* carries the reader along with a seventeen-year-old American airman in Korea. No social studies teacher should be without Stephen Meader's books.

Fortunately for teachers and students in the social studies, many excellent writers have provided us with superb biographies and historical novels. Indeed, most of those referred to in this suggested list will also be acceptable as literature by English teachers. Plot, description, characterization, use of literary devices, and other aspects, are often of high quality. One fine book is *Johnny Tremain,* by Esther Forbes. Others among Esther Forbes's excellent books for the social studies (published by Houghton-Mifflin, in Boston) are *America's Paul Revere, The General's Lady, A Mirror for Witches,* and *The Rising of the Tide.*

Besse Streeter Aldrich is another all-time favorite. Mention of *A Lantern in Her Hand* and *The Lieutenant's Lady* is enough to remind the teacher of others by this fine writer.

Among the authors who have written books set in several eras of American life is Jim Kjelgaard, a favorite among young people. His many books include

Buckskin Brigade, Snow Dog, Rebel Siege (set during the American Revolution), *Desert Dog,* and *Wolf Brother* (a story of the Apaches in the 1880s).

Perhaps the most careful writer of historical novels and biographies is Jean Lee Latham, who spends a great deal of time in on-the-spot research, with the result that her excellent books are historically authentic and her characters and plots are true reflections of the times. Happily, her books are exciting as well. *This Dear Bought Land,* on Captain John Smith, won the Newberry Award. *Carry On, Mr. Bowditch* portrays the life of an eighteenth-century sailor from Salem. *On Stage, Mr. Jefferson* is a frontier story of an actor and friend of Lincoln. *Young Man in a Hurry* is an accurate account of Cyrus Field; and *Man of the Monitor* painstakingly tells of the persistence of John Ericsson. Some of her other titles are *Sam Houston, George W. Goethals, Samuel F. B. Morse,* and *Eli Whitney.*

One of the most prolific writers of historical novels and biographies for young people was Clara Ingram Judson who, just before her death in 1960, was honored with ALA's Laura Ingalls Wilder Award. She has done at least ten biographies of famous Americans: Carnegie, Washington, Holmes, Franklin, Jackson, Lincoln, McCormick, Jane Addams, Jefferson, and Theodore Roosevelt. They are all written at about a sixth-grade reading level, with an interest level ranging through grade 10. Judson has also written biographies of foreign-born Americans which portray life among the pioneer immigrant groups who came to America in the 1800s from Dalamatia, Bohemia, Ireland, Sweden, and Scotland. Her story of the French, of course, is set in the mid 1700s. Many of her books have been published by Follett.

Special mention must be made of Follett, since its entire operation is geared for the production of supplementary and enrichment books in the subject areas of the secondary school. Those books are by well-known writers, edited for a broad distribution over many units in the subject areas, and written and selected at "easy" and "fair" levels of readability. Consequently, every social studies teacher, together with the librarian, should explore the Follett list and make its titles available in quantity to the students.

Garrard (Champaign, Illinois) is another company dedicated mainly to the production of supplementary and enrichment materials for school subject areas. Much of the Garrard materials are appropriate for junior and senior high school content areas, and Garrard has assembled a consulting staff of noted reading specialists who serve as editors for the various series, helping authors understand the problems of readability. The result has been an enviable collection of materials, written by well-known authors and directly selected to fit specific needs in the high school subjects. Garrard's "Discovery" books cover biographies of eight presidents, four statesmen, dozens of war heroes, colonial and pioneer heroes and heroines, explorers, and reformers. In the Garrard collection are books on people who made America great, written in a style and at a reading level that even the poor reader in the secondary school can enjoy. Garrard's "Rivers of the World" series is a must for geography and area studies.

A number of other publishers have started series which should be investigated by the social studies teacher, in cooperation with the librarian. The reading teacher should also be consulted, to aid in classification according to readability levels; for many of these books have not been edited by reading specialists, but have been published more as books for the general public. Care must be exercised in classifying them at a particular grade level.

For example, a series called "Milestones in History" is published by Messner (a division of Simon and Schuster). These are nonfiction books containing maps, bibliographies, and other classroom aids; some of the titles are The '49ers (by Bob and Jan Young), Mr. Madison's War: 1812 (by Noel Gerson), After The Alamo (by Burt Hirschfeld), and From Tsars to Commissars (by Kaye Moulton Teall). Messner also publishes a biography series on some rather hard-to-get subjects, such as Fighter Against Slavery (the story of a New England missionary who helped in the fight for freedom of the people of Liberia), Empress of All Russia, and Oliver Cromwell.

A factual series published by Fiedler (Grand Rapids, Michigan) is especially useful for good readers who are engaged in geography or area studies. Each book treats the geography, economics, politics, sociology, and customs of one country. These Fiedler books are comprehensive and accurate, since the author of each is an expert on the country described. The books are more expensive than the less complete treatment in other series. They are recommended for students with high ability, since no attempt has been made to control readability; but even the student with poor reading ability will be able to obtain considerable information from the excellent photographs reproduced in these books.

Melmont (Chicago)—better known as Children's Press—has recently made a number of outstanding series available. "People of Destiny" is a set of twenty biographies of leaders who have made an impact on history. Many are quite recent historical figures. These books have the added feature of almost fifty historical photographs and illustrations in each biography. They are written at a sixth-grade reading level.

Children's Press also publishes the excellent "Young People's Story of Our Heritage"—a fifteen-volume survey of world civilization, beautifully illustrated. Their seventeen-volume Pictorial Encyclopedia of American History is highly motivational to the junior high school student. The "Enchantment of America" series has long been well received as authentic regional studies of eight parts of the United States, Canada, and Mexico. More recently, the "Enchantment of American State Books" have been completed. Two new series in the social studies are beginning to come from Children's Press: "Biographies of Living American Negroes" and the "Enchantment of South America" books. In geography, the "Let's Travel" books provide excellent source materials on the geography, people, culture, and history of more than two dozen countries and regions of the world.

Watts has started an ambitious series called the "Immortals" books; one of these is on Simon Bolivar.

An interesting book on people who have led their nations from obscurity to the news of the world is *From Prison to Power*, by Emil Lengyel. This volume contains dramatic stories of Ben Bella, Nkrumah, Bourguiba, Kenyatta, Sukarno, Kadar, Gomulka, and Makarios, describing their roles in their nations' bids for freedom. This book provides some hard-to-get facts for the secondary school social studies student.

John Day (New York) has started a series of nonfiction books appropriate for the average and poor reader. Their shortness (they are only about 112 pages each) and photographs appeal to the less mature reader. They are published as part of the series called "Young Historian Books" and include various ancient and classical eras of history (*Republican Rome* and *Ancient Crete* are two of the titles), as well as others.

Houghton-Mifflin is continuing a historical adventure series which could well be called the "He Went With . . . " series. The titles in the series—all starting with that phrase—cover the adventures and explorations of Marco Polo, John Paul Jones, Columbus, DaGama, Magellan, and others. Louise A. Kent is the author.

Meindert DeJong has written a number of novels for young adults, set in his native Holland. Among them are *Tower By The Sea* and the *Wheel on the School*, the latter a Newberry Award winner. DeJong's stories impart the flavor of life for young people in the Netherlands; this is an area rarely handled by American authors.

South Africa is the setting for Alan Paton's *Cry, The Beloved Country*, which was an adult best-seller for many months and is now being discovered as having some extremely significant truths for today's young adults. The fair and good readers consider it a most important book.

Anne Frank's *Diary* has become a must among teen-age classics. It has been bought in paperback by hundreds of thousands of teen-agers, as have *Darkness at Noon* (about the Moscow Trials); *The Last Hurrah* (Edwin O'Connor's searching account of Boston politics); William Golding's *Lord of the Flies*, that disturbing symbolic story of the defects of human nature; and *On the Beach*, a story about nuclear annihilation and perhaps one of the most disturbing novels of its time.

John Gunther's books are also a must in any secondary school's social studies collection, although they are beyond the ability of about 80 percent of high school readers. *Inside Africa, Inside Asia*, and the others, however, provide a kaleidoscopic view of each of those regions, impossible to obtain elsewhere in one volume.

In an attempt to do this at the secondary level are the books in the Scribners (New York) "World Background Series," such as *The New Africa*, by Gatti. The Public Affairs Pamphlets are well-known for the valuable information they provide. The North Central Association of Colleges and Secondary Schools has recently started a series on current problem areas, and McCormick Mathers has done similarly.

Thomas B. Costain's huge novels appeal to the good readers and are significant for the social studies. It is necessary to mention only a few: *The Silver Chalice, Son of a Hundred Kings, Black Rose, Joshua, For My Great Folly, Ride With Me.*

Better readers are still enjoying Alexander Dumas' *The Three Musketeers, Twenty Years After, The Count of Monte Cristo,* and others. A word of caution should be raised here: these should be *free* selections — not required reading.

Similarly, James Fenimore Cooper's books are still popular as free-reading selections, and hundreds are sold in paperbacks. *The Last of the Mohicans, The Pathfinder, The Deerslayer,* and *The Spy* are still favorites with good readers.

Robert Louis Stevenson's *Black Arrow, Kidnapped, Treasure Island* and others also are surefire with the better reader who is not afraid of a large volume. These too should be given as suggested choices.

More modern and perhaps more significant to the realities of our day are John Hersey's books: *A Bell for Adano, Hiroshima, Into the Valley, Men of Bataan,* and *A Single Pebble,* all for good high school readers. Other books dealing with the Second World War and postwar problems are too numerous to mention. Remember that many boys in secondary school will soon be in the armed services — and perhaps not far from the battlefield and death. They are acutely aware of this, and books dealing with war are especially important to them. Examples are *Exodus* and *Mila 18,* by Leon Uris; the *Bridge at Andau; This Was Your War* (edited by Brookhouser and containing articles by Irwin Shaw, Ernie Pyle, James Michener, Herman Wouk, Norman Mailer, and others); *PT 109,* by John F. Kennedy; *Three Came Home,* by Keith;

Lord's Day of Infamy; They Were Expendable, by W. L. White; *Battle Stations,* by James Scroggin; *Up Front,* by Bill Mauldin; and Pierre Boulle's *Bridge Over the River Kwai:* such books are necessities in a social studies library designed to have immediacy and significance to young people today.

The social studies, more than any other subject area in the secondary school curriculum, have the opportunity to capitalize on the needs and concerns of today's generation of young people.

This is the age of protest, and never before in history have such large numbers and such a great percentage of young people become concerned with their future and that of society. The teacher who ignores or evades this readiness for reading should not be a social studies teacher, for this is what the social studies are all about.

Much of the concern of young people centers upon war, social arrangements, racism, honesty, decency, commitment. As they grow into maturity, they want to "tell it like it is." The social studies can give them an opportunity, as never before, to read about their pressing concerns. Both black and white students, for example, will become readers of books by black authors telling it like it is. To be sure, these books cover controversial subjects; similarly, the books of today's protest movements are controversial. Such books are often considered "dangerous," because their insight is different from that of middle-class society. And indeed they are dangerous to teachers and school administrators, for they will be very likely to draw a negative reaction from the public. Yet, they are the stuff of social studies today. They cannot be ignored.

One such book, considered very dangerous in its day, was Harriet Beecher Stowe's *Uncle Tom's Cabin.* The impact of that book on American history is incalculable. Today, it has been revived and is a popular book with young people. *Uncle Tom's Cabin* is a must in the study of contemporary American problems. *Black Like Me*, an insightful look at more recent discrimination may be considered more "safe," since it was written by a white reporter who disguised himself as a Negro. In *Black Boy*, Richard Wright discusses his boyhood and youth in the Deep South. Who can read it without becoming deeply involved in the insults and erosion of self which this "black boy" had to endure? Young people, black and white, identify with him and therefore can *feel* the problem as they read.

Probably the best book for better readers who wish to understand the background of the black power movement is the *Autobiography of Malcolm X.* In it, Malcolm X describes his growing understanding of the black man's place in the scheme of things, and his break with the extreme militants. This is for good students who can read critically.

Background or follow-up should be provided through the writings of W. E. B. DuBois, a socialist of the 1920s and 1930s, and Marcus Garvey, a leader of the back-to-Africa movement a half-century ago.

Any of James Baldwin's books can be handled by the average reader, and these books are essential in contemporary affairs classes: *Another Country; Blues for Mister Charley;* and of course *The Fire Next Time.* Background or follow-up could be provided by recordings of the speeches of Dr. Martin Luther King (he also warned of "the fire next time").

Much more controversial is *Soul on Ice,* Eldridge Cleaver's writings from prison. They are well-written essays and provide a point of discussion for the best students who can identify with the problems which Cleaver exposes.

It should be obvious that secondary school students must have books written by black authors, rather than simply books written by whites about black problems, for who can speak better than the black who is experiencing the erosion of his own personality and his children's future?

Once young people begin reading works such as those cited above, the library will be obligated to obtain many copies of each title. Indeed many schools have been selling these works in paperbacks by the hundreds to their students. Carrying paperbacks such as these, reading them, talking about them, and swapping them has now become the thing to do among students who are in the top groups. Paperbacks therefore deserve some discussion.

Carrying a paperback is more than just a "status symbol," although we must not discount that aspect. Paperbacks are symbols of adulthood, and may represent acceptance into the adult world. A paperback, then, may be the very vehicle for entering the world of books, for a reluctant and retarded youth. Through a paperback, the teacher may be able to involve his interest in books for the first time. It is almost unbelievable how many high school students consider textbooks forbidding but will be willing to risk a try at a paperback.

Dr. Charles G. Spiegler, one of the charter members of the IRA's Commission on Lifetime Reading, provides an interesting discussion on "Paperbacks for Reluctant Readers." It is reprinted here by permission.

PAPERBACKS FOR RELUCTANT READERS[3]
by Charles G. Spiegler
Charter Member, Commission on Lifetime Reading, International Reading Association

Until David Sanders was intoduced to The Men Who Won the West, by Franklin Folsom, he had never, voluntarily, read a book cover-to-cover in all of his 13 years.

"I hate books," he would tell you when, at book report time, you caught him repeating publishers' blurbs, or paraphrasing first and last pages of books, or reviewing TV stories as if they were books—until he was trapped by referring to the heroes as "the stars."

It was TV, in fact that had helped him find the bridge from the desert island of "no books" to the land of literature. One day his eye had caught the TV bulletin board in his English class called "If You Watch, Why Not Read?" If you watch Wagon Train, the notice suggested, why not read The Men Who Won the West? Both as a Westerns fan and a TV devotee, David was in fact a Wagon Train regular. A book about Western heroes? Maybe. His interest piqued, he dug into his pants for some change and made his first book investment. It was to prove a perfect prescription for David Sanders, reluctant reader.

We knew it from his book report which, this time, in his own words, described his genuine amazement at how "the men who won the West fooled their enemies!"

---

[3]Charles G. Spiegler, "Paperbacks for Reluctant Readers," Printed in Pamphlet #RR6, Scholastic Book Services, 1966.

We knew it from the first two books he bought at a Book Fair. We knew it when, at long last, he agreed to try membership in a paperback book club "only if they got mysteries and detectives and stuff like that." We promised. He joined. David Sanders was on his way from a desert island to the mainland.

There isn't a school district in all this land without its fair share of David Sanderses, whose reluctance to read is home-made or school-made, not inborn. It is a reluctance spawned in homes at cultural ebb tide where never is heard an encouraging word about books or ideas or the exciting world they come from. It is a reluctance forged from the zeroes in the record books issued for failure to read a prescribed book from the prescribed book list fashioned by the predilections of the pedagogues. Small wonder that a vast number of American youth (and particularly those not bound for college) have lost all ardor and curiosity about books, and have never sought the pleasure of their company.

Three vigorous revolutions have begun to change all that. The first is the paperback revolution, which has made it possible, at little or no more than it costs him to down a milk shake, for any youngster to buy anything from *The Story of Ferdinand* to *War and Peace*.

The second is the revolution in writing for youth. With all due reverence to the titans of literature, the fact is that theirs is a content beyond the ken of many non-academic millions in our classes; theirs is a style beyond such children's grasp. To fill the need for content and style more closely related to the interests and capacities of average youth, there has arrived a Golden Age of Writing for Youth, represented, for example, by an Anne Terry White who brings a crystal lucidity, combined with dramatic excitement, to whatever she essays: from stolid stone, *Rocks All Around Us;* to prehistoric man, *The First Men in the World;* to pure biography, *George Washington Carver.* A Glenn Balch in the animal kingdom, a Herbert Zim in the world of science speak the language of youth on the subjects of youth—and without infantilizing either.

The third revolution has been in our concept of the genus "reluctant reader." The evidence keeps piling up! It isn't that Johnny doesn't read because he can't. Rather, Johnny can't read (as well as he should) because he doesn't! And he doesn't because he finds it a bore! Give him a title, a book jacket that rings true. Let the world and its infinite wonders be the subjects he may choose from. Appeal to his interests—and Johnny reads.

It is with this in mind that the lists below have been prepared—with this caution: A book list must describe, not make decision; suggest, not give command. It is, at best, a way to catch an interest by the toe; then never, never let it go. Is your reluctant reader a sports fan? *How to Star in Baseball* may be the appetizer to whet the taste for richer fare. A horse lover? He will find it difficult to put down T. C. Hinkle's *Black Storm*, a true story of a horse with unflinching loyalty to the man who had "broken" him. The homemade zoo keeper with a flare for odd pets can read all about them in *Odd Pets;* the one who wonders how a hurricane starts, what it destroys, why, despite its power, it is named for girls—finds his answers in *Hurricanes and Twisters.* For answers to everything from why we get goose pimples to where baloons go when they're lost—there is a book: *Arrow Book of Answers.* Reluctant readers, like all readers, will respond to adventure as real and alive as in *Snow Treasure*, the story of Norwegian teens sleigh-riding their country's treasure right under the noses of the Nazis and on into safety.

They, too, can identify with the great and moving lives of a Helen Keller, a Nellie Bly, a George Washington Carver when these are written with the pace and style of the biographies listed below. They, too, may begin with the simple joke in *School Daze*, then grow to know the satire of a *Homer Price*. And, when they meet the word "herculean" in their daily lives, they too (though they are some years removed from Bulfinch and his Mythology) have a right to know that it comes from Hercules, whose exploits are revealed in *Hercules And Other Tales from Greek Myths* as adapted just for them.

"Give children books," it has been urged, "to respond to their nature, attract their eye, help them dream." This is the rationale on which the list below[4] is based. May it serve as Rx for your Reluctant Reader.

CRITICAL READING IN THE SOCIAL STUDIES

Unfortunately some teachers feel that the one and only objective of the social studies is to provide "information" to students. As a consequence, teaching is directed toward finding answers, memorizing facts, and being tested on retention of those facts.

Such an approach to the social studies may be considered to be at a most primitive and elementary level of learning. It may be achieved by memorization, and the process may be speeded by means of reward and punishment. But learning in this manner results in severely limited appreciation and understanding. Moreover, studies indicate that facts in the social studies memorized by rote are not retained long. This should lead the thoughtful social studies teacher to a critical examination of whether or not the quality and quantity of long-term learning justifies the effort. An honest evaluation will inevitably lead to a search for a better way.

Moreover, critical analysis will also reveal that all information in the social studies is selective. Such enormous quantities of information are available that authors are forced to select and concentrate upon those things which provide the best all-round support for their frame of reference. An author of a world history book, for example, may take the position that World War I was a turning point in history, marking the end of the era of royalty and the beginning of the rise of democracies throughout the world. His selection of materials may accordingly be almost wholly directed toward discussing the Hohenzollerns, the Hapsburgs, the Romanoffs, and other royal families, their marriages and intermarriages, and so on; the troops, ships, guns, and lands at their command; and the democracies that came after them. To expect

[4]This refers to the Readers' Choice Catalog, available from Scholastic Books Services, Englewood Cliffs, N.J.

that a modern secondary school student will memorize such facts as an adjunct to learning American history is to create distaste for the subject, the book, and the teacher.

Another author may approach World War I from the standpoint of power politics, and provide a different but equally formidable array of facts, for memorization. Still another author may be concerned with these same aspects of World War I (the downfall of despotism, the rise of democracies, shifts in power politics) but approach the era entirely from a sociological and economic point of view. Another may present a humanitarian point of view, extolling America's role in saving the world.

Naturally, every author must be selective, for there is neither time nor space to provide all the available facts. From a huge mountain of facts, only a small sampling will be selected. Why, then, should it be a matter of life or death, pass or fail, that the facts in a particular text be memorized? Does the student who learns "facts" from one text actually know more about World War I than an equally good student who has studied from a different text? For that matter, does any student actually know about World War I and its impact upon a nation or the world just by reading facts and memorizing them? The answer is obvious: Learning facts is a limited, primitive way of studying the social studies.

There must be facts, of course, but those facts must be transferable into a structure of ideas forming the main idea. Within the framework of the main idea, there must be knowledge and understanding of *who, what, when, where, how, how much, how many,* and *why.* In order to answer those questions, the social studies student must go beyond a mere accumulation of facts; he must relate facts to each other. Here, the whole is greater than the sum of its parts. Facts do not exist independently; they modify, color, and add substance to each other.

The opportunity to help secondary school students develop skills in critical reading is one of the most rewarding aspects of teaching social studies. When students are encouraged to discover for themselves that one author has said one thing and another author has presented a conflicting point of view, the social studies teacher has progressed a long way toward fulfilling the obligation of preparing students for responsible and thoughtful citizenship.

Citizenship in America is based upon the freedom of individuals to make choices—where they will live; what they will do to earn a living; how much they will spend and on what; how much they will save; whom they will marry; how, or if, they will worship; when and where they will travel; what they will write and read; who they will select to represent them in governing the nation. To prepare for the responsibility of making such choices, the student must learn how to select, and he must be allowed practice in decision making. The decisions of everyday citizenship require critical thinking, based upon adequate information concerning all the alternatives. Here critical reading plays a most significant role; the student, then, must learn to read critically and must have the opportunity to read critically.

Within the social studies classroom, students should be given the opportunity to sample the writings of a number of authors. For example, on the subject of the Negro revolt and civil rights, there are scores of books written pro and con. Each presents a point of view, either that of the author or that of a group for whom he speaks. Many books on this subject are written at a sufficiently easy level of readability that large numbers of secondary school students can handle them; a few, however, are written at a level beyond the conceptual ability of most high school upperclassmen. A unit on civil rights or black power (or both) would provide an opportunity for social studies students to read critically to discover, first, the author's point of view. Each student could and should determine what position the author is taking. By so doing, each student will then be ready to read what the author has written within the framework of his position. It is not a matter of discounting what the author has to say because of his position, but rather a matter of expecting certain things to be said because of the position taken by the author. Reading to discover an author's prejudices is an analogous process. Having established the setting for the argument, the reader then is able to evaluate whether or not the author has been able to justify his stand with facts.

Social studies students can learn that there are degrees of quality of writing, depth of scholarship, and honesty. Moreover, they can learn that there are partial truths and half-truths, deliberate omissions, sweeping generalizations, and downright lies; and also that there can be honest and careful presentation of both sides of controversial issues. Critical reading is not just a classroom exercise; it is a skill essential to the survival of freedom of choice in a democratic society.

In the social studies, students can learn how to read editorials and editorialized news, in contrast with factual news. The "managed news" produced by many organizations and groups can be studied and compared with the managed news produced by governmental agencies. Students can learn to go beyond managed news in their search for truth. The more able readers will respond to training and practice in critical reading with an almost insatiable appetite for digging up more and more discrepancies in the information available on the controversial social issues of the day.

It is through critical reading that the best minds can be trained for a lifetime of alertness, dedicated to preserving honesty and integrity in the giving of information—and dedicated to preserving democracy. The social studies, more than all other areas of the curriculum, bear this fundamental responsibility. Social studies teachers can respond to this challenge only by training their students in critical reading.

Questions and Activities for Discussion and Growth

1. Conduct a survey of secondary schools in your community to determine what percentage of classrooms are textbook-centered for social studies instruction. Find out what provisions are made for making textbooks of high, medium, and low readability available to classes of good, average, and slow readers. What is your reaction to your findings?

2. Examine three textbooks in each of the social studies and list their organizational patterns and themes. Note the frame of reference of each author (or team of authors). Compare, contrast, and summarize your findings, together with your own reactions.

3. Make a list of the vocabulary specific to each of the social studies. How would you help students learn the meanings of these words in their social studies contexts?

4. Develop a lesson plan in one of the social studies other than history. Include a directed-study lesson, alternatives for students at three levels of reading ability, and an assignment lesson.

5. Use the plan for estimating readability (described in Chapter 2) on six texts in world history, history of civilization, or both. Rank them from highest to lowest readability. What have you discovered?

6. Team up with another person and compare your estimates of the number of abstract concepts in a chapter (or a section of a chapter). What does this project tell you? How can differences be resolved?

7. What help can you expect from another teacher, from the librarian, and from the reading specialist in developing a list of books for information and enrichment in the social studies? To check your expectations, note the responses of a teacher, a librarian, and a reading specialist to your request for help. Be sure you present a definite problem to each of them, asking for a definite amount of help on a specific number of books in one area of the social studies. What do your findings tell you?

8. Make a list of books (other than those mentioned in this chapter) that the public might consider "safe" and "dangerous" for a class in problems of democracy consisting of (a) upper-middle-class whites; (b) lower-middle-class whites; (c) middle-class blacks; (d) lower-class blacks.

9. Present the lists developed for question 8 to (a) a teacher; (b) a librarian; (c) a reading specialist; (d) an English teacher; (e) a principal; (f) a school board member; (g) a sociologist; (h) a politician; and (i) to some members of the public. To get their reactions, tell them that you are thinking of using these books in your classroom, and would like their opinions of the value of the books in studying American problems. Summarize the responding and state your reactions and conclusions.

10. Collect paperback catalogs and develop a comprehensive annotated bibliography of paperbacks under the following categories: low, average, and high readability in the following subjects—American history, world history; economics, geography, sociology, government, contemporary problems. Categorize also by price, source, and length. You may find it is necessary to develop your bibliography on 3- by 5-inch cards. You may want to annotate your bibliography with such terms as "significant," "relevant," "safe," "controversial," "dangerous," "informative," "biased," "revealing," "thought-provoking," "for critical reading."

Selected References

Aukerman, Robert C.: "The Reading Status of Good and Poor Eleventh-Grade American History Students," *Social Education,* vol. XI, no. 8 (December, 1947), pp. 351–353.

Ambrose A. Clegg, Jr.: "Developing and Using Behavioral Objectives in Geography," *Focus on Geography,* 40th Yearbook, National Council for the Social Studies, Washington, D.C., 1970, pp. 291–303.

Crump, Kenneth Jr., and William P. Mulhair: "A Proposal for a Revitalized High School Social Studies Program," *Journal of Secondary Education,* vol. 43, no. 8 (December, 1968), pp. 366–372.

Estes, Thomas H.: "Reading in the Social Science Classroom: Research," Chapter 8 in James L. Laffey, ed., *Reading in the Content Areas,* International Reading Association—ERIC/CRIER, Newark, Delaware, 1972.

Foreign Policy Association: "Simulation Games For Social Studies Classrooms," *New Dimensions,* vol. I, no. 1, 1968.

Hafnew, Lawrence E.: *Improving Reading in Secondary Schools,* The Macmillan Company, New York, 1967. (A paperback of selected readings. Section 10 contains especially pertinent selections in the content areas.)

Herber, Harold L.: "Reading in the Social Science Classroom: Application of Research in the Classroom," Chapter 9 in James L. Laffey, ed., *Reading in the Content Areas,* International Reading Association—ERIC/CRIER, Newark, Delaware, 1972.

Herber, Harold L.: "Teaching Secondary School Students to Read History," *Reading Instruction in Secondary Schools,* International Reading Association, Newark, Delaware, 1964, pp. 73–86.

McDonald, Arthur S.: "Reading in History: Concept Development or Myth Making," *Proceedings: Reading and Inquiry,* International Reading Association, Newark, Delaware, vol. 10, 1965, pp. 102–103.

The Paperback Goes to School: Bureau of Independent Publishers and Distributors, 122 East 42 St., New York 10017. (A list of 5,000 inexpensive paperbacks, selected by a committee from the NEA, NCTE, and AASL.)

Roberts, Maxine G.: "Organizing a Reading Program in the Social Studies," University of Pittsburg Report on Annual Conference on Reading in Content Areas, 1959.

Shepherd, David L.: *Effective Reading in Social Studies,* Harper and Row, Evanston, 1960.

"Social Studies and Slow Learners": Issue of *Social Education.* National Council for the Social Studies, vol. 34, no. 2 (February, 1970).

8. READING IN THE ENGLISH CLASSROOM

Reading in secondary school English involves the student in the many facets of literature, with its special characteristics of style and beauty. Literature is the one academic content that does not depend upon a factual, structured textbook. The text in secondary English has the unique characteristics of an anthology.

In secondary school, the student moves up from children's literature, through the more sophisticated juvenile trade books, to the adolescent novel— and many of the college-bound students enter the world of mature literature. This transition is planned in the anthologies and in the curriculum. What often is *not* planned is a provision for helping the student develop the reading skills necessary to handle the progressively more difficult materials. To accomplish this with the least amount of stress, it would be wise for the English teacher to utilize some of the reading techniques developed especially for high school students. Certain reading skills are necessary if the objectives of literature are to be achieved.

BEHAVIORAL OBJECTIVES IN LITERATURE

The objectives of courses in literature fall into two categories: technical and psychological. But many educators have been blind to the existence of the second category; as a result there has been massive criticism of the teaching of literature in secondary schools, and this criticism is justified.

Dissection of literary works to identify setting, tone, characterization, theme, subtheme, conflict, climax, figurative language, alliteration, denouement, and genre—this sort of thing has bored generations of adolescents who should rather have been excited by literature. Apparently, the ability to identify the technical aspects of literature is an important objective for the teacher but a disastrous one for the student. The technical approach, of course, does have instructional advantages: achievement in this class of objectives may be tested easily. Such an idea is behind the development, by the Instructional Objectives Exchange, of objectives in English Literature for the senior high school.[1] Eight types of objectives for poetry were catalogued; nine for the novel; seven for the short story; and seven for drama. The behavioral objectives listed under each heading were accompanied by six measurement items "designed to test student's ability to perform the desired behavior." For example:

> What kind of poem is the poem "Edward, Edward"? List four characteristics of the poem that identify its type.

The student is supposed to be able to identify the poem as a ballad and to list characteristics of the ballad form, such as tragic theme, repetition, dialogue, and dramatic situation. Under the classification "genre," the high school student is tested on his ability to identify the apprenticeship novel, detective novel, historical novel, novel of incident, novel of manners, picaresque novel, psychological novel, regional novel, and novel of character.

Psychological objectives have to do with mental processes on a higher level, removing learning from memorization and application of learned categories. The behavioral objectives classed as psychological are related to introspection and empathy.

Psychologically, all real learning is related to one's self-concept, needs, and desires; it is a process of self-improvement. All real literature, similarly, is directed toward the reader's inner self. The objectives of literature courses, therefore, should be quite personal, individual, and self-centered. They can, however, be classified.

Cognitive objectives, which involve knowing (as opposed to memorizing) may be achieved through good historical novels or biographies. The reader comes to *know* a period of history or a great historical figure. The reader

---

[1] Instructional Objectives Exchange, *English Literature, Grades 10–12*, UCLA Center for the Study of Evaluation, UCLA, Los Angeles, 1970.

identifies with what is being portrayed—a figure, an era, a role, or a series of events. Cognitive learning is achieved also through literature portraying contemporary life. Such a novel can also transport the reader into the ghetto or hill country or factory or mine, providing the substance which lets him identify with the problems of the characters. This is also true, naturally, of the drama, biography, and short story with a contemporary setting. If these deal with subjects of particular contemporary concern, the possibility for cognitive learning is enhanced.

Psychological objectives call for behaviors which give evidence of certain reactions: empathy, compassion, dismay, disgust, a sense of fun, revulsion, love, hate, fear, or foreboding; or a feeling of power, helplessness, achievement, failure, futility. Past experiences of the reader are to be used in making value judgments (as in the case of "Horseman in the Sky," discussed later in this chapter). Some literature serves the psychological purpose of catharsis. Some may serve to release pent-up feelings. Some may serve a social as well as a personal end, as in the explusion of prejudices. And in many cases literature provides an escape from the realities of life, giving the reader a pleasant dream world or another time and place. It may provide a noble hero—a figure like King Arthur, Sir Gawain, Joan of Arc, Davy Crockett, or Sergeant York— with whom the reader can identify. It is often out of such idealized literary experiences that paintings are painted, songs are written and sung, and life plans are made. The achievements of others may well be an inspiration and motivation for the young reader.

Another objective may be the transmission of universal values. Myths, folktales, legends, and fanciful tales transmit culture and provide a frame of reference for the thought and behavior of the reader.

An interesting approach to behavioral objectives in literature was proposed recently. It is called the "Profundity Scale,"[2] and it provides the student with a way of assessing the depth of any narrative material. It suggests that there are five levels of profundity: (1) physical, (2) mental, (3) moral, (4) psychological, and (5) philosophical. Notice that these same levels may also be applied to the reader's involvement with the material. As an example, let us apply this analysis to a novel wildly popular at the time of this writing— Erich Segal's *Love Story*. At level 1 we have (awareness of) the actions of Oliver (the hero), Jennifer (heroine), and Oliver's father; at level 2, the intellectual conversations between Oliver and Jennifer; at level 3, the conflict between the heroine and hero over their break with his parents; at level 4, the hero's jealousy of his father; and at level 5, the themes of love, the rejection of false values and acceptance of simple values, the need for others.

[2]Eileen E. Sargent, Helen Huus, and Oliver Andresen, *How to Read a Book*, International Reading Association, Newark, Delaware, 1970, chap. 4 [based on Andresen's original article, "Evaluating Profundity in Literature," *Journal of Reading*, 8 (May, 1965), pp. 387–388].

Understanding of these levels of profundity is another objective valid for literature courses, and it may be considered as among the psychological objectives because, as has been noted, the "profundity levels" are matched by levels of personal reactions.

TO DEAL WITH INDIVIDUAL DIFFERENCES IN READING ABILITY: THE GUIDED READING LESSON

The most persistent problem faced by the English teacher is individual differences in reading ability. It would be ideal if the teacher could provide a variety of materials to match all the individual differences within a class and among all his classes. To this end, some teachers have made strenuous efforts to find different materials for different classes, and even to locate special literary selections for individuals or groups within classes. Some good results have been obtained. Realistically, however, the English teacher is still quite often confronted with the problem of working with a single anthology or list of works, some of which will probably not be suitable for the class as a whole and some of which will certainly not be suitable for certain individuals in the class.

One practical, if not complete, solution to this problem is the "guided reading lesson." This approach stresses extensive teaching *before* students undertake their independent reading. If this kind of teaching is done, even poor readers can manage fairly well with a textbook that is too difficult for them. Better readers, too, will gain as the constant review of skills of which they already have some grasp produces increased security and competence.

Some of the skills developed in guided reading lessons in English are:

Reading to follow narrative sequence
Reading to make inferences about characters, setting, etc.
Reading to recognize mood or tone
Reading for sensory imagery
Reading figurative language
Reacting to types of organization typical of different kinds of literature; the formal essay, various poetic forms, etc.
Oral reading of drama and poetry
Reading to feel the rhythm of poetry and good prose

The guided reading lesson is basic to teaching literature when a group of students of varying abilities are all working with the same material. Its strength lies in its emphasis upon teaching *before the students undertake their silent reading and study* and in the way it alerts both teachers and students to precisely what reading-study skills they need to use. Instead of reading with a kind of diffused and general objective, the student knows what he is doing.

The pattern of the guided reading lesson is determined largely by genre at hand. But with almost any piece of literature, the teacher should take time to do the following things with the students.

1. Consider the probable or possible significance of the title.
2. Note who the author is and discuss whatever they may know about him and his work.
3. Examine any headnote the editor may have written.
4. Look at the illustrations (if any).
5. Check the length of the selection that is to be read.
6. If the editor has provided questions in connection with the material, the students should read them before reading the selection. This helps the students to read with purpose. Good questions stimulate thinking; they do not "give the story away."

The six steps listed above, as has been mentioned, are appropriate with almost all types of literature. There are additional techniques that aid in the reading of certain specific types. For example, a quick first reading of a whole poem to get the general idea and tone before reading in close detail may be just the right approach. A formal essay with logical organization will be read with more understanding if the students are helped in skimming it first to discover the basic pattern of organization.

English teachers are sensitive to these differences and will have no difficulty in making modifications.

DESIRED SKILLS

In preparing a lesson plan for any specific piece of literature, the English teacher must answer two questions about the skills he hopes to teach in the lesson:

What skill or skills do my students most need to work on?
What skill or skills does this particular piece of literature *permit* me to work on effectively?

Day-by-day contact with the students plus, perhaps, some informal tests (either written or oral) prepared by the teacher, will supply the answer to the first question. The teacher must be able to recognize which skills need more work than others, and be willing to apportion work accordingly, depending on the abilities of each class.

The teacher's own analytical reading of the literature in question is necessary to determine its possibilities for teaching skills. One piece, for example, may lend itself to a study of imagery, another to concentration on figurative language, another to examination of the author's logic. Naturally, as the sample lesson plans given below were drawn up, it was *only* this second question which was considered.

The short story "A Horseman in the Sky," reproduced on pages 143–145, has been used to draw up sample lesson plans. (These sample plans have been adapted from plans made up by a subcommittee of the New England School Development Council Group.) A short story was chosen because this genre is common in all literature courses; however, the general approach illustrated by the sample lessons would be the same for other genres.

Of the various different lesson plans that would be possible with "A Horseman in the Sky," four have been selected here. Each covers the essential content of the story, but the four approaches focus on different reading skills. Only the teacher could choose the best of the four lesson plans for a particular class, by answering the question, What skill or skills does my class most need to work on?

It is suggested that the teacher examining these four sample plans first familiarize himself thoroughly with the story and then note, as he goes over the plans, the following points:

> The essential content of the story is taught in each of the four lesson plans.
>
> The skills that receive major emphasis differ from plan to plan.
>
> The reading discussion before reading is at least as extensive as the discussion after reading, if not more extensive. (Teachers will find, however, that the actual time spent on the lesson as a whole is no greater than they have been accustomed to spend. Students are alerted to read with purpose and understanding. Their work after reading, then, moves rapidly and efficiently.)

LESSON PLAN 1

Behavioral objectives:

1. To develop appreciation of the content of the story.
2. To provide an experience in reading for visual imagery.
3. To teach two word families (structural analysis).

Preparing the Class for Reading

After you have alerted the students to the fact that this is a Civil War story (you may need to remind them what *civil* means), you may wish to discuss the title of the story. What does it suggest? How does it arouse interest?

Then, ask the students to recall what they have learned about visual imagery. What do we mean by this term? Why does imagery make reading more interesting? What have the students read in which visual imagery was especially helpful? You may even want to ask why students today are probably less efficient in dealing with visual imagery than students of a generation ago. (The answer, of course, is television, which makes visual imagery unnecessary. Some students, however, may want to argue that television has made visual imagery easier to deal with because people today have "seen" so many more things than previous generations.)

Tell the students that many visual images in literature are brief, one-picture images. There are also, however, cumulative images, in which a picture gradually unfolds.

A HORSEMAN IN THE SKY

by Ambrose Bierce

I

One sunny afternoon in the autumn of the year 1861 a soldier lay in a clump of laurel by the side of a road in western Virginia. He lay at full length upon his stomach, his feet resting upon the toes, his head upon the left forearm. His extended right hand loosely grasped his rifle. But for a slight rhythmic movement of the cartridge box at the back of his belt he might have been thought to be dead. He was asleep at his post of duty. If detected he would be dead shortly afterward, death being the just and legal penalty of his crime.

The clump of laurel in which the criminal lay was in the angle of a road which went zigzagging downward through the forest. At a second angle in the road was a large flat rock, jutting out northward, overlooking the deep valley from which the road ascended. The rock capped a high cliff; a stone dropped from its outer edge would have fallen sheer downward one thousand feet to the tops of the pines. The angle where the soldier lay was on the same cliff. Had he been awake it might well have made him giddy to look below.

The country was wooded everywhere except at the bottom of the valley to the northward, where there was a small natural meadow, through which flowed a stream scarcely visible from the valley's rim. This open ground looked hardly larger than an ordinary dooryard, but was really several acres in extent. Its green was more vivid than that of the enclosing forest. Away beyond it rose a similar line of giant cliffs. The valley, indeed, from this point of observation seemed entirely shut in, and one could but have wondered how the road had found a way into it.

No country is so wild and difficult but men will make it a theater of war; concealed in the forest at the bottom of that military rattrap, in which half a hundred men in possession of the exits might have starved an army to submission, lay five regiments of Federal infantry. They had marched all the previous day and night and were resting. At nightfall they would take to the road again, climb to the place where their unfaithful sentinel now slept, and descending the other slope of the ridge fall upon a camp of the enemy at about midnight. Their hope was to surprise it, for the road led to the rear of it. In case of failure, their position would be perilous in the extreme; and fail they surely would should accident or vigilance apprise the enemy of the movement.

II

The sleeping sentinel in the clump of laurel was a young Virginian named Carter Druse. He was the son of wealthy parents, an only child, and had known such ease and cultivation and high living as wealth and taste were able to command in the mountain country of western Virginia. His home was but a few miles from where he now lay. One morning he had risen from the breakfast table and said, quietly but gravely: "Father, a Union regiment has arrived at Grafton. I am going to join it."

The father lifted his head, looked at the son a moment in silence, and replied: "Well, go, sir, and whatever may occur do what you conceive to be your duty. Virginia, to which you are a traitor, must get on without you. Should we both live to the end of the war, we will speak further of the matter. Your mother, as the physician has informed you, is in a most critical condition; at the best she cannot be with us longer than a few weeks, but that time is precious. It would be better not to disturb her."

So Carter Druse, bowing to his father, who returned the salute with a stately courtesy that masked a breaking heart, left the home of his childhood. By conscience and courage, devotion and daring, he soon commended himself to his fellows and his officers; and it was to these qualities and to some knowledge of the country that he owed his selection for his present duty at the extreme outpost. Nevertheless, fatigue had been stronger than resolution and he had fallen asleep. What good or bad angel came in a dream to rouse him, who shall say? He quietly raised his forehead from his arm and looked between the masking stems of the laurels, instinctively closing his right hand about the stock of his rifle.

His first feeling was a keen artistic delight. On the cliff—motionless at the extreme edge of the capping rock, and sharply outlined against the sky—was an equestrian statue of impressive dignity. The figure of a man sat the figure of a horse, straight and soldierly, but with the repose of a god carved in marble. The gray costume harmonized with its background, softened and subdued by the shadow. A carbine lay across the pommel of the saddle, kept in place by the right hand grasping it at the "grip"; the left hand, holding the bridle rein, was invisible. In silhouette against the sky the profile of the horse was cut with the sharpness of a cameo; it looked across the heights of air to the confronting cliffs beyond. The face of the rider, turned slightly away, showed only an outline of temple and beard; he was looking downward to the bottom of the valley.

For an instant Druse had a strange, half-defined feeling that he had slept to the end of the war and was looking upon a noble work of art. The feeling was dispelled by a slight movement of the horse which had drawn its body slightly backward from the verge; the man remained immobile as before. Broad awake and keenly alive to the significance of the situation, Druse now brought the butt of his rifle against his cheek by cautiously pushing the barrel forward through the bushes and, glancing through the sights, covered a vital spot of the horseman's breast. A touch upon the trigger and all would have been well with Carter Druse. At that instant the horseman turned his head and looked in the direction of his concealed foeman—seemed to look into his face, into his eyes.

Carter Druse grew pale; he shook in every limb, turned faint. His hand fell away from his weapon, his head slowly dropped until his face rested on the leaves in which he lay.

It was not for long; in another moment his face was raised from earth, his hands resumed their places on the rifle, his forefinger sought the trigger; mind, heart, and eyes were clear, conscience and reason sound. He could not hope to capture that enemy; to alarm him would but send him dashing to his camp. The duty of the soldier was plain: the man must be shot dead from ambush—without warning. But no—there is a hope; he may have discovered nothing—perhaps he is but admiring the landscape. If permitted, he may turn and ride carelessly away. Surely it will be possible to judge at the instant of his withdrawing whether he knows. It may well be that his fixity of attention. . . . Druse turned his head and looked downward. He saw creeping across the green meadow a sinuous line of blue figures and horses—some foolish commander was permitting the soldiers of his escort to water their beasts in the open, in plain view from a dozen summits!

Druse withdrew his eyes from the valley and fixed them again upon the man and horse in the sky, and again it was through the sights of his rifle. But this time his aim was at the horse. In his memory rang the words of his father at their parting: "Whatever may occur, do what you conceive to be your duty." He was calm now; not a tremor affected any muscle of his body; his breathing, until suspended in the act of taking aim, was regular and slow.

He fired.

III

An officer of the Federal force had left the hidden bivouac in the valley, and with aimless feet had made his way to the lower edge of a small open space near the foot of the cliff. At a distance of a quarter-mile before him, but apparently at a stone's throw, the gigantic face of a rock rose from its fringe of pines. Lifting his eyes to the dizzy altitude of its summit the officer saw an astonishing sight—a man on horseback riding down into the valley through the air!

His hands were concealed in the cloud of the horse's lifted mane. The animal's body was as level as if every hoof stroke encountered the resistant earth. Its motions were those of a wild gallop, but even as the officer looked they ceased, with all the legs thrown sharply forward as in the act of alighting from a leap.

Filled with amazement and terror by this apparition of a horseman in the sky, the officer was overcome, his legs failed him and he fell. Almost at the same instant he heard a crashing sound in the trees—a sound that died without an echo—and all was still.

The officer rose to his feet, trembling. The familiar sensation of an abraded shin recalled his dazed faculties. Pulling himself together he ran rapidly, obliquely, away from the cliff to a point distant from its foot where he expected to find the objects of his search at the very foot of the cliff. A half-hour later he returned to tell an incredible truth. He said nothing of what he had seen.

IV

After firing his shot, Private Carter Druse reloaded his rifle and resumed his watch. Ten minutes had hardly passed when a Federal sergeant crept cautiously to him on hands and knees. Druse neither turned his head nor looked at him, but lay without motion or sign of recognition.

"Did you fire?" the sergeant whispered.

"Yes."

"At what?"

"A horse. It was standing on yonder rock—pretty far out. You see it is no longer there. It went over the cliff." The man's face was white, but he showed no other sign of emotion. Having answered, he turned away his eyes and said no more.

The sergeant did not understand. "See here, Druse," he said, after a moment's silence, "it's no use making a mystery. I order you to report. Was there anybody on the horse?"

"Yes."

"Well?"

"My father."

The sergeant slowly rose to his feet and walked away. "Good God!" he said.

Ask the students to close their books as you read the first paragraph of the story aloud as given below, pausing wherever a slash mark occurs. Suggest that they note how the picture comes gradually into focus. You may wish to pause at some points for discussion.

One sunny afternoon in the autumn in the year 1861/ a soldier/ lay in a clump of laurel/ by the side of a road in western Virginia./ He lay at full length/ upon his stomach,/ his feet resting upon his toes,/ his head upon his left forearm./ His extended right hand/ grasped his rifle./ But for a slight rhythmic movement of the cartridge box at the back of his belt he might have been thought to be dead./ He was asleep at his post of duty. If detected he would be dead shortly afterward, death being the just and legal penalty of his crime.

To provide a second experience of the same sort, continue with the second paragraph, as given below:

The clump of laurel in which the criminal lay/ was in the angle of a road/ which went zigzagging downward/ through the forest./ At a second angle in the road/ was a large flat rock,/ jutting out northward,/ overlooking the deep valley from which the road ascended./ The rock capped a high cliff;/ a stone dropped from its outer edge would have fallen sheer downward one thousand feet/ to the tops of the pines./ The angle where the soldier lay was on the same cliff./ Had he been awake/ it might well have made him giddy to look below./

You may wish to have the students state in their own words the picture the author has developed. Ask: Do you think the setting will be an important element in this story? Why? How has the author aroused interest in his first two paragraphs?

Assignment (Setting a Purpose)

Ask the class to finish reading the story to discover the meaning of the title and also to:

1. Locate another vivid cumulative image
2. Find these two key words, make sure of their meaning and note why they are key words: *vigilance, immobile*

After the Class Has Read

You may wish to open the discussion by asking about the meaning of the title. Does the class like the title? Why?

Ask the students to indicate other cumulative images, and perhaps read them aloud. (A particularly good one is in the paragraph beginning "His first feeling . . . ").

Why are *vigilance* and *immobile* key words in this story? What are some other words that belong to the "families" of these words? (*vigil, vigilant, vigilante; mobile, immobility, immobilize, immobilization, movable, movement, mover,* etc.) In what sense do these words belong to "families"? What is the origin of each of their families? You may wish to work on some of the prefixes, suffixes, or both at this point. (For example, what is the function of *-ize?*)

Ask the class to note the interruption in the time sequence of the story starting with the paragraph that begins "The sleeping sentinel . . . " Why hasn't the author told the story "straight"?

You will probably want to discuss the nature of the conflict in this story. Why does Carter shoot the horse instead of the man?

When did the class first suspect who the horseman is? Why do they think the author withheld his identity to the very end of the story? Discuss the brevity of the ending. Is it good that way? Why?

LESSON PLAN 2

Behavioral objectives:

1. To develop appreciation of the content of the story
2. To practice derivation of word meaning from contextual clues
3. To provide an experience in analyzing a flashback

Preparing the Class for Reading

Read the first sentence with the class. Discuss the date and the fact that the young man is a soldier. Be sure your students understand in which war he is involved. What does the fact that he is involved in a *civil* war suggest about the possible conflict in the story? (What you probably will want to do here is encourage the student to anticipate what may happen.)

Ask the students to note that the story is divided by Roman numerals into four sections. Read aloud just the first paragraph of sections I and II. Is there a difference in the time setting between the first paragraph of section I and the first paragraph of section II? What do the students now suspect may be the reason for the division of the story into four sections? (You will be making them aware of possible time shifts in the story.)

Examine the last sentence in section I. What does *apprise* mean? Have the class note that a single sentence gives adequate clues to the meaning of the difficult word. Then ask them to find *cultivation* in the first paragraph of section II. What meaning do they usually associate with this word? How does this paragraph as a whole suggest a different meaning for the word? You may wish to remind the class that most words have multiple meanings, and that context usually determines which meaning is indicated. Ask the class what they think the title of the story means. They may have ideas, but they will have no way at this point in their study of knowing for sure. Suggest that reading in context may help them discover the meaning of a title just as it helped them discover the meaning of a single word.

Assignment

Ask the class to discover the meaning of the title from context and also the meanings of the following words:

verge (section II, paragraph 5)
sinuous (section II, paragraph 7)
conceive (section II, paragraph 8)
abraded (section III, paragraph 4)

Ask them to note where the contextual clues are located. (For your convenience, the following information is given: the clue to *verge* is in the preceding paragraph; the clue to *conceive* is in the same sentence as the word; the clue to *abraded* is in the whole situation, not in any specific words; there is no real clue for the word *sinuous*.) Students need to understand that this contextual method has its limitations.

Ask the students also to decide

1. What the approximate time span of the story is
2. In what order the various events happened

After the Class Has Read

With a slow class you may wish to start the discussion by having the students retell the story in chronological order. With a faster group, you might go right into some of these questions:

1. With what paragraph do the events of the story really begin?
2. What reasons can the class see why the author chose not to begin the story with this paragraph?
3. What necessary information does the main flashback provide? In what ways would the story be less effective without this information?
4. How could you support the statement that Carter Druse has been in the army for some time?
5. Can you find another minor flashback in the story?

Ask the class to define the four words assigned for study. Ask them also to discuss the contextual clues (or lack of them) which they discovered.

Ask the class to find in context and comment on the following:

1. "The figure of a man sat the figure of a horse. . . . "
2. "He fired."
3. " 'My father.' "

(What should come out of this discussion would be an appreciation of the dramatic impact of the author's economy of words.)

LESSON PLAN 3

Behavioral objectives:

1. To develop appreciation of the content of the story
2. To provide an experience in character analysis

Preparing the Class for Reading

You might like to start by telling the class something about Ambrose Bierce. He was nicknamed "Bitter Bierce" because of his sharp wit and the rather cynical attitudes he displayed in some of his work as a cartoonist, journalist, and writer. He was a drummer boy during the Civil War. Most of his life was spent in San Francisco, where he was well known and admired. When he was in his seventies he went to Mexico. One letter from him said he had joined the army of rebel Pancho Villa. He was probably killed in the civil war then raging in Mexico, but the facts of his death have never been certainly known.

Read with the class the first paragraph of section I of the story. What impression do the students have of the young soldier? Why? (They will probably jump to the wrong conclusions at this point.)

Then read with them the first three paragraphs in section II. Ask them to restate their impressions of Carter Druse. Have these impressions changed? Why? (This may be a good time to get the class to verbalize the danger of making hasty judgments about people—in or out of books.)

Remind the class of the four basic ways in which authors reveal character:

What the author says or implies about the character
What the character himself does
What the character himself says
What other characters say about him

Ask which of the four basic methods they have noticed so far in reading this story.

Assignment

Ask the students to write a one-page theme in which they answer the following question and support their opinion: In the light of what you know from the story, is Carter Druse an honorable man?

After the Class Has Read

You may wish to start the discussion by having a few of the students read their papers. (A more interesting discussion will develop if you have students read who have taken differing points of view about Carter Druse.)

You may wish to have the class analyze ways in which the author has given them evidence about Carter Druse's character. Which facts did he tell them directly? Which points have they inferred from Carter Druse's actions? From things he said?

You may wish to explore some of the deeper meanings suggested by this story as it relates to life today. A lead question might be: When (and where) might a young man today find himself in Carter Druse's position?

Note. In these first three lesson plans, the teacher has done most of the planning. Gradually, however, the students should develop the ability to set their own purposes. In Lesson plan 4, which follows, the students are in charge of their own study, which, to be successful, will have to be intensive. Role playing is used to help students interpret the story.

LESSON PLAN 4

Behavioral objectives:

(1) To develop appreciation of the content of the story.
(2) To give the students experience in independent analysis of a story.
(3) To develop a sense of the universality of the experience recorded in the story.

Preparing the Class for Reading

Have the class read the story quickly just to see what it is about.

Assignment

Explain to the class the following points of military law:

1. Military law is usually enforced through military courts, or "courts martial." These consist of boards of officers, convened, by order of the president or a military commander, for the trial of such cases as may be submitted to them.

The sentences of these courts have no effect until they are approved by the authority convening the court, or by the President of the United States.

2. A "general court martial" consists of a board of officers, not less than five in number, of rank appropriate to the rank of the accused, if an officer. It possesses jurisdiction over every offense triable under the Articles of War, and has power to impose a sentence of dishonorable dismissal or of death.[3]

Ask students to prepare the "case" of Carter Druse and, by playing various roles, to bring out the character of the man and the theme of the story. Allow adequate time for preparation.

Students should be as free as possible to develop their own ground rules and build their own case. However, if they need help, one or more of the following suggestions might be made:

1. The class may divide into two parts—prosecution and defense.
2. The students will have to determine the charges against Carter Druse. Some of these might be: falling asleep at post of duty; revealing the army's position by firing instead of engaging in hand-to-hand combat; failing to capture an enemy who was in a poor defensive position on the edge of a cliff; shooting the horse instead of the man.
3. Students may volunteer to play the following roles at the trial: Carter Druse; the officer; the sergeant; Druse's mother. Other persons who do not appear in the story itself might also be dramatized, such as a longtime friend of Carter Druse who knows the family background.
4. The chalkboard may be used for diagrams of terrain and location of the characters.

Students should have time to present their case as forcefully as they can do. Then, after the case has been given depending on what charges Carter Druse was tried on and upon what the verdict is, the teacher may wish to explore students' reactions—particularly, the reactions of those who "lost." What clues to the universality of the story can students bring out?

After the mock "court martial" of Carter Druse, students could easily be motivated to read some of the testimony of the trial of Captain Lloyd Bucher in the Pueblo spy case of 1969 or the newspaper reports of the trials connected with the My Lai massacre in South Vietnam (1970). Better students enjoy reading the court-martial scenes in *The Caine Mutiny*, Herman Wouk's novel of World War II. (These court scenes have been made into a play, *The Caine Mutiny Court-Martial*, which is complete in itself and makes interesting reading also.)

ASSESSING READING DISABILITY IN LITERATURE

One way to determine whether or not a particular student may anticipate difficulty in reading English literature is to administer the "Prognostic Test of Reading Disability in Secondary School Literature." It is based on the idea that literature is full of abstract and unusual terms and that inability to recognize and pronounce such words will indicate that the individual will have difficulty reading secondary school literature. (It should be noted that it is difficult to select a representative sampling of vocabulary in English literature,

[3]Lincoln Library of Essential Information, V2, p. 1480, copyright by The Frontier Press and reprinted with their permission.

chiefly because (1) vocabulary varies greatly from century to century, (2) it varies among writers even in one period of time, and (3) it varies from one literary form to another. Poetry, drama, the short story, and the novel generate the most difficulty as far as vocabulary is concerned.)

The test is given individually. Each student reads directly from the page of this book. (One or two minutes are enough.) Use only one of the three alternative forms.

*PROGNOSTIC TEST OF READING DISABILITY
IN SECONDARY SCHOOL LITERATURE*[4]

Directions. Cover the two alternative forms not being used (5- x 7-inch cards will do).

Ask the student to read from left to right, pronouncing each word and then the next at his normal rate.

Observe his facial expression as he reads. Note hesitations, repeats and regressions, uncertainties, gross mispronunciations, incorrect stress.

The student who is *not* able to move along smoothly, at about one word every two seconds, will have great difficulty in reading literature materials.

Alternative Form A

direful	compassionate	demeanor	concede
furtive	cynical	infinitesimal	malicious
nocturnal	intuitive	improvise	exuberant
nymph	gable	fluently	conservative
yearling	genteel	subtle	taut
trudge	placidly	haggard	deliberately
absurdly	dazedly	cranny	indignant
miserable	swaggered	shrieked	vicious
renegade	solemnly	horrible	ironically
bridled	audience	colossal	girth
eddied	dulling	magpies	realization
prudence	muttered	sufficed	sodden

Alternative Form B

aversion	asunder	beguile	lament
impropriety	grizzled	gloaming	congeniality
antithesis	foundling	ingenuous	poignant
troubadour	chronicle	foreshadowing	apparition
plague	hypocrite	lenient	naive
scrutiny	simultaneous	vulnerable	profuse
despondent	condone	affliction	animated
derisive	gingerly	uncanny	suffice
oblivious	indulgence	exasperate	detached
compassionate	complementary	apprehensive	brusque
enmity	commendable	austere	abashed
insinuate	listless	knave	obsession

[4] Copyright 1971 by Robert C. Aukerman.

Alternative Form C

acquisition	denunciation	ostentation	ponderous
multitudinous	mercenary	embodiment	subjugation
quagmire	provocative	reconnoiter	heinous
imperturbable	insinuating	imperceptible	dubious
semblance	reticent	unpretentious	verbose
superfluous	impetuous	gnarled	adversity
commensurate	boisterous	expedient	sublime
visage	translucent	supplication	impropriety
gangling	inquisition	ludicrous	awesome
circumstantial	beseech	exultant	distraught
intermediary	premonition	mediocrity	retraction
stipulate	venerable	terrestrial	comely

THE READABILITY OF LITERATURE ANTHOLOGIES

The textbook for literature courses in secondary schools in the past half century has been, as it still is, the anthology—although the use of individual paperbacks is gaining some popularity. The anthology of American, European, English, or world literature is a collection of literary selections arranged in units according to some scheme of classification.

The "authors" of secondary school literature books are actually compilers. They select poems; short stories; excerpts from articles, novels and journals; plays; and examples of other literary forms. Their authorship is generally limited to the introductions and summaries which open and close each unit, to "headnotes" preceding individual selections or groups of selections, and to questions and selected activities which follow each selection or unit. The actual authors of the selections in such an anthology probably knew nothing about the reading ability of secondary school youth and were unaware of any need to control the readability of their literary output. They are likely to have been men of literature, not educators, addressing an audience by no means limited to students.

It might be assumed that the compilers of anthologies would select literary materials of the same difficulty throughout the entire textbook. This is far from the case. Not only are literature anthologies very different from each other, as far as readability is concerned, but the contents of any one anthology may range in difficulty over as much as nine grades. This seems incredible, but it is borne out by studies of the readability of literature anthologies. One such study was reported to the National Council of Teachers of English in 1964.[5] In that study, more than eighty junior high school and senior high literature textbooks were analyzed for readability. They were listed in

[5]Robert C. Aukerman, "Readability of Secondary School Literature Textbooks: A First Report," English Journal vol. 54, no. 6 (September, 1965), pp. 533–540.

order from lowest readability to extremely high readability. However, grade-level indications were deliberately avoided. (As has been suggested previously, it is naive to classify a book's readability by grade level, for this is to assume that all students in that grade would be able to read it—which is of course never the case. A ranking from "easy" to "difficult" gives an English department some guidelines for selecting a text: an easy text for poor readers; a harder one for the average readers; and a more difficult one for gifted readers.)

The task of assessing the readability of English texts is far from finished. Still, it is clear that there are alternatives and that choices should be made not only among books but within a single book. Anthologies are merely samplings from our literary wealth. There is neither need nor justification for "covering the entire book." On the contrary, there is justification for selecting only those materials appropriate to the interests and abilities of each group of students.

FINDING APPROPRIATE LITERATURE FOR MODERN STUDENTS

Literature is frequently presented in units, classified according to themes. Some popular themes of this sort are courage, humor, kindness, human nature, war, peace, beauty, nature, survival, adventure, protest. Anthologies in which literature is classified according to historical eras are less inspiring; such eras might be the Puritan Age, colonial America, the westward movement, the Victorian era, the Reform movement.

Themes call for identification and involvement by the reader; fortunately, there is a wide variety of fiction, poetry, drama, and humor on almost any theme. The key to motivation is "relevance"; for the classroom teacher of English, this fact has enormous implications. Ideally, the teacher would know the experiences, needs, interests, and reading ability of each student well enough to assign appropriate literary works individually. But of course the practical solution, given the realities of classroom teaching, must be a compromise. The teacher has the option of assigning the same reading to everyone, regardless of the intellectual capacity and reading ability, or of classifying reading materials as "easy," "average," and "difficult" under the themes most popular with the students in his particular school.

A survey made by this author to determine the interests of today's generation of youth revealed that boys in secondary school are most interested in earning money, cars, girls, sports, travel, and adventure; and that girls are most interested in money, travel, boys, clothes, grooming, riding horses, surfing, imitating some "significant other" (such as an actress or singer), and personal problems. Some of these themes are, of course, universal; others are more peculiar to the young people now in school.

Casey at the Bat

The outlook wasn't brilliant for the Mudville nine that day—
The score was four to two with but one inning more to play;
And so when Cooney died at first and Barrows did the same,
A sickly silence fell upon the patrons of the game.

A straggling few got up to go in deep despair. The rest
Clung to that hope which springs eternal in the human breast;
They thought that if only Casey could but get a whack at bat—
We'd put up even money now, with Casey at the bat.

But Flynn preceded Casey, as did also Jimmy Blake,
And the former was a pudding and the latter was a fake;
So upon that stricken multitude grim melancholy sat,
For there seemed but little chance of Casey's getting to the bat.

But Flynn let drive a single to the wonderment of all.
And Blake, the much despised, tore the cover off the ball;
And when the dust had lifted, and they saw what had occurred.
There was Jimmy safe at second, and Flynn a'hugging third.

Then from five thousand throats or more went up a lusty yell—
It rumbled through the valley, it rattled in the dell;
It knocked upon the mountain top and recoiled upon the flat,
For Casey, mighty Casey, was advancing to the bat.

There was ease in Casey's manner as he stepped into his place;
There was pride in Casey's bearing, and a smile on Casey's face.
And when, responding to the cheers, he lightly doffed his hat,
No stranger in the crowd could doubt 'twas Casey at the bat.

Ten thousand eyes were on him as he rubbed his hands in dirt,
Five thousand tongues applauded as he wiped them on his shirt;
Then while the writhing pitcher ground the ball into his hip.
Defiance gleamed in Casey's eye, a sneer curled Casey's lip.

And now the leather-covered sphere came hurtling through the air,
And Casey stood a-watching it in haughty grandeur there.
Close by the sturdy batsman the ball unheeded sped—
"That ain't my style," said Casey. "Strike one!" the umpire said.

From the benches black with people there went up a muffled roar
Like the beating of the storm waves on a stern and distant shore
"Kill him! Kill the umpire!" shouted someone in the stand;
And it's likely they'd have killed him had not Casey raised his hand.

With a smile of Christian charity great Casey's visage shone;
He stilled the rising tumult, he bade the game go on.
He signaled to the pitcher, and once more the spheroid flew,
But Casey still ignored it and the umpire cried, "Strike two!"

"Fraud!" cried the maddened thousands, and echo answered, "Fraud!"
But one scornful look from Casey and the multitude was awed.
They saw his face grown stern and cold, they saw his muscles strain,
And they knew that Casey wouldn't let that ball go by again.

The sneer is gone from Casey's lips, his teeth are clenched in hate,
He pounds with hideous violence his bat upon the plate.
And now the pitcher holds the ball, and now he lets it go,
And now the air is shattered by the force of Casey's blow.

Oh, somewhere in this favored land the sun is shining bright;
Somewhere bands are playing, and somewhere hearts are light:
And somewhere men are laughing, and somewhere children shout,
But there is no joy in Mudville—mighty Casey has struck out.

SOURCE: National Baseball Hall of Fame and Museum, Cooperstown, New York.

It does not necessarily follow that all short stories, novels, poems, or non-fiction works dealing with young people's interests are, *ipso facto,* appropriate. The deciding factors are numerous and include relevance, style, and the ease with which readers can identify with the people being written about. The common characteristic of all the important factors is that they are *modern,* or —more precisely—ageless.

For example, a short story about baseball will probably be relevant to high school boys now, regardless of when it was written. The challenge and excitement of the game at anytime involves victory, pathos, daring, defeat, integrity performance, skill, and cunning—and these are universal. Baseball has celebrated its centennial, but the short stories, poems, novels, and anecdotes of the game provide the English teacher with a wealth of relevant materials. For example, consider the poem "Casey at the Bat." Compared with the "classic" epic poems so often included in literature anthologies, "Casey at the Bat" is both far more relevant and far easier for the poor reader, to whom making sense of a "classic" is often a hopeless task.

What may the English teacher accomplish with "Casey at the Bat"? First, it should be read aloud to the class. This brings together an important interest of at least the boys with an important interest of the teacher—literature. "Casey at the Bat" is, of course, hardly "great literature"; nonetheless, it is a poem, and it contains certain literary elements: setting, plot, characterization, situation, suspense, climax, and denouement; plus meter and rhyme. The students can enjoy the identification with a character and a situation pertaining to one of their own major interests. The vocabulary is often difficult, but if the poem is read aloud to the class there will be opportunity for clarifying it.

MONEY

Richard Armour

Workers earn it,
Spendthrifts burn it,
Bankers lend it,
Women spend it,
Forgers fake it,
Taxes take it,
Dying leave it,
Heirs receive it,
Thrifty save it,
Misers crave it,
Robbers seize it,
Rich increase it,
Gamblers lose it . . .
I could use it.

SOURCE: "Money," by Richard Armour, is reprinted from the International Pocket Library edition of Armoury of Light Verse by permission of Branden Press. Copyright 1964 by Bruce Humphries.

Factors like these can make the difference between literature that bores or even antagonizes young students and literature that they will enjoy.

Much humorous verse is universal in its appeal, and a great many themes have been treated by writers of light verse. For example, Richard Armour's little poem "Money" will surely seem relevant to high school boys and girls.

What may an English teacher do with "Money?" First, it is not difficult to read. Even the poor reader may enjoy it. It provides a theme with which students can identify, for earning money seems to be high on the list of interests for high school boys and girls. This little verse also has an interesting style, using repetition for humor (each line contains *it* as an object). Students can learn from such a poem that much modern verse is straightforward and simple. Finally, it may be used for vocabulary study: *spendthrifts, forgers, fake, heirs, seize, crave,* and *misers* are likely to be new words to many students.

Automobiles, another important item on the list of young people's interests, provide another theme for reaching students. William Saroyan's short story "Locomotive 38, the Ojibway" is a good example of this theme. Although it is set in 1922, it has a universal appeal (the hero and narrator is a fourteen-year-old boy attempting to drive a car). The title of the story does not reveal the theme, however, and the teacher will have the task of "selling" it to the students. This may be done by giving some of Saroyan's background. He was the son of immigrant Armenian parents and dropped out of junior high school. The story, told in the first person largely through dialogues, could be about a real episode in Saroyan's life. The fourteen-year-old narrator has the opportunity to drive a new Packard for a rich Indian. The boy claims he can drive. . . .

This will provide enough readiness. Identification with the boy and the situation, plus the intrinsic interest in automobiles, will motivate students to read the story. The readability level is very low; the level of interest high—and this is the ideal combination for self-motivation and relevance in literature.

There is also available a good deal of writing about hot rods; and the so-called "nonreader," or the reluctant reader may be *lured* into reading if the English teacher suggests *and makes available* some of this material in paper-back form. A few suggestions will indicate what highly motivational books are available: *Hot Rod Angels,* by R. S. Bowen; the many novels by Gregor Felson, among them *The Crash Club, Hot Rod, Street Rod, Road Rocket,* and *To My Son, the Teen-Age Driver.* Philip Harkins concentrates on hot rodding, and has written the popular *Day of the Drag Race* and *Argentine Road Race,* among others. The editors of *Hot Rod Magazine* (an excellent periodical for hot rod enthusiasts) publish a do-it-yourself paperback, *Supertuning. Stock Car Races* (by Caary Jackson) illustrates a slightly different form of interest in hot rods (as a spectator sport). *The Hot Rod Handbook* (by Fred Horsley) is more factual and is not the type of material that would be part of a "literature" program.

The main principle of learning, essential to success with the nonacademic students, is to *start where they are.* A student's interest in hot rods provides natural motivation. The follow-up must be a subtle transition to more sophisticated literature on related themes.

Sport is hugely important to many high school students. Only a few novels and biographies on this theme need be listed. Most are paperbacks, although Garrard and Follett both have published some excellent hard-cover novels and biographies about sports, written especially at a low readability level.

A few of the paperback novels that are easily available are *Perfect Game, Keeper Play, Winning Pitcher, The Quarterbacks, The Coach Nobody Liked, Hot Shot, Overtime Upset, Schoolboy Johnson, Young Razzle, Kid From Tomkinsville,* and *World Series.*

Scholastic Magazine has recently assembled a collection of paperbacks in what is called the "Reluctant Reader Library." The books are especially relevant to young adults interested in athletics, automobile racing, teen-age problems, and adventure.

Biographies and autobiographies include *The Babe Ruth Story, Basketball is My Life* (Bob Cousy), *Baseball is a Funny Game* (Joe Garagiola), *Stan Musial, Baseball's Unforgettables, Willie Mays, Baseball's Greatest Players Today,* and *Baseball's Hall of Fame.*

Hardbacks for the better reader include *The Bobby Richardson Story* (autobiography), the Garrard books *Stories of Champions, The Game of Baseball,* and *On the Mound* (biographies of three pitchers, Bob Feller, Carl Hubbell, and Howard Ehmke). Similar biographies are available in *Decathlon Men, Yea Coach* (football coaches), *100 Greatest Sports Heroes,* and *Baseball's Unforgettable Games.* The latter two were written by two Associated Press sports writers.

Teen-age girls who are reluctant readers may be reached through such novels as *First Love, True Love, First Orchid for Pat, Senior Year, Seventeenth Summer, Junior Miss, Co-ed in White, Hootenanny Nurse, Peace Corps Nurse,* and *Student Nurse.*

Adventure in our time is a theme today's young people find relevant. Charles A. Lindberg's *Spirit of St. Louis* and *We Seven* (the true story written by Scott Carpenter, Virgil Grissom, John Glenn, and four other American astronauts in Project Mercury) provide reading that is real and is related to another major interest: the airplane and space flight. (Science fiction is a related theme, but only a small group of especially able students enjoy it, as a rule.)

Another topic that is especially relevant to young people now is protest. It takes many forms, but there are three that concern young people most today: war, poverty, and racial hatred. Fortunately, protest is not peculiar only to this decade. It has been a social phenomenon and factor for change all through history. The literature of protest is almost as old as any of the writings of man. To start where the learner is, it would be wise to introduce this theme through some of today's writings of protest: songs, ballads, folk music, poetry, short stories, essays, nonfiction, autobiographies, and novels. Some titles were suggested in Chapter 6 for use in the social studies classroom; it may be helpful to repeat some of the recommendations here: *Black Like Me, Black Boy,* and *Uncle Tom's Cabin* are suitable for students with minimal reading ability; *Another Country, Blues for Mister Charley,* and *The Fire Next Time* are appropriate for students with average ability. More sophisticated reading ability is necessary for such books as the *Autobiography of Malcolm X, Soul on Ice* (by Eldridge Cleaver), and an excellent new anthology, *From Black Africa.*

Protest literature also directs itself to such topics as pollution, politics, business, health, war, and morals. Protest literature includes both fiction and nonfiction. John Gunther's series (once referred to as "John Gunther's Insides") present the theme of protest subtly. Dramas of protest include *Raisin in the Sun;* novels include Alan Paton's *Cry, the Beloved Country.* Where exposition ends and where fiction begins in protest literature is difficult to judge. For example, Rachel Carson's *Silent Spring* is an expository protest; Richard Llewellen's *How Green Was My Valley,* a novel, is also an exposition of the desolation of a valley and its people through coal mining operations.

The protest literature of the American radicals of the 1920s was thought to be subversive in its day. The protest literature of American colonial writers in the 1760s and 1770s, however, was more effective. The Abolitionist writers, who were extremely influential, belonged to the protest movement of their day. Protest is, indeed, a most viable theme throughout all literary periods. Moreover, it has special appeal to the idealism and restlessness of youth. Young people can identify with those who through the ages have written about the wrongs of their own societies and have risked disfavor and persecution as a result.

Many novels and short stories about the other themes which hold strong appeal to young adults are available: works on boy-girl relationships, growing into adulthood, riding horses, and personal relationships in problem situations. There are far too many to mention here; instead, sources of annotated lists are cited.

George Spache's *Good Reading for Poor Readers*[6] is the basic source for books of high interest and low readability. Spache gives estimates of readability and comments on the books he lists. A second sourcebook,[7] published by the National Council of Teachers of English, was prepared especially for use with secondary school youth. The best-seller in this field is Daniel Fader's *Hooked*

---

[6] George Spache, *Good Reading for Poor Readers,* Garrard Publishing Co., Champaign, Ill., 1971.

[7] Raymond C. Emery and Margaret B. Houshower, *High Interest Easy Reading for Junior and Senior High School Reluctant Readers,* National Council of Teachers of English, Champaign, Ill., 1965.

on Books,[8] a paperback which every English teacher should own and read. Dr. Fader reports his personal experiences in visiting secondary school English classrooms. His book recounts the amazement and dismay he felt on observing the totally ineffective methods and materials employed by the teachers whose classes he visited; it then describes Fader's significantly successful program of reading, devised for young people, of whom many were considered socially deviant and held in custodial institutions. *Hooked on Books* gives enough suggestions for dynamic reading programs to cover all six grades of the secondary school. The success of the program was the result of several elements; making books available in great quantity (many in paperback); putting significant, relevant, and readable books into the hands of concerned youth; not expecting anyone to "give a book report"; not demanding that anyone read a whole book; and providing for the entire range of individual differences found in a class of adolescents.

SUMMARY

Literature is meant to be read, and the teacher of literature is indeed a teacher of reading. Readiness for reading high school literature does not just happen; it must be taught. It is a developmental process.

The English classroom must be filled with books that provide a wide spectrum of choice based upon individual interests, abilities, needs, and goals. Since the English teacher cannot often know all his students well enough to aid each individually in making choices, it is practical to provide books at several levels of difficulty in each of the many themes of interest to today's youth. In that way, for each theme the reading levels of the students can be matched with the readability of the available books. If this is to be done, the literature anthology may have to be replaced by paperbacks, as is suggested by Daniel Fader in *Hooked on Books*. The anthology, as it has been devised in past years, is inconsistent as regards the difficulty of selections. Paperbacks are not only plentiful but are more easily managed when the teacher is attempting to match materials to students.

Secondary school students in literature will experience significant improvement in their academic work if the teacher will plan carefully for (1) reading assignments, (2) study of vocabulary in context, (3) reading for main ideas, (4) selection of books based upon individual differences, and (5) lessons which are designed for groups of varying abilities and interests. The improvement of learning in the literature classroom is closely related to the attention given by the English teacher to these guidelines for reading improvement.

[8] Daniel Fader and Elton B. McNeil, *Hooked on Books*, Berkley Publishing Corporation, New York, 1968.

Questions and Activities for Discussion and Growth

1. Read the paperback *Hooked on Books*. Investigate what you can do in your community to get a similar program into operation.

2. Select a short story with a modern theme and devise a lesson plan, similar to Sample lesson 1, in which visual imagery is utilized. This will place emphasis on vocabulary usage.

3. Select a different short story with a theme of special interest to today's youth. Develop a lesson plan, patterned after Lesson plan 3, in which character analysis is done.

4. The English teacher is still often confronted with the problem of working in a class using a single set of literature anthologies or novels not suitable to all students. What should be done with those students with low reading ability?

5. Develop a guided lesson plan for a literature selection, stressing the reading skill of following a story sequence. What visuals could you use?

6. Select a character description, and plan and teach a lesson on reading for implications about character.

7. Plan a guided reading lesson using the following outline:

> Determining the significance of the title
> Discussing the background of the author
> Examining the headnotes written by the editor
> Examining illustrations (if any)
> Noting the length of the selection
> Pondering questions before reading (to give direction to the thinking which accompanies the reading)
> Utilizing the past experiences of each reader

What improvement in learning do you anticipate from such a guided reading lesson, compared with the usual assignment in English? Try to be specific in making the contrast.

8. Select a portion of a story and develop a lesson in reading to interpret figurative language. What aspects of past experience must be utilized by the young reader? What should be done for those who do not possess such readiness for reading figurative language?

9. Obtain three literature anthologies that publishers claim are for one particular grade—the ninth grade, for example. Select a 500-word sample from three places in each book, choosing what appears to be of "average" difficulty. Use the readability form in Chapter 2 to arrive at relative placement of each anthology according to level of readability. Are you satisfied with your results? How do the three books compare? Why would one sample not be enough? What should be done to improve your estimate of the readability of each anthology?

10. Make a chart with themes of special interest to secondary school boys and girls as headings across the top (see page 153 of this chapter). List under each theme as many books as you can locate in your school library or in your local public library. Make a readability estimate of each book. Make a note of the themes in which the library's holdings are inadequate, as well as the levels of difficulty in which books are not available for each theme. Then make a plan for the acquisition of books to fill the needs shown on your chart. To do this, you may need the aid of your school's librarian and reading specialist, and catalogs from publishers.

Why should an undertaking of this magnitude be a project of the entire English department?

Selected References

Alm, Richard S.: "What is a Good Unit in English?" in *The English Language Arts in the Secondary School,* Appleton-Century-Crofts, New York, 1956, pp. 69–70. (Good suggestions on planning the assignment.)

Aukerman, Robert C.: "Readability of Secondary School Literature Textbooks: A First Report," *English Journal,* vol. 54, no. 6 (September, 1965), pp. 533–540.

Burton, Dwight L.: "Teaching Students to Read Literature," *Reading Instruction in Secondary Schools,* International Reading Association, Newark, Delaware, 1964, pp. 87–102.

Caldwell, Marguerite J.: "Teaching Reading Through a Play," *Journal of Reading,* vol. 11, no. 2 (November, 1967), pp. 105–110.

Cohen, S. Alan: "Paperbacks in the Classroom," *Journal of Reading,* vol. 12, no. 4 (January, 1969), pp. 295–298 ff.

Early, Margaret J.: "Reading: In and Out of the English Curriculum," *Bulletin* of the National Association of Secondary School Principals, 51 (April, 1967), pp. 47–59.

Fader, Daniel, and Elton B. McNeil: *Hooked on Books,* Berkley Publishing Corporation, New York, 1968.

Gallo, Donald R.: "Reading in the Literature Classroom: Research," Chapter 2 in James L. Laffey, ed., *Reading in the Content Areas,* International Reading Association—ERIC/CRIER, Newark, Delaware, 1972.

Gordon, Edward J.: "The Reading of Fiction," *Bulletin* of the National Association of Secondary School Principals, 39 (September, 1955), pp. 44–49.

Hook, J. N.: *The Teaching of High School English.* The Ronald Press Company, New York, 1965. (Chapter 4, "Improvement of Reading," on improving reading in the English classroom, is pertinent.)

Moore, Walter T.: "What Does Research Reveal About Reading in the Content Areas?" *English Journal* (May, 1969).

National Council of Teachers of English: *Your Reading, A Booklist for Junior High Schools,* Champaign, Illinois, 1966.

Nealon, Thomas E.: "The Adapted Classic in the Junior High School," *Journal of Reading,* vol. 9, no. 4 (March, 1966), pp. 256–262.

New York Board of Education: *Reading, Grades 7, 8, 9,* 1959. (A curriculum guide for reading in junior high school literature.)

Niles, Olive S.: "Developing Essential Reading Skills in the English Program," in International Reading Association, *Proceedings: Reading and Inquiry,* vol. 10, Newark, Delaware, 1965, pp. 34–36.

The Paperback Goes to School, Bureau of Independent Publishers and Distributors, 122 East 42 St., New York, New York 10017. (Lists 5,000 paperbacks by subjects: fiction, drama, short stories.)

Pitcole, Marcia: "*Black Boy* and Role Playing," *English Journal,* vol. 57, pp. 1140-2.

Siedow, Mary D., and Peter Hasselrus: "Reading in the Literature Classroom: Application of Research in the Classroom," Chapter 3 in James L. Laffey, ed., *Reading in the Content Areas,* International Reading Association—ERIC/CRIER, Newark, Delaware, 1972.

Simmons, John S.: "Teaching Levels of Literary Understanding," *English Journal,* vol. 54 (February, 1965), pp. 101 ff.

————: "The Reading of Literature: Poetry as an Example," in International Reading Association, *11th Annual Proceedings: Vistas in Reading,* Newark, Delaware, 1966, pp. 93-100.

Simpson, Elizabeth A.: *Helping High School Students Read Better,* Science Research Associates, Chicago, 1954. (Has excellent sections describing programs in several high schools. Chapter 3 is of special significance for the English teacher.)

Sipay, Edward R.: "Selecting Suitable Material for the Literature Program," in International Reading Association, *Proceedings: Improvement of Reading Through Classroom Practice,* vol. 9, Newark, Delaware, 1964, pp. 120-121.

Sohn, David A.: *Ten Top Stories,* Bantam Books, Inc., New York, 1964. (Excellent short stories, in paperback, for young adults.)

Spache, George: *Good Reading For Poor Readers,* Garrard Publishing Co., Champaign, Ill., 1971

Squire, James R.: "Reading in American High Schools Today," in International Reading Association, *Proceedings: Reading and Inquiry,* vol. 10, Newark, Delaware, 1965, pp. 468-472. (This is specific to the English classroom.)

Weiss, M. Jerry: *An English Teacher's Reader,* The Odyssey Press, Inc., New York, 1962. (A large paperback of readings.)

9. READING IN THE SCIENCE CLASSROOM

The study of science in the secondary school is no longer confined to cook-book-type texts and to the memorization of facts and formula. The texts in secondary school science now being published by major textbook houses are a far cry from those of a half-century ago. Today's texts are concept-oriented, with emphasis on cognitive learning. Consequently, they depend entirely upon the reading ability of the students. Reading is the means of learning science content, and the textbook is, more than ever, the medium of learning.

BEHAVIORAL OBJECTIVES IN SCIENCE

Science education objectives should never be static. They should evolve, in response to present factors and to the fact that there will be many exigencies in the future. Objectives common to many generations of young people have come to be called "behavioral" objectives, for they are what society expects concerning the mental and overt behaviors that should result from the study of science.

Through much of the 1960s, several groups worked on the task of enunciating objectives in science for the secondary school. The National Assessment of Educational Progress set up four primary objectives:

1. To know fundamental facts and principles of science
2. To possess the abilities and skills needed to engage in the processes of science
3. To understand and investigate the nature of science
4. To have attitudes about and appreciations of scientists, science, and the consequences of science that stem from adequate understanding[1]

It is understandable that these behavioral objectives, and the subheadings that were delineated by the Committee on Assessing the Progress of Education (CAPE), reflect the stance of the Educational Testing Service of Princeton. CAPE wisely stated, however, that "a comprehensive program in science education must consider two unequal groups of students, those who may eventually pursue scientific careers, and the great majority of those who will not."[2] These broad objectives formed the basis for the test items developed by ETS for the National Assessment project in science.

At the same time that the objectives listed above were being developed, the Graduate School of Education of the University of California at Los Angeles had a team working on behavioral objectives under a contract from the U.S. Office of Education. The Center for the Study of Evaluation at UCLA established the Instructional Objectives Exchange, which takes the form of monographs in most of the secondary school subject-matter areas. The one concerning biology, grades 10 to 12, is given as an example here.

Much of the material is an outgrowth of the "themes" developed by the Biological Sciences Curriculum Study (BSCS). Fourteen objectives were proposed. Briefly stated, they are:

1. To differentiate phenomena as being quantitative or qualitative
2. To be able to formulate and test hypotheses
3. To demonstrate competence in laboratory techniques
4. To be able to explain organic life processes
5. To be able to compare the similarities and differences in life structures and processes
6. To be able to explain the process of continuity of life
7. To handle hypothetical problems in genetics
8. To handle specific test cross problems
9. To understand structure related to the function it performs
10. To understand internal regulation and homeostasis
11. To understand the biological roots of behavior

[1] National Assessment of Educational Progress, *Science Objectives*, Committee on Assessing the Progress of Education, Ann Arbor, Michigan, 1969.
[2] Ralph Tyler and Jack Merwin, "Working Paper on Objectives," Exploratory Committee on Assessing the Progress of Education, The Carnegie Foundation, New York, 1965, p. 30.

12. To understand the relationship and interaction of organisms and their environments
13. To explain chemical bases of biological processes
14. To understand the historical evolution of biological concepts[3]

These fourteen behavioral objectives in biology may be categorized under the four general behavioral objectives in science delineated by the National Assessment Project. It should be obvious that secondary school science textbooks are built around those four objectives. Restated in terms of the textbook, the behavioral objectives are as follows.

1. Each secondary school science should provide the means for understanding the fundamental facts and principles of its particular subject matter.
2. The science text should help the student learn to operate in a scientific manner, using scientific processes.
3. The science text should provide instructions and information that will help the student experiment in science.
4. The text should help the student formulate positive attitudes, appreciation, concepts, and values related to the responsibilities and consequences of science in today's world.

STRUCTURE OF SCIENCE TEXTBOOKS

Secondary school science textbooks do not necessarily present materials in the sequence in which these objectives have been listed. Nonetheless, up-to-date texts do provide substance leading toward those behavioral objectives.

The student who can visualize organization and knows what elements to anticipate in written material will read science textbooks more efficiently. To illustrate the organization common to many science textbooks, one section of *PSSC Physics*, Chapter 4, ("PSSC" stands for the Physical Science Study Committee; see page 166); and one part of *BSCS High School Biology*, *Green Version*, Chapter 12, are analyzed here.

The pattern of the physics text includes the following elements:

1. Definition
2. Example
3. Introduction of new factors
4. Explanation
5. Formula, or "idea shorthand"
6. Generalization
7. Statement of purpose

[3]*Biology, 10–12*, Instructional Objectives Exchange (mimeographed), UCLA, 1969.

FUNCTIONS AND SCALING

CHAPTER 4

introduction → **4-1. Mathematical Relations**

Many of the laws of physical science are most usefully expressed by mathematical relations, which show how one thing that we can measure depends upon other things that we can measure. In this section we shall discuss some of these relations.

Direct Proportion

partial definition → One of the simplest relations between two quantities is called direct proportion. For ex-

example → ample, let us look at the relation between the volume of a piece of iron and its weight. If we make measurements on pieces of iron we find that 1 ft³ weighs 440 pounds, 2 ft³ weighs 880 pounds, 3 ft³ weighs 1320 pounds, and so on.

definition → This kind of relation, in which doubling the volume doubles the weight, tripling the volume triples the weight, etc., is what we mean by direct pro-

explanation; past experience → portion. You will meet many cases of direct proportion in physics, so it is well to understand the various ways of describing this relation. We can say weight "is proportional to" volume of iron, or weight "varies directly as" volume of iron. Both mean the same thing: twice the volume, twice the weight; ten times the volume, ten times the weight, and so on.

We can write the relation in the shorter form

formula → $$W \propto V,$$

where W is the weight of a piece of iron, V its volume, and the symbol ∝ means "is proportional

clue to new element to." If we have two different volumes of iron, *in* V and V', the fact that their weights W and W' *problem* are proportional to their volumes can also be expressed as

$$\frac{W'}{W} = \frac{V'}{V}. \quad \textit{alternate formula}$$

$W \propto V$ is just another way of making this statement.

Another useful form of this relation expresses the fact that when weight and volume are related by direct proportion they have a constant ratio. If we divide the weight of a sample of iron *new* by its volume, the result will be the same as that *clue* obtained by dividing the weight of any other sample by its volume.

$$\left(\frac{W}{V}\right)_{\text{one sample}} = \left(\frac{W}{V}\right)_{\text{another sample}} = k. \quad \textit{formula}$$

The constant ratio k is called the *proportionality constant*. In our example of iron, $k = 440$ *definition* pounds per cubic foot. We can express this relation as an equation for *any* piece of iron:

$$\frac{W}{V} = k$$

or

$$W = kV.$$

Notice that this expression is very similar to the relation $W \propto V$. Indeed, if we do not know the numerical value of k it is just the same thing.

SOURCE: Physical Science Study Committee, PSSC Physics, D. C. Heath and Company, Lexington, Mass., 1960, p. 39. Reprinted by permission of The Education Development Center, Newton, Massachusets.

An analysis of Section 4-1 in *PSSC Physics* (reproduced on this page) provides examples of many of the writing patterns found in science reading materials. It is not only helpful but essential that secondary school students learn to recognize such patterns and pick up the clues to the framework that the author is using.

Facts are not the all-important ingredient in science, but comprehension, emerging from the way groups of words are put together, *is* very important. The interdependence of materials is tighter in science than in, say, social studies, so that a sentence out of context is rarely useful. But although logical connection is of prime importance in scientific writing, the connectives used by authors are often obscure. Instead of such words as *therefore, firstly, secondly, because, on the other hand,* the scientist often uses *if we, you will, we can, another useful form,* etc. This sort of style may at first confuse the student. He will be helped by repeated teaching of these connective elements in science reading.

Next, let us examine some patterns in a biology text (the section is called "Cell Structure").

1. Definition
2. Process
3. Location
4. Example
5. Historical fact
6. Explanation
7. Appearance

Note that some elements of writing shown in the biology text (reproduced on pages 168–169) are different from those of the physics text, although some are the same. (Earth science and chemistry have still other patterns or elements.)

It is suggested that the teacher look at reading material from the point of view of *learning*, and become conscious of the patterns in the text so as to teach them one at a time. The teacher might, perhaps, start with "connectives" in physics and with "process" in biology, and then gradually introduce the other types of patterns until they are recognized by the students. Patterns can be utilized as a way to organize answers to quiz questions. The aim is to teach patterns, not for their own sake, but as an aid to visualizing the structure of the chapter, and as facets of the total scientific concept being studied.

UTILIZING THE SURVEY TECHNIQUE IN SCIENCE READING

Because of the nature of scientific subjects, a scientist must be very methodological. Accordingly, writers of science textbooks tend to provide highly structured chapters, with sections and subsections clearly delineated by headings. This suggests that the survey technique described in Chapter 4 will be very successful in the science classroom.

An example of the manner in which the survey technique may be applied to science textbooks is taken from *Modern Chemistry*, Chapter 26 ("The Halogen Family"). The chapters of this text are arranged in highly structured and orderly format. The selection used as an example here (see page 170–171) shows how easily the survey technique may be applied. The introductory paragraph consists of only one sentence, which indicates that the halogen group comprises fluorine, chlorine, bromine, iodine, and astatine. These five nonmetallic elements constitute the main subheadings in the chapter (the subheadings are set in color, for reinforcement). Each subheading is in boldface type; sub-subheadings, which indicate processes, uses, or characteristics, are in italics. Processes, uses, and characteristics are reinforced through the visuals in the chapter. The summary of Chapter 26 is set apart, with a large heading, "Summary" (also in color).

Schwann wrote, "We have thrown down a great barrier of separation between the animal and vegetable kingdoms."

In so doing they began the joining of botany and zoology into the unified science of all life—into biology. The word itself had already been originated in its French form by Lamarck in 1802.

THE CELL THEORY

Thus "cell," which once referred to an empty space, came to mean a unit of living matter. Leeuwenhoek's "little animals" were interpreted as the least possible degree of cellular organization—that is, single cells. All other organisms could then be regarded as aggregations (groupings) of cells—very highly organized and differentiated aggregations, to be sure, but nevertheless reducible to cell units.

The cell theory did not lead immediately to a great new era of research. Despite the microscope's usefulness, detailed studies of cells had to await another technological development—dyes that could make cellular structures more clearly visible. This came with a great spurt in chemical knowledge in the 1850's and 1860's. Soon thereafter every life process was being associated with one type of cell or another. The cell quickly came to be regarded as not only the unit of structure but the unit of function as well.

Already, in the decade after Schleiden and Schwann, investigators had begun to find that cells normally and

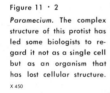

aggregations [Latin: *ad*, to, + *gregare*, to herd]

differentiate [dĭf'ə rĕn'shē āt; Latin: *dis-*, apart, + *ferre*, to carry]: become distinct or different

Such dyes came to be called stains by microscopists. What stains have you used?

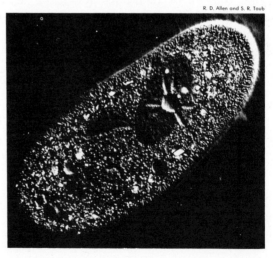

R. D. Allen and S. R. Taub

Figure 11 · 2

Paramecium. The complex structure of this protist has led some biologists to regard it not as a single cell but as an organism that has lost cellular structure.

X 450

regularly come into being through the division of parent cells. Soon the ideas were established that since the beginning of life there has been no break in the descent of living cells from other cells of the past and that all of heredity and all of evolution must be embodied in cells.

Today the cell theory may be summarized as three main ideas: (1) The cell is the unit of structure of living organisms. (2) The cell is the unit of function in living organisms. (3) All cells come from preexisting cells.

Why is this generalization called a theory?

CELL STRUCTURE

Differences among cells are great—in size, shape, and internal structure. When you study Figure 11 · 3, do not assume that all the structures shown are to be found in all cells or that all structures known to occur in cells are included. The diagram is intended only to assist you in remembering some of the principal structures of cells. Therefore, some structures that you may encounter in more advanced studies have been omitted. And it would be impossible to find any cell that, in every way, looks like the diagram.

Nearly every cell contains at least one *nucleus* (plural, "nuclei"). Under the microscope the nuclei of living cells are usually difficult to see, but they are readily visible when stained with various kinds of dyes. Compared with the rest

nucleus [noo'kli us; Latin: *nux*, nut]

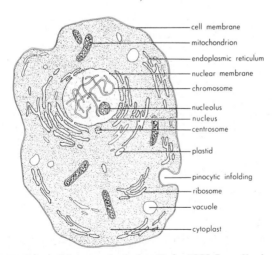

cell membrane
mitochondrion
endoplasmic reticulum
nuclear membrane
chromosome
nucleolus
nucleus
centrosome
plastid
pinocytic infolding
ribosome
vacuole
cytoplast

Figure 11 · 3

Cell structures. This is a *diagram*; it does not picture any particular kind of cell.

SOURCE: Biological Sciences Curriculum Study, BSCS Green Version High School Biology, 2d ed., Rand McNally & Company, Chicago, 1968. Copyright 1968 by The Regents of the University of Colorado and reprinted with their permission.

Chapter  THE

HALOGEN FAMILY

1. The Halogen Family is Group VIIA of the Periodic Table. It consists of the nonmetallic elements fluorine, chlorine, bromine, iodine, and astatine, as shown in the table on page 359.

From this table we learn that each of these elements has seven electrons in its outermost shell. In order to attain an outer octet of electrons, a halogen atom must acquire one electron. Since the atoms of these elements have such a strong affinity for electrons, they are all active elements which have never been found free in nature. In the elementary state they exist as covalent diatomic molecules. Fluorine, having the smallest atoms, shows the greatest affinity for electrons. Fluorine is consequently the most active nonmetallic

element, and cannot be prepared from its compounds by any purely chemical reduction. The other halogens, with increasingly larger atoms, show less activity than fluorine. As a result, the smaller, lighter halogens are able to replace the larger, heavier halogens from their compounds (see Activity Series, Chapter 12, Section 12). Astatine is a synthetic radioactive halogen produced in 1940 at the University of California by Corson, MacKenzie, and Segre. Very little is known of its properties. However, what study has been made of this element indicates that it is a halogen with properties which correspond to its position in the family.

We also see from the table that there is a regular change in properties shown

VOCABULARY

Antichlor. A substance used to remove traces of chlorine left in bleached goods.

Halogen (*hal*-oh-jen). The name given to the family of elements having seven valence electrons.

Mother liquor. The saturated solution remaining after the separation of a crop of crystals.

Pickling. Removing the surface impurities from a metal by dipping it into an acid bath.

ELEMENT	ATOMIC NUMBER	ATOMIC WEIGHT	ELECTRON CONFIGURA- TION	PRINCI- PAL OXIDA- TION NUMBER	MELT- ING POINT, °C	BOIL- ING POINT, °C	COLOR	DENSITY, 15° C
FLUORINE	9	19.00	2,7	−1	−223	−187	pale-yellow gas	1.69 g/l
CHLORINE	17	35.457	2,8,7	−1	−101.6	−34.6	greenish-yellow gas	3.214 g/l
BROMINE	35	79.916	2,8,18,7	−1	−7.2	58.78	reddish-brown liquid	3.12 g/ml
IODINE	53	126.91	2,8,18,18,7	−1	113.5	184.35	grayish-black crystals	4.93 g/ml
ASTATINE	85	210.	2,8,18,32,18,7					

by the members of this family as we proceed from the smallest and lightest to the largest and heaviest.

Each of the halogens combines with hydrogen. Hydrogen fluoride molecules are so polar that they associate by hydrogen bonding. The remaining hydrogen halides do not show this property. Each of the hydrogen halides is a colorless gas which is ionized in water solution. With the exception of hydrofluoric acid, these acids are highly ionized and are strong acids.

Each of the halogens forms ionic salts with metals. Hence the name *halogens,* which means "salt producers."

1. FLUORINE

2. The preparation of fluorine. Fluorine was first prepared in 1886 by Henri Moissan (1852–1907). He prepared it by electrolyzing a solution of potassium hydrogen fluoride, KHF_2, in liquid anhydrous hydrogen fluoride in a platinum tube. He used platinum-iridium electrodes. Today it is prepared by electrolyzing a mixture of potassium fluoride and hydrogen fluoride. Stainless steel or copper is used for the electrolytic cell. The fluoride coating formed on these metals protects them from further attack. Graphite is used for the anode.

3. What are the properties of fluorine? Fluorine is the most active nonmetallic element. A fluorine atom, with seven electrons in its outer L shell, has a great affinity for an additional electron to complete its octet. An acquired electron is very strongly attracted by the positively-charged nucleus due to the small size of the fluorine atom. This accounts for its extreme electronegativity. It unites with hydrogen explosively, even in the dark. It forms compounds with all of the elements except the inert gases. There are no known positive oxidation states of fluorine. It forms

SOURCE: Charles E. Dull, H. Clarke Metcalfe, and John E. Williams, Modern Chemistry, Holt, Rinehart, and Winston, Inc., New York, 1958, pp. 358–359. Copyright © 1958, and reprinted by permission.

Additional aids to reading are the vocabulary definitions at the beginning of the chapter and the concepts listed at the end of the chapter under the heading "Test yourself on these items."

The survey of the chapter, consequently, will quickly reveal that the material has been neatly written and edited in the following format:

(Title) The Halogen Family
  (Subtitles)
  Fluorine
  Chlorine
  Bromine
  Iodine
  Astatine
    (Sub-subtitles)
    Characteristics
    Uses
    Processes
    (Visuals)
    Table of characteristics
    Diagrams of preparation
    Photos of everyday uses
    Vocabulary: glossary at beginning of chapter
    Introductory and summary paragraphs

Any secondary school science class that surveys such a well-organized format will have taken a giant step toward significantly increased reading comprehension.

PREDICTING READING DISABILITY IN SCIENCE

Identifying the secondary school student who will have difficulty in reading science materials is not too difficult a task.

Readability depends chiefly on three factors: general vocabulary, specific scientific vocabulary, and complexity of writing. Complexity of writing is a problem for everyone; and scientific vocabulary is usually defined within the context and again in a glossary at the end of the text (see the example on page 173). Consequently, the student who will have particular difficulty is the one who cannot handle the general vocabulary. To assess a student's general reading ability, the general reading test described in Chapter 2 is useful. To forecast reading problems with a specific subject, a quick prognostic test should be used. A prognosis of difficulty with science materials has been developed on the assumption that students who cannot readily recognize general vocabulary used in a specific way in the field of science will have extreme difficulty reading science texts, on the basis of that factor alone.

Glossary

A battery. The battery used to supply power for the heaters of electronic tubes.

Absolute temperature scale. A thermodynamic scale not based on the physical behavior of water. The starting point is absolute zero with degree divisions equal to those of the Celsius scale.

Absolute zero. The lowest possible temperature.

Absorption spectrum. A spectrum having dark lines because of the absorption of some wavelengths caused by the radiation being filtered through a material medium.

Acceleration. The rate of change of velocity with respect to time.

Accelerator (particle). Device to give high velocities, and thus high energies, to atomic and elementary particles.

Amplifier. Thermionic tube or transistorized circuit used to increase the strength of an input signal voltage or current.

Amplitude. The crest or maximum value of a periodic wave or motion.

Amplitude modulation (AM). Variation of a carrier wave by changes in the amplitude of the wave.

Analysis. The breaking down of anything complex in order to learn its structure.

Angle of incidence. The angle formed by the perpendicular to a surface and the incident ray.

Angle of reflection. The angle formed by the perpendicular to a surface and the reflected ray.

Angle of refraction. The angle formed by the perpendicular to a surface and the refracted ray.

SOURCE: Frank L. Verweibe, Gordon E. Van Hooft, and Bryan W. Saxon, Physics, American Book Company, New York, 1970, p. 519. Copyright © 1970; reprinted by permission.

The secondary school student who cannot recognize the general vocabulary that is used in a specialized way in physics, chemistry, and biology will be in trouble—and, of course, it is likely that such a student will have even more trouble handling specific vocabulary such as that shown in the glossary.

The following prognostic text is to be given individually. Each student reads directly from the page of this book. One or two minutes is sufficient time in which to determine whether or not he will have trouble in reading a science text. Three alternative forms of the test are included, so that students will not be able to memorize the content from hearing it read over and over by the students who are tested first. No student will know which form he will be asked to read.

*PROGNOSTIC TEST OF READING DISABILITY
IN SECONDARY SCHOOL SCIENCE*[4]

Directions. Cover the other forms not being used (5- by 7-inch cards will do).

Ask the student to read from left to right, pronouncing each word in turn at his normal rate.

Observe his facial expression as he reads. Note hesitations, repetitions, regressions, uncertainties, gross mispronunciations, and incorrect stress.

The student who is *not* able to move along smoothly at about one word every two seconds will most probably have great difficulty reading in the field of science because he lacks adequate proficiency in general vocabulary. He will be at a total loss in the technical vocabulary of science.

[4]Copyright 1971 by Robert C. Aukerman.

Alternative Form A

translucent	radioactive	concentration	expansion
nuclear	precipitation	digestion	fission
vaporization	bacteria	synthesize	impurities
heredity	fusion	transmission	environment
equations	essential	formula	converted
coefficient	potential	homogeneous	impenetrable
decomposition	malleable	pulverize	attitude
condensation	parallel	friction	saturated
humidity	resistance	compensate	dehydrated
vaporize	contraction	disintegrate	acceleration

Alternative Form B

elements	gaseous	liberated	properties
substance	evaporation	material	matter
spontaneous	insoluble	process	oxidize
heaviness	characterize	decompose	density
solution	ignite	gravity	quantity
dilute	principle	proportion	existence
volume	relationship	behavior	capacity
formation	particles	liquids	reaction
assumption	solids	absorb	constant
characteristics	combustible	inverse	temperature

Alternative Form C

dissolve	varies	experiment	constituents
theory	pressure	emit	hypothesis
distinguish	atmosphere	factors	conductor
abundance	predict	phenomenon	periodic
structure	transformed	comprise	positive
unite	negative	porous	component
compressed	resistance	mixture	agents
compound	filament	attraction	equivalent
applications	repulsion	fluorescent	emulsion
immerse	transparent	nonmetallic	filtration

READABILITY OF SCIENCE TEXTS

Science textbooks present unique problems of readability. They are generally much too difficult for the average reader in the grade for which they are intended. Indeed, of textbooks surveyed by this author, 70 percent contained reading material considered beyond the average reading ability of the grade levels for which they were written.

At least three factors may account for this disparity between the readability of science materials and the reading ability of the students:

1. Scientific writers are not reading specialists and are not aware of the factors determining readability (described in Chapter 6).
2. The concepts of science are entirely new and foreign to most young people in high school, yet many textbook writers plunge into the subjects with little or no development, leaving the task of producing readiness to the classroom teacher.
3. The vocabulary of science is forbidding to many students because it is strange, complex, and full of polysyllabic words.

The task of the reader is somewhat like learning a foreign language. Moreover, the gap between the readability of the textbook and the reading skill of the *average* high school student is real and must be reckoned with by the classroom teacher.

One of the problems is the length and complexity of sentences. This may be no problem to the authors of the texts, and therefore they may assume that it is no problem to the reader. Here is an example (from Section 4–2, page 40, of the physics text shown on page 166). "Extrapolation from the behavior of gasses at normal temperatures leads to the idea of a lowest possible temperature, absolute zero, but about objects traveling close to the speed of light, extrapolation from ordinary experience leads to nonsense." And here is an excellent example of the specific vocabulary load encountered by the student reading scientific material:

81. Units of Work

Every unit for measuring work is arrived at by multiplying a force $\times$ a distance. Some of the units have names which show this; feet of distance $\times$ pounds of force give *foot-pounds* of work, and grams $\times$ centimeters give gram-centimeters. But dynes (force) $\times$ centimeters gives work in *ergs*; newtons (force) $\times$ meters $=$ *joules* of work (roughly $\frac{3}{4}$ of a foot-pound). Foot-poundal and inch-pound are also used. Engineers use the kilowatt-hour (which you will use when you study electricity), the foot-pound, and the inch-pound. Scientists use the erg (for tiny jobs) and the joule for larger ones.

SOURCE: Elements of Physics, revised by Paul J. Boylan, Allyn and Bacon, Inc., Boston, © 1958, 1962. P. 115.

Another example (from the same text) illustrates writing at an extremely high level of readability, far beyond the capabilities of the average high school student:

By using magnets of different strength placed at different distances from each other, it can be shown by careful measurements, that the force of attraction between two unlike poles (or of repulsion between two like poles) is equal to:

$$\frac{\text{strength of magnet A} \times \text{strength of magnet B}}{\text{square of the distance between the poles}}$$

(Coulomb's Law). The strength of a magnet pole is said to be unity (meaning 1) *if it attracts a similar pole at a distance of 1 cm with a force of 1 dyne.* (Review the dyne, § 94.) If magnet *A* has a pole strength of 8 units and *B* of 10 units, at 1 cm distance apart the force of attraction of one for the other will be 80 dynes; at 2 cm, 20 dynes; at 3 cm, about 9 dynes; and at 4 cm, 5 dynes. The variation of the magnetic force with the inverse square of distance follows the same law as do similar variations in gravitational and electrical forces. The attractive force of a magnet falls off sharply as it is moved farther from the object to be attracted.

SOURCE: Elements of Physics, revised by Paul J. Boylan, Allyn and Bacon, Inc., Boston, © 1958, 1962. Pp. 402–403.

It may be argued that it is necessary to present the scientific facts of physics in this way and that it is not possible to simplify either the concepts or the complexity of writing. Consequently, the burden of explanation falls to the classroom teacher. But the following example, from another physics text, might indicate that is not necessarily true:

As you perform these experiments you will find that the stronger the magnets you use, the greater will be the force exerted between them. You will also find that the farther the poles of the magnets are from each other, the weaker the force between them will be. These ideas are stated more precisely in **Coulomb's Law for Magnetic Poles** which says:

The force exerted by two magnetic poles on each other is directly proportional to the product of the pole strengths and inversely proportional to the square of the distance between them.

This law may be written in the following way:

$$F = \frac{km_1 m^2}{r^2}$$

F is the force, m_1 and m_2 are the pole strengths, *r* is the distance between them, and *k* is a constant. This is another example of an "inverse square law."

SOURCE: From EXPLORING PHYSICS, by Richard F. Brickerhoff, Judson B. Cross, and Arthur Lazarus, © 1970, Harcourt Brace Jovanovich, Inc., and printed with their permission. P. 368.

The sentences in the example above are less complex, yet the concept of magnetic force being discussed here is just as abstract as the concept discussed in the preceding example; an actual experiment with magnets is needed to provide some degree of reality.

Still, in general, length of sentences, complexity of sentence construction, general vocabulary, specific scientific vocabulary, and abstract concepts conspire to make science textbook materials difficult to read. Chapter 3 provides directions for assessing the readability of secondary school science texts; it is recommended that the available texts be ranked according to difficulty.

ADJUSTING READING ASSIGNMENTS TO READING ABILITY

Chapter 6 presents a workable philosophy on reading assignments. The "Reading Assignment Planning Form" provides space for listing textbooks and supplementary materials for good, average, and poor readers. It also provides space to list four alternatives for completing the assignment. Science teachers should use this form, noting, as did the ETS report referred to earlier, that "a comprehensive program in science education must consider two unequal groups of students, those who may eventually pursue scientific careers, and the great majority of those who will not."

In junior high school general science courses, difficult vocabulary and complex concepts are usually omitted. General science covers the more general notions in a simplified manner and embellishes them with applications in the everyday environmental experiences of youth.

Whereas general science texts tend to have a readability well within the range of "average" seventh and eighth grade students, secondary school physics and chemistry texts have measurable readabilities ranging into the senior college levels. Consequently, it is futile to attempt to have students work in such physics and chemistry texts unless they have adequate reading ability to handle such texts. This presents a real problem to the teacher of science.

There are several alternatives:

1. *Teach the student to read better, so that he may be able to read the science text.* This is *not* a feasible alternative for the science teacher who has neither the time nor the know-how for such remedial or developmental teaching. This is the specific responsibility of the reading specialist.

2. *Advise the student not to take (or to drop) physics, chemistry, or biology.* This might be the wisest thing to do, but it may not be practical for the college-bound student, who will be advised by college admissions offices to take a course in high school physics, chemistry, or biology.

3. *Select science materials that have been written specifically for students with average reading ability.* This should be a departmental, team project, undertaken with the aid of the reading specialist. Fortunately, materials written at lower levels of readability are now available, as a result of several years' effort by curricular materials task forces of the several science associations. (Their efforts have been aided financially by a number of foundations.) The Physical Science Study Committee, for example, was a group of high school and college physics teachers whose curriculum study was originated by the National Science Foundation in 1956. (The Ford Foundation and the Alfred P. Sloan Foundation also contributed financial support.) During the early days of the study, it was often referred to as the "MIT Study." The curricular materials developed by the Committee and several hundred associated and interested teachers consist of the text *PSSC Physics*, a laboratory guide, films, tests, related paperbacks, and a teachers' resource book. The PSSC materials were

tried with 37,800 students over a three-year period; the textbook is a revision of the materials based upon feedback from the tryouts.

Trial materials for biology were similarly developed, tried out on 150,000 high school students, and revised accordingly. Several different approaches were devised by the Biological Sciences Curriculum Study group, established by the American Institute of Biological Sciences. The text *BSCS High School Biology, Green Version,* is used here for illustrative purposes (see pages 168 and 169).

It could be argued that the PSSC and BSCS texts would undoubtedly have been improved if the committees had obtained the help of reading specialists. Since that was not done, some suggestions are given in this book for using these excellent texts in physics and biology.

The success of the PSSC and BSCS materials during the 1960s generated interest in the development of other textbooks in secondary school science for the great majority of students, who will not become scientists. It is incumbent upon the teacher of science to seek, find, and utilize these new texts to provide a comprehensive, stratified program for students with various degrees of ability. This may require changes in attitude on the part of the teacher.

Let us assume that the science teacher is committed to providing for the success of all students who are really interested in learning something about the particular science course he teaches: biology, physics, chemistry, etc. The best way to scuttle that high commitment is to assign the same materials to all students. The alternative is to provide opportunities to read about the same topics in materials which vary in difficulty. A few suggestions should indicate how easily this may be done.

First, for the very lowest group—the poorest readers—there is an abundance of excellent books written at the third- and fourth-grade level of readability. These are not baby books; they have been written by science educators for use in elementary schools and are parts of elementary science series published by many of the major textbook houses. Almost every subject in science can be found in such books, presented at very low levels of readability. The concepts of science are given by means of concrete examples and are beautifully illustrated. Most secondary school science teachers are totally unaware of the existence of these resources.

A number of years ago the Educational Division of Readers Digest Association started *Readers Digest Skill Builders in Science,* a series similar to the well-known *Skill Builders.* The science *Skill Builders* were edited by a reading specialist and rewritten for students with second-, third- and fourth-grade reading ability. Although the series was never completed, the titles that are available provide interesting human-interest stories which help achieve the fourth behavioral objective in science: formulation of a positive attitude about, and appreciation of, scientists, science, and the consequences of science, stemming from an adequate understanding of science. Such an objective can be achieved only through materials that the reader can understand.

The second ability group can best be served by some of the many excellent science texts at the junior high school level. The fact that such texts have been written for junior high school students does not mean that they must be confined to junior high schoolers. In fact, most of the newer texts at that level are admirably suited for the medium-ability groups in secondary school. One example will illustrate this point.

Compare the excerpt on page 180 with the illustration previously given from the BSCS biology text (see page 168). Both examples are on cell structure. Notice that the subject—cells and cell structure—is quite adequately covered in the lower-level text. Most of the other topics in biology (for example, bacteria, fungi, algae, mosses, vascular green plants, anthropods, and vertebrates) are also covered satisfactorily. The earth sciences book by the same team of authors is a superb example of the newer trends in science materials for the average reader.

There is no dearth of science materials for the college-bound students, who include the future scientists. The problem frequently is that texts supposedly written for readers at the level expected of college-bound students are loaded with extremely difficult material actually more suitable for college students or even graduate students. The secondary school teacher must adjust his expectations to include the many college-bound students who are not going to become scientists and who may well have difficulty with such material. Consequently, in college-bound classes, it will be wise to provide at least two texts each in chemistry, physics, biology, earth sciences, etc. If further persuasion is needed, consider this: the average reading ability of the beginning college freshman is between the sixth- and seventh-grade levels. Moreover, the average reading speed of college freshmen is between 300 and 350 words per minute for narrative materials, and much lower for technical and scientific materials. Assignments in science must, therefore, attempt to match the required reading materials with the *actual* abilities of the learners. Anything else is unrealistic.

READING SKILLS IN THE SCIENCES

Specific details of teaching reading skills in secondary school subjects have been presented in Chapter 5. Consequently, a few examples pertaining to science should suffice here.

Reading for Main Ideas

Two of the four behavioral objectives in science depend on the ability of the student to pick out main ideas; these are (1) the understanding of fundamental facts and principles, and (2) the formulation of a positive attitude toward and

Note once again the structure of the cells, especially the three parts that are labeled. Now compare the plant cell illustrated in the investigation on the opposite page with the cheek cell above. Each plant and animal cell has a **nucleus, cytoplasm,** and a **cell membrane.** In fact, all the cells of your body (except one kind) have a similar structure—a nucleus, cytoplasm, and cell membrane. **Figure 1-7** shows different types of cells—muscle, bone, blood, nerve, and skin cells. In which type of cell do you not see a nucleus? (It does, however, have a nucleus in its early stages of growth.)

It is true that you are made up of cells, but let us look more closely and see whether we can find a difference between plant and animal cells.

Bend a twig. When you let go, it will straighten out again. Look at a corn plant. It stands upright but bends back and forth in the wind. Push against a small tree, and it will bend. Branches of large trees sway back and forth in a heavy wind and sometimes break if the wind bends them too far.

These plants, although they have no skeleton as you do, have a structure rigid enough to hold them upright, but flexible enough to permit them to bend. In this characteristic of rigidity combined with flexibility is a clue to one major difference between plants and animals. This clue is a difference in cell structure which helps to distinguish plant cells from animal cells.

Every plant cell contains a substance that is not found in animal cells. This substance is **cellulose** (SEL–yuh–lohs), which makes up the **cell wall** in all plants. Refer to the drawing in the investigation on the following page. This substance helps give plants their relatively rigid form.

Chapter 1: Matter, Energy, and Life   **11**

SOURCE: From THE EARTH: ITS LIVING THINGS, by Paul F. Brandwein, Alfred D. Beck, Violet R. Strahler, Matthew J. Brennan, and Daniel S. Turner, © 1970, 1964 by Harcourt Brace Jovanovich, Inc., and reprinted with their permission. P. 11.

appreciation of science, scientific concepts, and scientific values. Some of the seven patterns of paragraph structure described in Chapter 3 apply to scientific writing. Three examples are given here.

1. Main ideas + examples

Energy is the lifeblood of the scientific technology that activates our world. As populations and scientific applications increase at explosive rates, so does the hunger for energy. Energy is needed to heat our homes in winter, to cool them in summer. Energy is required to run the machines that manufacture our clothing. Energy must be provided for the farm machinery used to plant and harvest our crops and for the factories that prepare our foods. The energy of fuels must be available to drive our cars and trucks, our ships and planes to transport us and the thousand and one things we use in our daily lives.

SOURCE: Frank W. Verwiebe, Gordon E. Van Hooft, and Bryant W. Saxon, Physics, American Book Company, New York, 1970, p. 106.

2. Examples + main idea at end

Catalysts

In the laboratory you found that when potassium chlorate ($KClO_3$) was heated in a test tube, oxygen was produced—but very slowly. By increasing the temperature, the rate at which the oxygen formed was increased. But the oxygen formed quite rapidly, and at a comparatively low temperature, if a little manganese dioxide (MnO_2) was added to potassium chlorate. Evidently, manganese dioxide in some way takes the place of heat energy in this chemical reaction. After all the oxygen has been freed from the mixture of $KClO_3$ and MnO_2, the materials that remain can be separated from one another by adding water to them and then filtering. When this is done, a dark gray solid is left in the filter paper. This solid, the MnO_2, can be used repeatedly with new supplies of $KClO_3$ to speed up the rate at which oxygen is produced. The MnO_2 does not break down to release oxygen.

Only by repeated experiments have chemists discovered such substances which can cause specific reactions to occur rapidly, even at temperatures which are quite low. They have also uncovered other substances which can slow down specific reactions at relatively high temperatures. In both cases the substances themselves, although they affect chemical reactions, do not seem to be changed by the reactions. Such substances that either speed up or slow down the rate of a chemical reaction yet themselves remain unchanged are called **catalysts.**

SOURCE: From CONCEPTS IN CHEMISTRY, by Arthur W. Greenstone, Sidney P. Harris, Frank X. Sutman, and Leland G. Hollingworth, © 1970 by Harcourt Brace Jovanovich, Inc., and reprinted with their permission. P. 165.

3. Main Idea + examples + main idea restated

As we subdivide and reorient plane mirrors in space, we construct closer and closer approximations to a mirror with a continuously curved surface; and we can imagine the indefinite continuation of the process which results in a smooth mirror which focuses the parallel light. The shape of the smooth surface (called a paraboloid of revolution or parabolic mirror) is determined exactly by our imaginary procedure. The spot F to which all the reflected light converges is called the *principal focus* of the parabolic mirror. In Fig. 12–16 a cross section is shown through the principal focus parallel to the direction of the incident light. Each of the rays we draw indicates how the light is reflected. It stays in the plane of the figure according to the laws of reflection; and the angle of reflection of each ray equals the angle of incidence. If we choose one point on the mirror and the focal point to which we wish to bring the light, only one smooth surface can be constructed which will do the job. The curve cut by this surface on the plane in Fig. 12–16 is a parabola, and the whole surface is called a paraboloid of revolution because by revolving the figure about the ray through F the parabola would be moved around over the whole surface of the mirror.

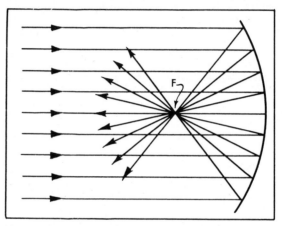

12–16. The converging of light by a curved mirror.

SOURCE: Physical Science Study Committee, Physics, D. C. Heath and Company, Boston, 1960 pp. 198–199. Reproduced by permission of the Education Development Center, Newton, Massachusetts.

Skimming

Skimming to get the gist of a section (the technique is detailed in Chapter 5) has a place in science. It is most appropriate for human-interest stories, descriptions of recent discoveries, and many of the other day-to-day contemporary news items that should be utilized to enrich the science period and give relevance to the science classroom.

Scanning

When a student is working with several source books in science to collect information on a topic, scanning is a valuable technique. (The teacher should *not* assume that the student knows how to do this efficiently.) Moreover, scanning may be the best technique to follow in the survey of a section by the entire class, especially with low-ability groups.

Usually there are questions at the end of a chapter. In texts that are easy to read, the questions can generally be answered by means of scanning. If this is by the whole class together, even the students with lowest reading ability will have some feeling of success. The pattern may be as follows:

1. The teacher reads a question from the text, as all in the class follow in their own texts.
2. The students scan for the answer. The teacher waits until several indicate that they think they have found it.
3. One student gives the answer. Others confirm or challenge his answer.
4. (This is the most important step.) The student is told, "Read the sentence which proves what you have said."
5. The student reads the entire sentence.
6. The teacher asks one or more of the other students to put this same idea into their own words.

Scanning makes it possible to follow this routine in thinking, proving, and understanding.

Understanding Vocabulary

Because scientific material is written for step-by-step analysis, each word or groups of words must be understood before a student can learn effectively. Vocabulary problems in science fall into four areas:

1. Words which are used only in science; for example, *molecule, diffraction, solenoid.*
2. Words which have a special meaning in science, but a different meaning in other content areas; for example, *current, uniform, incline.*
3. A group of words giving one concept: *Along the perpendicular to the diameter of the circle is the axis.* Here, *Along the perpendicular to the diameter of the circle* should be considered a single concept. Students need help with this. Most such groups of words can be replaced by one word; but if this is done too soon, the students may not understand the concept.
4. Symbols in formulas: $\dfrac{W}{V} = K$

Following Directions

The ability to follow directions is closely related to achievement in laboratory sciences. The laboratory manuals are like cookbooks in nature, and they assume that the reader has been taught to follow stepwise directions. But students— even adults—ignore directions more than they follow them. The quip "When all else fails, follow the directions" is evidence of this quirk of human nature.

The best technique for teaching students to follow directions in science is to provide a worksheet with each project. On such a sheet, the student is to reproduce the step-by-step directions *in his own words.*

Making Inferences

One of the skills that is part of the "spiral concept" of reading discussed in Chapters 1 and 5 is perceiving cause-and-effect relationships: the mature reader has learned to draw inferences from facts. The ability to read for inferences is an essential skill in science, since progress toward solutions of scientific problems depends on inferences. In elementary school, the teacher often stops in the middle of the story and asks a "thought question": "And now, what do you think will happen next?" "Why do you think that will happen?" In the sciences, the same routine is used, although it is not exploited for cognitive learning as often as it should be, or as thoroughly. Memorization of facts and formulas, as the end product of science teaching, is totally unacceptable in today's world. Students must confront problems and must make inferences from their reading. This is the essence of the fourth behavioral objective in science education.

ENRICHMENT IN SCIENCE READING MATERIALS

A wealth of supplementary reading materials is available to every secondary school science teacher, and unless he uses them, he must be textbook-bound. By using them, the teacher provides his students with a broad spectrum of interesting, significant, and relevant books.

Enrichment books include biographical, autobiographical, factual, and science-fiction materials. The science teacher should always be seeking books on subjects of high interest, written at low levels of readability, as most readers enjoy enrichment reading if it is relatively easy. For most students, it is no fun to struggle through difficult material.

It is fortunate that many materials of high interest and low readability have been developed. Some of these are in series. The following are a few suggestions which, if followed through with the help of the librarian and the reading specialist, will open a whole special library of reading materials in science.

The "How and Why Wonder Book" series includes many titles, such as *How and Why Wonder Book of Beginning Science* and *How and Why Wonder Book of Electricity;* others in the same series include *Oceanography, Reptiles and Amphibians, Birds, Rockets and Missiles, Ants and Bees, Chemistry, Wild Animals, Prehistoric Mammals, Human Body,* and many others. The series is published in paperback by Grossett and Dunlap and in hardcover editions by Merrill. Other paperbacks that are well received by teen-agers are *The Silent World, The Living Sea, A Planet Called Earth, The Human Side of Animals, Report on Unidentified Flying Objects,* and *The Strange Story of Our Earth.*

The college-bound secondary school student will enjoy reading Thor Heyerdahl's *Kon Tiki* and *Aku-Aku;* Herman Melville's *Moby Dick;* and Rachel Carson's *The Sea Around Us* and *Silent Spring*. *Life* magazine's hardcover science volumes *The Sea, The Desert, The Forest,* and *The Mind* are comprehensive and highly accurate treatments of scientific materials in a popular and fascinating format. Since the reading level is difficult, these books are suitable primarily for the best readers, although others may gain much from the excellent color illustrations.

Science fiction is also for the better reader. Jules Verne, of course, tops the list; other excellent writers are H. G. Wells, Paul deKruif, G. Conklin, A. C. Clarke, I. Asimov, and Edgar Rice Burroughs (who wrote as many science-fiction books as his famous Tarzan books).

Several series high in interest but with a low vocabulary load are available, and these are assets in any program seeking to improve learning in science by attending to the students' reading needs. For example, the "Allabout Books," published by Random House, are excellent for junior high school students with low reading ability. The very slow readers will find the Harr Wagner Publishing Company's "Deep Sea Adventure Series" just about right for their abilities. In addition, it captures the interest generated by television series, such as "Sea Hunt" and other underwater adventures. *Parents Magazine* publishes a series on nature under the general title "Finding Out Books."

The Prentice-Hall series "Junior Research Library" is also written with low readability. In contrast, Basic Books publishes a series, "Science and Discovery," that is challenging to the best readers. The "Science Works Like This" series (Roy Publishers) and Dr. Glenn Blough's "Science-Nature" series (published by McGraw-Hill) are especially good for junior high school students, as are the science-fiction novels in a series published by Holt, Rinehart and Winston.

Finally, Scholastic Magazine Book Services, through its Science World Book Club, provides students, teachers, and school libraries with an annotated bimonthly listing of excellent science paperbacks at very reasonable prices. (The idea for this book club was developed by Dr. William Boutwell.)

These are only a few of the large and ever-growing number of titles available to the science teacher in the secondary school. The teacher who helps students discover that reading in science is a multifaceted experience, and who supplements the textbooks with novels, biographies, autobiographies, poems, short stories, science fiction, and factual scientific books will have helped his students move into the world of science through the medium of reading. Reading in science opens the world of imagination to the student even more than does literature or, in fact, any other academic area of the secondary school curriculum.

SUMMARY: GUIDELINES FOR THE SCIENCE TEACHER

The basic pattern of the science text provides the framework and structure for the main ideas, concepts, and details. It is the job of the teacher of science to spend considerable time training the class to recognize the structure of each chapter in the text. This is ordinarily not a difficult task, for most science texts are written and edited in a highly structured pattern; consequently, the survey technique is a "natural" with science materials. Scientific writing is also full of clues to meaning. These are usually well marked in a text, by the use of numerals and ordinals, boldface type, italics, and print in contrasting color. Definitions are often so labeled. Visuals are cross-referenced within the text. Indeed, it may be said that the structure of science texts is their greatest asset.

On the other hand, the high readability level of many senior high school science texts is their greatest liability. The main guideline for the teacher of science is: find reading materials that your students can read. This is a task which, when completed, will greatly improve learning.

Questions and Activities for Discussion and Growth

1. Give the Prognostic Test of Reading Disability for Secondary School Science to a class of tenth-grade students. Compare the performances of those who do poorly with their performances in junior high school general science. What adjustments should be made in their science reading in the senior high school?
2. Prepare a lesson on the survey technique for a specific chapter in a physics textbook. Be sure to include the questions that should be asked to improve reading. (See Chapter 4 for a full treatment of this technique.)
3. Prepare a lesson on finding main ideas in a biology text. Indicate how you would help a class implement this technique in their biology reading.
4. Using the form in Chapter 2, measure the readability of three different general science texts and rate them as "most difficult," "average," "easy."
5. Attend a conference where publishers are displaying new supplementary reading materials in science. Ask them to indicate how the readability level of the materials is determined. What did you learn from your interviews?
6. Ask the librarian to help you locate some of the new science-fiction books. Use the information in Chapter 2 to assess their readability level.
7. Make an annotated list of biographies of scientists arranged according to levels of readability and categorized by sciences: physics, chemistry, biology, astronomy, geology, anthropology, etc. Have the list available— and in separate parts—for students with various abilities and interests.

8. Develop a lesson which will involve reading for contextual meanings. Carefully selected materials should be chosen, from which the students are to ascertain the meanings of terms from the context rather than by reference to a dictionary. Include in the lesson plans an introduction, an objective, methodological directions, and outcomes.

9. Plan a unit of science reading on a subject in science that is of interest to the nonacademic student. Indicate what specific reading materials you will need to assemble. You may decide to use some texts of low readability and some supplementary enrichment materials. Be specific in indicating exactly what materials are to be used and why.

10. Plan a reading assignment for a science class in which there are two or more ability groups. Use Chapter 6 as a guide.

Selected References

Ausubel, David P.: "An Evaluation of the BSCS Approach to High School Biology," *American Biology Teacher,* vol. 28, no. 3 (March, 1966), pp. 176–186.

Bamman, Henry A.: "Reading in Science and Mathematics," in International Reading Association, *Reading in Secondary Schools,* Newark, Delaware, 1964, pp. 59–72.

Ferguson, Jerry: "Teaching the Reading of Biology," in International Reading Association, *Fusing Reading Skills and Content,* Newark, Delaware, 1969, pp. 114–119.

Herber, Harold L.: "Teaching Reading and Physics Simultaneously," in International Reading Association, *Proceedings: Improvement of Reading Through Classroom Practice,* vol. 9, Newark, Delaware, 1964, pp. 84–85.

Lockwood, J. Bryce: "Research on Problems in Reading Science," *School Science and Mathematics,* 59 (October, 1959), pp. 551–556.

Mallinson, George G.: "The Development of a Vocabulary for General Physical Science," in National Council on Measurements in Education, *Twelfth Yearbook,* 1955, pp. 6–8.

——: "Reading in the Science Classroom: Research," Chapter 6 in James L. Laffey, ed., **Reading in the Content Areas,** International Reading Association—ERIC/CRIER, Newark, Delaware, 1972.

Marksheffel, Ned. D.: *Better Reading in the Secondary School,* The Ronald Press Company, New York, 1966. (See section on science.)

Moore, Arnold J.: "Science Instructional Materials for the Low-Ability Junior High School Student," *School Science And Mathematics,* vol. LXII (November, 1962), pp. 556–563.

Shepherd, David L.: *Effective Reading in Science,* Harper & Row, Publishers, Incorporated, New York, 1960.

——: "Reading and Science: Problems Peculiar to the Area," in International Reading Association, *Fusing Reading Skills and Content,* Newark, Delaware, 1969, pp. 151–161.

Smith, Carl Bernard: "Reading in the Science Classroom: Application of Research in the Classroom," Chapter 7 in James L. Laffey, ed., *Reading in the Content Areas,* International Reading Association—ERIC/CRIER, Newark, Delaware, 1972.

Smith, Nila B.: "Patterns of Writing in Different Subject Areas," *Journal of Reading,* vol. VIII, no. 1 (October, 1964). (Especially pertinent to the field of science)

10. READING IN THE MATHEMATICS CLASSROOM

The study of mathematics requires much more reading than it did twenty-five years ago. Mathematics teachers are aware of the fact that many high school youth have trouble comprehending mathematics materials. This has always been the case, and attention has usually been directed toward the symptoms rather than the cause. As a result, the usual explanation has been to say that a student who has difficulties has low intelligence or "no bent for math."

It is true that there is a high correlation between intelligence and achievement in mathematics. But there is also a close relationship between good reading ability and achievement in mathematics, and this fact is seldom recognized. Indeed, so little attention has been given to this key factor in secondary mathematics achievement that the classroom teacher generally is completely unaware of it.

Intensive, exacting reading—as well as good intelligence and good general reading ability—is the key to success in handling mathematics materials. The mathematics teacher will observe an improvement in class achievement as soon as effort is expended in teaching the students how to read the mathematics textbook.

BEHAVIORAL OBJECTIVES IN MATHEMATICS

The Instructional Objectives Exchange—a clearing house for behavioral objectives in subject matter areas (it was set up under a grant from USOE to UCLA)—published in 1970 two large mimeographed pamphlets, *Mathematics, Grades 7-9;* and *General Math, Grades 10-12.* The material dealing with junior high school contains 265 specific objectives organized under ten categories. For senior high school, 123 specific objectives are classified into nine categories. The objectives were listed for the purpose of designing test questions that could be used to determine whether or not students had attained them. In a sense, then, they are both instructional objectives and behavioral objectives.

The categories for junior high school are: sets; numbers; numerals and numeration systems; mathematical operations and their properties; measurement; geometry; relations, functions, and graphs; probability and statistics; applications and problem solving; and mathematical sentences, order, and logic.[1] Some of the behavioral objectives under those categories are: demonstration of knowledge of modern mathematics symbols; ability to perform a large number of operations and measurements; ability to apply knowledge of geometry to problems; ability to construct graphs; demonstration of knowledge of probability; and the ability to convert word problems into mathematical and logical operations.

The senior high school categories[2] are similar: modern mathematical terms and symbols; arithmetic operations involving modern mathematical procedures and operations with weights and measures; word problems in weights, measures, and percents; operations in simple plain geometry; construction and interpretation of simple graphs; everyday problems in probability; a few exercises in elementary logic; and some word problems calling for the application of simple arithmetic.

The School Mathematics Study Group, meeting in 1969 at Yale and Stanford Universities, and the study groups of the National Council of Teachers of Mathematics have been active in delineating behavioral objectives that, in turn, have been adopted by the authors of a number of texts published in 1970 and 1971. The most obvious behavioral objectives in the new appraoch to secondary mathematics are aimed at cognitive learning.

Relevance to the present and the future is an important element in much of the material found in the newer texts. Human-interest stories about mathematicians of the past; problems in the form of brain teasers; applications to radar, space travel, sports, and other areas of interest—such elements give vitality to what otherwise would be rote learning and thus aid understanding. Appreciating the relevance of mathematics to present, past, and future problems of life is one of the behavioral objectives that demands attention to reading skills and the readability of textbooks.

[1] *Mathematics, Grades 7-9,* Instructional Objectives Exchange, UCLA, Los Angeles, 1970.
[2] *General Math, Grades 10-12,* Behavioral Objectives Exchange, UCLA, 1970.

Another behavioral objective now considered essential in all grade levels is the ability to handle proof. Concepts of proof are presented in verbal form, and the reading ability necessary for dealing with those concepts must be developed by the mathematics teacher.

The general and specific vocabulary of mathematics is now receiving increased attention by textbook writers in an effort to provide the means for achieving understanding of mathematical terms. The significance of this may easily be demonstrated by asking the students in any university liberal arts class (or majors in education) to define such terms as *minuend, commutative, quadratic, radicand, dividend, factoring.* In the past it was considered enough to memorize such terms at the same time as one memorized the algorithm and related procedures: meaning might well be absent.

Mathematics is a skill, and there is an old saying, "No skill without drill." Although that idea is valid, drill without understanding provides skill that is limited to mechanical operations. The swing toward understanding in mathematics tended to make drill unpopular, but it must be remembered that drill and understanding are both important. The authors of *Mathematics 1, Discovery and Practice* state this position succinctly: "The authors are convinced there is a solid middle ground. Many students who seem to gain little appreciation for the structure of mathematics can certainly successfully learn its algorithms and develop computational skill. However, these goals do not have to be achieved at the expense of rote learning without understanding."[3]

THE SURVEY TECHNIQUE IN MATHEMATICS

Many mathematics texts are written and edited in a structured framework that makes the use of the survey technique (Chapter 4) a most effective approach.

Often the title of a chapter, although it introduces a new concept in mathematics, contains what linguists call "cognates"—words that have the same meaning in both technical and nontechnical language. The following chapter headings are examples:

"Probability"
"Cones, Cylinders, and Spheres"
"Equations and Inequalities"

The structure of a well-written and carefully designed mathematics text will include subheadings; definitions; visuals; clues in boldface, color, or italic type; and a chapter introduction and summary.

A unique format is employed in two new texts in junior high school mathematics. The authors (Gerardi, Jones, and Foster) have incorporated material

---

[3] Russell F. Jacobs and Richard A. Meyer, *Mathematics 1, Discovery and Practice,* Harcourt Brace Jovanovich, New York, 1971, Preface, p. *vi.*

25	*Introduction to Probability*
2	**THE PROBABILITY RATIO**

Warm Up

1. Everett wanted to go to the movies, but Fred wanted to stay home and watch television. What is one fair way to settle this?

2. There are 13 girls in the choir. "This means that at least two of us have a birthday in the same month," shouted Ida. Was she right?

3. The coach will pick 25 boys for the baseball team. Does probability have anything to do with Conrad making the team?

Discussion

The chances are slim, but it still may rain.

1. "The chances of rain tomorrow are 10%," announced the weather man. Do you think it is likely to rain tomorrow?
   • The 10% tells the chance or <u>probability</u> that it will rain.

$$10\% \longrightarrow 10 \text{ chances out of } 100 \longrightarrow \frac{10}{100}, \text{ or } \frac{1}{10}$$

2. In this game, 10 red marbles and 6 white marbles are placed in a bowl. Without looking, what is the probability of selecting a white marble?
   ❶ How many white marbles are in the bowl?
   ❷ What is the total number of marbles?
   ❸ Use the **probability ratio**.

$$\frac{\text{Number of Successful Ways} \longrightarrow 6}{\text{Number of Possible Ways} \longrightarrow 16} = \frac{3}{8}$$

The probability, then, is $\frac{3}{8}$.
   • What is the probability of selecting a red marble?

A **die** is one of a pair of **dice**.

3. There are 6 possible ways for a <u>die</u> to turn up.

$$\{1, 2, 3, 4, 5, 6\}$$

   • What is the probability of rolling a 1? a 2? a 3?
   • How many ways are there to roll an even number? What is the probability of rolling an even number?

KEY IDEA

You use this ratio to find the probability of an event.

Number of Successful Ways
──────────────────────────
Number of Possible Ways

4. What is the probability of getting a 5 by spinning the arrow? a 4?

5. What is the probability of getting an even number? an odd number?

6. What is the probability of landing on the red region?

Answers: **4.** $\frac{1}{6}$; $\frac{1}{6}$ **5.** $\frac{3}{6}$, or $\frac{1}{2}$ **6.** $\frac{3}{6}$, or $\frac{1}{2}$

Exercises

A bag contains 8 red, 6 white, and 10 green marbles.

1. How many marbles are in the bag?

2. What is the probability of picking a red one?

3. What is the probability of picking a white one?

4. What is the probability of picking a green one?

5. How many red and white marbles are in the bag?

6. What is the probability of picking a red **or** a white one?

No peeking!

Use the spinner at the right for Exercises 7–13.

7. What is the probability of getting a 2?

8. If the arrow lands on a 2 or a 3 you win. What is the probability of winning?

9. How many of the numbers are greater than 5?

10. What is the probability that it lands on a number greater than 5?

11. Name the prime numbers on the spinner.

12. What is the probability of landing on a prime number?

13. If the arrow lands on 2, 3, 8, or 9 you win. What is the probability of winning?

14. In this game, you toss a coin twice. Tossing 2 heads in a row wins. What is the probability of winning?

1st	2nd	1st	2nd	1st	2nd	1st	2nd
H	T	H	H	T	H	T	T

245

SOURCE: From KEY IDEAS IN MATHEMATICS 2, by William J. Gerardi, Wilmer L. Jones, and Thomas R. Foster, copyright © 1971 by Harcourt Brace Jovanovich, Inc., New York, and reprinted with their permission. Pp. 244–245.

designed to fit the behavioral objectives of national study groups. Their textbooks are examples of the new trend toward better, more readable, more relevant, more comprehendable texts. (See the sections reproduced on pages 192–193.) The books are structured with these features: each lesson is contained on two facing pages; a warmup (for readiness) ties the new lesson to past experience; the discussion is divided into a problem and the solution (designated by a gray overlay); a practice problem similar to the first one is given; the "key idea" is noted; and a few exercises are suggested. Several visual devices are used to appeal to the student: the owl is a reminder that the student learned this fact previously; the man gives hints in cartoon fashion; and the key pinpoints the main ("key") idea. All these aids contribute much to the readability of the textbook.

READING SKILLS IN MATHEMATICS

The secondary school student who has the habit of skimming all reading material and being satisfied with a general idea of the content may have difficulty adapting himself to the more exacting type of reading demanded by mathematics, even if he knows that he must adjust his rate of reading to fit his purpose and so reads mathematical materials at a moderate rate. The poor reader, too, will read slowly but lack conceptual power; although he reads the words, he misses the ideas and relationships that the words embody. He lacks sufficient ability to integrate words into unified thoughts.

In general, mathematics reading is approached in the same manner as any difficult study-type reading that requires simultaneous reading and reasoning and a slow, scientific approach. To complete mathematics assignments successfully, the student should:

1. Read at a moderate rate to get an overall view of the content, and to answer these questions:
   "What is to be proved?"
   "What is the unknown?"
   "What vocabulary needs clarification?"
   "What must I know to solve for the unknown?"
   "What information am I given?"
2. Reread at a slower rate (but not word by word) to note the relationships and the logical development of the problem.

Because word problems in mathematics are so succinct and precise, there is little of the redundancy present in some other types of reading. The contextual clues on which the poor reader depends so heavily are largely lacking in mathematics. The reader is left with the task of comprehending each phrase and relating it to the whole. This becomes a most difficult undertaking for the poor reader.

By the **Product Rule for Fractions,** the product of numbers named by fractions can be written as a fraction. The numerator is the product of the numerators, and the denominator is the product of the denominators of the fractions.

SOURCE: From MATHEMATICS 1: DISCOVERY AND PRACTICE, by Russell F. Jacobs and Richard A. Meyer, copyright © 1971 by Harcourt Brace Jovanovich, Inc., New York, and reprinted with their permission. P. 233.

When you multiply with fractions, multiply the numerators to get the numerator of the product, and multiply the denominators to get the denominator of the product.

 KEY IDEA

SOURCE: From KEY IDEAS IN MATHEMATICS 1, by William J. Gerardi, Wilmer L. Jones, and Thomas R. Foster, copyright © 1971 by Harcourt Brace Jovanovich, Inc., New York, and reprinted with their permission. P. 121.

If reading ability is to be improved, some informal diagnosis should be made through recorded observations of each student's daily performance in class. It is probable that the comprehension problems can be categorized under five headings:

1. A lack of ability to understand and interpret a statement
2. The inability to interpret the author's examples and illustrations because of insufficient mathematical knowledge
3. The inability to relate words to the appropriate illustrations
4. Insufficient intensity and preciseness in reading
5. A lack of analytical ability (analytical ability is a factor associated with intelligence)

Ability to Pick Out Main Ideas

Mathematics texts, like all academic subjects, are built around a framework of main ideas, supported by details. The chapter headings and the subheadings within each chapter provide a developmental outline of the main ideas and the details.

In addition, many newer texts provide visual aids highlighting main ideas. Two examples are shown above. Note how, in the passage reproduced on page 196, the chapter summary gives a restatement of the main ideas.

CHAPTER SUMMARY

A fraction is a symbol that represents the quotient of two numbers. Thus, if a and b are any numbers, then $\dfrac{a}{b}$ is a fraction, where $b \neq 0$.

A fraction is in simplest form when the numerator and denominator are relatively prime. This means they have no factors in common except 1.

In simplifying and operating with fractions, it is necessary to be constantly aware of any and all restrictions on the variables. For example, in the fraction $\dfrac{(x+1)(x-2)}{(x+2)(x-3)}$, $x \neq -2$ and $x \neq 3$.

Every division problem may be written in the form $n = qd + r$ where n is the dividend, q is the quotient, d is the divisor, and r is the remainder. When $r = 0$, the division is said to come out evenly.

In division of polynomials, both divisor and dividend should be arranged in descending powers of a variable. For example, the following polynomial has its terms arranged in descending powers of the variable:

$$2x^3 + 3x^2 - 5x - 2$$

The fundamental theorem for multiplication of fractions is

$$\frac{a}{b} \cdot \frac{c}{d} = \frac{ac}{bd}, \text{ where } b \neq 0 \text{ and } d \neq 0$$

The least common multiple of two or more numbers is the smallest number into which each of the given numbers will divide evenly. The LCM may be determined by first finding the intersection set of the set of multiples of each of the given numbers. The LCM of $3x$, x^2, and $x^2 + 3x$ is $3x^2(x + 3)$. Note that $x^2 + 3x = x(x + 3)$.

The fundamental theorem for addition of fractions is

$$\frac{a}{b} + \frac{c}{b} = \frac{a + c}{b}, \text{ where } b \neq 0$$

SOURCE: J. Houston Banks, Max A. Sobel, and William Walsh, Algebra: Its Elements and Structure, McGraw-Hill, Webster Division, St. Louis, 1965, pp. 353–354. Copyright © 1965 by McGraw-Hill, Inc., and reprinted with their permission.

Vocabulary

The vocabulary that must be mastered for success in mathematics tends to fall into three groups:

1. Words which are not peculiar to mathematics but which may prove difficult to the student.
2. Words which have a general usage but which are used in a special way in mathematics. (*Power, product, root, square,* and *exponent* are examples.)
3. Words peculiar to mathematics (technical terms).

The vocabulary load is increased by mathematical abbreviations and symbols. Vocabulary alone may be the major cause of comprehension problems for a large percentage of poor achievers in mathematics.

Much mathematics vocabulary is a legacy from the Greeks and Romans; hence it lends itself to what reading specialists call "structural analysis"—a study of the parts of the word. Many specific terms can be analyzed for meaning of prefixes and roots. The following are examples of mathematical terms which may be studied structurally:

Mathematical term	Source	Related word in common use
binary	Latin *bi*, "two"	bicycle
binomial	Latin *nomen*, "name"	nominate (to name)
trinomial	Latin *tri*, "three"	trio, tricycle
triangle		
monary	Greek *mono*, "one"	monograph
transportation	Latin *trans*, "across"	transfer, transform
polygon	Greek *poly*, "many"	polychrome
	Greek *gon*, "angle"	Pentagon

The mathematics teacher cannot assume that secondary school students know the Latin and Greek derivations of words. Because of this, some teachers attempt to teach the Greek and Latin roots and affixes, not realizing that merely learning these is adding one more abstraction which requires meaningless memorization. In contrast to that procedure, however, a study of word structure by the class as a whole can be an enlightening and positive learning experience when examples from everyday usage are included with the Latin and Greek derivations.

Vocabulary study, like all learning, is best when it utilizes past experiences. When new words, such as *variable, number, square root,* and *equation,* are being introduced, class discussion will elicit many concepts from experiences of the students. For example, weather forecasts make extensive reference to *variable winds;* thus all students are aware of one meaning of *variable.* Similarly, most mathematics terms have counterparts in everyday speech which should be exploited to enrich their mathematical meaning.

HOW'S YOUR MATHEMATICAL VOCABULARY?

The key words and phrases of the chapter are listed below. How many do you know and understand?

Zero exponent	Radical equation
Negative exponent	Pythagorean numbers
Law of exponents in	Radicand
multiplication	Rationalizing a denominator
Square root of a number	Pythagorean theorem
Radical sign	Law of exponents in division
Radical	Extraneous solution

SOURCE: J. Houston Banks, Max A. Sobel, and William Walsh, Algebra: Its Elements and Structure, McGraw-Hill, Webster Division, St. Louis, 1965, p. 401. Copyright © 1965 by McGraw-Hill, Inc., and reprinted with their permission.

Vocabulary study is an essential phase of a program of improvement in mathematics reading, with resulting improvement in mathematics achievement. It can be done only by the mathematics teacher. Some mathematics textbooks do provide vocabulary aids in special sections; others define vocabulary within the context, and when this is the case the mathematics teacher must give special attention to teaching and reteaching the skill of contextual analysis. The "learning spiral" mentioned earlier is an important concept here. Two examples, reproduced on pages 198 and 199, will illustrate this point. (Vocabulary as it affects the task of understanding and following directions is discussed on pages 211–212.)

The Grammar of Mathematics

There are a considerable number of relationships between mathematical statements and grammatical statements. Numerals, variables, geometric points, and many other mathematical elements work the same way as nouns do; and there is a strong similarity between verbs and such symbols of relation as equality ($=$), size ($<$), congruence ($\cong$), and membership (Σ). Punctuation plays an important role in removing ambiguity in both grammatical and mathematical sentences. For example, consider this road sign in a suburban community: SLOW CHILDREN PLAYING. What does the sign mean? Does this mean that the children are slow, or that one should proceed slowly? The ambiguity of the statement is removed by inserting a period: SLOW. CHILDREN PLAYING. Here is a mathematical example: $2 \times 3 + 4 = ?$ Is the answer 10 or 14? The ambiguity must be removed by inserting punctuation: $(2 \times 3) + 4 = 10$, or

CONSECUTIVE NUMBERS ▪ 13.4

Recall that an *even integer* is an integer that is divisible by 2. For example, -6, -4, 0, 10, and 18 are even integers. An *odd integer* is an integer that is not divisible by 2. For example, -5, -1, 3, 7, and 29 are odd integers.

Consecutive integers are integers which follow in order such that the difference between any of the integers and the one before it is 1. For example, -3, -2, -1, 0, 1, 2, 3, 4 are consecutive integers. *Consecutive even integers* are even integers which follow in order such that the difference between any of the even integers and the one before it is 2. For example, -6, -4, -2, 0, 2, 4, 6, 8 are consecutive even integers. *Consecutive odd integers* are odd integers which follow in order such that the difference between any of the odd integers and the one before it is 2. For example, -5, -3, -1, 1, 3, 5, 7 are consecutive odd integers.

SOURCE: Max Peters and William L. Schaaf, Fundamentals of Algebra, American Book Company, New York, 1970, p. 263. Copyright © 1970; reprinted by permission.

$2 \times (3 + 4) = 14$. Again notice how punctuation makes statement 1 different in meaning from statement 2:

1. In making the following measurements, would you use 5-gallon containers?
2. In making the following measurements, would you use 5 gallon containers?

One very rewarding exercise for students to do from time to time is "punctuating" a mathematics formula or problem. The objective of such an assignment is to provide meaningful practice in understanding the relationships among parts of a formula and in separating the parts of a problem.

The following "punctuation marks" are used in modern mathematics instruction and represent the "shorthand" of mathematics reading. Each mark represents vocabulary and concepts specific to mathematics reading:

$+$	$-$	$\div$	$\cdot$	$=$	¢	$\times$	$<$	$>$
gcf	cos	tan	sin	$\rightarrow$	$\leftarrow$	$\pm$	$\downarrow$	✔
$\circ$	©	®	$\triangle$	$\square$	$\neq$	$\cong$	[ ]	( )
†	‡	$\therefore$	{ }	π	∞	μ	β	Δ

Grammar and punctuation are essential elements in reading comprehension. The mathematics teacher who gives adequate attention to the development of the "grammar" and "punctuation" of mathematics by relating verbal usage will be building significantly increased comprehension skills.

Following Directions

Following directions is another important skill in mathematics reading. Lack of comprehension may, of course, be caused by a weak mathematics background, or it may result from failure to interpret relationships. One incorrect interpretation may change the entire meaning of a passage. A sound knowledge of mathematics vocabulary, including symbols, is absolutely essential.

5.5
GRAPHING STATEMENTS OF INEQUALITY

Statements of inequality may also be graphed on the coordinate plane, as in the following examples.

Example 1. Graph the solution set: $\{(x,y) \mid y > x - 2\}$.

> **Solution:** It is usually best to graph the statement of equality first. We know the nature of the graph of $y = x - 2$ from the last section, and we draw this first, using a dotted line.

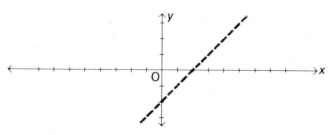

Every line divides the entire coordinate plane into two parts that are known as *half-planes*. For any point x, we now want to locate all of the points greater than $x - 2$. This will be a half-plane consisting of the set of points above the line $y = x - 2$. We indicate this by shading above the line as follows:

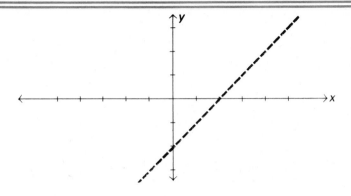

The dotted line indicates that the points on the line do *not* belong to the solution set.

There is another convenient way to graph a statement of in-equality, such as $y > x - 2$. First draw the graph of $y = x - 2$, again with a dotted line. We need to determine which half-plane to select as the graph of $y > x - 2$. To do this, test to see whether a particular point, such as the origin, $(0,0)$, is a member of the solution set.

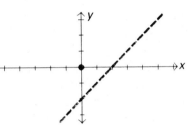

Thus, for $(0,0)$ we have $0 > 0 - 2$. What information does this give us? Our original inequality was $y > x - 2$. The ordered pair, $(0,0)$, not only gives us the replacement of 0 for x, and 0 for y, it also gives us an easy check for the x-coordinate and the y-co-ordinate of a point to be tested. This test tells us that the origin (the point being tested) is included in the solution set. Therefore, we conclude that the graph is the half-plane above the line $y = x - 2$. Why did we pick the point $(0,0)$? Simply because the computation is easier.

This method will not work if the line passes through the origin. Why not? In this case merely select any other convenient point, not on the line, to make your test. The origin was chosen arbitrarily

SOURCE: J. Houston Banks, Max A. Sobel, and William Walsh, Algebra: Its Elements and Structure, McGraw-Hill, Webster Division, St. Louis, 1965, pp. 206–207. Copyright © 1965 by McGraw-Hill, Inc., and reprinted with their permission.

If directions are long and difficult, the material should be divided into sections. As the teacher previews these, he should pause for interpretation in the students' own words, and for questions. Consider the following examples:

Bisect $\angle$ A.
To solve the following, would you use sin, cos, or tan?
Which of the following figures have sides $=$ and $||$ and therefore form a $\square$?
Find the quotient of the following numbers: . . .
What is the number by which 13 exceeds 8?
Show the relationship between the following: . . .

The excerpt from a mathematics text on pages 200–201 will serve as an example of the need for skill in following directions.

An observation of most junior high and senior high school mathematics texts will lead one to the conclusion that the example selected here is more common than unusual. Since mathematics textbooks are written by mathematics experts, not reading experts, improved achievement in following mathematical directions can be obtained only if the mathematics teacher provides skillful aid in reading.

Two elements of learning are involved in following directions. First, a large number of new terms must be learned within a short period; this will require rote learning, which is the most difficult type of learning. However, memorization can be made easier for the student, as has been mentioned, if the teacher utilizes class discussion on the meanings of related words that are part of students' past experiences. The following examples and those on page 196 are useful.

axis—axle
coordinate—cooperate
intersect—street intersection
horizontal—horizontal bars in gym
vertical—vertical hold on TV sets
quadrants—quarters

Second, learning by doing must go along with the verbal directions; the teacher must therefore have materials available for directed learning activities in the classroom. (This would include, for example, graph paper and pencils supplied by the teacher.) In classes of slower learners, the teacher can have everyone work simultaneously under careful step-by-step directions demonstrated by one student working at the chalkboard while another reads each step in the directions. Unless this is done, it is likely that more than half of the students in the secondary school will not succeed in mathematics because they will not be able to understand the directions they must follow.

Reading Mathematical Graphs, Charts, and Tables

Graphs and charts are frequently used in mathematics textbooks. They are not new to most secondary students, who will have seen or examined them

Final, Unofficial Fielding Averages

American League

Compiled by Howe News Bureau
CLUB FIELDING

Club	G.	PO.	A.	E.	DP.	PB.	Pct.
Detroit	162	4407	1748	106	156	12	.983
New York	162	4356	1984	126	159	10	.981
Cleveland	..162	4320	1711	115	159	18	.981
Baltimore	..158	4246	1672	112	148	16	.981
Oakland	161	4408	1660	117	157	17	.981
Boston	162	4329	1623	116	149	18	.981
California	..162	4443	1899	131	159	23	.980
Minnesota	..160	4250	1604	118	134	12	.980
Kansas City	161	4261	1807	132	178	11	.979
Washington	159	4256	1765	141	170	23	.977
Milwaukee	..161	4249	1692	138	152	9	.977
Chicago	162	4351	1844	160	128	32	.975

TRIPLE PLAY—Milwaukee 1.

National League

Compiled by Elias Sports Bureau
CLUB FIELDING

Club	G.	PO.	A.	E.	DP.	PB.	Pct.
Cincinnati	.162	4332	1870	103	174	11	.984
Houston	162	4414	1750	104	152	18	.983
Philadelphia	162	4412	1945	120	156	28	.981
New York	.162	4399	1572	113	134	13	.981
Chicago	162	4332	1825	126	149	18	.980
Los Angeles..162		4349	1852	131	159	14	.979
Pittsburgh	.162	4383	1834	133	164	17	.979
St. Louis	163	4401	1773	142	155	24	.978
Atlanta	162	4427	1814	146	177	33	.977
Montreal	162	4303	1812	150	164	13	.976
San Diego	.161	4309	1772	161	143	5	.974
San Fran.	..162	4364	1750	179	153	23	.972

TRIPLE PLAYS—Houston 2; Pittsburgh; San Diego, one each.

SOURCE: The Sporting News, October 30, 1971. Reprinted by permission.

in the form of box scores, batting averages, temperature reports, stock market reports, and television schedules. The teacher should start by introducing charts and graphs with which the students are already acquainted. It will help produce readiness if enlargements of such charts and tables, taken from current sources, are displayed. One example (baseball statistics) is shown on this page. Another example—Ruth's baseball record—appears on page 204.

The mathematics student (as well as the student in economics or merchandising) should learn the following steps for understanding data and comparisons presented as visuals:

1. Read the title. Know exactly what is being compared with what.
2. Read the labels and figures on the graph. (The teacher should be sure that the students understand what they stand for.) Read the titles on each axis.
3. Study the graph to make comparisons among the different items on it.
4. Interpret the significance of the graph as a whole. Draw conclusions.

To demonstrate these steps, use different types of graphs (including bar graphs, line graphs, and circle graphs).

Numerical tables have been developed to present series of numbers systematically. The guidelines for understanding tables are similar to those for graphs.

1. Read the title thoughtfully.
2. Find out what is being compared with what, and how.
3. Decide which columns show the most meaningful data.
4. Interpret the meaning of the table as a whole. Draw conclusions on the meaning of the data in each column.

The bar chart (see the example on page 205) is probably the most simple means of visualizing a statement of arithmetical fact. The statement for our

GEORGE HERMAN (BABE) RUTH

Born, February 6, 1895, at Baltimore, Md.
Died August 16, 1948, at New York, N. Y.
Height, 6.02. Weight, 215.
Threw and batted lefthanded.
Married Claire Merritt Hodgson, April 17, 1929.

Holds major league record for highest slugging percentage, season (.847), 1920; Ruth followed this record year with an .846 slugging percentage for the 1921 season; led American League in slugging percentage 13 years—a major league record, 1918 to 1931, except 1925; holds major league record for most years leading league in runs scored (8); holds modern major league record for runs scored, season (177), 1921.

Established the following major league home run records; most home runs in major leagues (714); most home runs, American League (708); most home runs two consecutive seasons (114), 1927-28; most years leading league in home runs (12); most years 50 or more home runs (4); most times, three or more home runs in a double-header (connecting in both games), league (7); most times, two or more home runs in a game (72); most home runs with bases filled, two consecutive games (2) (tied for mark), September 27-29, 1927, also August 6 (second game), August 7 (first game), 1929; most home runs two consecutive days (6) (tied for mark), May 21-21-22-22, 1930; most home runs, one week (9) (tied for mark), May 18 to 24, second game, 1930. Hit 60 home runs (1927) in 154-game schedule; in World Series, twice hit three home runs in one game, October 6, 1926, and October 9, 1928.

Hit seven home runs in five consecutive games, with at least one homer in each game, June 10-11-12-13-14, 1921.

Hit three home runs in a game, May 21, 1930 (first game) and May 25, 1935.

Named Most Valuable Player, American League, 1923.

Named as Outfielder on THE SPORTING NEWS All-Star Major League Teams. 1926-27-28-29-30-31.

Coach, Brooklyn Dodgers, 1938.

Named to Hall of Fame, 1936.

Year	Club	League	Pos.	G.	AB.	R.	H.	2B.	3B.	HR.	RBI.	B.A.	PO.	A.	E.	F.A.
1914—Balt.-Prov	Int.	P-OF	46	121	22	28	2	10	1	....	.231	20	87	4	.964
1914—Boston	Amer.	P	5	10	1	2	1	0	0	0	.200	0	8	0	1.000
1915—Boston	Amer.	P.-OF	42	92	16	29	10	1	4	20	.315	17	63	2	.976
1916—Boston	Amer.	P-OF	67	136	18	37	5	3	3	16	.272	24	83	3	.973
1917—Boston	Amer.	P-OF	52	123	14	40	6	3	2	10	.325	19	101	2	.984
1918—Boston(a)	Am.	OF-P-1	95	317	50	95	26	11	•11	64	.300	270	72	18	.950
1919—Boston(a)	Am.	OF-P	130	432	*103	139	34	12	*29	*112	.322	270	53	4	*.988
1920—New York	Am.	OF-1-P	142	458	*158	172	36	9	*54	*137	.376	259	21	19	.936
1921—New York	Am.	OF-1-P	152	540	*177	204	44	16	*59	*170	.378	348	17	13	.966
1922—New York	Amer.	OF	110	406	94	128	24	8	35	96	.315	226	14	9	.964
1923—New York	Am.	OF-1B	152	522	*151	205	45	13	*41	•130	.393	378	20	11	.973
1924—New York	Amer.	OF	153	529	*143	200	39	7	*46	121	*.378	340	18	14	.962
1925—New York	Amer	OF	98	359	61	104	12	2	25	66	.290	207	15	6	.974
1926—New York	Amer.	OF	152	495	*139	184	30	5	*47	*155	.372	308	11	7	.979
1927—New York	Amer.	OF	151	540	*158	192	29	8	*60	164	.356	328	14	13	.963
1928—New York	Amer.	OF	154	536	*163	173	29	8	*54	•142	.323	304	9	8	.975
1929—New York	Amer.	OF	135	499	121	172	26	6	*46	154	.345	240	5	4	.984
1930—New York	Amer.	OF-P	145	518	150	186	28	9	*49	153	.359	266	10	10	.965
1931—New York	Am.	OF-1B	145	534	149	199	31	3	•46	163	.373	237	5	7	.972
1932—New York	Am.	OF-1B	133	457	120	156	13	5	41	137	.341	212	10	9	.961
1933—New York	Amer.	OF-P	137	459	97	138	21	3	34	103	.301	215	9	7	.970
1934—New York(b)	Amer.	OF	125	365	78	105	17	4	22	84	.288	197	3	8	.962
1935—Boston	Nat.	OF	28	72	13	13	0	0	6	12	.181	39	1	2	.952

		G.	AB.	R.	H.	2B.	3B.	HR.	RBI.	B.A.	PO.	A.	E.	F.A.
American League Totals		2475	8327	2161	2860	506	136	708	2197	.343	4665	561	174	.968
National League Totals		28	72	13	13	0	0	6	12	.181	39	1	2	.952
Major League Totals		2503	8399	2174	2873	506	136	714	2209	.342	4704	562	176	.968

aSold to New York Yankees for $125,000, January 3, 1920.
bReleased to Boston Braves, February 26, 1935.

WORLD SERIES RECORD

Year	Club	League	Pos.	G.	AB.	R.	H.	2B.	3B.	HR.	RBI.	B.A.	PO.	A.	E.	F.A.
1915—Boston	Amer.	PH	1	1	0	0	0	0	0	0	.000	0	0	0	.000
1916—Boston	Amer.	P	1	5	0	0	0	0	0	1	.000	2	4	0	1.000
1918—Boston	Amer.	P-OF	3	5	0	1	0	1	0	2	.200	1	5	0	1.000
1921—New York	Amer.	OF	6	16	3	5	0	0	1	4	.313	9	0	0	1.000
1922—New York	Amer.	OF	5	17	1	2	1	0	1	1	.118	9	0	0	1.000
1923—New York	Amer.	O-1B	6	19	8	7	1	1	3	3	.368	17	0	1	.944
1926—New York	Amer.	OF	7	20	6	6	0	0	4	5	.300	8	2	0	1.000
1927—New York	Amer.	OF	4	15	4	6	0	0	2	7	.400	10	0	0	1.000
1928—New York	Amer.	OF	4	16	9	10	3	0	3	4	.625	9	1	0	1.000
1932—New York	Amer.	OF	4	15	6	5	0	0	2	6	.333	8	0	1	.889

		G.	AB.	R.	H.	2B.	3B.	HR.	RBI.	B.A.	PO.	A.	E.	F.A.
World Series Totals		41	129	37	42	5	2	15	33	.326	73	12	2	.977

PITCHING RECORD

Year	Club	League	IP.	W.	L.	Pct.	H.	R.	ER.	SO.	BB.	ERA.
1914—Baltimore-Providence	Int.		•22	9	*.710						101	
											7	3.91
												2.44
												.75

SOURCE: Daguerrotypes of Great Stars of Baseball, published by The Sporting News, 1968, p. 181.
Reprinted by permission.

example could read: "Coal production in the United States rose from little under 50 million tons in 1870 to almost 550 million tons in 1915. Students reading such a statement might not be as impressed as they would be at seeing it presented graphically. Another means of presenting the same facts would be in a table; but this also might be uninteresting. The bar graph, on the other hand, presents the facts vividly; it is thus a good way for the student to explore the concepts of the x-axis, the y-axis, and coordinates.

The statistical table is another form that may be utilized by the mathematics teacher. One giving world population is shown on page 206. Data presented in tabular form like this may be used for practice in relationships, since it is interesting "real-life" material. Activities of this type are valuable in creating readiness for reading. The creative teacher can find countless similar, equally valuable, situations.

In the graph shown on page 207 (a line graph illustrating personal income), the student will discover the meaning of several basic concepts: x-axis, y-axis,

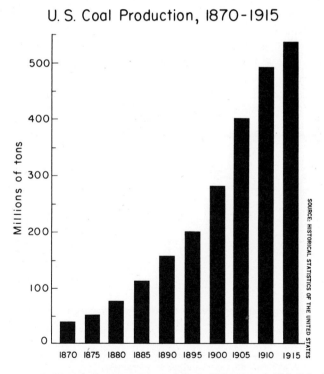

U. S. Coal Production, 1870-1915

SOURCE: HISTORICAL STATISTICS OF THE UNITED STATES

SOURCE: Boyd C. Shafer, Everett Augspurger, and R. A. McLemore, A High School History of Modern America, Laidlaw Brothers, River Forest, Ill., 1970, p. 376. Copyright © 1970. Reprinted by permission of Laidlaw Brothers.

coordinates; indication of main idea by the title of a graph; the appropriateness of line graphs for showing longitudinal movement; index numbers; "key" or "code" to the meaning of a graph; and methods of visual comparison. For example, when the student finds that the line graph in this example is based upon index numbers, he will have to read about index numbers in an economics or business education book, or an encyclopedia. The teacher could, in addition, point out that the format of this graph also suggests a bar graph.

By moving from the known to the unknown, the data in such graphs may be converted into algebraic equations, as is illustrated in the passage shown on page 208, "Relations and Functions."

Solving Verbal Problems in Mathematics through Increased Attention to Reading Skills

The most serious difficulty in mathematics is the inability of many students to read and interpret verbal problems ("word problems") adequately. The cause of this may be low reading ability, inadequate knowledge of mathematical shorthand and punctuation, inadequate knowledge of mathematical processes, or the fact that the problems themselves are poorly written. Naturally, any combination of these factors, or any one factor, will produce difficulty in understanding. Moreover, every reading skill necessary for mathematics in general is needed for reading word problems, so difficulties will also arise if any of the general skills is deficient.

ESTIMATES OF WORLD POPULATION BY REGIONS, 1650–1960
(Estimated population in millions)

Date	World Total	Africa	Anglo-America	Latin America	Asia (except U.S.S.R.)	Europe and Asiatic U.S.S.R.	Oceania	Area of European Settlement
1650	545	100	1	12	327	103	2	118
1750	728	95	1	11	475	144	2	158
1800	906	90	6	19	597	192	2	219
1850	1,171	95	26	33	741	274	2	335
1900	1,608	120	81	63	915	423	6	573
1920	1,834	136	115	92	997	485	9	701
1930	2,008	155	134	110	1,069	530	10	784
1940	2,216	177	144	132	1,173	579	11	866
1950	2,406	199	166	162	1,272	594	13	935
1960	2,995	254	199	206	1,679	641	16.5	—

Source: United Nations, *The Determinants and Consequences of Population Trends,* Population Studies No. 17 (New York: United Nations, Department of Social Affairs, Population Division, 1953), p. 11. The figures for 1960 are from United Nations, *Demographic Yearbook,* 1961, Table 2, p. 120.

SOURCE: Donald H. Riddle, ed., **Contemporary Issues in American Democracy,** 2d ed., 1969, p. 74. Copyright © 1969, McGraw-Hill, Inc. Reprinted by permission.

Three lesson plans are shown on pages 209 and 210. These plans are based upon a reading-study approach to word problems.

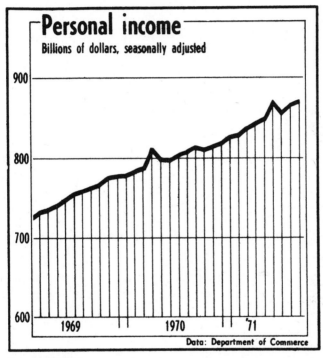

By a staff artist

Personal income rose $3,200 million in September to a seasonally adjusted annual rate of $870,800 million, the U.S. Commerce Department reported. Wage and salary disbursements held unchanged at an adjusted rate of $580,900 million.

SOURCE: Christian Science Monitor, October 26, 1971. Reprinted by permission.

538 ▪ RELATIONS AND FUNCTIONS

2. STATING THE RELATIONSHIP
BY MEANS OF A GRAPH

The graph below represents temperature readings in the town of Springfield for the hours shown.

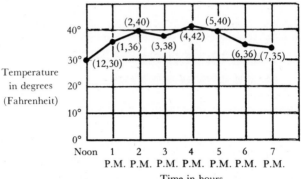

In this case, the domain is the set of natural numbers designating time, and the range is the set of numbers representing temperature readings. The pairing of a member of the domain with a corresponding member of the range simply depends upon the thermometer reading at a particular time. *The rule is the association pictured by the graph.*

3. STATING THE ASSOCIATION
BY MEANS OF AN EQUATION

The solution set of an open sentence such as $y = 3x + 2$ is a function. For each value of x, there is *determined* exactly one value of y. For example,

$$\text{if } x = 1, y = 3(1) + 2, \text{ or } 5;$$
$$\text{if } x = -4, y = 3(-4) + 2, \text{ or } -10.$$

Thus, the equation gives us an infinite number of ordered pairs such as

$$(1,\ 5),\quad (-4,\ -10),\quad (0,\ 2),\quad (5,\ 17),\quad \left(2\tfrac{1}{2},\ 9\tfrac{1}{2}\right),\quad \ldots$$

Since the domain of x is not stated, we assume it to be the set of real numbers. In this case, the domain of the function is the set of real numbers and the range of the function is also the set of real numbers.

For convenience, functions are often given names and written by using the set-builder notation. In this case *the rule is the equation.*

$$f = \{(x, y) \mid y = 3x + 2\}.$$

SOURCE: Max Peters and William L. Schaaf, Fundamentals of Algebra, American Book Company, New York, 1970, p. 538. Copyright © 1970. Reprinted by permission.

LESSON PLAN 1

Word problem: A boy collecting for UNICEF gets four times as many dimes as quarters. If his dimes and quarters total $1.95, how many of each has he?

Procedure:
1. The students should read the problem through at a moderate rate to get a general understanding of the problem and determine definitely what they must find.
2. Then question them:
   a. What are you asked to find?
   b. Have you ever seen this type of problem before?
   c. What must you know in order to solve the problem?
3. The students should reread the problem very carefully, considering the known facts necessary for solving the problem.
4. Continue your questions to the students:
   a. What two known facts have you found? (He has 4 times as many dimes as quarters. They total $1.95.)
   b. What must be done to balance these two factors? (Use value of coins.)
   c. Chart the known facts before setting up the equation:

	Dimes	Quarters
Number of coins	4x	x
Value of coins	4 (.10x)	.25x

5. Can the students estimate the answer? ($.40x + .25x = 1.95)

LESSON PLAN 2

Word problem: A man is working in a factory that makes drinking glasses. His job is to pack them for shipment. He gets 8 cents for each glass he packs, but he is fined 25 cents for each glass he breaks while packing it. His net earnings for one day were $18. The records show that on that day he packed 10 more than 30 times as many glasses as he broke. How many glasses did he pack without breaking that day?

Vocabulary: The students must understand the meaning of *fined* and *net earnings*. They must also understand how to calculate net earnings and what effect fines would have.

Procedure:
1. The students should read the problem through slowly enough to get the main idea (that the packer is paid for the articles he packs without breaking and in fined for each article he breaks).
2. Then the students must answer these questions:
   a. What am I asked to find?
   b. Have I worked with similar problems?
   c. If so, how did I solve them?
   d. What must be done to solve the problem?
3. Question the students: What facts are given?
4. Make an open sentence:

Number packed	Number broken (x)	
Earnings on number packed	Fine for number broken	Net earnings
.08 (10 + 30x)	.25x	$18.00

LESSON PLAN 3

Word problem: If one side of a square is increased by 8 feet and an adjacent side is decreased by 2 feet, a rectangle is formed whose perimeter is 40 feet. Find the length of a side of the square.

Vocabulary: The students must understand the following terms: *square, adjacent, rectangle,* and *perimeter.*

Procedure: The students should reread the problem, sketching a figure that includes the elements given.

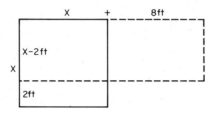

This enables the students to visualize the problem. They can now set down the elements in algebraic terms:

x = side of square

$2(x + 8)$ = length of 2 sides of the rectangle

$2(x - 2)$ = length of the other two sides

And they can formulate the equation:

$$2(x + 8) + 2(x - 2) = 40$$

Some students may find it necessary to verbalize the equation as an intermediate step before putting it into algebraic form.

There are two major objectives for Lesson plan 3. The first objective is to help students identify the "core" of a verbal statement—that is, the essential elements. This tends to clarify the meaning for them. Eliminating unnecessary words should bring into sharper profile the significant words in the statement. The second objective of the lesson (the teacher may find that he wishes to devote a separate lesson to this idea) is to let the student arrive inductively at the functional role of the vital elements in the verbal statement.

Finding the "core" of a verbal statement. The teacher should say to the students: "Study the word problem. If you wanted to telegraph this problem to someone, you would naturally want to make it as short as possible. Go through the problem, then, and mark out any word that you think is unnecessary. Be careful not to distort the meaning of the problem. (Be sure that you can defend your reason for eliminating a word.)" The student might produce something like this from the problem given for Lesson plan 3:

> If one side of a square is increased by 8 feet; and an adjacent side decreased by 2 feet: a rectangle is formed whose perimeter is 40 feet. Find the length of a side of the square.

Go on to say to the students:

> "Now that you have isolated the core of the statement, restate this core in your own words, keeping the meaning of the statement without making it any longer."

This might produce the following:

> One side of square is increased by 8 feet; adjacent side decreased by 2 feet.
> Resulting rectangle has perimeter of 40 feet.
> How long is side of square?

Identifying the functional role of words and symbols. To elicit this skill, the teacher might say this to the students: "Using the words and symbols that are left in the problem, arrange them in groups according to similarities among them. Be prepared to explain your reason for grouping words together." The students might come up with this sort of arrangement:

First Group	Second Group	Third Group
length	twice (times 2)	resulting
width	is equal to (is)	
perimeter	plus	
side	increased	
square	decreased	
adjacent side		
rectangle		

Ask the students:

> What is the basis for grouping the words in the first group? (They are names of things.)
> Is there a grammatical term for those words? (Nouns.)
> Would numbers and symbols fall in that category? (Some would.) These words and symbols may be called "mathematical individuals."
> What was your basis for grouping the words in the second group? (They require you to do something to the mathematical individuals.) These words and symbols are usually referred to as "operators.". They are similar in function to verbs.
> The third group includes only one word:
> resulting. What functional role does it perform in this statement? (It states a relationship between parts of the problem.)
> Is there a grammatical equivalent to this "relation" symbol or word? (No.)

Students should have an opportunity to try this approach on several problems under the direction of the teacher. They should then be asked to list all the words and symbols that they have encountered in all the problems and classify them into the three suggested categories. In this way the relationships between the elements in the statement will be spotlighted and the direction the solution must take will be made clear.

INCREASING COMPREHENSION IN MATHEMATICS READING

Comprehension in reading mathematics materials is essentially the same as comprehension of general reading. The difference lies only in the fact that mathematics utilizes far more "shorthand" than most other subjects.

The preceding lesson plans have illustrated several means of increasing comprehension of word problems. The techniques may be summarized as follows:

1. Have the students restate the problem in their own words.
2. Discuss the vocabulary with the entire group, comparing as many terms as possible with everyday usage. Study all vocabulary in relationship to context— never in isolation.
3. Have the students note the relationships between the parts of the problem. This can often be visualized by means of a graph or chart.
4. Have the students draw a diagram which will evolve from a step-by-step rereading of the problem.
5. Help the students as a group to devise an equation which correctly states the problem.
6. Discuss the estimated or probable answer on a basis of "educated guesses." This is a good check on the adequacy of comprehension.
7. Have the students solve the problem and check the answer against the educated estimate. Then double-check it within the equation to see if it satisfies the conditions of the equation.

SOLVING REAL-LIFE MATHEMATICAL PROBLEMS

One of the major obstacles to successful learning in mathematics is the fact that many of the word problems are far removed from the real-life experiences of today's youth. One psychological principle of learning is clear: all learning must be related to past experience. Another principle of learning is that comprehension depends on the ability of the learner to identify with the material being learned and relate it to his own interests. The mathematics teacher who selects problems that deal with the events and realities of importance to modern young people will be providing materials with which his students can identify.

The following problem is one with which a high school boy could easily identify.

> *Problem:* The list price of a new sports car is $4,235, and the book value of your trade-in is $1,925. The dealer says he will allow you $2,450 on your old car because he can sell it to someone who is eager to get one just like it. This sounds like a good deal, and you sign up.
>
> The next day your friend tells you that he went to the same dealer and looked at the same car with a few extras amounting to a list price of $4,375. His old car has a book value of $2,000, but he is selling it to a neighbor for $2,100. Since he has no trade-in, the dealer told him that he could have a special discount of $300 on the list price, and he signed up.
>
> You are discouraged because the dealer didn't give you a discount. Are you right? Who got the best deal? What are the figures? What mathematics did you use to find the answers?

Another problem relevant to modern living is computing the percent of interest on borrowed money. Any number of different problems could be devised or selected from the operations of finance companies and time-payment plans, based on the *real* interest charged, as regulated by the "Truth-in-Lending" Act of 1969.

Other interesting problems have to do with gasoline consumption; clothes budgets; air-travel package deals; international sports championships; sales; income tax deductions; and space travel. Some of those problems call for simple arithmetic; others are complicated enough to require advanced algebra.

Real-life problems in geometry are also rather easy to find. They should be used to replace the abstract and often absurdly meaningless problems found in older texts.

The principle of learning that is the recurrent theme throughout this discussion may be summed up in one currently popular word: "involvement." Until a student identifies with a problem that is meaningful to him because of his own past experience, present needs, or both, the problem will remain in the realm of the abstract as far as he is concerned. Once a student does identify with a problem because it has relevance to his own experiences, he becomes involved and is motivated to find a meaningful solution.

A CASE STUDY: A CLASS DISCUSSION ON MATHEMATICAL VOCABULARY

The following discussion, by one mathematics class, was recorded at the Needham, Massachusetts, Junior-Senior High School with the aid of William Cogswell, Mathematics Coordinator, and Richard Hubbard, Director of Mathematics. It illustrates many of the practices which the subcommittee suggests will be effective in solving some of the problems of teaching the reading skills associated with good achievement in secondary school mathematics.

The objective of the lesson was to teach mathematics vocabulary in a meaningful context. The dialogue reproduced here is from a lively discussion which erupted on the concept of "infinity."

A student remarked, "But I can imagine the smallest possible number."

Another responded, "You tell me what it is, and I will divide it by 2. Don't you remember about 'halfway to the wall'?"

A third student supported this, and drew a quick sketch of the room on a transparency for the overhead projector. He explained, "If we start from here and go halfway to the wall each time, we never get there. Therefore, there is no possible smallest number, just as there is no largest number."

A girl observed, "You can always divide or add, and your concept of infinity can be packed in closely, or it can be spread out." She added, "You can go all the way up to zero or all the way down."

The class became more lively. One boy went to the overhead projector and demonstrated the concept another way. "You can picture it with rays and half-lines":

Ray $x \geq 0$

$\circ\longrightarrow$

Half-line $x > 0$

The discussion then concentrated upon vocabulary concepts: *cardinality, one-to-one correspondence, including, excluding,* etc. A misunderstanding developed around the meaning of *infinity.* As a student supplied directions, the teacher sketched this figure on the chalkboard:

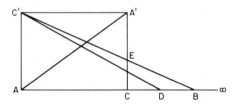

After extensive discussion, the class concluded that as points were placed farther out on line *AB*, eventually *E* would coincide with *A'* at infinity.

Another student asked about *infinity minus one,* and that led to a discussion of the geometrical relationship between *plus infinity* and *minus infinity.* The class agreed that it would be possible to establish a one-to-one relationship between the intervals containing [0, —1] and [—∞, +∞], diagrammed thus:

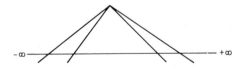

The students suggested that infinity —1 is an extremely large number, and that the farther out one goes in the approach to infinity, the smaller become the units or intervals.

One boy suggested that infinity is "sort of like absolute zero." To which a girl asked, "Which absolute zero, —273 °C or —460°F?"

In this way, verbalizing concepts, the students were able to develop both generalizations and specific statements. By setting the direction and readiness for learning, the teacher had prepared the students for the assignment.

On other occasions in the same mathematics class, new mathematics "shorthand" symbols were discussed:

"Congruency is just an equals sign with a squiggle over it: $\cong$. When two line segments are equal, we write it in symbols like this: $AB = m\ (\overline{AB})$." Other vocabulary concepts elicited discussion and resulted in concrete examples: "Triangles can be classified according to their sides, or according to the size of their angles." The class developed acceptable definitions and examples of *scalene, isosceles, equilateral, right,* and *obtuse* triangles. One boy argued the point that "it is impossible to have an *obtuse* triangle, for three obtuse angles would total more than 180°."

Another student had trouble understanding and explaining the meaning of *isosceles triangle.* With the help of other students in the class, who sketched isosceles triangles and provided definitions in their own words, he reached a more adequate understanding of its properties.

Among many other concepts enriched through discussion were such *equilateral, equiangular,* and *derivation.*

The main feature of this mathematics lesson was the dialogue, which centered on mathematical concepts expressed in the vocabulary of mathematics. Reading ability in mathematics is greatly improved through such discussion. This is a realistic approach, providing a concrete element to what would otherwise be memorization of abstract terms and meaningless processes.

PROGNOSIS OF READING DISABILITY IN MATHEMATICS

Comprehension in any academic subject depends upon the student's knowledge and understanding of the vocabulary, as well as upon the readability of the texts. This is especially true in mathematics, where the specific vocabulary load is extremely heavy.

One simple way of determining who will have difficulty is to administer to each student one of the alternative forms of the Prognostic Test of Reading Disability in Mathematics. Because a substantial number of common words are used in a specific way in mathematics, inability to recognize and read these words will predict a distinct handicap to comprehension of textual materials. Naturally, the specialized vocabulary of the various mathematics subjects will present even more difficulty. The test will *not* determine a student's grade-level reading ability in mathematics (that is not necessary); but it will provide a means by which the teacher can quickly identify the student who will not be able to read secondary school mathematics textbooks.

The prognosis is given individually. Each student reads directly from the page in this book, pronouncing the words aloud. One or two minutes are enough. Use only one of the three alternative forms for each student. (Using several forms prevents the students from memorizing words as they hear others reading aloud.)

PROGNOSTIC TEST OF READING DISABILITY IN SECONDARY SCHOOL MATHEMATICS[4]

Directions: Cover the two forms not being used (5- x 7-inch cards will do).

Ask the student to read from left to right, pronouncing each word in turn, at his normal rate.

Observe his facial expression as he reads. Note hesitation, repetition, regression, uncertainty, gross mispronunciation, and incorrect stress.

Identify the student who is *not* able to move along smoothly at about one word every two seconds. He will most probably have great difficulty reading the textbook because he lacks proficiency in general vocabulary. He will be at a total loss when faced with the technical vocabulary of mathematics.

Alternative Form A

horizontal	conclusions	numerical	equivalent
vertical	polygon	measurement	perpendicular
geometrical	estimate	equally	segment
intersect	equidistant	diagonal	surface
symbol	corresponding	definition	indicate
negative	represent	diagram	midpoint
operations	properties	coordinates	irrational
conditional	substitution	congruent	formula
rational	inverse	inconsistent	eliminated
solution	approximation	intercept	determine

Alternative Form B

coincide	difference	variation	circumference
graphically	connecting	velocity	computing
infinite	inequality	multiple	parentheses
projection	approximately	conceptual	probability
demonstrated	derivation	illustrated	relationship
assigning	unspecified	principle	expression
absolute	frequency	associated	distributive
assumptions	numerical	cancellation	reciprocal

Alternative Form C

symmetry	replacement	conditional	significant
consecutive	supplementary	alternate	variable
constant	cumulative	fractional	combination
displacement	deviation	successive	mutually
approximation	exclusive	origin	relationship
proportion	numerical	simultaneous	terminate
transform	parallel	unsolvable	reduce
multiply	corresponds	simplify	characteristics

[4] Copyright 1971 by Robert C. Aukerman.

READABILITY OF MATHEMATICS TEXTBOOKS

Word problems make up only a small percentage of mathematics work, but they generate most of the reading difficulty which occurs. Difficulty also occurs, however, with introductory and descriptive reading material. These two elements—word problems and introductory discussions—cause many mathematics textbooks to be excessively difficult.

Some authors and editors of mathematics textbooks obviously make a conscious effort to control readability. Others, unfortunately, produce extremely difficult reading loads. Examples have been selected here from three secondary school geometry texts (see pages 218–222).

Consider first the material from the chapter called "Postulates in Geometry." The sample shown here runs through postulate 3 and contains a little over 500 words. There are five paragraphs containing twenty-four sentences. The average sentence length is 21 words. The first paragraph, however, contains sentences with word counts of 33, 39, 49, 17, 19, and 19. Moreover, sentence construction is very sophisticated: the first sentence is compound; the second half of the second sentence is complex; the third is a triple compound; the fourth has inverted word order with inadequate punctuation; the sixth, although technically a simple sentence, has an involved subject. Only the fifth sentence is actually simple.

Difficult vocabulary and abstract concepts abound: *mathematician, laid the foundation for his work, self-evident truths, reflected the world about him, sophisticated modern mathematician, principles from which he evolves his subject, properties about figures, frame of reference, divorced a postulate,* and many others.

Could this not all be written at a lower level of readability, thus gaining lucidity? Even a skillful reader would have difficulty with this level of readability.

The second example is also from a geometry text; here geometric construction is explained. Even though a specific, concrete process is being described, there is a high degree of abstraction, created by the use of such terminology as the following:

> *A construction is a theoretically exact method of determining a required point or line. Geometric points, lines, and circles are mental concepts.*
> *A construction, however carefully performed, is merely an approximate representation of the geometric situation.*

Note that the incidence of difficult words in this last example is almost 100 percent. It couldn't be more difficult if it were written for graduate students. Other examples could be cited, but these should be enough to prove that even concrete ideas can be and often are presented in a complex manner and with difficult vocabulary.

■ Postulates in Geometry

The early Greek mathematician laid the foundation for his work on certain "beliefs" that he referred to as "self-evident truths," for to him they reflected the world about him as he saw it. The more sophisticated modern mathematician, however, recognizes the principles from which he evolves his subject for what they really are; that is, no more than *a set of mutually agreed upon properties about figures that he himself has created*. To illustrate, he created the line and the real number system; he then linked the two together by the property that to every real number there exists one and only one point on this line and further, that to every point there exists one and only one real number. A statement such as this the mathematician accepts in order to lay the foundation for further discussion. This discussion can not take place without some core of ideas or frame of reference from which to begin. These fundamental principles from which mathematics springs are the *postulates* or, as they are often called, *axioms* or *assumptions*.

Current interpretation of mathematics has divorced a postulate from its original interpretation as a "belief." When considering a belief, we are sometimes left with a feeling of vagueness as to the truth or falsity of the statement. On the other hand, a postulate carries with it no such squeamishness; it is like asking, "Are the rules of baseball true or false?" The question, obviously, makes little sense. These are the rules established to create the game; they are neither true nor false! So, too, are the postulates, the "rules" to create the subject of mathematics.

It would be inaccurate to leave you with the impression that creating mathematics is comparable to creating a game where the rules are established at the whim of the creator. Far from this! Mathematicians frequently formulate their postulates as a model of what they perceive in the world that exists about them. It is true that some aspects of modern mathematics appear to bear no remote resemblance to any practical application. However, as has happened almost always in the past, future scientists will very likely discover a need for these branches of mathematics in their work.

In view of the foregoing analysis, it would seem wise if we, too, placed our cards face up on the table and admitted to a number of postulates we had failed to establish in Chapters 1 and 2, although we had made use of them. Briefly, they were concerned with these points:

(1) The possibility of extending a line as far as desired in either direction.

(2) The notion of "betweenness" that implied that between any two points on a line there existed a third point.

(3) The existence of a pairing between the points on a line and the real numbers.

These principles we will now state formally as our first three postulates:

POSTULATE 1: A line may be extended as far as desired in either direction.

POSTULATE 2: For any two points on a line, there exists a third point that is between them.

POSTULATE 3: There exists a one-to-one correspondence between the points on a line and the real numbers.

The last of the principles concerning a line that we want to consider at this time is one that you have used each time you drew a margin on a piece of paper. In drawing a "half-inch" margin, it is likely that ou placed a point $\frac{1}{2}$ inch from the edge near the top of the paper and repeated this process at the bottom. After which you laid the ruler along these two points

SOURCE: Harry Lewis, Geometry: A Contemporary Course, Van Nostrand-Reinhold Books, 1968, pp. 53–54. Copyright © 1968. Reprinted by permission of American Book Company.

Finally, the explanation of coordinate geometry is included to illustrate the fact that "advanced mathematics" can be and occasionally is written with improved comprehension as a goal. In this third example, the construction of a coordinate system is explained in concrete terms. Wherever new mathematics vocabulary is introduced, it appears in italics and is defined within the context. Although the reading is not what we would consider "easy," it is evident that the authors and editor have made a conscious effort to produce good readability.

Excerpts are now presented that show the levels of readability of three algebra texts (see pages 223–225). For purposes of comparison, passages on the same topic (polynomials) have been chosen.

All three examples have a degree of readability beyond the ability of students whose IQs place them in the lower quartile or whose performances on standardized reading tests place them in the lower quartile in reading. Indeed, it is likely that students in the lower 50 percentile in reading will not be able to handle the abstract concepts presented in these texts.

These are representative of substantial, sound mathematics texts on the market today. Two things should be obvious from an examination of them. First, these texts were written and edited by people who are unaware of the readability problems they contain. Second, the mathematics teacher is the only person who can help students with the comprehension problems produced by mathematics reading materials.

Constructions

The diagrams we have made so far have been used as illustrations. They have helped us visualize the successive steps of a proof. It is not necessary that such diagrams be accurate, though they should not be misleading.

A part of geometry, however, is concerned with the possibility of constructing accurate diagrams to satisfy certain conditions, and with methods of performing the constructions. The traditional tools permitted in these constructions are a straightedge and a compass (or dividers). The straightedge is not to be used as a measuring device but merely as a means of ruling straight lines. The compass is used to construct circles, and to mark off equal line segments.

A construction is a theoretically exact method of determining a required point or line. The theoretical exactness rests on the supposition that compasses enable us to reproduce a line segment equal to any given line segment. This idea was examined in chapter 2. The use of compasses is formalized by the following definition and postulate.

▶ **Definition:** A circle is the set of all points in a plane which are at a fixed distance, r units, from a fixed point O of the plane.

The fixed point O is called the *center* of the circle, and the fixed distance, r units, is called the *radius* of the circle. A point P of the plane is inside, on, or outside the circle, according as OP is less than, equal to, or greater than r units. If P is on the circle, then OP is called a radius of the circle, and the circle is said to contain P.

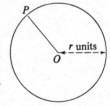

▶ **Postulate for Circles.** A circle can be drawn in a given plane with any given point as center and any given line segment as radius. With a specified center and radius, only one circle can be drawn in the plane.

If A and B are points of a circle with center O, then:

(a) A and B divide the circle into two parts called *arcs*. The arc AB consists of A, B, and the set of points of the circle in the interior of $\angle AOB$.

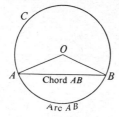

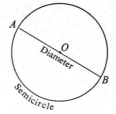

The other arc is usually indicated by assigning a third letter to one of its points. In the left-hand diagram it would be referred to as the arc ACB.

(b) The line segment AB is called a *chord* of the circle.

(c) If AB contains O, AB is called a *diameter* of the circle, and each of the arcs is then called a *semicircle*.

Geometric points, lines, and circles are mental concepts. A construction, however carefully performed, is merely an approximate representation of the geometric situation. In giving the proof of a construction, however, we accept the theoretical accuracy of each step as part of our hypothesis.

Thus, if we have two lines intersecting at a point O, and we construct a circle with center O cutting the lines at points A, B, C, D, we say

(1)

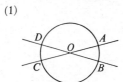

(2)

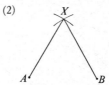

$OA = OB = OC = OD$. (Figure (1).) The definition of a circle justifies the statement. Again, if arcs of circles are constructed with centers A, B, and having the same radius, then if the arcs intersect at X, we say $AX = BX$. (Figure (2).)

We accept the result illustrated in figure (3), that if the distance between the centers of two circles is less than the sum of the radii and greater than the difference of the radii, then the circles intersect in two points. These points are on opposite sides of the line through the centers of the circles.

(3)

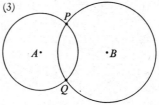

SOURCE: Arthur W. Weeks and Hackson B. Adkins, A Course in Geometry, Plain and Solid, Ginn and Company, Boston, 1961, pp. 85–86. Copyright 1961 by Ginn and Company. Reprinted by permission.

COORDINATE GEOMETRY   **201**

Exercises

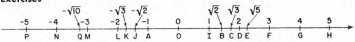

Using the coordinate line shown above, evaluate the following:

1. $|AB| + |BA|$
2. $|KM| + |MN|$
3. $|AO| + |OI|$
4. $|DE| + |EH|$
5. $|PN| + |NM|$

6. $|OM| + |MO|$
7. $|OM| - |OM|$
8. $|AO| + |OI| + |IH|$
9. $|CE| + |FE| + |DG|$
10. $|dd. CE|$

Rectangular coordinate system

If the methods of analytic geometry were restricted to a single coordinate line in the Euclidean plane, the methods would not be very powerful. Descartes extended this coordinatization of a line to a plane, however, and in this extension you can begin to see the power of analytic geometry. You are familiar with the rectangular coordinate system, but we shall here review its construction. First, two mutually perpendicular lines are constructed. (Note. We could develop a coordinate system based upon any two intersecting lines, but the algebra involved would in general be more complicated if the lines were not perpendicular.) The point of intersection of our perpendicular lines we designate as the *origin*, *O*. The horizontal axis we call the *x* axis, and on this axis we construct a coordinate line with zero at the origin, with the positive real numbers to the right of *O* and with the negative real numbers to the left of *O*. The axis that runs vertically we call the *y* axis, and again we construct a coordinate line upon this axis with the positive reals above *O* and with the negative reals below *O*. Although it is not necessary or customary in general, we shall indicate by arrows that the positive reals are to the right of *O* and above *O*.

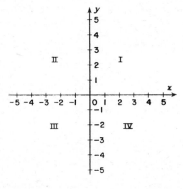

The perpendicular lines divide the plane into four parts which, you remember, are called *quadrants* and designated as quadrants I, II, III, and IV as shown in the figure. We then say that the *x* and *y* axes form a rectangular coordinate system on the plane.

4

Operations with Polynomials

Introduction

4-1 Vocabulary

Before a student can completely develop the study of equations and in-equalities, he must learn how to operate with algebraic expressions.

We have already found that an *algebraic expression* is composed of:

(1) a numeral naming a number like 7;
(2) one variable or the product of two or more variables like d or a^3xy;
(3) both numerals and variables joined as a product, like $-7a^2b$, or by opera-tional symbols, like $x - 5y$ or $2a^2 - 7a + 8$ or $4b^3 - 2b^2c + 5bc^2 - 10c^3$, etc.

A *term*, also called a *monomial*, is a numeral, or a variable, or a product of variables, or a product of a numeral and a variable or variables. 9, s, cd, and $-8x^2y$ are monomials. When a term consists only of a numeral, it is called the *constant term*.

An algebraic expression consisting of one term or the sum of two or more terms is called a *polynomial*. If the only variable in the expression is x, it is called a *polynomial in x*. If y is the only variable, then it is a *polynomial in y*.

The polynomial $5x^3 + 7x^2 + 3x + 8$ has four terms: $5x^3$, $7x^2$, $3x$, and 8.

The expression $a^2 - 2ab + 9b^2$ is also a polynomial, since it can be expressed as $a^2 + (-2ab) + 9b^2$, in which a^2, $-2ab$, and $9b^2$ are the terms. A plus sign is not required to indicate addition when a term has a negative coefficient or the constant term is a negative number. $x^2 + (-3x) + (-5)$ is written as $x^2 - 3x - 5$.

A polynomial is sometimes described as a monomial or the sum of two or more monomials. When the polynomial consists of only two terms, like $4x - 3y$, it is called a *binomial*; when it consists of only three terms, like $c^2 - 5c + 7$, it is called a *trinomial*. Mathematicians generally use the word polynomial to describe an expression of two or more terms and the word monomial for an expression of only one term.

245

SOURCE: Albert I. Stein, Modern Algebra, Step by Step, American Book Company, New York, 1970, p. 245. Copyright © 1970. Reprinted by permission.

THE NATURE OF POLYNOMIALS ▪ 16.2

We will now consider a special kind of algebraic expression called a *polynomial*. The following are examples of polynomials:

$$2x^2 + 3x - 1$$
$$a^2b^2 + \frac{1}{2}a$$
$$5 - 2x^2 - 3xy$$

Observe that, in each case, the only operations that involve variables are addition, subtraction, and multiplication. Division and root extraction may be used if these operations are applied to the real numbers only and not to the variables. Thus,

$$\frac{5x}{3}, \quad \frac{2a - \sqrt{7}}{6}, \quad \text{and} \quad x^3 + 5x^2 - \frac{x}{\sqrt{2}}$$

are also polynomials. However, algebraic expressions such as

$$\frac{x + y}{x}, \quad \sqrt{a^2 + b^2}, \quad \text{and} \quad \frac{3a + 4b + c}{5ab}$$

are *not* polynomials.

If a polynomial has *one term* it is called a *monomial*. For example:

$$7a^2b, \quad 5xyz^3, \quad -\frac{7}{9}c, \quad \text{and} \quad \frac{1}{2}x^3y \quad \text{are monomials.}$$

If a polynomial has *two terms* it is called a *binomial*. For example:

$$2c - d, \quad 5a^2b^2 - 3ab, \quad 7x^2 - \frac{x}{3} \quad \text{are binomials.}$$

If a polynomial has *three terms* it is called a *trinomial*. For example:

$$a + 2b + 3c, \quad x^2 + \frac{3x}{10} - 7, \quad 2p^2 - pq + q^2 \quad \text{are trinomials.}$$

Polynomials which have more than three terms have no special names. They are simply called polynomials.

The *degree of a polynomial* in one variable is determined by the greatest exponent that appears in the polynomial. For example, the degree of the polynomial $x - 3x^5 + x^4 - 7x^3 + 8$ is 5.

SOURCE: Max Peters and William L. Schaaf, Fundamentals of Algebra, American Book Company, New York, 1970, pp. 331–332. Copyright © 1970. Reprinted by permission.

7.1

TYPES OF POLYNOMIALS

Much of our work this year has been centered about operations with monomials. It is necessary to extend our thinking to include expressions such as $x^2 + 3x$, $\frac{1}{2}a + b - c$, and $y^2 - 2$. Expressions such as these are called *polynomials over the real numbers*. They are formed by combining a finite number of multiplication and addition operations with real numbers and variables. The only restriction is that the exponent of a variable must be a nonnegative integer.

Each of the expressions $x^2 + 3x$, $\frac{1}{2}a + b - c$, and $y^2 - 2$ is also a *polynomial over the rational numbers* (or a rational polynomial), since each expression contains only rational numbers and variables.

> A *polynomial over the real numbers* is an expression formed by a finite number of addition and multiplication operations with real numbers and variables. The exponent to which any variable is raised must be a nonnegative integer.

According to this definition, $\dfrac{x}{y}$ is *not* a polynomial, but $\dfrac{x}{2}$ *is* a polynomial. Note that $\dfrac{x}{2}$ means $\frac{1}{2} \cdot x$ and thus is the *product* of a real number and a variable.

In this text the word polynomial will mean polynomial over the real numbers, unless another domain is specified.

The simplest of all polynomials is the monomial. Does our definition of a monomial seem to fit the definition of a polynomial over the real numbers?

In the expression $x^2 + 3x$, x^2 is one term and $3x$ is another term. The common name for a two-term polynomial is *binomial*.

The expression $\frac{1}{2}a + b - c$ contains the three terms $\frac{1}{2}a$, b, and $-c$. Polynomials which contain three terms are called *trinomials*.

SOURCE: J. Houston Banks, Max A. Sobel, and William Walsh, Algebra: Its Elements and Structure, Book I, McGraw-Hill, Webster Division, St. Louis, 1965, pp. 279–280. Copyright © 1965. Reprinted by permission of McGraw-Hill, Inc.

The first thing that should be done is to encourage students, working in pairs, to reword the statements in the book in their own words. When they have accomplished that, they will have demonstrated comprehension of the textual reading material. The next step is to understand the "word problems." Here, the procedure described earlier in this chapter is helpful.

The New SMSG Multilevel Mathematics Texts

For several years, a group of distinguished mathematicians and secondary school mathematics teachers worked to produce a series of secondary school mathematics texts on three parallel levels of readability. The first fruits of their efforts were produced in 1972 as the Blue, Green, and Gold versions of "Secondary School Mathematics," Byrne Publishing.

The Blue text was written and edited for above-average students (roughly the top 25 percent); the Green version, for average and low-average students; and the Gold version, for low achievers. The lower the level, the less material treated and the lower the readability task. The authors assumed that readers above grade level would be able to handle the Blue version; Green version students would be reading one or two grades below grade level; and the Gold version would be for those whose reading ability was even lower.

Purely technical vocabulary was, as far as possible, used in its mathematical sense, and terms such as *determine, locate, thus,* and *therefore* were replaced with more common words. Traditional mathematical phraseology, such as *it is necessary,* was replaced with straightforward, simple structure, such as *you must* and *you should.*

Sentence structure has been simplified through the elimination (as far as possible) of subordinate clauses and parenthetical phrases—both mentioned in Chapter 3 as major contributors to high readability.

In any mathematics text, of course, it is necessary to use the technical vocabulary of the subject, as well as common vocabulary used in ways specific to mathematics. The SMSG material helps mitigate this problem by providing vernacular synonyms in many places when technical vocabulary is first introduced, and, in addition, by making extensive use of marginal notes alongside technical terms. In a sense, this provides for the contextual meaning (see Chapter 3) that is preferred to dictionary usage, especially for students with low reading ability.

The materials in all three textual levels are arranged in what their editor calls "small assimilable chunks." All exercises are printed in a second color to distinguish them from the main textual copy. Other editorial features also make the texts more easily readable: consistency of length of printed lines; many illustrations; elimination of hyphenated (broken) words at the ends of lines of print; simplified punctuation; and an abundance of white space.

The following three examples will serve to illustrate the three levels of readability of the Secondary School Mathematics series:

From the Blue (highest level):

Introduction

Over the course of centuries, as life has become increasingly technological, man has been forced to invent new and different kinds of numbers in order to solve his problems. Learning how to use those numbers is a very important part of your study of mathematics. For example, you must learn how to add them or to multiply them. In this chapter you will learn about the set of numbers called the integers.

As you continue to study the number system, you may find it helpful to think of the various sets of numbers as members of a club; we'll call it the Number Club. Like most clubs, the Number Club has certain rules that must be followed by any new member. Each new member must pay an initiation fee, that is, must contribute something to the club. Each new member must also agree to follow the rules of the club.

The first members of the Number Club are the counting numbers. As the founders of the club, they set the rules which all members must obey. Those rules are the properties of addition and multiplication on the set of counting numbers. You know about those properties, although you may not remember their names. This Class Discussion will remind you about them.

SOURCE: From Secondary School Mathematics, Blue Version, Byrne Publishing, New York, 1972. Reprinted with permission.

The Green version (for the middle range of readability) provides this introduction to the same material:

The Number Club 4-1.

You can think about numbers as if they belong to a club, which we will call the Number Club.

The first members of this club were the counting numbers,

$$1, 2, 3, 4, \ldots$$

so that to begin with, the club was called the Counting Number Club.

Before new members allowed to join the Counting Number Club they have to agree:

(1) **to behave like the other members of the club,**
and (2) as an initiation fee, **to supply ways by which the club can expand its operations.**

The first new member to be admitted to the Number Club is the number zero **0**. The new member has to behave like the other members, but, this new member allows the club to expand its operations to give answers to problems that had no answer before. Problems such as

$$3 - 3 = ?, \quad 5 - 5 = ?, \quad 97 - 97 = ?$$

could not be answered before zero became a member. Even more importantly, the result of adding zero to any member of the club is always identical to that member.

$$5 + 0 = 5, \quad 6 + 0 = 6, \quad 127 + 0 = 127$$

For this reason, we give zero a special name,

The Identity Member for Addition

and change the name of the club to the Whole Number Club,

0, 1, 2, 3, . . .

In the rest of this chapter we will see the club grow to include certain numbers which lie to the left of zero on the number line. We will see how they behave and what they contribute to the club.

SOURCE: From Secondary School Mathematics, Green Version, Byrne Publishing, New York, 1972. Reprinted with permission.

The Gold version (the simplified version for poor readers) introduces the same material without any reference to a "number club," thus:

In the last two chapters you have used negative numbers to help you locate points in the coordinate plane. In this chapter you will learn, among other things, to add and multiply both positive and negative numbers.

To begin, look at this number line:

[*Here a number line is shown.*]

The numbers **0, 1, 2, 3, 4, 5,** and so on are called whole numbers.

If you take a compass and put the needle point at **0** and the pencil point at **1**, you can draw a half circle that intersects the number line at a point to the left of zero. The pencil will also be at the same distance from zero that positive **1** is.

[*Here the number line is shown
intersected by a semicircle.*]

The coordinate of this point is called the negative of one. In symbols, it is written—**1**.

If you do the same thing for other points on the number line, you will locate points to the left of zero whose coordinates are negative numbers.

SOURCE: From Secondary School Mathematics, Gold version, Byrne Publishing, New York, 1972. Reprinted with permission.

The graphic technique called "comic stripping" is used to show the steps of an operation in progressive detail and aids immeasurably in adding concrete imagery to the reading material of the text. An example is shown on page 229. A second color overlay (not shown here) is used to highlight each successive step in the section ("Solving Mathematical Sentences"). Diagrammatical aids to understanding are provided in a slightly different manner (also in color) in the excerpt shown on page 230.

6-3.   Solving Mathematical Sentences

Suppose you are given the equation

$$2(5 \cdot x + 3) + 4 = 3(4 - x) + 9$$

and you are asked to find the solution set. You could draw graphs of the functions or you could guess and test some numbers to see if they result in a true statement. In either case, it would be difficult to arrive at the solution set which is $\left\{\dfrac{11}{13}\right\}$ with what you have learned so far. We need some better methods for finding the solution set to equations like this.

Look at the equation $2 \cdot x - 3 = 7$. First, we will rewrite the sentence as:

$$2 \cdot x + {}^{-}3 = 7$$

We changed from "**subtracting 3**" to "**adding the opposite of 3**" because we will be using some of the Number Club rules, or properties, of addition to help us to solve equations. Subtraction does not have these properties.

We will see how the phrase $2 \cdot x + {}^{-}3$ is "built up." First,

we start with a number **x**

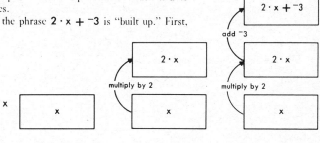

Next, we multiply by **2** and get $2 \cdot \mathbf{x}$,   and then we add $^{-}3$
to get $2 \cdot \mathbf{x} + {}^{-}3$

SOURCE: From Secondary School Mathematics, Green Version, Byrne Publishing, New York, 1972, p. 231. Reprinted by permission.

When the Physical Science Study Committee produced multilevel *PSSC Physics* texts and the Biological Sciences Curriculum Study group wrote the three versions of *BSCS High School Biology* (see Chapter 9), an immediate impact was observable in the science texts that followed. It is to be expected that, with the publication of the first three-track secondary school mathematics texts described here, other authors and publishers of mathematics texts will become more aware of the need for texts of lower readability.

CONCLUSIONS

Reading in the secondary school mathematics classroom is textbook-oriented. Mathematics—contrary to the commonly held belief that it is primarily the

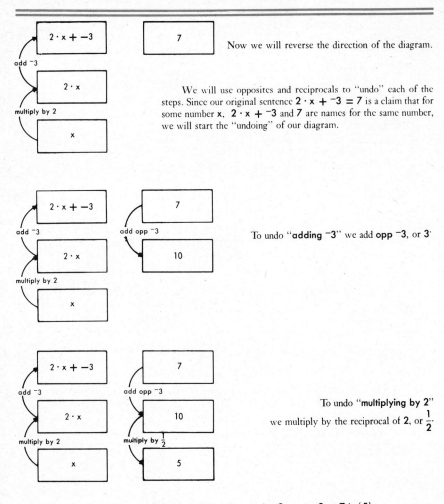

Now we will reverse the direction of the diagram.

We will use opposites and reciprocals to "undo" each of the steps. Since our original sentence $2 \cdot x + {}^-3 = 7$ is a claim that for some number x, $2 \cdot x + {}^-3$ and 7 are names for the same number, we will start the "undoing" of our diagram.

To undo "**adding** $^-3$" we add **opp** $^-3$, or 3·

To undo "**multiplying by 2**" we multiply by the reciprocal of 2, or $\dfrac{1}{2}$.

The solution to the equation $2 \cdot x + {}^-3 = 7$ is $\{5\}$.

SOURCE: Secondary School Mathematics, Green Version, Byrne Publishing, New York, 1972, p. 232. Reprinted with permission.

manipulation of numerals, symbols, and algorisms—is chiefly concerned with comprehension.

The student who learns to substitute numerals for symbols and to "work problems" has merely arrived at the level of memorization. When vocabulary, introductory and descriptive materials, and word problems are introduced, readability becomes the dominant factor to be dealt with and indeed frequently makes the difference between success and failure. Improvement in mathematics is, consequently, directly related to the attention which the classroom mathematics teacher gives to the application of helpful, efficient reading techniques such as those suggested in this chapter.

Questions and Activities for Discussion and Growth

1. Obtain some graphs and charts and make up problems about them, using the simplest vocabulary and sentence construction. Observe the improved mathematics performance of your poorest mathematics students when the readability of problems is lowered to their level.

2. Select ten word problems from a secondary school mathematics text, being certain that they are in keeping with the topic currently being studied. Make one typed "test" using the problems as they appear in the text and administer this to your class. Two days later, administer a second "test" made up of the same problems which you have rewritten at the lowest possible level of readability. Note the significant difference in achievement.

3. Devise a lesson plan for handling the readability problem cited in the first paragraph of "Postulates in Geometry" on pages 218–219.

4. Work up directed reading lessons with step-by-step directions on one or more reading problems in mathematics. Some of the suggestions in Chapter 7 may be applied here.

5. Develop a series of worksheets for practice in memorizing the "punctuation marks" of modern mathematics. Each worksheet in the series should contain some new punctuation marks as well as provision for review and reinforcement of previously memorized marks. The first worksheet should contain those symbols which most students already know:

"Punctuation mark"	Meaning	Example of use
$+$		
$-$		
$\div$		
$=$		
$\times$		
$\triangle$		

6. Develop a list of mathematical terms which have counterparts in everyday speech. Such a list will be valuable to you as a teacher as you help students apply their past experiences to the new vocabulary of mathematics.

7. Administer the Prognostic Test of Reading Disability in Secondary School Mathematics to a class of eighth-graders. Do the same with tenth-graders. Compare the results on the prognostic test with the performance of the tenth-graders in mathematics. What significance do your findings have as regards the eighth-graders who scored low on the test?

8. Select four mathematics textbooks on the same subject and attempt to rate them in the order of their readability.

9. Select an introductory discussion from a mathematics textbook and rewrite it at the lowest possible level of readability. What conclusions did you reach?

10. Plan a lesson in which you concentrate on the survey technique of reading (see Chapter 4) in a chapter of a mathematics textbook.

Selected References

Aaron, Ira E.: "Reading in Mathematics," *Journal of Reading,* vol. VIII, no. 6 (May, 1965), pp. 391–401.

Bamman, Henry A.: "Reading in Science and Mathematics," in International Reading Association, *Reading Instruction in Secondary Schools,* Newark, Delaware, 1964, pp. 59–71.

Call, Russell J., and Neal A. Wiggin: "Reading and Mathematics," *Mathematics Teacher,* 59 (February, 1966), pp. 149–157.

Corle, Clyde G.: "Reading in the Mathematics Classroom: Research," chap. 4 in James L. Laffey, ed., *Reading in the Content Areas,* International Reading Association—ERIC/CRIER, Newark, Delaware, 1972.

Coulter, Myron L.: "Reading in the Mathematics Classroom: Application of Research in the Classroom," chap. 5 in James L. Laffey, ed., *Reading in the Content Areas,* International Reading Association—ERIC/CRIER, Newark, Delaware, 1972.

Eagle, Edwin: "The Relationship of Certain Reading Abilities to Success in Mathematics," *Mathematics Teacher,* 41 (April, 1948), pp. 175–179.

Earle, Richard A.: "Reading and Mathematics: Research in the Classroom," in International Reading Association, *Fusing Reading Skills and Content,* Newark, Delaware, 1969, pp. 162–170.

Earp, N. Wesley: "Observations on Teaching Reading in Mathematics," *Journal of Reading,* vol. 13, no. 7 (April, 1970), pp. 529–532.

Henderson, Kenneth B.: "Interpreting Reading Material in Mathematics," in University of Chicago Annual Conference on Reading, *Proceedings: Improving Reading in All Curriculum Areas,* 1952, pp. 159–163.

McCallister, James M.: "Paragraph Clues as Aids to Understanding," *Journal of Reading,* vol. VIII, no. 1 (October, 1964). (Special attention to reading tasks in mathematics.)

Muelder, Richard H.: "Reading in a Mathematics Class," in International Reading Association, *Fusing Reading Skills and Content,* Newark, Delaware, 1969, pp. 75–80.

Olander, Herbert: "Developing Competence in the Reading of Arithmetic and Mathematics Material," in *Reading in the Content Areas,* University of Pittsburgh Annual Conference Report, 1959, pp. 107–123.

Shepherd, David L.: "Teaching Science and Mathematics to the Seriously Retarded in the High School," *Reading Teacher,* vol. 17 (September, 1963), pp. 25–30.

11. READING IN BUSINESS EDUCATION, INDUSTRIAL ARTS, AND VOCATIONAL CLASSROOMS

Reading problems are common in secondary school business, industrial arts, and vocational classes. However, there is an occasional urge on the part of some teachers to assume that students in those classes are necessarily those with the lowest ability in school, and that reading difficulties are therefore inevitable. There may be some evidence in specific instances to support such a position, but as a generalization the idea is unwarranted. On the contrary, there is considerable evidence that many business, industrial arts, and vocational students would demonstrate significantly improved achievement if more attention were given to certain reading skills as an integral part of the instructional program in those subject areas.

BEHAVIORAL OBJECTIVES

Over the years, the objectives in the various vocational fields have emphasized such psychological and performance achievements as a positive attitude toward tools and machines, a positive attitude toward the world's work, a healthy self-concept, care and efficiency in planning one's work, care and efficiency in carrying out the mechanical operations of a project, pride in the completed task, understanding the basic elements of a process, following directions, and mastery of certain skills (including making accurate measurements; computation; use of machines, tools, and instruments; blueprint reading; understanding symbols; and following safety practices). Although it is difficult to find those objectives stated in the modern terms of "behavioral objectives," they could well be divided into three behavioral categories: attitudes and concepts; cognitive understanding; and skills related to performance.

Attitudinal objectives are achieved as a result of thinking at a fairly high level—the kind of thinking that produces value judgments and develops attitudes toward people, places, organizations, things, and (most important) oneself. Since vocational students often have very low self-concepts, producing good self-concepts is a prime objective. But if a student is unable to read the materials in an assignment, a negative self-concept will be produced or reinforced—and this is the *first step* toward becoming a school dropout.

Cognitive understanding is the core of industrial, mechanical, vocational and business education. Yet, this is the objective most often unattained. Whether or not understanding should come first or last is an academic question. Learning to do something without insight into the process must be memorization devoid of knowing. It may be true that the students with IQs in the lowest 10th percentile may never go much beyond the stage of memorization; but for the other 90 percent, cognitive objectives within the limits of their various abilities should be established. Some of the students may be able to understand the process of atomic fission; others may only be able to understand the process of cutting wood grain. In either case, understanding of the process in question is an essential part of reading.

Performance skills are the easiest of the behavioral objectives to measure. The Educational Objectives Exchange, set up in the Center for the Study of Evaluation of the University of California at Los Angeles under a USOE grant, defined fifty-five objectives in woodworking and eighty-five objectives in mechanical drawing for grades 7 through 12. In both cases the objectives were skills, related to performance, that may be measured objectively, such as basic skills, dimensioning, making drawings to scale, doing rough and finished work, and understanding symbols. Performance skills are equally important in typing, running office machines, the trades, studying diversified occupations, and working in the print shop, machine shop, and foundry. In other specialized vocational subjects as well, performance skills are important; indeed, too often they are the only behavioral objectives.

READING THE STRUCTURED TEXTBOOK

Although textbooks in most business, industrial arts, and vocational subjects continue to be how-to-do-it manuals, some changes are appearing, especially in areas whose graduates will be meeting the public. Textbooks for such subjects include materials aimed at developing the various attitudinal objectives. Sometimes, attention is also given to developing understanding—that is, to achieving certain cognitive objectives.

In any event, textbooks for all business, industrial arts, and vocational subjects are highly structured and depend heavily upon the students' reading ability, in spite of the many diagrams and other visuals so lavishly provided. It may be surprising to discover that the format of books in these areas is identical to that of informational reading for, say, civics, science, or home economics. The page from an industrial arts text reproduced on page 236 illustrates this point.

Using the Survey Technique

The survey technique of reading was described in Chapter 4 and an extension of the SQ3R method was discussed. A few examples from current textbooks will illustrate the type of reading materials that lend themselves to a survey by the class as a whole. An example from retailing is shown on page 237. This retailing text is structured, but its primary interest is to convey information that will aid the student in understanding various operations of retail management before he learns the methods of carrying out these operations. The reasons and philosophy behind each phase of retailing are fully presented. The format of each chapter is such that a survey is in order. The teacher will notice, by the way, that there are fewer visuals in this text than in most modern texts, a situation which suggests that the text has not been adequately updated since its first appearance in 1935 (although the authors do refer in the preface to "the liberal use of illustrative materials").

The two examples shown on pages 238 and 239 are from texts by Chris H. Groneman—one in general shop and the other in general woodworking. Unit 20, "Safety," from the *General Shop* textbook, shows the use of screening, boldface type, numerals, and a short introduction. The entire text is organized using all the essential elements which the survey technique touches. Although the book is replete with excellent and up-to-date illustrations, the major portion of its content is entirely dependent upon the reading ability of the student. Consequently, learning in general shop, when a text like this is used, will be greatly improved through use of the survey technique and development of the other skills described in Chapter 4. Groneman's *General Woodworking* also illustrates a text admirably adaptable to the survey technique.

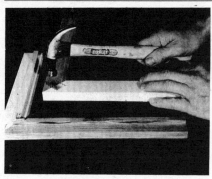

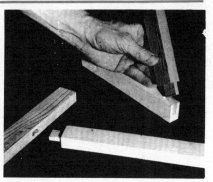

30-7. The miter joint is used to make frames, moldings, and corners on modern furniture. This window-screen frame is being fastened with corrugated fasteners.

30-9. The mortise-and-tenon joint is found in the best type furniture. The blind mortise-and-tenon joint (at the left) is used to fasten rails to legs on tables, chairs, and similar furniture. The one on the right is called an open mortise-and-tenon joint.

DADO JOINT. A *dado* joint is a good one for shelves, steps, bookcases, book racks, chests and other types of cabinets. Fig. 30-6. A blind *dado*, or *gain*, is one in which the dado is cut only part way across the board. A notch must be cut out of the second piece. This makes it look better from the front edge because the dado doesn't show. The *dado and rabbet* is a good joint for drawers.

MITER JOINT. In a *miter joint* the corners are cut at an angle, usually 45 degrees, forming a right angle. A picture frame is a good example. Trim around doors and windows is made with a miter joint. A way to strengthen

this joint is to use a dowel, spline, or key (a thin piece of wood inserted across the corner) Fig. 30-7.

LAP JOINT. The *cross-lap joint* is made when two pieces of wood must cross. You find it on frames, table legs, and some kinds of chairs (especially summer furniture). Fig. 30-8. The carpenter often uses it to strengthen the frame of a house. The pieces may cross at any angle. Other common kinds are the *middle lap* and the *end lap*. Lap joints are made in the same way as rabbet or dado joints.

MORTISE-AND-TENON JOINT. The *mortise-and-tenon* joint is one of the strong-

30-8. The cross-lap joint is used in making modern furniture. Outdoor furniture frequently has this kind of joint.

30-10. The dovetail joint is found in fine box and drawer construction. The most difficult joint to make, it is found only in highest quality furniture.

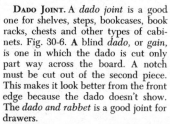

6

STORE ORGANIZATION

What organization is. The purpose of store organization is to bring the various parts of the store into systematic relation so that the coordinated whole functions efficiently and harmoniously. Each part performs its services not as an end in itself but as a means of helping the whole machine or organization reach the common goal. Thus, in any store the creation of the proper organization is an important step toward successful operation.

The organization of a store may be said to consist of the store personnel and their duties and the relationship between those duties. Therefore, in a one-man store, where all the duties in the store are performed by one person, there is no need for organization except in the sense that the individual should organize or divide his time among the various duties. As soon as he hires someone, the work of the store must be divided between them; thus the need for organization appears. As the store grows in size and its activities become more varied, it becomes increasingly necessary for the head of the store to delegate his authority and duties by means of the proper organization.[1]

The need for organization. Although the need for organization is immediately apparent in the large store, its importance in the small store is likely to be overlooked or undervalued. Both the large and the small store are buying, selling, and advertising merchandise, hiring and training employees, and performing the other common functions of a store. It is just as necessary in the small store as in the large one that each person knows his job and that he does it. Much time is lost in many small stores because of the lack of proper allocation of duties among the em-

---

[1] "While a soundly conceived organizational structure does not ensure successful business operation, it does provide an atmosphere in which the institutional objectives are most likely to be realized." By permission from *Retail Personnel Management,* by William R. Spriegel and Joseph W. Towle, copyright 1951, McGraw-Hill Book Company, Inc., p. 8.

158

SOURCE: From Principles of Retailing, by Clare W. Baker, Ira D. Anderson, and J. Donald Butterworth, McGraw-Hill, New York, 1956, p. 158. Copyright © 1956. Used with permission of McGraw-Hill Book Company.

Unit 20. Safety

Working with wood is enjoyable if you have the proper respect for safety. This means you should learn to care for yourself, the tools, and the materials. You should follow safe-conduct rules with fellow students. More accidents occur in the morning around ten o'clock than at any other time of the day. Facts show that more accidents happen on Wednesdays, except on days immediately before and after vacations.

The wood chisel is the hand tool which causes most injuries in woodworking. The jointer is responsible for the greatest number of accidents among the power-tool machines. Inexperienced people, or beginners, have more injuries than those who have skill. Carelessness and improper use of tools are the causes.

The general safety rules which follow apply to both hand and machine tools. Special rules for using machine tools are included in the units on these machines.

Physical Safety

1. Use your leg and arm muscles to lift heavy objects. Never depend on your back muscles. Ask someone to help you.
2. Test the sharpness of edge-cutting tools on wood or paper, not on your hand.
3. Be careful when you are using your thumb as a guide in crosscutting and ripping.
4. Always cut away from your body when you are using a knife.
5. Make sure that your hands are not in front of sharp-edged tools while you are using them.

Clothing Safety

1. Wear a shop or laboratory apron or some other protective clothing when you work in the industrial laboratory or shop.

2. Tuck your tie in your shirt, and roll up your sleeves.

Tool Safety

1. Place tools in an orderly arrangement on a bench top with the cutting edges pointed away from you. Sharp tools should not rub against each other or extend over the edges of the bench.
2. Keep screw drivers properly pointed to prevent injury to hands and to the wood fiber.
3. Fasten handles firmly on planes, hammers, mallets, and chisels.
4. Make sure that files have suitable handles.
5. Use all tools properly and only for their intended purpose. Do not try to pry with a file, a screw driver, or a wood chisel.

Materials Safety

1. Always fasten or hold wood properly. You may use a vise with clamps or sawhorses.
2. Put waste pieces of lumber in a storage rack or in a scrap box.
3. Keep oily or finishing rags in closed metal containers.

Shop or Laboratory Courtesy

1. Report an accident immediately after it occurs so that first aid can be given.
2. Warn others to clear out of the way when you handle long pieces of lumber.
3. Walk carefully—do not run—in the industrial laboratory or shop or home workshop. Running can be dangerous.
4. Carry only a few tools at a time.
5. Cooperate with your fellow worker to help prevent accidents.

105

SOURCE: Chris H. Groneman and John L. Feirer, General Shop, 4th ed., McGraw-Hill, Webster Division, St. Louis, 1969. Copyright © 1969. Reprinted by permission of McGraw-Hill, Inc.

UNIT **37** CUTTING WITH THE PORTABLE JIG SAW

The decorative cutting which you did in Unit 30 on the table-model jig saw could also have been done with the portable type. The feature of the portable jig saw is that it can be taken to the place where you are working. This tool is sometimes called a saber saw or a bayonet saw. Piercing or internal cutting can be done easily with this saw, as shown in Fig. 37-2.

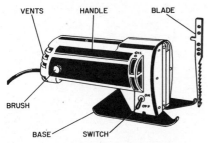

Fig. 37-1. Portable electric jig saw.

Fig. 37-2. Cutting with a portable electric jig saw.

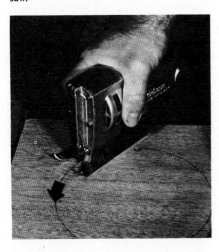

The blade works up and down, just as it does on the table model. Blades are available for cutting different types of materials in addition to wood. Some of these are ferrous and nonferrous metals, felt, leather, rubber, plastics, insulating materials, composition board, and linoleum.

The portable jig saw weighs about 3½ pounds. Figure 37-1 shows the various parts. Manufacturers have their own recommended methods for inserting and removing blades. Study their instructions.

■ *CAUTION:* <u>Before using the portable jig saw, make certain that the electrical connection is grounded. This will protect you from a possible shock.</u>

⬡ SAFETY RULES

1. Always secure permission from your teacher to use the portable jig saw.
2. Disconnect the plug from the electric-power outlet before you inspect parts, make adjustments, or insert the blade.
3. Check to see that the electrical connection is grounded.
4. Hold or clamp the board to be cut so that it will not vibrate.
5. Always hold this tool firmly.
6. Allow the blade to come to full speed before starting to cut.
7. Protect your clothing.
8. Concentrate on what you are doing.

SAWING

1. Lay out or mark the board to be cut.
2. Disconnect the plug from the electric-power outlet; then insert a blade suitable for your job. Replace the plug in the outlet.

SOURCE: Chris H. Groneman, General Woodworking, 3d ed., McGraw-Hill, Webster Division, St. Louis, 1964, p. 146. Copyright © 1964. Reprinted by permission of McGraw-Hill, Inc.

CHAPTER 10

QUENCH AND SQUISH AREA

WEDGE   HEMISPHERIC

Automotive-engine Fuels

This chapter discusses the origin and characteristics of various fuels used in automotive-type engines, including gasoline, LPG (liquefied petroleum gas), and diesel-engine fuel oil.

§ 10–1. GASOLINE Gasoline is a hydrocarbon (made up of hydrogen and carbon compounds). These compounds split into hydrogen and carbon atoms when gasoline burns; these atoms then unite with oxygen atoms. Gasoline is produced by a complex refining process from crude oil, or petroleum. No one knows exactly how petroleum originated. It is found in "pools," or reservoirs, underground. When a well is drilled down to a reservoir, the underground pressure forces the petroleum up and out of the well. The petroleum must then be put through an intricate refining process; the resulting products include gasoline, many grades and kinds of lubricating oil and fuel oil, and many other products.

§ 10–2. VOLATILITY OF GASOLINE Actually, gasoline is not a simple substance. It is a mixture of a number of different hydrocarbons; each has its own characteristics. Aside from its combustibility, one of the important properties of gasoline is *volatility*.

Volatility refers to the ease with which a liquid vaporizes. The volatility of a simple compound like water or alcohol is determined by increasing its temperature until it boils, or vaporizes. A liquid that vaporizes at a relatively low temperature has a high volatility; it is highly volatile. If its boiling point is high, its volatility is low. A certain heavy oil with a boiling point of 600° F has a very low volatility. Water has a relatively high volatility; it boils at 212° F at atmospheric pressure.

Gasoline is blended from different hydrocarbon compounds, each having a different volatility, or boiling point. The proportions of high-volatility and low-volatility hydrocarbons must be correct for the operating conditions, as noted below.

1. *Easy starting.* For easy starting with a cold engine, gasoline must be highly volatile so that it will vaporize readily at a low temperature. Thus, a percentage of the gasoline must be highly volatile. For the colder Northern states, the percentage must be higher than for the South.

2. *Freedom from vapor lock.* If the gasoline is too volatile, engine heat will cause it to vaporize in the fuel pump. This can cause vapor lock, which prevents normal fuel delivery to the carburetor and would probably produce stalling of the engine. Thus, the percentage of highly volatile gasoline must be kept low to prevent vapor lock. The use of a vapor-return line to return vaporized fuel from the fuel pump to the fuel tank, and also to circulate extra fuel through the fuel pump to keep it cool, is discussed in § 9–7.

3. *Quick warm-up.* The speed with which the engine warms up depends in part on the percentage of gasoline that will vaporize immediately after the engine starts and thus contribute to engine operation. Volatility for this purpose does not have to be quite so high as for easy starting. But, all the same, it must be fairly high.

4. *Smooth acceleration.* When the throttle is opened for acceleration, there is a sudden increase in the amount of air passing through the throttle valve. At the same time, the accelerator pump delivers an extra amount of gasoline. If this gasoline does not vaporize quickly, there will be a momentary interval during which the air-fuel mixture will be too lean. This will cause the engine to hesitate, or stutter. Immediately after, as the gasoline begins to evaporate, the mixture will become temporarily too rich. Here again there will be poor combustion and a tendency for the engine to hesitate. A sufficient proportion of the gasoline must

178

SOURCE: William H. Crouse, *Automotive Mechanics*, McGraw-Hill, Webster Division, St. Louis, 1970, p. 178. Copyright © 1970. Reprinted by permission of McGraw-Hill, Inc.

9

Auxiliary views and revolutions

Fig. 9-1. Revolution about a vertical axis. A 15-ton, 80-ft-boom shipyard traveling crane. (McKiernan-Terry Corporation)

9•1 Explanatory views projected on other planes. In the previous chapters views have been drawn on the three regular planes with the object in a normal (regular) position. The three regular planes are the top, or horizontal plane; the front, or frontal plane; and the side, or profile plane. In this chapter views are drawn of inclined surfaces on planes which are parallel to the inclined surfaces and of objects which have been revolved, or turned about an axis (Fig. 9-1).

9•2 Auxiliary views are "helper views." When an object has slanting surfaces, the usual views do not show the true shapes of such surfaces (Fig. 9-2a at A). However, a view on a plane parallel to the slanting surface will show the true shape of the slanting surface, as at B. This, together with the side view, a bottom view of the base, and a partial front view, will give a better description than the views at A.

◄ *An auxiliary view is a projection on an auxiliary plane parallel to a slant-*

ing surface. It is a view looking directly at the slanting surface in a direction perpendicular to it.

Observe the anchor pictured in Fig. 9-2b in Space 1 and that the position of the auxiliary plane in Space 2 is parallel to the inclined face and perpendicular to the frontal plane. In Space

Fig. 9-2b. An auxiliary view is drawn on a plane parallel to the inclined surface.

Fig. 9-2a. An auxiliary view gives a better description than regular views.

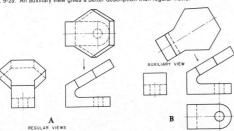

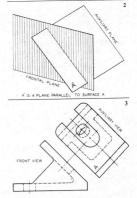

SOURCE: Thomas E. French and Carl L. Svensen, *Mechanical Drawing,* 7th ed., McGraw-Hill, Webster Division, St. Louis, 1966, p. 102. Copyright © 1966. Reprinted by permission of McGraw-Hill, Inc.

The passage from Crouse's *Automotive Mechanics* reproduced on page 240 illustrates a number of aids to reading that are evidence of careful writing and editing. New vocabulary (such as *hydrocarbon* and *volatility*) is defined in the text immediately following the word. Paragraph sections are numbered, and headings are printed in brown. Subheadings are numbered and printed in italics. Each chapter heading carries an accompanying foreword telling exactly what the chapter discusses. With such format, it would be wasteful not to utilize the survey technique. In spite of the excellent organization, however, the readability of this textbook is far from easy, and it would be useless for students of low intelligence or low reading ability to undertake it.

Our next example (reproduced on page 241) is from one of the most amazing textbooks ever written for a secondary school subject—the late Thomas E. French's *Mechanical Drawing*, which was originally copyrighted in 1919 and is now in its seventh revised edition. It should be noted that in this text, as in many other industrial arts texts, modern numbering practice has been adopted for the subheadings. Italic type is used for definitions; headings and subheadings appear in boldface type. Illustrations are plentiful and have been updated. Because of the vocabulary and the new concepts presented, the readability of this textbook is high; therefore, students with low intelligence or low reading ability should not be expected to handle it.

To the five illustrations given here there might easily be added numerous examples from other textbooks in business, industrial arts, and vocational education. But our examples should be adequate evidence that textbooks in these subject areas are highly "academic" in content and format. Few people realize this. Even professional educators and organizations have failed to recognize the significant relationship between reading ability and success or failure in these areas. The relationship exists, obviously, because success in those areas depends upon textual materials and the ability to deal with them. As far as orientation to a textbook is concerned, there is no significant difference between academic and technical subjects at the secondary level.

The classroom teacher in each of those areas is responsible for learning. Attention to reading skills is therefore one of his essential responsibilities.

Reading to Follow Directions

Reading to follow directions is an important objective of many texts and supplementary books in business education, industrial arts, and vocational education. The books tend to be how-to-do-it manuals and are designed for training in specific skills, such as office practices, running office machines, bookkeeping, merchandise control, secretarial practices, office management, receptionists' duties, retail and house-to-house selling techniques, profitable management of small shops, and organizing small businesses. Technical skills are usually described in detail in shop manuals for repairing automobiles, implements such as lawnmowers, radios and television sets, and appliances; in books on hair styling; and in texts for such fields as greenhouse management, air conditioning installation, and gasoline station operation.

The classroom teacher may help the student by providing guidelines for reading to follow directions. A helpful method is to provide a written form with spaces for the student to fill in answers to such questions as the following:

What is the objective of the project? What are we trying to do?

What tools are needed? Implements, tools, supplies, measuring tools, materials, etc., should be listed.

How much material is needed?

Where may it be obtained?

Is everything on hand before we start? The answer to this question might form a sort of checklist.

What do you do first? Why?

What are the directions? The student should list them step by step in his own words, and number the steps.

Has anything been left out? The student should check the manual, step by step, to be sure nothing has been omitted. If everything is all right, he is ready to start.

Did the manual provide all the necessary information?

What words gave trouble?

What was not clear? Why?

Following directions calls for memory and ability to visualize. The directions are necessarily given in words, only some of which (if any) will be accompanied by visuals. The reader must visualize as necessary and make a mental storage of the sequence. If he has poor reading ability, poor ability to visualize, or poor memory, he will have difficulty comprehending or following the directions. If he suffers from more than one of these lacks, he will be in real difficulty. Students with such disabilities should be given simple tasks which require a minimum of verbalization and should not be expected to handle reading materials that contain extensive directions, references to diagrams, symbols, and relationships (such as are found in shop manuals), complex directions for assembly, and sophisticated procedures and diagrams.

Here is an example from a junior high school general shop text, written at a comparatively low readability level:

Applying Oil Stain

1. Select the desired color of stain.
2. Shake the stain container thoroughly before opening it.
3. Brush some stain on a scrap of the same wood as the project to test the color.
4. Apply a coat of linseed oil to all end grain.
5. Apply the stain with a medium-size brush to the exposed parts of the entire project. Brush with long, even strokes (Fig. 49-1). You can get the same results by using a cloth.
6. Wipe off surplus stain quickly with a cloth (Fig. 49-2).
7. Allow the stain to dry overnight.

SOURCE: Chris H. Groneman and John L. Feirer, General Shop, McGraw-Hill Book Company, New York, 1969, p. 187.

Other texts, such as the two in automotive mechanics and mechanical drawing previously cited, may be found to have extremely high levels of readability.

§ 32–3. TRANSMISSION REMOVAL AND IN-STALLATION Because of the variations in construction of transmissions on different automobiles, different procedures must be followed in the removal, disassembly, repair, assembly, and installation of their transmissions. These operations require about 5 to 7 hours, the difference in time being due to variations in the procedures. Basically, the procedures are similar. However, refer to the manufacturer's shop manual before attempting such work. In general, the following steps are required:

1. Drain lubricant. Some manufacturers recommend flushing the transmission before removal. This is done by filling the transmission with gasoline or kerosene, after the lubricant is drained, and then operating the engine with the transmission in neutral for 15 seconds. Then the cleaner should be drained.

2. Disconnect the rear axle or the front end of the propeller shaft or the universal joint, according to type. Where needle bearings are used, tape the bearing retainers to the shaft to avoid losing needles.

3. Disconnect shifting linkages from transmission, hand-brake linkage or spring, and speedometer cable.

4. Install engine support, where specified (see Fig. 32–1).

5. Remove attaching bolts or stud nuts. Where recommended, two pilot, or guide, pins should be used. These pins are substituted for transmission bolts and prevent damage to the clutch friction disk as the transmission is moved back. The transmission is then moved toward the rear until the main gear shaft clears the clutch disk. It can then be lowered to the floor.

6. In general, installation is the reverse of removal. Be sure the matching faces of the trans-

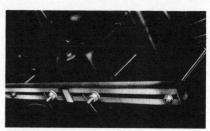

Fig. 32–1. Installing engine support prior to removal of transmission.

mission and the flywheel housing are clean. Place a small amount of lubricant on the splines of the main gear shaft. Carefully support the transmission (using guide pins if specified), and move it forward into position. Turn the shaft, if necessary, to secure alignment of the shaft and the clutch-disk hub splines. Put bolts in place, and tighten them to the correct tension.

● **CAUTION:** If the transmission does not fit snugly against the flywheel housing, do not force it. Roughness or dirt, or possibly a loose snap ring or other parts, may be blocking the transmission. If the bolts are tightened under such circumstances, the transmission case may be broken.

§ 32–4. TRANSMISSION AND OVERDRIVE OVERHAUL The overhaul procedures differ for each model of transmission and overdrive. Thus, before disassembling, servicing, and reassembling a transmission or overdrive, always refer to the shop manual that covers the specific model being repaired. Follow the instructions step by step.

426

SOURCE: William H. Crouse, Automotive Mechanics, McGraw-Hill, Webster Division, St. Louis, 1970, p. 426. Copyright © 1970. Reprinted by permission of McGraw-Hill, Inc.

Poor readers would not be able to follow the directions given in such textbooks as they appear. Two examples, shown on pages 244 and 245, will illustrate the problem. The solution depends upon the ability of the classroom teacher to provide instruction in following directions. The best procedure is to have the students reword the directions, taking each step of the procedure separately. Unless the directions can be reworded, they have not been understood: the student has only been pronouncing words. Being able to restate the directions in one's own words is proof of understanding.

"DRAFTING PRACTICES APPLICABLE
TO GRAPHIC SYMBOLS

1. A symbol shall be considered as the aggregate of all its parts.
2. The orientation of a symbol on a drawing, including a mirror image, does not alter the meaning . . . .
3. The width of a line does not affect the meaning of the symbol. In specific cases a wider line may be used for emphasis.
4. The symbols shown in this standard are in their correct relative size. This relationship shall be maintained as nearly as possible on any particular drawing, regardless of the size of the symbol used.
5. A symbol may be drawn to any proportional size that suits a particular drawing, depending on reduction or enlargement anticipated. If essential for purposes of contrast, some symbols may be drawn relatively smaller than the other symbols on a diagram.
6. The arrowhead of a symbol may be closed ——▶ or open ——▶ unless otherwise noted in this standard.
7. The standard symbol for a TERMINAL (○) may be added to each point of attachment to connecting lines to any one of the graphic symbols. Such added terminal symbols should not be considered as part of the individual graphic symbol unless the terminal symbol is included in the symbol shown in this standard.
8. For simplification of a diagram parts of a symbol for a device, such as a relay or contactor, may be separated. If this is done provide suitable designations to show proper correlation of the parts.
9. In general, the angle at which a connecting line is brought to a graphic symbol has no particular significance unless otherwise noted in this standard.
10. Associated or future paths and equipment shall be shown by lines composed of short dashes: – – –.
11. Details of type, impedance, rating, etc., may be added, when required, adjacent to any symbol. If used, abbreviations should be from the American Standard Abbreviations for Use on Drawings (Z32.13-1950). Letter combinations used as parts of graphic symbols are not abbreviations."

SOURCE: Thomas E. French and Carl L. Svensen, *Mechanical Drawing,* 7th ed., McGraw-Hill, Webster Division, St. Louis, © 1966, p. 260; quoted in "American Standard Graphic Symbols for Electrical and Electronics Diagrams," Institute of Electrical and Electronic Engineers.

THE READING ASSIGNMENT

Reading in business, industrial arts, and vocational classrooms does create problems for the classroom teacher, and some suggestions may be helpful as guidelines.

Three typical reading problems are described below from the point of view of the classroom teacher. Following each problem are some practical solutions offered by reading specialists.

Problem 1

Certain students of average reading ability cannot understand the content of a textbook reading assignment in an industrial arts class.

> "In my woodworking class I frequently assign eight or ten pages to be read in our textbook, and I do this especially when we are about to begin a new phase of work.
>
> "These assignments are made because I want the boys to gain sufficient background on the topic to enable them to participate in class discussions. I find, however, that my students come to class unable to discuss the material intelligently. I honestly believe most of the boys *are* reading the assignments, but they just don't seem to understand what they are reading.
>
> "At first I thought the textbook might be too difficult for them to read; but when I checked the office records, I found that all the boys had made satisfactory scores on reading achievement tests.
>
> "I am willing to make an effort to help the boys. Can you make a suggestion?"

Possible solution. Although the textbook may be difficult to read, students can learn to read it more successfully with some direct instruction and guidance from the classroom teacher. It will take only one or two class periods to help students learn how to "study-read" an assignment. While doing this, they will be working on a textbook assignment that is a regular requirement for the course. The difference is that they will do the reading, not on their own, but under supervision. They will be led through a series of sequential steps and activities to show them how to *study* an assignment.

A directed reading lesson, based on a ten-page reading assignment in an industrial arts textbook, is described in the lesson plan that follows.

Though this is a "practice lesson" on how to begin and carry out the requirements of a textbook reading assignment, it does not require special reading materials. Students will be working on material they would ordinarily read for an assignment. The major difference between this assignment and others that the class may have done is that the teacher will guide the students through the reading.

Students should learn that the "study-reading" techniques they are learning as they do this reading assignment can be used also in reading textbooks in other subjects.

This lesson will offer opportunity to evaluate the average reading level of the class and find out which students are most in need of help in reading the special materials of industrial arts.

LESSON PLAN

Behavioral objective. To teach the students to read a textbook assignment more efficiently and with greater understanding.

Materials needed
1. Textbook for each student
2. Overhead projector, if available
3. Transparency or chart of
   a. Technical words
   b. Common words that have a different meaning when used in woodworking
   c. Nontechnical polysyllabic or unusual words
4. Copy of vocabulary for each student
5. Copy for each student of steps to follow in "study-reading" an assignment
6. Transparency (if an overhead projector is available) of the material in item 5; or a chart prepared for display

Teacher's preparation

1. Decide on length of assignment and major points to be emphasized.
2. Prepare transparencies, chart, and vocabulary sheets.
   a. Vocabulary does not need to be limited to single words. Choose key words, phrases, technical words, and common words whose meanings are different in woodworking. Divide some of the more difficult words into syllables and add accent marks.
   b. Indicate that simple words like "stock" and "plane" have different meanings when used in woodworking classes.
3. The following words from Units 16 and 17 are examples of technical words, common words with uncommon meanings in this field, and difficult words.[1] These should form the vocabulary list, with other such words. (The teaching plan might include all the words in these categories, but the transparency or chart would include only those that might give the most trouble.)
   a. Technical words:

cellulose	lignin	veneer
rotary cutter	resin	laminated
grain patterns	cypress	acetone

   b. Common words with uncommon meanings:

softwood	hardwood
close-grained	pressed wood
spirits	

   c. Difficult words:

conifers	impregnating
distillates	synthetic
edible	durable

4. Prepare at least five questions (as suggested below) to be answered by the students as a homework assignment.

The questions in step 4 above will direct the students' attention to a particular section of the textbook and should require the students to read and reread that section to locate answers or to organize information to answer the questions fully. For this lesson, the page or pages should be listed where information pertaining to a particular question can be found.

[1] These examples are typical of words found in a woodworking text.

Sample homework assignment

1. Name the five commercial forests of the United States. (Pages 50–55.)
2. What is the difference between veneer and plywood? (Pages 49 and 56.)
3. Describe how plywood stock is made. (Pages 49 and 56, and Fig. 17–3.)
4. What species of tree yields a product used widely in the paint industry? (Page 57.)
5. Name a tree which is used in the manufacture of lead pencils and cedar chests. (Page 51.)
6. What tree, valuable for its beautiful wood and delicious nuts, is used in the making of fine furniture and boatbuilding? (Pages 54–55.)
7. Approximately what percentage of the total timber harvested in America's five commercial forests is used in the manufacture of paper? (Page 56.)
8. Describe the process of making laminated paper products. (Page 56.)
9. What products are made from waste sawdust shavings? (Page 56.)
10. Wood consists of two classes of substances, cellulose and lignin.
    a. Name five products made from cellulose. (Page 57.)
    b. Name three products made from lignin. (Page 57.)
    c. What two substances can be found in plastic objects? (Page 57.)

Method. The first step in the approach is to establish a dialogue between teacher and students. This may be accomplished by considering the reasons for the directed reading lesson on Units 16 and 17. The discussion should be followed by a procedure planned on a basis of the following concepts and steps:

1. Most students may be capable of reading the textbook, but it is apparent that many are not getting enough out of their reading. Obviously, something is wrong.
2. Students need to know how to read many types of materials assigned in different subjects. Textbook assignments are read differently from the way a book is read for pleasure. When students read the textbook for industrial arts, they must apply certain study skills; they must also know when and where to concentrate and when to skim.
3. Take enough time for discussion, so that the students will be interested in learning how to "study-read" an assignment.
4. Apply the survey technique (see Chapter 2).
    a. Have the students open their textbooks and read the following:
        (1) All titles and subtitles, italicized print, pictures, and graphs.
        (2) The introduction and summary (if any) and discussion questions for the unit.
        (3) The first sentence of each paragraph.
    b. Discuss with the students what they have read.
    c. Point out key words and phrases, if there is enough time.
5. If an overhead projector is available, put the transparency of new vocabulary on the projector. Cover it with a sheet of paper, so that only the word or words you wish to discuss will be seen when you turn on the projector.
    a. Ask a student to read the first word. Tell the class the page where the word may be found and have them read the word silently in context. Discuss the word and its meaning in the sentence. (You will not need to do this with all the words; some may only need to be reviewed for the benefit of poor readers.)
    b. Discuss the common words with special meanings, such as "plane." Emphasize the special meaning this word has in the shop context.
4. Distribute the prepared questions to the students and ask them to be able to discuss their answers at the next class session.

Problem 2

Students in industrial arts classes cannot always read and interpret graphic materials.

> "Members of our Industrial Arts Department seem to have a common complaint. . . . Our students do not know how to gain the most information from reading graphic materials. We feel that when the boys look at a diagram. they do not realize all the information it offers. If they knew how to study a diagram, we are sure they would have a more thorough understanding of the project to be made, make better sketches of their projects, and ultimately produce the finished project with less difficulty."

Possible solution. It is true that many students enter junior high school without knowing the specific skills needed to read and interpret graphs, diagrams, and other graphic materials. Reading graphic materials involves three processes:

1. Recognition
2. Analysis
3. Interpretation

When introducing a diagram to the class, the teacher should help students *recognize* the visual aid as a method of offering information, *analyze* it for specific information, and *interpret* it by drawing generalizations from it. Students do not always carefully analyze the lines of a diagram and consequently often confuse them. The task of the classroom teacher is to make the students understand that graphic materials are a type of shorthand.

LESSON PLAN

Behavioral objective: To increase the students' ability to read and interpret diagrams.

Project. Half-round table.

Materials needed

1. A completed half-round table for display.
2. A transparency of the following technical words and phrases used in explaining the diagram of the half-round table:

router	back apron
aprons	mortise
pilot hole	braces
$\frac{3}{16}$ drill	tenon braces
$\frac{3}{8}$ C' bore	tapered legs

3. Duplicated sheets for each student of the following:
   a. Vocabulary used on the diagram of the half-round table and used to explain the half-round table.
   b. An "alphabet of lines" and steps to follow in reading and interpreting diagrams.

4. Transparency of the half-round table (see illustration below).

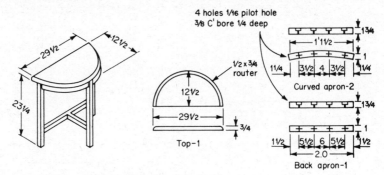

5. Transparency of the alphabet of lines:

——————— Visible outline line

– – – – – – – Hidden line

——— – ——— Center line

——————— Extension line

←—— 4 ——→ Dimension line

6. Transparency showing the steps to follow in reading and interpreting diagrams, as follows:
   a. Read the title of the diagram.
   b. Note the terms used in the diagram.
   c. Note the various lines and determine what they represent.
   d. Examine the diagram for unfamiliar lines.
   e. Refer to the chart for an explanation of the unfamiliar lines.
   f. Apply this information to the diagram.

Procedure

1. Display a completed half-round table.
2. Discuss the project and the need for knowing how to "read" graphic materials.
3. Project the transparency listing technical words (vocabulary) used in describing the half-round table.
4. Review the vocabulary.
5. The following suggested questions may be used to direct the students' attention to reading and interpreting the diagram:
   a. Why is the title of the diagram important?
   b. Find the measurement "24½" on the top. What does it mean?
   c. Look at the heavy black lines on the drawing of the completed table. What do these lines indicate?
   d. Look at the term "Apron-2." What does this tell you?
   e. Do all the lines in this diagram look alike? How are they different?
   f. Look at the label "Back Apron-1." Find the measurement "¾." What does it tell you?
   g. Find the circle illustration. What is the meaning of "⅜ x ½ tenon on braces"?
   h. Which number gives the diameter?
6. Emphasize that each type of line on a diagram has a specific meaning.
7. Project the transparency of the "alphabet of lines."

8. Project the transparency of the half-round table again. Ask the students to supply all the information they can about this half-round table by "reading the diagram."
9. Project the transparency that lists steps to follow in reading and interpreting a diagram efficiently. Review the steps with the students.
10. Distribute the following duplicated sheets to the students, to be kept in their notebooks for future reference in reading diagrams:
    Sheet (a)—Vocabulary of diagram
    Sheet (b)—Alphabet of lines
    Sheet (c)—Steps in reading diagrams
11. As a follow-up lesson, the students may be asked to write a short paragraph describing the half-round table, using as much technical vocabulary as they can.

Problem 3

Students in business subjects are unable to separate the main ideas from the details of a selection.

> "I have discovered that students in my classes underline everything in their textbooks. I asked them why they did this, and many responded that everything seemed to be important—otherwise, why did the author of the text include it?
>
> "They also said that they underline so that they will know what to look at again in preparation for a test.
>
> "It seems that they do not have any way of knowing the difference between main ideas and details."

Possible solution: Reading for main ideas. Many subjects in business, industrial arts, and vocational education textbooks are structured as a sequence of steps presented in the form of directions. Others, especially in business education, are presented in a format which calls for applying the technique of reading for main ideas described in Chapter 5. Many texts in general business, office practices, merchandising, selling, the psychology of advertising, business law, economic geography, and vocational information have materials which fall into this latter category. The techniques presented in Chapter 5 are applicable in textbooks for all these subjects; in fact, it is the obligation of the teachers of those subjects to devise exercises in the texts that will help students gain this important reading skill.

The most important checks on reading for main ideas in these areas are what? how? how much? how many? and why?—with less emphasis on where? when? and who? Consequently, the teacher must adjust the check on main ideas to the style of the textbook in each subject. The aspect of reading for main ideas that is probably least important in business and vocational texts is who. The material is factual, but, ordinarily, it does not deal with specific individuals in a historical setting.

The patterns and structure of the paragraphs and chapters in business and vocations texts are the same as those described in Chapter 5, and the technique of diagramming the patterns may be applied throughout.

Collision insurance does not provide for payment of damages in excess of the value of the car. For example, suppose that your old car is worth only $150. If as a result of an accident you find that it will cost at least $300 to repair the car, your insurance company would be obligated to pay only $150. For cars of little worth, it would probably be foolish to pay yearly premiums for collision insurance. Some insurance companies will not sell collision insurance for low-value cars. Remember, too, that collision insurance does not cover injuries to people or damage to the property of others.

AUTOMOBILE INSURANCE
A SUMMARY CHART OF PRINCIPAL APPLICATIONS OF BASIC COVERAGES

TYPE OF COVERAGE	PERSONS To Whom Coverage Principally Applies		PROPERTY To Which Coverage Principally Applies	
	Insured Including Family	Persons Other Than Insured	Policy-holder's Automobile	Property Other Than Policy-holder's
Bodily Injury Coverages				
1. Bodily Injury Liability	NO	YES		
2. Medical Payments	YES	YES		
3. Protection Against Uninsured Motorist	YES	YES		
Property Damage Coverages				
4. Property Damage Liability			NO	YES
5. Comprehensive Physical Damage			YES	NO
6. Collision			YES	NO

Insurance Information Institute

What does automobile insurance cost?   The cost of automobile insurance depends on several things such as:

1. Place of residence of insured person.
2. The value of the automobile.
3. The purpose for which the automobile is used.
4. The miles that are, on the average, driven in a year.
5. The age of the driver.
6. The safety record of the driver.

The cost is usually higher when one of the drivers in the family is under 30 years of age than it is if all are over 30. In general, the difference in cost increases as the age of young drivers decreases. If young drivers are included in a policy, the cost of insurance on one car may amount to two or three times more than

For example, examine the selection from a general business text reproduced on page 252. Reading for main ideas would bring out these elements:

What? Collision insurance to cover the value of the car.
How much? The cost is higher for those under 30.
How? See the chart to determine how insurance applies.
Why? Why does it not apply to cars of low value? Why does it cost more for young drivers?

The main idea of collision insurance escapes a huge percentage of automobile drivers. In order for this page to be understood adequately by students, it must be read to answer those questions noted above.

The following examples serve to illustrate some of the types of paragraph structure which may be analyzed for finding main ideas; they also indicate the relevance of analyzing structure in texts for business education, industrial arts, and vocational education. (The patterns are described in more detail in Chapter 5.)

The first is an example of pattern 1, in which the main idea is followed by examples and details:

It is most important that when the clutch pedal is released, the throw-out bearing will not be touching the release levers. The throw-out bearing must clear for two reasons. As long as it touches, it will continue to rotate. This will shorten its useful life. More important, if the throw-out bearing is not fully released, it may bear against the release levers hard enough to partially disengage the clutch. Any removal of pressure plate force will cause the clutch to slip. When slippage occurs, the clutch will overheat and burn.[2]

The throw-out bearing must clear. (*Main idea*)
  Touching will shorten its useful life.
  Removal of pressure will cause the clutch to overheat and burn up.

In the second example, the details are given first, followed by the main idea:

With the compensating port closed, the piston traps the fluid ahead of it, and creates pressure in the cylinder. This pressure forces the check valve inner rubber flap to open and pass fluid into the lines as the piston continues to move and force the shoes tightly against the spinning drum. As long as the pressure is maintained on the brake pedal, the shoes will remain pressed against the drum.[3]

Piston creates pressure in cylinder.
  Pressure forces fluid into lines.
    Pressure forces shoes against spinning drum.
      As long as there is pressure, the shoes will remain pressed against the drum.
      (*Main idea*)

[2] Martin W. Stockel, *Auto Mechanics Fundamentals*, Goodheart-Wilcox Company, 1963, p. 9–9.
[3] Stockel, *Auto Mechanics Fundamentals*, p. 9–9.

The next example illustrates the structure in which the main idea is followed by details and then is restated at the end of the paragraph:

> Above all else, GRADUATE FROM HIGH SCHOOL. High school dropouts are considered poor risks by employers, and for good reasons. National figures on salaries and employment show that the average dropout is unemployed a great deal of the time. When he is able to find work, it is usually some low-pay job. The world today is moving forward at an ever-increasing speed and there will be little chance for the unskilled and uneducated dropout. STAY IN SCHOOL.[4]

Graduate from high school. (*Main idea*)
  Dropouts are poor risks.
    Dropouts are often unemployed.
      Dropouts get low pay.
        Dropouts have little chance in today's world.
          Stay in school. (*Main idea restated*)

Where several details are given, as in the example above, one detail may be implied rather than stated directly. If this is the case, the students may be asked to supply the implied detail.

Occasionally, it requires more than one paragraph to provide a complete main idea. This is illustrated by the following selection, in which details are presented first, the main idea follows, and more details are given after the main idea to complete the concept:

> It is difficult to say what salary you can expect, as much depends on type of work performed, location of the job, employer, prevailing business conditions, and job supply and demand. All of these exert a definite influence on mechanics' salaries.
> Suffice it to say that most mechanics earn a good living and that their salaries are in line with other types of technical jobs.
> Many auto mechanics receive a certain percentage of the customer labor charge. As the rates for various jobs are fixed, the skilled mechanic will be able to do more jobs in one day than the unskilled mechanic, and as a result, will earn more money.[5]

Salary depends upon:
  Work performed
  Location
  Employer
  Business conditions
  Supply and demand.
Skilled mechanics earn a good salary. (*Main idea*)
  Salary also depends upon:
    Percentage of charge to customers for labor
    Rate of work of the mechanic

[4] *Career Opportunities in the Retail Automobile Business*, General Motors Corporation, Detroit.
[5] Stockel, *Auto Mechanics Fundamentals*, p. 17-7.

The next example illustrates an exposition of the main idea in two parts. Main idea, part 1, is followed by details; contrast is signaled by the word *however*, which is followed by main idea, part 2, plus details:

> In many dealerships the dealer acts as his own general manager, supervising and directing the overall operation of the business. If the dealership is a large one, however, the dealer often needs a capable executive to share his duties, so he appoints a general manager.
>
> The full responsibility of seeing that all departments are properly organized and operated falls on the general manager's shoulders. Consequently, he must be a thoroughly capable director—he must know how to manage men—and he must exercise sound business judgment in all important dealership matters.[6]

The dealer can be his own general manager. (*Main idea, part 1*)
　As such, he supervises and directs the business.
However, (*Signal*)
large dealerships need a separate general manager. (*Main idea, part 2*)
　The manager must be:
　　A capable executive
　　A capable director
　　Able to manage men
　　Able to exercise sound judgment

The final example illustrates how the reader of an industrial arts textbook may check for the factors that constitute the main idea:

> 　　[Who]　　　　[What]
> The body painter is a specialist whose work has come into greater demand as,
> 　[When]　　　　　　　　　　　　　　　　　　　　[When]
> in recent years, cars have been made more colorful and attractive. Now it seems everyone is interested in keeping up the appearance of the car he drives . . . and
> 　　　　　　　　　　[Where]
> this means more business for a dealer's body painting activity. This department
> 　　　　　　　　　[How many]
> must keep up with the great varieties of new colors and color combinations introduced every year by different manufacturers and must have body painters who
> 　[What]　　　　[Where]
> can do color work on all makes of cars.
> 　　　　[What]
> 　　When he has a body part to be refinished after it has been repaired, the body
> [Who]　　　　　　　　　　　　　　　　　　[What]
> painter must be able to match color perfectly and assume a job that will be both
> 　　　　　　　[What]
> pleasing to the customer and a credit to the dealership. Considering the many shades of color used on cars today, you can see that getting a perfect match with
> 　　　　　　　　　　　[How]
> paint takes an experienced eye and an expert hand with a spray gun.[7]

[6] *Career Opportunities in the Retail Automobile Business*, General Motors Corporation.
[7] Stockel, *Auto Mechanics Fundamentals*, p. 95.

PREDICTING THE READING DISABILITY OF BUSINESS, INDUSTRIAL ARTS, AND VOCATIONAL STUDENTS

General reading ability is important in all subject-matter areas. As has been repeatedly stated, there is a significant relationship between reading ability and achievement in these content subjects. An assessment of students' reading ability may be obtained from the permanent records and translated into percentiles (see Chapter 2). This takes some time, but it must be done eventually to identify students as good, average, and poor readers.

A quick method of determining reading disability, to discover those students who will not be able to handle the material in these subject areas, is provided here. This prognostic test is based upon the idea that the general terms which are used in a specific way in business, industrial arts, and vocational classes will handicap very poor readers (to say nothing of the technical vocabulary in each subject area, which will create an even greater handicap). Inability to recognize the common general terms is closely related to failure in these subjects.

The prognostic test is given individually; each student reads directly from the page in this book. (One or two minutes are enough to administer the test.) Use only one of the three alternative forms for each student (this is to prevent students from memorizing the words as they wait their turn and hear others reading).

PROGNOSTIC TEST OF READING DISABILITY IN SECONDARY SCHOOL BUSINESS, INDUSTRIAL ARTS, AND VOCATIONAL EDUCATION[8]

Directions. Cover the other two forms not being used (5- x 7-inch cards will do.) Ask the student to read from left to right, pronouncing each word in turn at his normal rate. Observe his facial expression as he reads. Note hesitation, repetition, regression, uncertainty, gross mispronunciation, and incorrect accent.

Identify the student who is *not* able to move along smoothly at about one word every two seconds. He will most probably have great difficulty reading the textbook because he lacks adequate proficiency in general vocabulary (and he will be at a total loss when confronted with the technical vocabulary).

Alternative Form A

functional	assistance	indicative	inexperienced
measurements	representative	characteristics	synchronizing
expenditures	communication	sensitivity	orientation
tabulation	evaluation	detecting	attainment
impulse	identification	neglected	balancing
facilities	transportation	responsibility	standardized
discrepancy	arrangement	consignment	mechanized
computorized	percentage	transaction	deliberately
resistance	policy	techniques	routine
inventory	courteous	electronic	absenteeism
application	mechanism	horizontal	diameter

[8] Copyright 1971 by Robert C. Aukerman.

Alternative Form B

maintenance	potential	unethical	dependability
manufacturer	workmanship	discrimination	concessions
established	destination	justified	consolidate
demonstrator	seasonally	allowance	disadvantage
misunderstanding	confirmation	reconsider	reasonable
automatic	arrangements	diagram	processing
suspension	placement	combination	replacement
automotive	accomplished	requirements	fluctuations
mechanism	determining	thicknesses	inclination
clearance	projection	appreciable	residual
specifications	approximate	accessories	appropriate

Alternative Form C

compulsory	unconditionally	representation	charitable
reasonable	indebtedness	indorsement	contractual
collective	independent	bargaining	authorized
reputable	comprehensive	residential	contending
mechanization	dimensions	measurements	lengthening
application	intersection	horizontally	fluctuating
determine	arrangement	graduated	construction
advantageous	supervision	integrity	accommodations
merchandise	eliminating	specialized	proprietorship
preferences	suburban	neighborhood	departmental
equipment	minimize	adjustments	personality

READABILITY OF BUSINESS, INDUSTRIAL ARTS, AND VOCATIONAL TEXTBOOKS

Because a large percentage of students in business, industrial arts, and vocational education classes will not go on to college, most authors of textbooks in those subjects, although many of them are not acquainted with the concept of "readability," have made a conscious effort to produce relatively easy materials. They know that students in these subjects are often poor readers.

Despite these efforts, however, there still remain considerable differences in readability, and there are no definitive standards for, say, eighth-grade texts as opposed to eleventh-grade texts. It appears that there is no consistency, because the authors are not reading specialists and follow no specific guidelines for length or complexity of sentences, or for difficulty of vocabulary.

Given this situation, there are some choices open to teachers in business, industrial arts, and vocational subjects. The textbooks may be classified by means of the check points noted in Chapter 3. The result will be a listing of available texts ranked from "easy" to "difficult," from which the department may select texts appropriate for the students in particular classes.

Factors in the Sales Load

Many factors enter into what may be called the *sales load*, the amount of selling effort required to make a sale. The amount of customer assistance required for a given sale depends on many things called "sales variables" which may be grouped under (1) the product, (2) the store, (3) the competition, (4) the salesperson, and (5) the customer. Understanding the *sales variables*, factors contributing to the difficulty of a sale, helps the salesperson in adapting his sales presentation to his customer.

Benefits from Understanding the Sales Variables.   When you understand the sales variables, you will be in a good position to size up a sales load. As a result, you should: (1) be able to do a better job of planning sales presentations, (2) have a clearer idea of the relative position of the various occupations in the retail sales hierarchy, (3) know what kinds of jobs may be considered advancements over others, (4) have a better understanding of the relationship of your job to other sales positions, (5) be able to decide what sales practices are best suited to the kind of selling you do, and (6) have a better understanding of the reasons for differences in remuneration for sales occupations.

Variable Group 1: The Product

The first sales variable is the nature of the product. Obviously, it is more difficult to sell an adding machine than a box of breakfast cereal. The adding machine is an example of *business goods*, products usually used in the operation of a business. Breakfast cereal is an example of *consumer goods*, products used by ultimate consumers. The purchasers of these two kinds of goods buy for entirely different reasons—one to improve business efficiency, the other for personal satisfaction. Business goods are usually purchased by trained, cautious buyers who, as compared to consumer-purchasers, strike a hard bargain.

Within the consumer-goods classification, there are convenience goods, shopping goods, and specialty goods. The nature of these goods was described in Unit 7 on pages 147–148 along with the need for the salesperson's having product information about them.

Another consideration in exploring the sales variables as these relate to the product is the classification of merchandise lines into "hard lines, soft lines, and foods." Durable goods—such as hardware, appliances, furniture, and electrical supplies—make up the *hard lines*. Textile merchandise—such as ready-to-wear, fabrics and domestics, along with shoes—is known as *soft-lines* merchandise. Dry groceries, produce, meats, dairy and bakery products are examples of *food-line* merchandise. Soft lines and foods are considered to be nondurable goods. Each kind of merchandise has its characteristic sales practices that influence the weight of the sales load.

In retailing, the need for technical product information plays an important part in determining the sales load. For example, the electric-appliance salesman needs a great deal more technical product knowledge than does the person

226   *Unit 10* ■ *Becoming a Consumer Consultant*

SOURCE: From Retailing: Principles and Practices, by G. Henry Richert, Warren G. Meyer, and Peter G. Haines, McGraw-Hill, Gregg Division, New York, 1962, p. 226. Copyright © 1962. Used with permission of McGraw-Hill Book Company.

A passage taken from a text in retailing (reproduced on page 258) will serve to illustrate the significance of readability. The difficulty encountered in this particular selection is such that many "general business" students could not possibly achieve adequate comprehension. The text is one of the most popular in the field, having gone through four editions over a period of more than twenty-five years; nevertheless, its use in a classroom which includes poor readers would certainly call for special reading instruction by the teacher. To provide a five-hundred word sample from this section of the text, thirty words must be added from page 227. Our sample then contains 22 sentences; the average sentence length is almost 23 words. One sentence has 90 words, one has 34 words, and one has 33 words. Such lengths are excessive; they are difficult even for proficient readers. Because of the sentence length, readability should be rated "high."

Half of the sentences contain complex construction, and at least two are in reverse order. Such a high degree of complexity is a serious problem to poor readers. On this factor, too, then, the level of readability must be rated "high."

Vocabulary is also difficult; difficult words make up 15 percent of the sample. The nature of the material lends itself to the use of specialized and somewhat technical vocabulary. A few are listed below to indicate the nature of the vocabulary; besides those cited, fifty other difficult words are used.

assistance	variables
competition	contributing
hierarchy	advancements
efficiency	classification
cautious	convenience
determining	consequently
installation	maintenance
characteristic	

The incidence of abstraction is also high, with such terms as the following appearing: *factors, sales variables, sales load, nondurable, relative position, sales hierarchy, hard bargain*. Some of these terms are explained within the context; others are not.

The readability level of the selection is thus extremely high. On the other hand, the text is comprehensive, factual, and thorough, and for those reasons it appeals to the teacher. It is virtually a handbook on retailing and merchandising management. If one assumes that students in retailing are highly motivated to becoming top sales people and store owners, there would be good reason to use such a text. If, on the other hand, the teacher assesses the reading ability of his students and finds some who are potential failures, some alternative must be found for these poorer readers. The only acceptable solution is to use reading materials appropriate to the different reading abilities of the students. Enough textbooks and supplementary handbooks are available so that the classroom teacher can provide materials at several readability levels in most subjects. In the more technical subjects, however, it is a miscarriage of educational justice to expect students of low intelligence or low reading ability to succeed at all. Indeed, some of the textbooks for very technical subjects—such as the mechanical drawing text cited previously—are suitable only for gifted students attending highly selective technical high schools (such as Cass Technical High School in Detroit, which is the high school equivalent of M.I.T.).

ENRICHMENT MATERIALS

Teachers sometimes believe, erroneously, that students who cannot read textbooks can read newspapers and magazines. This is not necessarily true. In fact, most reputable newspapers and periodicals are written at the sixth-grade level, or higher. The readability of *Popular Mechanics,* for example, is far from low; *Mechanics Illustrated* is also of average or above-average reading difficulty. Still, trade journals and trade newspapers are often appropriate for very poor readers, since they do provide the motivation of current news. In addition, nonacademic students are often more attracted to them than to general news media. They therefore provide the most likely medium of reading for poor readers in nonacademic classes. The classroom teacher should utilize as many trade journals as possible.

A number of very good novels appropriate for use in vocations or careers classes are also available. They usually present a hero or heroine who is successful in a career. Such books are of high interest and low readability and have the added feature of furnishing a "significant other" with whom the non-academic reader may identify. A few such novels are: Zelda Bates's *Roses Are Blue* (florist); Harriet Hubbell's *The Friendship Tree* (workers with disturbed children); Lucy Graves Mayo's *Wendy Scott, Secretary* (office work); Harry Neal's *Nature's Guardians* (conservationists); Phyllis Whitney's *The Highest Dream* (guide at the U.N.); Lee Wyndham's *Lady Architect.*

Librarians who are aware that a classroom teacher is interested in providing easy enrichments books for poor readers among the nonacademic students will work long extra hours to arrange for the acquisition of such books. Only by working to obtain such books, of high interest and low readability, can a classroom teacher reach many of the poorer readers in business education, industrial arts, and vocational classes.

CONCLUSIONS

Business, industrial arts, and vocational classrooms are quite similar to other subject areas of the secondary school in that they are most often textbook-oriented. Moreover, the textbooks are organized according to units and chapters, much the same as texts in history, science, home economics, and so on.

Reliance on reading as the medium of learning produces some very serious problems for the classroom teacher. Students in these areas have the reputation of being less motivated academically and of lower academic ability than students in the college-preparation curriculum. They have often met with failure in their reading assignments. The high readability of many textbooks in business, industrial arts, and vocational education confronts the students with a situation in which reading failure is probable.

The classroom teacher can increase the students' achievement by applying the survey technique (described in Chapter 4) to the many textbooks which are structured in a way that makes this technique appropriate. Reading for main ideas is called for by some materials. Most important, perhaps, is the ability to follow directions.

The readability of textbooks should be assessed, and those which are too difficult should be replaced by texts that are appropriate for the students who will be using them. Materials of low readability but high interest provide motivation. Those which hold the most promise are the trade journals and novels about vocations and careers.

Probably in no other area of the curriculum is reading such a problem as in the nonacademic subjects. Many, though of course not all, of the students enrolled in business, industrial arts, and vocational classrooms have had considerable experience with failure. The classroom teacher has a wonderful opportunity to change this, to provide experiences of success by providing texts of high interest and low readability—materials relevant to the subject and the interests of the students.

Questions and Activities for Discussion and Growth

1. Select a textbook in office practices and develop a reading lesson using the survey technique (see Chapter 4).
2. Select a textbook in automobile mechanics and plan a reading assignment according to the suggestions for lesson plans in Chapter 6. Be sure to observe the various aspects of the reading assignment. Give the assignment to an automobile shop class and observe the students' reactions. Then follow through and note the results.
3. Make an annotated list of many books and booklets on various vocations. Classify the books according to categories of vocations and according to readability, (see Chapter 3). When the list is long enough, check with the librarian to be certain that there are an adequate number of copies available in the library. Use the list—and have the books and booklets in the classroom for the students to use.

4. Make transparencies for the overhead projector, similar to those described in this chapter. Their objective will be to help the students improve their reading of a particular text.

5. Select one part of a chapter in a text in business or industrial arts— preferably one the majority of students have trouble reading. Make a tape recording of this reading material, along with directions that will help the students as they read the same material in their texts. Choose a small group of students and try the tape out with them, having them use their texts along with the tape. What results did you obtain? What may be improved? What should be discarded? Give reasons that seem to be valid.

6. Write to the following publishers for their latest catalogue of books on vocations and careers:

> Henry Z. Walck
> 19 Union Square
> New York, New York 10003
>
> E. P. Dutton & Co., Inc.
> 201 Park Avenue South
> New York, New York 10003
>
> Julian Messner, Publishers, Inc.
> 8 West 40 Street
> New York, New York 10018

Classify the titles you obtain and ask your librarian to acquire the books for your vocations class. Evaluate their readability.

7. Go to a wholesale magazine distributor and ask for sample copies of old trade publications. He will provide you with a sampling of journals for many trades, occupations, technologies, and businesses. Look those over and select some that you would like to have regularly for your industrial arts, business, or careers class and ask the administration of your school to order them.

8. Give the Prognostic Test of Reading Disability in Secondary School Business, Industrial Arts, and Vocational Subjects to as many students as possible. What results do you observe? What are the implications of your results?

9. Choose three textbooks from the same specific area (for example, wood-working, office practices, or general business), and compare their levels of readability, using the method of assessment suggested in Chapter 3. Rank them according to difficulty.

10. Plan several sessions of "individualized reading" for a class. Provide a "free selection" of some of the novels in the field of business, industrial arts, and careers. What choices seem to be most popular? Take action, with your librarian, on the basis of your findings.

Selected References

Coston, Frederick E.: "Reading and Vocational Education," in International Reading Association, *Fusing Reading Skills and Content,* Newark, Delaware, 1969, pp. 145–150.

Haehn, Faynelle: "Let's Have a 'Read-In' in Typewriting," in International Reading Association, *Fusing Reading Skills and Content,* Newark, Delaware, 1969, pp. 69–74.

Hafner, Lawrence E., Wayne Gwatney, and Richard Robinson: "Reading in Bookkeeping: Predictions and Performance," *Journal of Reading,* vol. 14, no. 8 (May, 1971), pp. 537–546.

Harris, Robert L.: "Salvaging Failures Through Improved Reading: Reading in Vocational Classes," Claremont Reading Conference, *29th Yearbook,* Claremont, California, 1965, pp. 160–167.

Harrison, Lincoln J.: "Teaching Accounting Students to Read," *Journal of Business Education,* vol. 35 (January, 1960), pp. 168–170.

Levine, Isidore N.: "Solving Reading Problems in Vocational Subjects," *High Points,* vol. XLIII (April, 1960), pp. 10–27.

Mehrer, Ron: "Improving Reading Ability of Vocational Agricultural Students," *The Agricultural Education Magazine,* vol. 32 (October, 1959), pp. 81–82.

Musselman, Vernon A.: "The Reading Problem in Teaching Bookkeeping," *Business Education Forum,* vol. XIV (December, 1959), pp. 5–7.

Robinson, Richard D.: "Business Teachers Are Reading Teachers," *Journal of Business Education,* vol. 44 (February, 1969), pp. 201–202.

Wood, Marion: "Help Your Students Develop Their Reading Skills," *Business Education World,* vol. XLIII (May, 1963), pp. 33–35.

12.
READING IN THE HOME ECONOMICS CLASSROOM

Home economics has far too frequently been classed together with shop, mechanical drawing, and other vocational skills. This reveals a certain ignorance of the nature of the home economics curriculum today. No longer are millinery, sewing, and cooking the elements of home economics, as they were half a century ago. Instead, the content of home economics is now generally divided into the following six categories: (1) home management and consumer education; (2) personal growth and personal relationships; (3) child growth and child care; (4) foods, nutrition, and health; (5) clothing and textiles; (6) housing and home furnishings. [1] These six categories may be varied, condensed, or expanded, but in any event home economics content today is overwhelmingly verbal in nature, rather than manual. The implication is obvious: if a student is to succeed in home economics, she must master the verbal content of home economics textbooks. The skills necessary for reading those materials must be taught by the home economics teacher. *No one else* is going to do the job.

[1] See the home economics curriculum guides available from the various state departments of education. The listing given here was taken from the Ohio guide, 1966.

THE BEHAVIORAL OBJECTIVES OF HOME ECONOMICS

The quality of individual and family life is the focus of all home economics textual materials today. The objectives of courses are interwoven strands including self-knowledge, self-fulfilment, efficiency as a consumer and planner, ability to weigh alternatives and make decisions, knowledge of health and safety practices, and the enhancement of personal relationships. Objectives in home economics for grades 7 through 9 and 10 through 12 were formulated by the staff of the UCLA Center for the Study of Evaluation under a USOE grant and published in 1970 in two pamphlets as part of the Instructional Objectives Exchange. The major concern of the Exchange was to design items for testing the student's acquisition of skills entailed by the behavioral objectives. In most cases, this means that the objective must be of a nature that can be tested by means of objective questions or mechanical performances. The Exchange delineated seventy-four objectives[2] for junior high school home economics.

In child growth and care, objectives include the identification of a developmental task; matching play functions with developmental tasks; analysis of appropriate conduct of a baby-sitter; selection of the best solution to a behavior problem.

Behavioral objectives in clothing and textiles include the ability to identify colors and fabrics and their origins; understanding of weaves, finishes, printing, and dyeing; ability to select clothing wisely; skill in design and construction of clothing; and care of textiles and clothing.

In foods and nutrition, the ability to identify the four basic foods and an understanding of the relationship among them remain the primary objectives, as they have been for many years. A secondary objective, listed for junior high school, actually seems more appropriate for students in senior high school: grading and classification of poultry and basic meat cuts. Knowledge of multi-ethnic foods is an objective described in some detail. A third major area within this category is the efficient preparation of foods and care of food equipment.

In the area of home management and family economics, knowledge of good manners and behavior is the first group of objectives listed, but efficient home management is really the primary objective.

The list of forty-one objectives[3] for senior high school calls for thinking at a high level and for problem-solving ability. For most of the objectives, a case study is given, and the objective includes selecting the appropriate action for the situation presented. For example, the student must be able to select appropriate rewards or punishments for hypothesized children's behavior; make decisions regarding clothing; decide on procedures for laundry; apply principles of family management; demonstrate ability to do financial planning;

[2] Instructional Objectives Exchange, *Home Economics, Grades 7–9*, UCLA, 1970.
[3] Instructional Objectives Exchange, *Home Economics, Grades 10–12*, UCLA, 1970.

make decisions about housing allotments and interior arrangements; and acquire an understanding of human reproductive systems, pregnancy, and birth.

The textbooks that provide the basic information necessary for attaining such objectives must, obviously, be verbally descriptive; the attainment of these goals must therefore depend upon the reading ability of the students and the readability of the texts.

HOME ECONOMICS TEXTBOOKS

Today's home economics classrooms are textbook-oriented. The content of the texts is structured according to three major patterns: (1) factual information, (2) discussion of problems, and (3) how-to-do-it directions. The textbooks provide the means for attaining the behavioral objectives and are the medium of instruction.

1. Factual Information

Books containing factual information exclusively tend to be a minor part of the curriculum. They are more often used as supplementary resource materials

---

Professional Nurses

About two-thirds of the professional nurses work in hospitals. Most of them are general-duty nurses who perform skilled bedside nursing, such as caring for patients after an operation, assisting with blood transfusions, and giving medication. They also observe, evaluate, and record such symptoms as temperature, blood pressure, and pulse. Some hospital nurses work primarily in operating rooms. Others limit their work to certain types of patients, such as children, the elderly, or the mentally ill.

In 1966 about 65,000 persons were private-duty nurses who cared for patients in hospitals and private homes. These nurses are employed by the patients whom they are nursing or by members of their families. They provide intensive care of one patient at a time, following the orders of the patient's physician. Nearly 50,000 nurses were employed in offices of physicians and dental surgeons. Such nurses assist with examinations and sterilize instruments. Sometimes they also have such office duties as making appointments and helping maintain patients' records. Public-health nurses in government agencies, visiting nurses' associations, and clinics, numbered nearly 40,000.

Licensed Practical Nurses

Under the direction of physicians and professional nurses, licensed practical nurses provide nursing care which requires technical knowledge but not the technical training of registered nurses. In hospitals they provide much of the bedside care needed by patients whose illnesses are not at a critical stage. They change dressings, administer certain prescribed medicines, and bathe patients. They may also give injections and assist physicians and professional nurses in examining patients. Some licensed practical nurses are employed in private homes to care for patients. In addition to providing nursing care, they may prepare the patient's meals, keep the rooms tidy, and teach family members to perform simple nursing tasks.

SOURCE: Reprinted by permission from Occupations and Careers, by S. Norman Feingold and Sol Swerdloff, McGraw-Hill, Webster Division, St. Louis, 1969, p. 155. Copyright © 1969 by McGraw-Hill, Inc.

✳ PLASTICS

BASIC FAMILIES
OF PLASTICS

The variety that makes plastics so useful divides the materials into eleven basic groups of family members.

Acrylic (*a·kr̃il'ĭc*), Acrylic plastic is a thermoplastic material introduced commercially in the United States in 1939.

It is used for watch crystals, compacts, TV and camera lenses, dentures, eyeglass frames, surgical instruments, outdoor signs, automotive taillights, book ends, light fixtures, costume jewelry, roofing, lamp bases, buttons, shower doors, and partitions.

Acrylic is strong and may be colorless or in many colors; transparent, translucent, or opaque. It resists weather and water, is an excellent insulator, is warm and pleasant to the touch, odorless, tasteless, nontoxic, and possesses exceptional clarity and good light transmission.

It should be hand washed with mild soap and lukewarm water. Abrasive and cleaning fluids should not be used in the cleaning of acrylic plastics.

Cellulosics (sĕl·u·lō'siks). There are four types of cellulosics, all thermoplastic:

1. *Cellulose acetate,* developed in 1927, is used in lamp shades, toys, vacuum-cleaner parts, and combs.
2. *Butyrate,* developed in 1938, is used in steering wheels, portable-radio cases, tool handles, pipes, and tubings.
3. *Nitrate,* developed in 1868, is used in shoe-heel covers and as a fabric coating.
4. *Ethyl cellulose,* developed in 1935, is favored for edge molding on cabinets, flashlights, electrical parts, and outdoor sporting goods.

The four types have certain features in common. They may be colorless, transparent, translucent, or opaque in a wide variety of colors. They are strong and durable. Normally rough usage will not break cellulose parts. They will withstand moderate heat. They have good electrical properties and are suitable insulators against normal domestic and industrial currents.

Cellulosic plastics may be washed with warm water and mild soap. Abrasives should not be used. Cleaning fluids should not be used on butyrate and ethyl cellulose.

Melamine and Urea (mĕl'a·mēn; u·rē'a). Melamine is a thermosetting material, developed in 1939, which is familiar in colorful dinnerware. It is also used for buttons, hearing-aid cases, table tops, and cutlery handles. Urea, developed in 1929, is thermosetting and used in radio cabinets, buttons, bottle tops, electric plugs, wall plates, appliances, stove knobs and handles.

Both melamine and urea offer a full range of translucent and opaque colors—colors that are light-fast. They are strong but not unbreakable. They perform satisfactorily over a wide temperature range and have good electrical qualities.

Melamine and urea plastics can be washed in very hot water, in dishwashers, using soap or detergents. Cleaning fluids can be used on them. These plastics should not be used in an oven or over a flame, as discoloration or charring may occur; however, neither will burn or soften in contact with a flame. Abrasives should not be used.

Nylon. Nylon, developed in 1938, is a thermoplastic material used for tumblers, slide fasteners, faucet washers, gears, combs, and funnels. It is used as a filament in brush bristles and fishing lines.

than as texts, although sometimes an entire course will be based on a particular factual text. Two examples of such texts are *Occupations and Careers* and *Facts About Merchandise*. Excerpts from these books are reproduced on pages 267 and 268. The preface to *Facts About Merchandise* states that its basic purpose is "to provide up-to-date information about products sold in the retail market." Texts or supplementary books which are concerned with providing this sort of information are necessarily descriptive and consequently are greatly affected by the degree of awareness and skill their authors and editors brought to bear on controlling the level of readability. The excerpts from our two examples will indicate the nature of factual content and typical formats for its presentation.

In these examples, three factors are important: (1) vocabulary, (2) readability, and (3) how much memorization is called for. The readability of home economics texts and the vocabulary load characteristic of them will be discussed at length later. Memorization is characteristically called for by any factual, informational book, regardless of its content. For memorization to become cognitive learning, there must be exposure to reality as well as to words on a page. Pronouncing words and memorizing specialized vocabulary does **not** by itself constitute reading for understanding. Reading should imply comprehension, knowing, and cognitive learning, and these depend upon experiencing. The task of the classroom teacher is to provide the materials and experiences necessary to ensure reading comprehension.

2. Discussion of Problems

Most home economics textbooks are primarily interested in discussing the problems which adolescents face in their high school years. Those problems essentially have to do with one's own personality and with interpersonal relationships. Textual discussion of such matters necessarily must utilize the readers' past experiences. Because experiences differ greatly from person to person, from one social class to another, and from one region to another, one would expect universal problems to generate the greatest interest and response in any heterogeneous group. Some home economics textbooks are consequently oriented toward such universal problems. One of the most popular, now in its third edition, provides a good example of material that is relevant to teen-agers; a passage is reproduced on page 270.

The reading task in problem-oriented textbooks is usually not complicated by specialized vocabulary, abstract concepts, or complicated directions. It is usually straight talk. However, two problems may cause trouble in reading. First, authors may lack knowledge concerning factors of readability, so that sentence construction and general vocabulary may be beyond most readers. Second, there may be discussion of problems that are not really relevant to today's youth. This is not only an obstacle to reading but also destroys motivation and prevents involvement in the material.

Shelton from Monkmeyer

In dating, each learns the other's moods, interests, role conceptions, and ways of thinking, all of which will be useful in choosing a life partner.

cannot make up for an unpleasant disposition or poor sportsmanship in a girl.

This period of "playing the field," or dating a number of different boys or girls, may go on for a few months or several years, but after a while one begins to discover that certain kinds of people always make for more enjoyable dates than do others. These dating discoveries are important in revealing the traits common to many members of the opposite sex. They tell a person a great deal about himself, too, and what kind of mate it will take to satisfy him. What one likes or dislikes in his dates is actually a reflection of his own personality and background.

HANDICAPS TO DATING

During the early teen years many take no part in dating. Even in later teens there are those who for one reason or another do not date or seldom date. And there are those who will eventually marry the first person they ever date.

The No-dates Teen-ager

Critics of the dating system feel that it is unjust to some because they have no chance

WHAT'S WRONG WITH THE OPPOSITE SEX IN DATING?

(Based on a Purdue University study of 8,000 teen-agers)

Girls say of boys:
1. Careless and thoughtless
2. Less inhibited
3. More disrespectful
4. Sex-driven
5. Loud
Are they, in your opinion, too critical?

Boys say of girls:
1. Less natural than boys
2. More touchy
3. Money-minded
4. Unresponsive
5. Childish and flighty
Are they, in your opinion, too critical?

Who is to blame for failure to get along on a date? According to the study:

Boys blamed girls.

Girls blamed themselves or a girl rival.

Which group do you think is the more honest here? On what do you base your opinion?

to date. What about the no-date teen-ager? Is this a serious matter?

Many a boy or girl who doesn't date doesn't even want to. They are not going to be pushed into it just because everyone else seems to be dating. Boys particularly lag in dating during the early teens.

But what about the girl who is ready to date but doesn't get asked? Part of her problem is the relative slowness of boys in growing up. There are not enough dating-minded boys to go around.

113

SOURCE: Paul H. Landis, Your Marriage and Family Living, 3d ed., McGraw-Hill, Webster Division, St. Louis, 1969, p. 113. Copyright © 1969. Reprinted by permission of McGraw-Hill, Inc.

3. Directions

Some modern home economics texts, like many in the past, are books of directions on such matters as how to prepare meals, how to entertain, how to make a budget, and how to sew a skirt. Texts of this sort are also verbal in nature and represent a wide range in levels of readability, from very easy to very difficult. The differences are caused by the manner in which the directions are worded. Fortunately, most how-to-do-it home economics books are written in straightforward, simple terms: "When meat is served with a sauce over it, vegetables should be plain." "Avoid drawing pictures for a child." "Keep all spending records to compare with those for previous months and years." "Check the length of the opening for the zipper."

Hurlock's *Child Growth and Development,* now in its fourth edition and one of the most successful texts in home economics, is essentially a book of directions telling what *should* be done and *why.* The words *should* and *because* are the two keys to understanding the author's point of view and the structure of the writing. An excerpt will illustrate this characteristic, which is common to many home economics texts.

Learning to pronounce words. The first task in learning to talk is the very difficult skill of pronouncing words correctly. The child learns to pronounce his words by imitation. This is difficult because, even though the child may hear the word correctly, he cannot always control his tongue and lip muscles well enough to reproduce accurately the word he has just heard.

Because of this difficulty, the child should be encouraged to try again and to keep on trying until he can say the word correctly. Before each trial, it is better to repeat the word for him so that he will have the correct sound clearly in mind as a model to imitate. It may require several days of persistent trying on the child's part, with help from the parent, to accomplish his goal.

In learning any new skill, there are certain to be errors at first. These errors should not be overlooked nor should there be the assumption that the child will outgrow them in time. Even more serious, they must never be encouraged because they are cute. They should be corrected early, and constant attention should be given by an adult to make sure that the child's errors are not repeated often enough to settle into a habit.

SOURCE: Elizabeth B. Hurlock, Child Growth and Development, McGraw-Hill Book Company, Webster Division, St. Louis, 1970, p. 188.

An examination of the various how-to-do-it texts indicates that difficulty in reading occurs chiefly when paragraphs are long. This problem can be easily overcome by having the students separate each long paragraph into groups of sentences, or single sentences, that present one concept. Here is an example:

Storage. Are your storage spaces used economically? Do a little research to see how efficiently each square foot is used. Most textbooks show elaborate setups for this, requiring more facilities, perhaps, than any householder could ever *manage successfully.* So think of the practical side: work systematically, with well-organized methods. First, *list* your belongings by groups as you take them from their original places. Next, *discard* things that have lost their value to you—but do not throw anything away just to have more room. *Pack* the "keepsakes" in cartons, labeled for identification. Then, look through your *storage drawers.* Can you divide them into sections to help keep articles in groups? A lumberyard employee will help you make dividers, or you can tape heavy cardboard in to make inexpensive sections. Gloves, scarves, cosmetics, and other accessories can be put in shallow boxes without lids and then placed in drawers. Notice the illustrations to help keep belongings neatly arranged and easily accessible. *Now put away* your belongings. Some of your possessions will go back into the same old places; others will be put into new places.

SOURCE: Margaret Raines, Managing Livingtime, Chas. A. Bennett Co., Inc., Peoria, Ill., 1964, pp. 178–179.

This paragraph should be divided so that its contents can be visualized. This may be done by printing the sentences on tagboard strips and arranging them on the chalkboard, or by using transparencies made by the teacher for the overhead projector, programmed in a series of overlays. Either method is simple and will greatly help in providing a visual image of the structure of the paragraph. The paragraph could be divided thus:

> **Storage:** Are your storage spaces used economically?
> Do a little research to see how efficiently each square foot is used.
> Most textbooks show elaborate setups for this, requiring more facilities, perhaps, than any householder could ever manage successfully.
> So think of the practical side: work systematically, with well-organized methods.
> 1. **List.** First, list your belongings by groups as you take them from their original places.
> 2. **Discard.** Next, discard things that have lost their value to you—but do not throw anything away just to have more room. Pack the "keepsakes" in cartons, labeled for identification.
> 3. **Organize storage.** Third, look through your storage drawers. Can you divide them into sections to help keep articles in groups?
> A lumberyard employee will help you make dividers, or you can tape in heavy cardboard to make inexpensive sections.
> Gloves, scarves, cosmetics, and other accessories can be put in shallow boxes without lids and then placed in drawers. Notice the illustrations; they show how to keep belongings neatly arranged and easily accessible.
> 4. **Put away.** Fourth and finally, put away your belongings. Some of your possessions will go back into the same old places; others will be put into new places.

CARE OF HANDBAGS

Avoid carrying too many articles in your handbag or purse.

Keep the inside of your bag clean by brushing or wiping the lining frequently.

Brush bags made of cloth or suede.

Clean scuffed places on leather bags with shoe polish.

Use white shoe polish or a cleaning fluid to clean white leather bags that cannot be washed.

To wash a leather bag, go over it lightly with a soapy cloth or sponge, rinse with a cloth wrung out in clear water, and polish with a dry cloth.

Before putting a bag away, remove the contents, stuff the bag with tissue paper, and place a covering over it.

DAILY CARE OF CLOTHES

1. Upon arriving home, brush your jacket or coat and hang it in the closet. If it is wet, place it on a hanger and let it dry before putting it away. Then change to other clothes.

2. When you put on and take off clothes, do so with care to avoid stretching, ripping, or soiling them. If you are wearing pins or clips, remove them before taking off your dress. Replace them after you have put on the dress next time.

3. When you take off a dress or sweater that does not unbutton down the front, lift it carefully over your head, easing the sleeves and waistline portion so that they slip up without tearing. Bend over so that you can grasp the skirt of the dress, and bring the whole garment up over your shoulders and head.

4. Put on and take off skirts over your head. This is a better method than stepping into them, especially if the floor is dusty and your slip or petticoat is full.

5. Hang coats, dresses, blouses, and skirts on hangers, never on hooks or nails. Take time to put a garment on a hanger properly, adjusting shoulder lines and collars.

6. If the garment will not be worn again very soon, protect it from dust with a cloth or plastic cover.

7. Remove spots on clothes as soon as possible.

8. Air your sweater after removing it. Then fold it and put it into a dresser drawer, so it will not stretch.

9. Place dirty clothes in a clothes hamper or laundry bag, drying them first if necessary.

10. Before going to bed, see that the clothes to be worn the next day are clean, pressed, and laid out or hung up within easy reach.

11. Polish shoes the night before wearing them or just before putting them on.

CARE OF JEWELRY

Wash costume jewelry by dipping it quickly into warm suds and wiping dry.

Brighten dull-looking jewelry with colorless nail polish.

Keep costume jewelry in a box or drawer with separate compartments, so it will not become scratched or tangled.

CARE FOR CLOTHES AS YOU WEAR THEM

1. Avoid carrying bulky or heavy objects in your pockets.

2. Keep your hands out of your pockets.

3. Pull up a tight skirt slightly before sitting down.

4. Protect your clothing from food stains or spots by wearing an apron when cooking, by using a napkin during meals, and by sitting up straight at the table. Before sitting down in a place where food is served, look at the chair seat to be sure that no food has been spilled on it.

5. Unfasten a fitted suit jacket when you are seated. To avoid wrinkling it, adjust or straighten your skirt and the back of your jacket as you are seated.

6. When you are lounging or lying down, take off your dress so that it will not get wrinkled.

92

SOURCE: Reprinted by permission from Teen Guide to Homemaking, by Marion S. Barclay and Frances Champion, McGraw-Hill, Webster Division, St. Louis, 1961, p. 92. Copyright © 1961 by McGraw-Hill, Inc.

Many home economics texts, like the passage just discussed, are outright do-it-yourself manuals. For example, preface to *Teen Guide to Homemaking* identifies its objectives as follows: "Young high school girls, as well as some of their teen-age brothers, have immediate need for many how-to-do-it experiences . . . " The passage reproduced above is an example of the highly structured format characteristic of this type of home economics text. When such a format is encountered, the reading skills of the learners should be developed accordingly. To deal with reading material based on facts and directions, the readers should be aware of the format: *do this; now do this; then do this.* This will ensure better understanding of the content.

USING THE SURVEY TECHNIQUE

The survey technique (described in Chapter 4) is an excellent way to help disabled readers and poor readers acquire some meaning from the printed page. The survey is also the most important means of providing for students of all abilities an overview of the structure and contents of a chapter in home economics. All three types of home economics texts—factual, problematical, and directional—lend themselves to the survey technique of reading. Most, if not all, home economics textbooks have a format admirably suited to the survey technique. One example[4] will indicate how easily the survey may be applied:

> Chapter 6: Children Learn Through Activities (The chapter title is printed in red.)
> Introductory statement: "In this chapter we shall discuss activities . . . "
> PLAY (Subtitle, printed in red.)
> **Values of Play** (Second-level heading; boldface.)
> *Learning in play is the foundation for intellectual development.* (Third-level head; italicized.)
> *Play is a way to deal with anxieties.*
> *Play is also a way of expressing and communicating ideas and feelings.*
> LANGUAGE (Etc.)

When a chapter has a format like this, the survey alone will supply a framework for either discussion or reading. In the text we have just quoted, the carefully chosen illustrations tell the main points and subordinate ideas almost by themselves; the captions are short and pertinent. For each section of the chapter, suggested activities are set in boxes. Each section also has a summary of five things to do to ensure that the reader will learn through the particular activity being discussed.

The teacher should seek out such well-edited books. Their use will improve reading in the home economics classroom, for they are "naturals" for the survey technique. The selection from a text on foods and nutrition reproduced on page 275 is an example of the type of material that should always be introduced through the survey. The page layout in this selection provides an opportunity to visualize the structure. The running head is a clue that the information presented is related to the general topic "Breakfast." The section heading, "Pointers on Fruits," is accompanied by a border of fruits (not shown here), which may be used for motivation (the students may be challenged to identify the nine fruits shown.) The two subheadings on this page are "Fruit Juices" and "Fruits"; the latter is followed by sub-subheadings in italics. The entire section is structured in this manner. A survey which includes the headings and subheadings will provide a thorough preview of the topic, with *clues to content* and "set" or readiness for reading. A fifteen- or twenty-minute survey, using the

---

[4]Katherine R. Baker and Xenia F. Fane, *Understanding and Guiding Young Children,* Prentice-Hall, Inc., Englewood Cliffs, N.J., 1967. This is the format of Chapter 6.

POINTERS ON FRUITS

Fruits can be served at any meal. Eaten "out of hand," they are excellent as snack foods. Breakfast without fruit in one form or another seems incomplete to most Americans.

Because breakfasts are likely to be hurry-up meals, we prefer fruit juices or easy-to-eat fruits.

If we don't drink our fruit as juice, we are likely to eat it with our cereal. Sliced bananas, sliced peaches, strawberries, blueberries, and red raspberries are favorites with both cooked and ready-to-eat cereals.

Easy-to-eat fruits are cooked prunes, apricots, applesauce, sliced fresh oranges, melons, and fruit cups consisting of pieces of canned or fresh fruits.

When we enjoy a leisurely breakfast we may offer strawberries with the hulls left on, cherries unstemmed and unpitted, broiled grapefruit, or baked apples.

Fruit Juices

Most popular is orange juice—which may be freshly extracted, may be canned, may come shipped in cartons, or may be a diluted fresh-frozen concentrate. It's fortunate that we like orange juice, because it is rich in vitamin C. That's a vitamin, remember, not stored in the body, so every day we need a fresh supply.

Other fruit juices are: pineapple, tangerine, grapefruit, cranberry, apple, grape, and various combinations of any or all of these with each other or with lemon or orange juice.

Nectars are commercially canned fruit juices with some sieved pulp included; they may be diluted with other juices which have been strained.

Fruits

Apples. These may appear on the breakfast table in the form of applesauce or baked apples. Slices may be cooked with granular cereals (see *Pointers on Cereal Cookery*).

Bananas. The fruit is peeled, stringy fibers are removed, and the fruit is sliced. Because the cut surface darkens when exposed to air, it is good practice to slice the fruit just before serving, or, if that is impossible, to dip the slices into pineapple juice, into a sugar and water syrup, or into acidulated water.

Berries. The most popular ones are strawberries, blueberries, and red raspberries. Raspberries and strawberries are fragile. Wash them gently in warm water, drain, and pick them over. Hull strawberries. Sweeten or not, as desired . . .

SOURCE: From YOUR FOODS BOOK, by Florence L. C. G. Harris and Rex T. Withers, copyright © 1966 by D. C. Heath and Company, Boston, Mass., p. 223.

textbook with the entire class, will result in significantly better reading comprehension than would be obtained from the bare assignment of pages 223–230.

This particular book, however, does present some problems of readability. Reading difficulty is not unusual in home economics texts, for in general they are not written or edited by reading specialists. Examples of difficult material may be found on page 223 of *Your Foods Book.* The main problem is complexity and length of sentences. The following sentence, under heading "Bananas," is a case in point:

> Because the cut surface darkens when exposed to air, it is good practice to slice the fruit just before serving, or, if that is impossible, to dip the slices into pineapple juice, into a sugar and water syrup, or into acidulated water.

One way to handle a sentence like this, which states several alternatives, is to have the class break it down into its component parts. These should be printed by the teacher on large cardboard strips with a felt pen; each strip may then be affixed to the chalkboard or to any other surface in the room by means of one of the plastic adhesives (such as "Plasti-Tak"). After they have analyzed the structure of the sentence, the students should conduct experiments with bananas, using the four alternatives suggested in the sentence. This will give them a concrete understanding of what would otherwise be largely an abstract and hence meaningless concept. Only the home economics teacher can help with this sort of problem of readability.

RETEACHING CONTEXTUAL ANALYSIS

As is true for all subjects, there is a vocabulary specific to home economics and specialized meanings for words also in common use. The following words, taken from the example we have been discussing ("Pointers on Fruits") may have to be analyzed in context:

leisurely	diluted	sieved
broiled	concentrate	granular
extracted	commercially	"out of hand"
acidulated	fragile	

Much of the meaning of the passage depends on the use of these words in context. It is the task of the classroom teacher to help all the students to understand them. Assigning these words for "dictionary practice" will defeat the purpose of reading the section (that is, to understand the place of fruit in the American breakfast). Only occasional dictionary practice in class should be used, and this should be done only to provide a meaning which cannot be obtained from the context or from past experience. In this case, *acidulated* is the only word that should be looked up in the dictionary. It is a good idea to have two students do this simultaneously, rather than have the entire class do it.

READING TO FOLLOW DIRECTIONS

It has been noted that some home economics texts are essentially books of directions—do-it-yourself books. In courses where such books are used, the teacher must know how to teach students to follow directions. One teacher described the problem as follows:

"I teach home economic classes in a 1,100-student high school in an affluent suburban town. We have a very adequate budget for foods used in my cooking classes, but this year, because some of the students made many mistakes in preparing different foods, my supplies are being used up at an alarming rate.

"In my clothing course, the materials purchased by various students for their clothing projects often cost two or three dollars per yard. Some girls have ruined the material because they have misread the instructions for cutting.

"As I keep careful records on each girl's progress in both sections of the course, I have been able to judge that the same few girls are making most of the mistakes. As these girls are mainly in college-preparatory classes, isn't it unusual for them to be making careless errors on this simple type of reading? Should I have them read the recipes and pattern directions aloud to me?

If some home economics students are habitually making errors in reading recipes and directions, they are probably also making careless errors in their reading for other courses—mathematics problems, for example, and scientific experiments. But it should be realized that the types of directions students are asked to read and follow vary from subject to subject. Directions found in science and mathematics texts, for instance, involve experimenting, finding answers to problems, and applying principles. On the other hand, typical directions in a home economics class might involve following a recipe in sequence, or following plans for sewing a dress. Such directions have to do with parts or ingredients, and the order and manner in which they are assembled. The purpose unlike that of, say, an experiment in science, is to *create*.

Given a set of directions, home economics students will need help in understanding "when to do," "what to do," and "how to do."

LESSON PLAN: FOLLOWING DIRECTIONS

Behavioral objective. To develop the students' ability to read and follow printed directions more efficiently.

Project. Preparation of curried shrimp.

Materials. An overhead projector; a transparency of the recipe for curried shrimp; an individual copy of the recipe for each student.

(*Suggestion:* Inexpensive special masters can be used to produce a transparency which can then be placed on any duplicating machine to produce individual worksheets for your students. For best results, hand-print the recipe on the transparency unless you have access to a primer-sized typewriter.)

Procedure

1. Project the transparency of the recipe for curried shrimp.

CURRIED SHRIMP

2 lb fresh or frozen shrimp	2 tbsp seafood seasoning
2 tbsp salt	2 quarts hot water

Clean shrimp, removing shells and veins. Place in saucepan with salt and spice, Add hot water and bring to boil; simmer 5 minutes. Cool in water in which shrimp was cooked.

1/4 cup butter or margarine	1 cup chicken stock
1/4 cup onion flakes	2 cups milk
1/3 cup flour	1 tsp lemon juice
1 tsp salt	4 cups (approx.) shrimp,
3 tsp curry powder	cooked

Melt butter, add crushed onion flakes, and cook until soft. Stir in flour and seasonings. Add stock; cook until thick, stirring constantly. Add milk, lemon juice, and shrimp. Heat thoroughly. Prepare rice according to directions on the package. Add 1/2 tsp saffron to water in which rice is cooked. Serve rice in separate bowl. Serve the curry buffet style with one or more of the following accompaniments arranged in small bowls or on a "lazy susan." Arrange the buffet so guests can serve themselves first with rice, top the rice with a serving of curry, and add a spoonful of each condiment on top of the curry. Top with another spoonful of the curry mixture.

Accompaniments

Chopped pickles	Chopped peanuts
Diced celery	Chopped crisp bacon
Chopped hard-cooked eggs	Seedless raisins
Shredded moist coconut	Pineapple tidbits
Chopped orange rind	Currant jelly

2. Present new vocabulary:

buffet	onion flakes
condiment	saffron
curry	simmer
lazy susan	stock

   a. You may ask some students to find the dictionary meanings of the following technical words: *curry, saffron, condiment.*

   b. The following common words have different meanings when used in home economics classes (they may need further explanation): *stock, buffet.*

3. Distribute worksheets which contain the recipe.

4. Ask the students to read the entire recipe *silently* to get a general idea of the directions.

5. Give the students an opportunity to express their ideas about the recipe. Responses might be:

   "We are going to make a white sauce."

   "The shrimp will be placed on the rice."

6. Guide students in rereading the entire recipe; have them especially note the order of the steps. Ask them to try to form a mental picture of the steps.

7. Ask the following questions to determine whether or not the students have an under-standing of the correct sequence:
   a. "What are the ingredients we will need first?"
   b. "What will we do with them?"
   c. "What is the next step?"
8. In order to direct the students' attention to specific parts of the recipe, prepare a transparency of the following suggested questions. (These can be written on a 10- × 10-inch clear acetate sheet. Use a wax pencil or a special marking pen. As the correct answer is given you may add it to the transparency.)

Suggested Questions

   a. You are to_____the shrimp.
      (1) boil
      (2) simmer
      (3) broil
   b. You are asked to_____the sauce.
      (1) heat
      (2) simmer
      (3) boil
   c. You are asked to add_____saffron to the water in which the rice is cooked.
      (1) 1/2 tsp
      (2) 1/4 tsp
      (3) 1/8 tsp
9. Encourage the students to reread carefully, concentrating on the logical order of the steps.
10. Place the following summary on a large chart so that students may refer to it periodically.

Summary: Reading to follow directions

   a. Read the entire recipe silently to get the general idea.
   b. Review the steps to note the order in which the directions are to be followed.
   c. Make sure you understand each step.
   d. Reread the directions, this time concentrating on remembering the correct order of the steps.

THE READING ASSIGNMENT IN HOME ECONOMICS

The assignment of reading material in home economics is the essential and crucial step in the learning process. Complete suggestions for planning reading assignments are to be found in Chapter 6. The planning form shown on pages 94–96 should be adapted to each specific subject and textbook in home economics. There is absolutely no substitute for a well-planned reading assignment.

The contents of home economics textbooks are chiefly built around main ideas even though they may also be directional, informational, or problem-solving in nature. Unless a student is taught how to extract the main idea from a paragraph or section of textual material, he cannot be expected to read with any good degree of comprehension. The home economics teacher, as a conse-quence, has the specific responsibility of teaching students how to "see" structure and finding main ideas. This is very easy to do if one follows the suggestions in Chapter 5, where seven patterns of paragraph structure have been described and illustrated. Those are the seven ways in which main ideas and the facts related to them may appear in textbooks. We need not repeat this material here, and two examples will illustrate the sort of structure to be found in home economics materials.

In the first example, the main idea is stated at the outset, and details follow:

Blankets are usually necessary as bed covering, but the number needed and the kind selected will depend upon the amount of warmth desired. The yarn used in a blanket may be wool, cotton, rayon, nylon, Acrilan, or combinations of two or more of these. A good blanket is soft and springy, with a surface-nap finish. The warmest blankets are made of wool, but they are also most expensive. Cotton blankets are satisfactory for mild climates. Rayon, nylon, and Acrilan, used with wool or cotton, make fluffy, warm blankets and are usually less expensive than all-wool blankets.

SOURCE: Marion S. Barclay and Frances Champion, Teen Guide to Homemaking, McGraw-Hill Book Company, Webster Division, St. Louis, 1961, p. 222.

In our second example, the main idea is stated, then details are given, and finally the main idea is restated:

Frozen poultry. A great deal of poultry is frozen at packing plants for convenience and for safety in transportation. Most of this frozen poultry is in the ready-to-cook form. Chickens and turkeys are frozen whole or as parts. There are also boneless turkey roasts in rolled shape. These are made of all white meat, all dark meat, or of a combination of both kinds. They are packaged raw, fully cooked, or smoked. Turkeys and Rock Cornish hens that are stuffed and then frozen are other kinds of frozen poultry. Frozen poultry is convenient to use in meal preparation since it need only be cooked to be ready for serving.

SOURCE: Dorothy E. Shank, Natalie K. Fitch, Pauline A. Chapman, and Mary S. Sickler, Guide to Modern Meals, McGraw-Hill Book Company, Webster Division, St. Louis, 1970, p. 280.

PREDICTING READING DISABILITY IN HOME ECONOMICS

It is easy to identify the secondary school student who will probably have difficulty reading textbook materials in home economics. Those who are in the lowest percentiles in intelligence, in reading ability as determined by standardized tests, or in both, will most certainly find reading the textbook difficult, if not impossible. (The explanation for this is given in Chapter 2.)

Those below the 20th percentile on both measures will have trouble; those below the 10th percentile on either measure or both measures should not be expected to deal with reading as a medium for learning. .

Another method of determining who will have difficulty reading secondary school home economics texts is the Prognostic Test of Reading Disability in Secondary School Home Economics, of which three alternative forms are presented here. This test is simple and fast. The theory behind it is that a number of words in common use are appropriated by any subject and used in a specific way in the context of that subject; failure to recognize those essential common words will be a major handicap to understanding and a good predictor of failure.

The following prognosis is to be given individually. Each student reads aloud directly from the page of this book. One or two minutes is sufficient time to determine whether or not that student will have trouble with the textbook materials of home economics subjects.

The three alternative forms of the test are included so that students waiting to be tested will not be able to memorize the words as they hear others reading aloud.

PROGNOSTIC TEST OF READING DISABILITY IN SECONDARY SCHOOL HOME ECONOMICS[5]

Directions Cover the other two alternative forms not being used (5- x 7-inch cards will do). Ask the student to read from left to right, pronouncing each word in turn at his normal rate.

Observe his facial expression as he reads. Note hesitation, repetition, regression, uncertainty, gross mispronunciation, and incorrect accent.

Identify the student who is not able to move along smoothly, pronouncing at least one word every two seconds. That student will have difficulty reading in the field of home economics.

Alternative Form A

establishing	classifying	embroidery	inconveniences
accommodation	convenience	harmonize	preferences
management	maintenance	conflict	activities
adulthood	inferiority	adolescence	textured
frustration	measurements	communicating	establishment
complement	possibilities	recommended	experimenting
workmanship	judgment	perpendicular	housekeeping
inconspicuous	investigation	attractive	supervise
impulse	horizontal	resources	uncomfortable
capabilities	merchandise	temperament	possibilities

[5] Copyright 1971 by Robert C. Aukerman

Alternative Form B

simplifies	budgeting	household	livable
refreshments	centerpeice	harmonize	vegetables
accessories	essential	appliances	guarantee
preparation	cooperative	attractive	refrigerator
nonessentials	perishable	ingredients	appearance
occupations	careers	merchandise	textiles
rationalization	regression	psychological	compensation
mechanism	development	physiological	extrovert
maturation	organism	nutrition	frustration
psychological	prenatal	vitamins	vigorous

Alternative Form C

opportunities	inheritance	coordination	experiences
imaginative	characteristics	resourceful	self-confidence
acceptance	attractive	behavior	balanced
circumstances	conditions	initiative	qualities
approving	consequences	activities	expectations
guidance	independence	role	competencies
responsibilities	equipment	productive	appropriate
parental	suggestion	desirable	standards
encouragement	approval	fashionable	communicable
requirements	contagious	contaminated	utilities

THE READABILITY OF HOME ECONOMICS TEXTBOOKS

Note: The reader is referred to the more thorough treatment of this subject in Chapter 3.

Seldom, if ever, is an author of a home economics textbood paired with a reading specialist to produce textual materials appropriate to the reading abilities of the students for whom they are intended. Moreover, most home economics textbooks are written by college professors far removed from day-to-day exposure to the interests and abilities of junior and senior high school students. Consequently, the readability of home economics texts is often high. Even the best-organized and best-written text may be most difficult to read. Choice of such a text should be made, not on the basis of grade level, but on the teacher's knowledge of the reading ability and intelligence of his own students.

Two examples will illustrate the need for discrimination on the basis of readability. The first, taken from the Landis text *Your Marriage and Family Living,* indicates the extremely high readability created by difficult vocabulary and, in some cases, complicated sentence construction. This textbook would be appropriate only for those with high mental ability and superior reading ability:

Engagement period usually turbulent. The sociologists who made this study found that two-thirds of couples experience some degree of strain during their engagement. Jealousy, disagreement about friends, trouble over in-laws, quarrels over money matters, differences in philosophy of life are the kinds of problems that are likely to arise, once two people in love are serious about marriage. This is a period when real communication can and should take place. It is the time when facts and issues must be faced and not glossed over by insincere lovemaking.

Such areas of disagreement raise issues which must be settled in some way if the engagement is to last and marriage eventually take place. Most couples at some time doubt that they should go on with the marriage. Many discuss the advisability of their mate choice with relatives, friends, counselors, or others.

Some couples become so plagued with doubts about the desirability of the forthcoming marriage, and are involved in so much conflict, that they break off temporarily. All in all, research shows that the engagement period is quite a turbulent period for many.

Signs of hope and failure. How does one know whether these difficulties point to failure ahead, if the marriage is entered into, or are only the signs of normal adjustment of two people to each other?

If the various tensions and disagreements are worked out to the point where greater harmony and understanding result, the signs are hopeful for a successful marriage. If one of the pair is left humiliated after the disagreements, if tension builds up, if the atmosphere is one of increasing hopelessness that problems can ever be solved, then it is time for reassessment. If the engagement can not be made to work, neither can the marriage.

Finally, if one finds himself losing interest, it is a bad sign.

SOURCE: Paul H. Landis, Your Marriage and Family Living. McGraw-Hill Book Company, Webster Division, St. Louis, 1969, p. 206.

This material consists of approximately 300 words. The fourteen sentences, with an average length of 21 words, are longer than average, but not excessively long. The high readability is caused by the use of compound subjects or compound predicates. In some sentences, both subject and predicate are compound and consequently difficult to grasp. A good example of the several complicated constructions is found in this sentence: "If one of the pair is left humiliated after the disagreements, if tension builds up, if the atmosphere is one of increasing hopelessness that problems can never be solved, then it is time for reassessment."

In this sentence, the three modifying clauses which stand in initial position refer to the phrase *is is time for reassessment*, the final phrase of the sentence. Students with low intelligence or poor reading ability would be lost in such material.

MATCHING READING ABILITY AND READABILITY

In most areas of home economics there is some choice between textbooks of high readability and those of medium readability. There are, however, few texts of satisfactory quality and high interest written at a low readability level. This creates a problem for the many students with low reading ability.

The teacher should do whatever possible to provide readings of an appropriate level for students with differing abilities.

The traditional image of the home economics student has been of a girl who is not going on to college; but this picture is no longer accurate. The nature of the content of the home economics curriculum makes it a vital part of the total education of all young people—both boys and girls. Although this is not yet a universally accepted fact, many junior high schools do require home economics for all girls. This means, of course, that girls with various abilities and backgrounds are in the courses. For practical purposes, then, the classes should be grouped according to ability, including reading ability.

If this sort of grouping is not effected, the home economics teacher must at least know which students in class are likely to have difficulty in reading home economics textual materials. This is easily accomplished by examining scores on intelligence tests and reading tests and formulating percentile rankings (the process is described in Chapter 2).

It is *not* the task of the home economics teacher to attempt to correct reading disabilities. And if appropriate printed materials are lacking, the home economics teacher must devise other means of conveying information and providing background for discussion and learning. Unfortunately, as has been mentioned, there is little material available for the disabled reader in home economics. There are several alternatives, however. One is the use of junior high school texts in senior high school classes of poor readers (the text chosen should not, of course, have been used previously by the same group of students). But this will not necessarily solve the problem, since a large number of students in the lowest quartile cannot handle junior high school texts. Some are virtually nonreaders. Still, the use of the junior high school text for a senior high school class might be effective with those whose reading ability is equal to that of an average fourth- or fifth-grader, if it were not for the fact that the social maturity differences in the two age levels are so great.

A second alternative is to select materials from various issues of *Glamour*, *Co-Ed*, or *Charm*. These periodicals are generally written at about fourth- and fifth-grade readability levels, although some articles are more difficult.

Another alternative is to develop "experience charts" with severely disabled readers. This is referred to as the "language-experience approach," since it utilizes the language and experiences of the students. In class, the students dictate their ideas and the teacher prints their sentences on large ruled paper on an easel. The students then read the sentences back. In this way the retarded or disabled reader, who would experience failure in attempting to read a text, experiences success. The experience chart may be embellished with cutouts or sketches to illustrate the concepts it contains.

The next step is to move to individual language-experience booklets, dictated, printed, and illustrated by the students. Each student produces her own language-experience book. This gives a feeling of pride of accomplishment to the poorest readers and nonreaders. Moreover, it often is an effective substitute for remedial reading, since the student who can write words and sentences can certainly read them.

ENRICHMENT READING IN HOME ECONOMICS

Home economics education has as its goal the enrichment of individual, family, and community life. It would seem, therefore, that enrichment materials should be at the core of the reading program. This is especially true as regards supplementary reading materials to be used in the classroom.

The home economics classroom can be enlivened and made more relevant to today's teen-agers through utilization of the hundreds of fine teen-age books available. These are customarily referred to as "young adult" novels. The themes that correlate best with home economics are family life, girls and girls' problems, dating, boys, self-fulfilment, adventure in the world of business, vacations, love, travel, and popularity.

Old standbys, such as *Little Women, An Old-Fashioned Girl,* and some of the other novels by Louisa May Alcott, doubtless still appeal to some adolescents even today. The same probably is true of Kate Douglas Wiggins' *Rebecca of Sunnybrook Farm;* but a realistic appraisal of the interests of high school adolescents today would reveal that few would want to read such quaint books. The reason is, of course, that most teen-agers want to be sophisticated. The home economics teacher (or college student preparing to be a home economics teacher) must build a list of books that are relevant to the interests of today's young high school student, noting the themes listed above as areas of special interest.

A few suggestions will serve as examples of the type of books to select for enrichment in home economics. Two factors must be paramount in the selection of enrichment books: (1) the books chosen must be relevant and of high interest to today's youth—especially girls; (2) they must be written at a low readability level—preferrably the fourth- or fifth-grade reading level.

Head Into The Wind, by D. Robinson Barnwell (McKay, 1965), a story of the adjustment made by a teen-ager after the death of his father, is good for junior high school readers. *The Moffats,* by Eleanor Estes (Harcourt, 1941), has been a favorite with high school girls for several generations. The "Sue Barton" series, by Helen Boylston (Little, 1936), has been overwhelmingly popular for more than thirty years and continues to be the best of the vocational stories for young teen-age girls. Sue Barton lives in the imagination of millions of girls.

Growth of personality and self-reliance is the theme of Dorothy Canfield Fisher's best-seller, *Understood Betsy* (Holt, 1946), a "must" in any home economics collection.

Conflict between what one should do and what one wants to do seems to be a persistent problem of adolescence. One of the perennial favorites with that theme is Bess Streeter Aldrich's *A White Bird Flying* (Appleton, 1931). Equally relevant is *Window on the Sea* (Westminster, 1962), Adrien Stoutenberg's young-adult novel about the choice between college and marriage.

Junior high school girls especially enjoy books about girls in exciting jobs. Cathlyn Gay's *Girl Pilot* (Messner, 1966) and Shirley Sargent's *Ranger in Skirts* (Abington, 1966) appeal to girls seeking adventure.

Lots of Love, Lucinda, by Bianca Bradbury (Washborn, 1966), relates the relationships that develop when Lucinda, a Negro girl from the South, comes to live with a white family in New England.

One of the most popular stories of a teen-age girl's first love is Maureen Daly's *Seventeeth Summer* (Dodd, 1942).

Erich Segal's best-seller, *Love Story,* topped the list of supplementary reading for teen-age high school students at the time of this writing. It was not written particularly for high schoolers, but it captured their imagination the way Anne Frank's *Diary* and *On The Beach* did in the 1950s. Its appeal probably lay in its relevant theme, shortness (only 131 pages, broken into very short chapters of 4 or 5 pages each), youthfulness, pathos, and rebellion. It is now an "in" book for the marriage and family relations courses and really cannot be ignored as an excellent means for reaching today's youth.

Magazines are also popular with young people. Some of the stories in *American Girl*, the Girl Scout magazine, can be cut out and utilized as supplementary enrichment material; these often deal with teen-age problems. The same is true of the stories in *Seventeen, Glamour, Co-Ed,* and *Charm*. Teen-age girls are now avidly reading and swapping a whole new generation of "teen magazines." These often feature some current idol or singing group. Teen magazines represent one more aspect of the "generation gap." Adults find them ludicrous, but they provide for many an adolescent girl an important means of identification. The home economics teacher who ignores the fact that adolescent girls are reading such magazines from cover to cover will be out of touch with her students. But if she accepts and knows something about such magazines, they may provide a means of communication; a basis for discussion of fashions, behavior, modes of living, grooming, self-improvement, values, etc. The simple principle of learning that applies here is "Start where the learner is."

It should be admitted that one can hardly expect adolescents to be inspired by the home economics textbook alone. Using the many good enrichment materials of the types suggested above will reward any home economics teacher with increased interest, motivation, and commitment on the part of her students.

CONCLUSIONS: GUIDELINES FOR THE HOME ECONOMICS TEACHER

Home economics classrooms in the secondary school are textbook-oriented. The texts may be informational, directional, or problem-oriented, and their chief areas of concern are the teen-ager and his relationships with others. The main objective of the courses and texts is growth of the personality, the acquisition of self-confidence, the improvement of personal relationships, and self-fulfillment.

Reading in home economics textbooks, as in other areas of the curriculum, calls for special training in finding main ideas, following directions, and developing vocabulary. In addition, the structure of home economics textbooks makes it appropriate and effective to train students in the survey technique of reading.

The home economics teacher has the task of assessing the readability of the available textbooks and choosing materials appropriate to the reading ability of the students who will be using them. The choice of good enrichment materials will provide additional motivation and improve learning in the secondary home economics classroom.

Questions and Activities for Discussion and Growth

1. Home economics textbooks are structured like social studies, science, and business texts. What is the justification for this?
2. Make an informal survey of the problems which concern teen-agers today and compare your findings with the problems discussed in various home economics textbooks. Which problems are new? Which problems are overlooked in the texts? How can they be handled without textual materials?
3. Using the readability form in Chapter 3, assess at least three texts in each of the following areas: home management, personal relationships, child care, foods, clothing, and home furnishings. What differences in readability did you discover?
4. If you find a great range in readability in the texts examined for question 3, how do you interpret this? That is, what are (a) the causes and (b) the implications?
5. Make a survey of the "social maturity" of young people in several home economics classes. How do the contents of the texts being used correspond to the social maturity of the students who are reading them?
6. Using the same classes, run a general reading test on all students and compare the results with the levels of the texts being used.
7. Give the prognostic test to all the students in an eighth-grade home economics class and estimate what percentage will probably have trouble reading the texts in home economics. What do your findings imply?
8. Develop a lesson plan for surveying a chapter (or part of a chapter) in one home economics text. Specify the materials you will need, the questions you will ask, and the answers you anticipate.
9. Develop a lesson plan in which you utilize the sequence steps for following written directions, described on pages 277–279 of this chapter.

10. Start an annotated bibliography of enrichment books in home economics, listing titles under the six main categories of home economics. Assess the readability of each book. As the bibliography develops, try the books with good, average, and poor readers in home economics classes (using books relevant to the various units of the courses). This will enable you to make a list of relevant books at various levels of readability that are available in your library.

Selected References

Symkowicz, Dorothy: "Home Economics and Reading," in International Reading Association, *Fusing Reading Skills and Content*, Newark, Delaware, 1969, pp. 62–66.

13. IMPROVING THE READING SKILLS OF COLLEGE-BOUND STUDENTS

When the college-bound high school student graduates and then enters the freshman class in college, he is faced with an almost unbelievable load of reading assignments in such courses as English literature, history, sociology, government, economics, and psychology. These students, who are less than three months out of high school, are hit with a reading task for which many are totally unprepared even though they may have graduated in the college preparatory curriculum.

There are many reasons for the size of the college reading load. First is the availability of thousands of titles in paperback. Second is the explosion of knowledge, which has not been accompanied by any lengthening of the time required for a baccalaureate program; since more knowledge must be acquired in the same amount of time, assignments are longer. Third is the prevalence of huge lecture courses enrolling hundreds—sometimes more than a thousand—students; in these courses the student is truly on his own and must rely on reading for much of the information he is expected to acquire. Finally, since

no college or university library can stock enough books to cover all the outside reading requirements in large freshman and sophomore courses, most
classes utilize books of supplementary "readings". Instead of having different
students read different materials, the instructor now holds everyone responsible for all the readings. These factors working together have produced a reading load three to four times greater than that of a few years ago. This means
that the high school student in a college preparatory curriculum should plan
to improve his reading skills in anticipation of the college reading load.

IMPROVING READING SPEED

The Concept of "Speed Reading"

It is natural to think of "speed reading" as an obvious solution to the problem
of covering more reading material in limited amounts of time, particularly
since it has been proven that most high school students in the college preparatory curriculum can and should read faster than they do. But under practical
conditions, it is impossible for the school's reading specialist to run speed-
reading courses for all the college-bound students. The alternative is for the
classroom teacher to suggest, explain, and demonstrate a few simple techniques
that will produce an increase in speed with no significant loss in comprehension.

There has been sufficient advertising of various speed reading courses
in newspapers to alert students to the existence, popularity, and potential of
speed reading. The results claimed are impressive, and the concept itself
appeals to the desire for self-improvement. Speed reading, then, needs no
introduction, but it does need to be looked at critically. This may profitably
be done in the business, social studies, and English classes, and elsewhere.
Certain questions must be asked: "On what mathematical basis are the claims
valid?" "Is improvement in a skill the result of teaching or practice?" "How
does one define 'reading'?" "Are the people who make fantastic improvement
also extraordinary in other ways?" It is wise for the classroom teacher to discuss
the claims made by advertisements for speed-reading programs such as this:
"At least triple your present reading efficiency or your tuition will be
refunded."[1] "Most Optimum Rapid Reading Course students, from children
to senior citizens, learn to read at the rate of 5,000 words per minute."[2]
"So far over 300,000 people have [increased their reading speed]. . . . And
all of them have at least tripled their reading speed with equal or better
comprehension. . . . All of them—even the slowest—can now read an average
novel in less than two hours."[3] High school students have seen such advertising
and some, perhaps, have witnessed demonstrations by people who "read" at

[1]The New York Times Magazine, January 8, 1967, p. 65.
[2]Chicago Tribune, January 1, 1967, advertisement, p. 21.
[3]Providence Journal, January 13, 1970, advertisement, p. 8.

5,000 or 10,000 words per minute, or more, and recount the gist of the material read. Demonstrations of this type are usually quite impressive.

Every student anticipating a heavy reading load in college wants to learn to read faster. A critical discussion of the claims concerning speed reading will probably conclude with these ideas: (1) Everyone can read faster. (2) Speed reading may not actually involve reading every word. (3) Speed reading may be good for some materials. (4) One should learn to vary his reading speed selectively. (5) To succeed in college, the student should learn to read many types of materials faster. The only point that needs to be "sold" is the assurance that "you too can read faster." The following procedure will accomplish that:

Without any prior announcement of objectives or explanation, give the students in any class—English, social studies, science, home economics, etc.— a general reading test, consisting of a section from the textbook about 2,500 words in length.

The time of starting should be noted, and each student should note the number of minutes elapsed immediately upon his completion of the reading. He should divide the number of words read by the number of minutes elapsed to obtain his average rate per minute. He should then answer ten questions that have been prepared by the teacher to test comprehension. It should be observed that the test need not be a "standardized test," and the questions need not be subjected to factor analysis. This is not a scientific experiment, and the variables are not critical; the objective is simply to establish a rough idea of each student's normal speed and comprehension. Without any special training, the average college-bound student will probably read at a speed some- where between 250 and 300 words per minute. Some will be much slower. When everyone has finished reading and answering the questions, the students are asked to check their answers and find their percentages of accuracy. They should then multiply the percent of comprehension by the speed. For example, 80 percent comprehension at 300 words per minute equals a reading achieve- ment of 240; 70 percent comprehension at 343 words per minute equals a reading achievement of 240. The reading achievement thus calculated is the starting point.

Most of the students will be surprised to learn that a reading speed of 250 words per minute at 80 percent comprehension is not much better than that of the average sixth-grader. It is totally inadequate for college work. An effective way to prove this is for the teacher to assemble the required reading for a freshman course in the same academic area (the books can be borrowed from a college instructor). An English teacher would, for example, present a stack of hardcover books, collections of readings, and paperbacks for an introductory course in English literature at the college level. This will convince any student who is reading at the sixth-grade level that something must be done right away in preparation for the task ahead.

Finally, assurances from the teacher that help will be given within the class, and that there is a good probability of significant improvement, will create motivation.

Techniques for Increasing Speed

1. Awareness. Most college-bound students can increase their reading speed simply by becoming aware that they are reading far below their potentials. They have doubtless been told—often incorrectly—to "read every word *slowly* to get the meaning." Once they are assured that they not only can but should increase their reading speed, a number will make significant improvement on their own. Consciousness of the bad habit of reading slowly is a good start which can and should be made in every academic area. Even if no further training is given, the classroom teacher can give this encouragement.

Students should be told to practice increasing the speed at which they read their textbook, with the expectation that they will soon be given another speed and comprehension test.

A few minutes should be devoted each day to discussing the experiences students are having with their practice in speeding up their reading. After three days of such discussions, a second test (again of 2,500 words from the textbook and ten comprehension questions) should be given. As before, the students should note time elapsed in reading, calculate the average rate (words per minute), find the percent of comprehension, and derive their reading achievement. (Note that for most high school academic material a comprehension of 80 percent should be achieved by college-bound students. This figure can be reached through discussion by the class, rather than being stated by the teacher.)

2. Intensity of commitment and drill. The intensity of commitment to speed reading is an individual matter. But in any event speed reading, like any skill, requires intensive drill.

The intensity of drill may be increased by one or two simple techniques. Evelyn Wood, who developed the Evelyn Wood Reading Dynamics Institute method, has used the hand as a pacing device. The student learns to turn pages with one hand while the other hand sweeps down the middle or margin of the page in a regular rhythm—slowly at first and then with slightly increasing speed until a desired speed is attained.

There are some machines which can be adjusted to various rates and which force the reader to maintain an intense effort for speed. Such pacing devices are not usually found in the academic classroom; indeed, some research indicates that they are not necessary. Even if a student does use them at some point, he will still have to acquire some method or scheme for maintaining an intense effort and a consistent speed after the mechanical devices are no longer available to him. Another simpler device of this sort (which some students may own already at home) is the metronome.[4] It may be set to tick at a rate timed to correspond to the student's speed per line. When the student is first starting, it will be slow; later, its speed will be increased.

The purpose of any of these techniques is to keep the student semi-consciously aware of his rate and to help him intensify his efforts at speeding up.

3. The survey technique and SQ3R. All academic material is organized in almost exactly the same format. A student who is able to analyze the structure of a chapter in one academic subject may easily transfer that skill to most other subjects.

Textbooks are designed with the semester system as the time schedule. A semester is normally eighteen weeks long, and texts tend to be divided so that about one chapter per week is to be read.

Chapters are usually grouped in units. There is usually an introduction to each unit; and the relationship of the chapter titles to the unit as a whole is discernible.

The college-bound student should learn to preview units and chapters to see the structural framework of the text. This serves exactly the same purpose as examining the picture on the cover of the jigsaw puzzle box before attempting to assemble the pieces: it is the only sensible thing to do.

A more careful and detailed scrutiny of the framework of each chapter should also be a regular practice. The details of this surveying technique are described in Chapter 4. Application of the survey technique is also illustrated in each of the chapters dealing with content subjects. The survey takes some time, but it eventually produces greater speed and superior comprehension.

All college-bound students should also be proficient in Robinson's SQ3R technique (of which the survey is the most important element). Using the complete SQ3R sequence virtually ensures mastery of academic material. The entire routine should become automatic for college-bound students.

4. Reading for clues to meaning. The classroom teacher can provide significantly helpful instruction regarding the clues to meaning that are used by writers and editors of academic textbooks. Such clues are used for a purpose—a purpose which frequently goes unheeded by both teacher and student.

The chapter title, of course, is selected to set the direction of thinking. Much thought is expended in the development of meaningful chapter titles. They convey the meaning of the author, and the reader must bring to them meaning from his own past experience. The task of the subject-matter teacher is to exploit the chapter title as a meaningful clue, but its significance to each student will also depend partly on his own experience. Discussing a

[4]Gene S. Fazio and Thomas McDonald, "Using a Metronome in Reading Class," *Journal of Reading,* vol. 34, no. 4 (January, 1970), pp. 289–291.

chapter title enriches learning and is the first step in creating readiness for reading the chapter. College-bound students who acquire this habit will have made a valuable addition to their reading skills.

Other clues which are aids to faster reading with better comprehension include typographical distinctions. As has been mentioned, a survey of headings and various material set in special type (italics, boldface, color, boxed copy, and so on) will greatly improve the student's grasp of reading material.

Punctuation itself can also be an important source of clues. The college-bound student has probably learned the punctuation marks used in written English and has used them repeatedly in his compositions. Seldom is it pointed out to him that he can more easily grasp the meaning of printed matter by quickly giving attention to punctuation. Punctuation marks at the end of sentences need little emphasis to college-bound students: periods, exclamation points, question marks, and quotation marks are standard and are common knowledge. The internal signposts, however, although important, are most often neglected. The comma is almost completely ignored by poor readers. Those who wish to improve their reading ability should practice reading aloud, pronouncing the word "comma" whenever the comma appears. This will reveal the nature of the phrases set off by commas. The same technique of verbalizing punctuation marks should be used with colons, semicolons, and dashes—all important and meaningful clues which aid in rapid reading.

The two examples below, taken from a textbook in American government,[5] illustrate the importance of punctuation as a clue to meaning. Note the contrast between the selection whose internal punctuation has been removed and the one with punctuation. Two students in class should be sent out of the room, so that they will not know what they are to do. The rest of the students should be given mimeographed sheets containing the two selections. Then the first student should be called in, given the selection with no punctuation, and asked to read it at top speed. The class will be primed to note errors and speed. The second student is then called in to read the version *with* punctuation. Class discussion follows, and conclusions are reached.

PARTY DIRECTION [Punctuation removed]
Some states have attempted to abolish parties in their state legislatures in others notably in the South where only one party has the confidence of the people that party splits into factions under rival leadership. However for business to be conducted some advance agreement by the majority no matter what it is called is necessary. If all the lawmakers entered the chamber as individuals unorganized and with no preliminary understandings we would witness confusion like a tug of war in five directions. The unofficial and advance meeting of a majority or minority party of a faction or group of likeminded representatives is called a caucus or conference. It is not unlike the corridor gathering of a dozen or so seniors who a day or two before the class meeting say lets elect Tom Grumman president.

[5] Robert Rienow, *American Government in Today's World,* D.C. Heath and Company, Boston, 1962, p. 590.

PARTY DIRECTION [Punctuation retained]
Some states have attempted to abolish parties in their state legislatures; in others, notably in the South, where only one party has the confidence of the people, that party splits into factions under rival leadership. However, for business to be conducted, some advance agreement by the majority, no matter what it is called, is necessary. If all the lawmakers entered the chamber as individuals, unorganized, and with no preliminary understandings, we would witness confusion like a tug of war in five directions. The unofficial and advance meeting of a majority or minority party, of a faction or group of like-minded representatives, is called a "caucus" or conference. It is not unlike the corridor gathering of a dozen or so seniors who, a day or two before the class meeting, say, "Let's elect Tom Grumman president.

COGNITIVE LEARNING THROUGH READING

"Knowing" may be said to be in both the eye and the mind of the beholder.

The process of *knowing* consists of a sequence of events: looking, seeing, and comparing. Looking involves attending, that is, paying attention to the stimulus. Seeing is the process of registering the visual stimulus on the retina and receiving it in the brain. This process involves awareness. The higher mental process of comparing is, essentially, the core of cognitive learning. One may look and see, and yet not know. A reader may look at words, see them, register them in the brain, and still know nothing. Everyone has had the experience of "reading" a page of a text, and presumably "pronouncing" all the words, yet having no idea, when the bottom of the page is reached, of what has been read. It should be obvious, then, that we can look at words, pronounce them, and still not be *reading*. Cognition is not complete until the reader actively does something with the words he is seeing and pronouncing.

The essential feature of cognitive learning is categorizing ideas and relating them to the past experiences of the reader. This is a process which must be learned, and how fast a reader can do this depends on the amount of practice he has had. It has sometimes been suggested that speed is not an important part of this process—that the reader should tarry along the way, to take in the beauty of the landscape, to think, and to dream. This idea is often valid, for out of men's thinking and dreaming the great inventions, discoveries, and masterpieces are born. Nevertheless, speed of reading—including an intensity of effort in relating what is being read to one's own stored learning—has its place in the improvement of reading techniques. For some reading materials, in fact, it is a necessity.

Equally important, however, is reading in depth. This requires the reader to embellish the words he is reading with all gems from his storehouse of experiences. Naturally, some students have a richer store of experiences than others. For anyone, though, storing information and experiences is never a valid end in itself. It is the utilization of stored information and experience that brings reality to the printed and spoken word.

The technique for helping college-bound students enrich their reading through the retrieval of past experiences is a slow, deliberate construction of constellations of ideas around one word or phrase. The teacher will provide the most satisfying learning experience by encouraging the students to share their ideas with each other. The method is simple.

Select a term—any term which has large possibilities. In home economics, for example, it might be "quality of living." In social studies, it could be "the Arab World"; in science, "energy"; and so on.

Each student is alerted to record the first thing that rises to his consciousness when the term is presented. The students then share these ideas with each other. Four facts will become apparent as this is done: (1) Meaning is in the mind of the reader. (2) Meaning depends on past experience. (3) The many facets of meaning are related. (4) When various aspects of meaning are brought together, they form a constellation of ideas.

SKILLS FOR EFFICIENT READING

1. Breaking Bad Habits

Most courses in speed reading provide practice in breaking some of the habits that hinder efficient reading. When one is first learning to read, he learns to pronounce the sounds of letters (this is called "phonics instruction"). But anyone who continued to pronounce every letter sound in sequence would not learn to read properly. The results would be grotesque and unintelligible. Rather, the reader learns to synthesize sounds into words; he becomes a "word pronouncer." Later, he will become a pronouncer of phrases and meaningful clusters of words. Seldom is he taught that, to rise above the speed of pronunciation, he must *stop* pronouncing.

Some small effort is made by elementary teachers when they discourage "reading out loud" or "reading in whispers," (this is called "vocalizing"). It is, indeed, a handicap to speed. "Internal speech"—pronouncing the words to oneself with lip movements—has the same effect. Pronunciation slows reading. Improvement will result when a student practices reading with as little vocalizing as possible. This is difficult because most students have had many years of practice in pronouncing as they read.

Word-by-word reading is another handicap which can be overcome with practice. The student who discovers, through introspection, that he is a word-by-word reader has already made a step toward correcting this habit. The classroom teacher can help students understand this concept by showing them photographs of the eye movements of poor and good readers. Such photographs have been taken by the author (of teen-age readers), and they speak for themselves. They show the number of fixations made by the reader as his eyes stop to read words and parts of words along just one line of print, and the number of regressions made as his eyes go back to pick up parts of words that he must put together in his attempt to create meaning. The good reader makes fewer fixations per line and few, if any, regressions. The college-bound student should be able to reduce the number of fixations per line simply by being made aware of these facts and practicing for wider vision span. The shorter the line of print, the easier this is to do; students should therefore be encouraged to practice on a text that has two columns of print per page. The objective should be to read with no more than two fixations per line. One aid in doing this is a pointer (a finger or pencil will do) swinging back and forth like a pendulum across each line. As reading improves, the pendulum becomes more of a zigzag motion and eventually may be eliminated entirely.

2. Versatility

Mature readers do not read, or even look at, every word if they have been taught to select their method of reading according to their objectives. This is frequently referred to as "versatility."

The versatile reader is one who adjusts his speed and method to the type of material at hand and to his needs, just as a motorist varies his speed according to driving conditions and his desire to cover ground quickly or to proceed leisurely.

The college-bound student must learn several facts about versatility:

1. Mature readers do not read all materials at the same speed. Some things they skim over; some they read more slowly, for enjoyment; some they read still more slowly, with concentration.
2. It is not "cheating" to skip some materials if you are not interested in them or do not need to learn them, or if you already know about them.
3. There are efficient methods of skimming, skipping, and scanning.
4. Anyone who recommends reading *everything* "carefully and slowly so you will be sure to learn it" is unaware of the techniques that have been developed for versatility in reading.
5. The college-bound student must learn to be versatile in reading if he wants to read efficiently at the college level.

The first step for the classroom teacher is to suggest that students must learn several ways to read in the particular subject matter being studied.

Second, the teacher should plan a series of lessons in that subject (history, literature, science, or whatever) in which skimming and skipping are to be practiced. The material to be skimmed should be relatively easy, and the objective should be to get the gist of the selection. The material to be scanned should be such that the reader will quickly be able to find answers to specific questions. The material for skipping should be such that parts may be skipped entirely because the student presumably already is well acquainted with what they cover. Encouraging versatility of this type has the objective of helping students adjust their way of reading to the type of material without feeling guilty or worried about doing the "wrong" thing.

As the third step, the teacher may conduct the lessons as a learning exercise for the whole class. This step may include the following:

1. *Introduction to the concept of versatility.* The main idea to stress is that all mature readers learn to skim, scan, and skip when it is appropriate to do so.

2. *Answering the question, What kind of material may be skimmed?* The main idea is for the students to realize that the material must be easy and not of great importance or interest to them. The objective of skimming is just to get the gist of a selection.

3. *Skimming several short, easy selections.* (The selections will, of course, be in the academic area of the particular class.) This practice can demonstrate what type of material may appropriately be skimmed and how much information one may expect to get by this process. The emphasis is on the idea that skimming is good enough for material of a transitory nature. Most newspaper items reporting current events may be skimmed, for example.

4. *Answering the question, What type of material may be scanned?* The main idea to develop is that scanning is appropriate for finding quick answers to various questions (How many? Where? When? Who?). The answers can be found quickly if one looks for figures, names, dates, and various symbols, like the dollar sign for costs.

5. *Reproduction of several selections containing many facts, and giving questions to be answered quickly by skimming.* Time the class as they do this, and the students will soon discover that enormous amounts of material may be covered this way.

6. *Answering the question, What type of material may be skipped?* The main idea is to have students learn that much of what they read is unnecessary repetition of facts they already know.

7. *Reproduction of selections in which material can be skipped.* Be sure that the selections are almost entirely repetitious of materials which the students have already learned in junior high school or in elementary school. (For example, much on the Pilgrims is common knowledge to high school students.)

8. *Testing the students on the content of selections for skipping, before they read.* Have the students read the selections after taking this test. They will discover that they already knew the essential facts and information, and could easily skip much of the material.

3. Reading for Main Ideas

The concept and techniques of reading for main ideas have been discussed in Chapter 5, and we need not repeat them here. But it must be emphasized that the college-bound student will need to devise methods for finding main ideas quickly and efficiently. Observation of the way college students underline and otherwise mark their textbooks provides proof that many are unable to distinguish between main ideas and supporting details.

4. Developing a Superior Vocabulary

The possession of a superior vocabulary and the ability to use it are important assets for the college student. Vocabulary building begins long before elementary school but must be continued and intensified in the secondary school classroom. Merely acquiring vocabulary temporarily in order to pass the Friday vocabulary test is a total waste of time. This is not learning; it is merely going through the motions. Words are the building blocks of ideas. The acquisition of building blocks results in nothing unless they are utilized in a meaningful relationship to each other. Vocabulary must be used, and it must fit together. It must contribute just the right touch in the right place. It must be learned in context, never in isolation.

The content teacher has a special opportunity for helping college-bound students build vocabulary in context. The students should be encouraged to use the specialized vocabulary of each subject. Common vocabulary should not be accepted when there is a specific word or phrase indigenous to the field of study. For every content area, there is a vocabulary that is much more meaningful than everyday usage.

Use of the dictionary is to be encouraged as vocabulary in context is being developed. The best dictionary practice is finding synonyms—selecting the right word for the right meaning. This is the direct opposite of making an educated guess from contextual clues. When the contextual method is being used, the dictionary should be the last resort. But for building vocabulary, it is the dictionary which provides shades of meaning and alternatives.

5. Profiting from Library Resources

A college or university library contains hundreds of thousands—in some cases, millions—of books. A student who makes use of only the assigned readings is, indeed, impoverishing himself as well as handicapping his reading performance.

To cope with the explosion of knowledge, the college-bound student should learn to utilize the holdings of the high school library for his own enrichment. His reading performance will be improved in direct proportion to the skill he develops in using the library.

The college-bound student should be taught to read in abundance. The subject-matter teacher should provide an abundance of reading materials right in the high school classroom. The academic classroom should be an environment not of recitation but of learning. Books and periodicals should be in abundance everywhere in the room. They should surround the student so thoroughly that he becomes habituated to reading in abundance. When the college-bound secondary school student learns to read abundantly, he not only becomes an excellent student in his high school subjects, but is then truly ready for college.

CONCLUSIONS

No attempt has been made here to describe or propose a separate speed-reading course for college-bound secondary school students. There are a number of such courses given in high schools, but they are the province of trained specialists. There are, however, at least ten things that each subject-matter teacher may do in the classroom to help students prepare for the enormous reading load that faces them in college. If he does these things, the teacher will discover that the quality and quantity of learning in the high school content materials will be significantly increased; the teaching task will be made easier; and learning will become more pleasurable.

Increasing speed is only one of the skills that the college-bound student must acquire. He must also develop proficiency in surveying the chapter; using the SQ3R method; recognizing clues to meaning; reading critically; improving the mechanics of perception; skipping, skimming, and scanning; finding main ideas; developing a superior vocabulary; and reading in abundance.

Questions and Activities for Discussion and Growth

1. Find someone who has taken a speed-reading course and ask him to describe specifically how it has helped him. What aspects of the course are there in addition to those described in this chapter? Do they add to the validity of the course?

2. Read some of the material that is supposed to refute the claims of extraordinary speed-reading achievements. On what basis is it claimed that it is *impossible* to attain speeds of more than 1,000 words per minute? What do you think of this?

3. What is the basic essential for success in improving one's techniques in reading? What proof can you cite for your answer?

4. Plan a lesson in one content area in which you concentrate instruction on skipping and skimming. What questions must you ask to direct the students toward skipping and skimming as valid methods of reading?

5. Plan a lesson in which you demonstrate the need for versatility to a college-bound group. What visuals do you need for the lesson? What questions must you ask to involve the students in the discussion? What answers can you anticipate?

6. Obtain one of the several mechanical devices for pacing reading speed (such as the "Rateometer" or the "SRA Reading Accelerator"). Work with the device under relatively controlled conditions and record your experience. What factors operate when an individual is aware of his intention to increase his reading achievement?

7. Why is reading speed, multiplied by percentage of comprehension, a practical way of measuring reading achievement and comparing that achievement with past or future performance?
8. If possible, obtain an EDL eye-movement photography instrument and take pictures of the eye movements of several poor readers in the college-preparatory curriculum. Show each student the photographs of his own eye movements and discuss their significance with him. Without giving further teaching or discussion, note his self-motivation for improvement.
9. Plan a lesson for college-bound students on the development of a superior vocabulary. What factors must be included? Is it worthwhile to learn a large number of esoteric words? On what do you base your answer?
10. Start an outline or diagrammatic scheme of the associated concepts surrounding some specific topic (such as "power"). Let a high school class have a brainstorming session to find possible related topics (from physics, chemistry, economics, sociology, government, religion, and so forth). It should become apparent that one word may trigger a huge galaxy of related ideas. What is the significance of this for the secondary school student who is learning to read in abundance?

Selected References

Berger, Allen: *Speed Reading,* International Reading Association, Newark, Delaware, 1967. (An annotated bibliography.)

Bliesmer, Emery P., and Ralph C. Staiger (eds.): *Eleventh Yearbook,* National Reading Conference, Milwaukee, 1962. (This is devoted exclusively to reports and discussion on reading speed and comprehension.)

Ekwall, Eldon E.: "The Truth About Speed Reading," *Phi Delta Kappan,* vol. LI, no. 2 (October, 1969), pp. 97–98. (Includes a "Response" by Nancy B. Davis.)

Elkins, Deborah: *Reading Improvement in the Junior High School,* Bureau of Publications, Teachers College, Columbia University, New York, 1963.

Fazio, Gene S., and Thomas McDonald: "Using a Metronome in Reading Class," *Journal of Reading,* vol. 13, no. 4 (January, 1970), pp. 289–291.

Massey, Will J., and Virginia D. Moore: *Helping High School Students to Read Better,* Holt, Rinehart and Winston, Inc., New York, 1965.

Matthews, John H.: "Some Sour Notes on Speed Reading," *Journal of Reading,* vol. 9, no. 3, (December, 1965), pp. 179–181 ff.

McLaughlin, G. Harry: "Reading at 'Impossible' Speeds," *Journal of Reading,* vol. 12, no. 6 (March, 1969), pp. 449–454.

Pauk, Walter: "Reading and Study in Content Areas," *Reading Improvement,* vol. 2, no. 3 (Spring, 1965), pp. 63–64.

——: "Can the Mind Speed Read?" *Journal of the Reading Specialist,* vol. 10, no. 1 (October, 1970), pp. 14–18.

Rauch, Sidney J., and Alfred B. Weinstein: *Mastering Reading Skills.* American Book Company, New York, 1968. (An excellent reading-improvement manual for college-bound students, applied especially to the content areas.)

Sargent, Eileen E.: "College Reading Before College," *Journal of Reading*, vol. 14, no. 2 (November, 1970), pp. 83–88.

Schale, Florence: "Three Approaches to Faster Reading," *Reading Improvement*, vol. 2, no. 3 (Spring, 1965), pp. 69–71.

Shefter, Harry: *Faster Reading Self-Taught*. Washington Square Press, New York, 1962. (A do-it-yourself paperback manual for motivated high school students.)

Schmidt, Bernard: "Changing Patterns of Eye-Movement," *Journal of Reading*, vol. 9, no. 6 (May, 1966), pp. 379–385.

Spache, George D.: "Is This A Breakthrough in Reading?" *The Reading Teacher*, vol. 15, no. 4 (January, 1962), pp. 258–263. (An evaluation of the "Reading Dynamics" method of speed reading.)

Taylor, Stanford E.: "An Evaluation of Forty-One Who Had Recently Completed the 'Reading Dynamics' Program," in National Reading Conference, *Eleventh Yearbook*, Milwaukee, 1962.

Warren, Mary B.: "Description of a Reading Program for Pre-College Students in a High School," in College Reading Association, *Proceedings*, vol. VI (1965), Lafayette College, Easton, Pennsylvania, pp. 13–16.

Witty, Paul A.: "Rate of Reading—A Crucial Issue," *Journal of Reading*, vol. 13, no. 2 (November, 1969), pp. 102–163.

Wood, Evelyn Nielsen, and Marjorie W. Barrows: *Reading Skills*, Holt, Rinehart and Winston, Inc., New York, 1958. (By the originator of the "Reading Dynamics" method of speed reading.)

14. PROVIDING READING SUCCESS FOR ACADEMICALLY DISADVANTAGED STUDENTS

It is an obvious fact that young people who choose teaching as a career are above average in many ways. They are academically oriented; highly motivated; concerned for the welfare of others; and above average in intelligence, reading ability, and academic achievement. College students in teacher-training curriculums appear on the dean's list and other lists of honors students more consistently than any other group except engineering students. Many other instances of superior academic ability could be cited as evidence that people who become teachers have little or no problem with most academic work.

It is this situation which creates a serious gap between teacher and student in the secondary school. Teachers—especially those just out of college—assume that all high school students are just about like themselves. When they were high school students, teachers had no trouble handling most of their reading assignments. They were perfectly able to read most of their high school textbooks—found many of them quite easy, in fact.

But for more than 50 percent of the young people in secondary school today, this is not the case. There is ample evidence that a large percent of secondary school students are being asked to read materials which are beyond their ability. These students are faced with academic failure before they start.

There are many variables causing this unfortunate situation, and they should be explored thoroughly, for almost every teacher will have some poor students in his classes. To provide success in reading for many poor readers, both in nonacademic and in academic classes, the classroom teacher needs to know certain facts about his students and about the available reading materials in his subject.

IDENTIFYING DISADVANTAGED STUDENTS

It should never be assumed on the basis of a student's economic background that he will necessarily have low intelligence, poor reading ability, modest expectations, or poor motivation; that he comes from a broken home; that he has had substandard nutrition; that his vision is poor; that he is disadvantaged because of his home life; that he comes from a slum environment; that he has unacceptable speech habits; or, indeed, that he will show any of the characteristics assumed to be part of the makeup of the poor. Any or all of those factors may—or may not—be present in any student of any background. When they are present, singly or in combination, they will put a student at a disadvantage in the classroom. Nor should it be assumed that the nonacademic student— that is, the student enrolled in a general or vocational curriculum—will necessarily have any of these characteristics.

If a teacher has thirty or more academically disadvantaged young people in a required course in the secondary school, it will be disastrous for him to expect them to read the same textbook as the better students (who will include many of those in the college-preparatory curriculum).

It is evident that some of the factors just mentioned are beyond the control of the classroom teacher. The permanent records will give the teacher some information with which he can classify a student as "academically disadvantaged." The three factors that are of most significance to the classroom teacher are *intelligence, reading ability,* and *achievement.* Young people whose records show that they are below the 50th percentile in one or more of these three factors will probably be poor students. It should be emphasized again that nonacademic students will not necessarily be poor students. It should also be pointed out that a student who is high in intelligence and reading ability may be low in achievement because he lacks general motivation or has been going through the motions in academic subjects when his true motivation is in the direction of the nonacademic.

The classroom teacher has an obligation to collect the information necessary to construct a profile of the class, including intelligence, reading ability, and achievement. As he does this, he must remember that all tests of human abilities are *relative measures;* none can be absolute measures. This means that performance by a particular student on a particular test must be thought of as related to scores made by others on the same test and to scores by the same student on other tests. To make their relative nature clear, scores must be converted into percentiles; it is then possible to compare performance between individuals, between tests, and between the abilities of an individual in different areas. See Chapter 2 for a discussion of techniques for accomplishing the conversion into percentiles.

Sample Profile of a Secondary School Class of Poor Students

It may be helpful to provide a sample of the way in which a classroom teacher may develop a profile of a class. There are six steps in recording the information:

1. List the students' names and sex, and give each student a designating number.
2. Copy their IQs from the permanent records.
3. Copy their reading scores (or grade-level-equivalent scores) from the permanent records—noting the name of the reading test(s) from which they were derived.
4. Estimate and note the *average* marks in academic subjects received by each student in the two previous grades in school.
5. Use the conversion table on page 10 to enter the approximate percentile equivalents of the IQ scores.
6. Use the manual(s) from the reading test(s) to find the approximate percentile equivalents for the scores. Enlist the help of your reading specialist.

A sample table of scores, derived from recording the data collected in the six steps above, is shown below.

SCORES, PERCENTILES, AND AVERAGE MARKS OBTAINED BY 25 POOR STUDENTS IN THE TENTH GRADE

Student	Sex	Intelligence		Reading		Average of academic marks, Grades 8 and 9
		IQ	Percentile	Test scores	Percentile	
1	M	114	80	85	50	C—
2	M	96	43	78	36	D
3	M	99	48	80	41	C
4	F	104	58	84	48	B—
5	M	107	69	85	49	B—
6	F	105	61	72	27	C
7	F	95	40	73	29	D
8	M	86	21	59	17	D—
9	M	84	18	52	10	D—
10	F	81	11	51	9	D—
11	F	82	14	52	10	D
12	F	87	23	54	12	C
13	M	82	13	52	10	D—
14	M	79	9	39	4	D—
15	F	84	19	52	10	D
16	F	106	62	84	48	B—
17	M	99	49	75	33	C+
18	M	99	48	85	51	C
19	M	101	52	79	38	C
20	F	105	59	84	47	B—
21	M	100	51	80	41	B—
22	F	99	47	65	21	D
23	M	96	43	54	12	D—
24	M	95	41	59	16	D—
25	M	100	51	64	19	D—

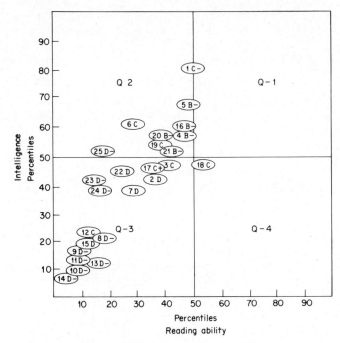

Scattergram obtained by plotting percentiles of intelligence and reading for one class.

The teacher is now ready to plot a profile of the class, the objective being to visualize the distribution of students according to intelligence, reading ability, and past academic performance.

The framework for the plotting is a grid consisting of a horizontal axis (X-axis) which is divided into ten segments, each representing 10 percent of the total population (100 percent); and a vertical axis (Y-axis) also divided into ten segments, each representing 10 percent of the total. The X-axis will be reading ability, and the Y-axis intelligence.

Intelligence test scores generally are concentrated, with approximately 35 percent above and 35 percent below the mean representing one standard deviation plus and minus ($\pm 1\sigma$). At the top of the $+1\sigma$ is an approximate IQ of 115–118. At the lower point of -1σ is an IQ of 85–83. These are *approximations* on the Stanford-Binet IQ and are close enough for our purposes of plotting.

Each student's percentile rank in intelligence and in reading is plotted, and the point plotted is labeled by the student's number. For example, student 1, with an IQ percentile of 80 and a reading score at the 50th percentile is on

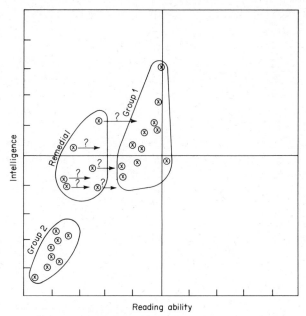

Class profile indicating grouping according to abilities.

the midpoint in reading and high up in IQ. Alongside the designation "1" is a small C—, representing his estimated average academic marks for the past two years. Student 2 is a boy in the lower lefthand quadrant (quadrant 3); he is below the median in both IQ and reading. Scores, converted into percentiles, are plotted in this way for the entire class.

Our profile of a sample class indicates that there are two distinct groups of achievers: the top group and the bottom group, with a third group that has average IQ but is below average in reading skill. This latter group would benefit by remedial reading instruction.

Group 1 has intellectual ability, but their reading ability is below their potential. Group 2 is low on both measures of ability, and may reasonably be designated as "nonreaders." It would be futile to expect pupils in group 2 to undertake reading in a secondary school textbook, and disastrous to demand it.

With concentrated remedial instruction by the school's reading specialist, it is reasonable to anticipate that some or all of the six students in the "remedial group" will move up from a virtual inability to read to an ability to read materials being studied by group 1.

It should be noted that most students in group 1 do not have reading ability commensurate with their IQ. It is the task of the teacher to seek materials with which they can relate and in which they can experience success.

The poorer students in group 1 are somewhat retarded in reading, but they are *not* subjects for remedial instruction.

Students in group 2 are severely retarded in reading. Their performance on the intelligence test also places them at the bottom. Since most intelligence tests are group tests done in booklets and requiring reading, the low IQs may, in some cases, result from poor reading ability. This can be factored out by the guidance counselor or reading specialist who can give a nonverbal individual IQ test. Because reading is likely to contaminate the IQ score, IQs must not be considered as *absolute* measures of potential. Nevertheless, students such as those in group 2 should be referred to the diagnostic specialist. The classroom teacher should not attempt to have them work in the normal way in textbooks. If individual testing reveals that a student's IQ is in fact low on the Stanford-Binet or the WISC intelligence test, then it is reasonable to conclude that he will not be able to benefit from ordinary remedial work. (Only those with adequate potential can benefit from the type of remedial reading instruction usually available in the public school.) Other reading materials must be employed, therefore, and additional modalities of learning tried.

PROVIDING SUCCESS IN READING FOR THE POOR STUDENT IN THE ACADEMIC CLASSROOM

The poor student, who is often enrolled in a general or vocational curriculum, is obligated to take certain required academic courses in American history, government, English, and perhaps other subjects. In addition, many of the textbooks or supplementary books used in the nonacademic curriculum are academic in style and format. Regardless of curriculum, reading is the common denominator of most secondary school learning. The student who does not possess adequate reading skills is a potential dropout, and even if he does not leave school, he feels inadequate and unsuccessful when confronted with the materials some teachers expect him to read.

The alternative to this unhealthy situation is to identify inadequate readers and provide them with materials in which they can succeed. This is an extremely simple solution, and teachers who try it see their students experience success almost immediately. It requires no remedial work. It applies a time-honored principle from the psychology of learning: *Start where the learner is*. This is done by providing materials of high interest and low readability.

High Interest–Low Readability Materials for Academically Disadvantaged Students

Note: The reader is also referred to Chapters 7 through 12, which discuss various levels on which reading in the content areas may be approached.

To provide success in academic subjects for poor students, provide books that they can, and will, read. Such books must have two important character-istics: (1) They must be related to the real interests of the students who are to read them. (2) They must be written at a level of readability with which these students feel comfortable. Most secondary school textbooks will not meet these two requirements. But there is a growing body of materials that meet both criteria. These are referred to as books of high interest and low readability. They are available in many subject-matter areas.

Using these books in place of inappropriate textbooks is entirely justifiable. Textbooks themselves consist of topics and facts selected from the ponderous amounts of knowledge in each field. Obviously, only some things can be presented at the secondary school level. In the secondary school textbook, groups of selected concepts are arranged around main topics or units. The classroom teacher can list the main topics or units for his course, and then, instead of using the textbook with students who cannot read it, he can provide high interest–low readability materials for each unit or topic. In doing this, the classroom teacher should enlist the aid of the librarian and the reading special-ist. There are also several excellent annotated lists of books of high interest and low readability that every secondary school should make available to its teachers and librarians. (See the Selected References at the end of this chapter, page 314.)

A few suggestions are given here which should provide the teacher with an understanding of the type of books that should be used, all available in large numbers.

Social studies. Whether it be for ninth-grade world history or eleventh-grade American history, the historical novel provides the reader with the most relevant reading material. However, other types of readings are also effective.

The historical novel. More can be learned about life in a particular period of history through the historical novel than through any other reading material. In a pleasant package, the historical novel presents setting, plot, and charac-terization; problems and solutions; conversation; vocabulary; and situations and historical facts. The teacher who surrounds the students with historical novels, written at their reading levels, is filling the classroom with social studies materials of high interest and thus enriching the classroom environment.

Biography. Young people love biographies, and many biographies are avail-able at low readability levels. There are biographies of figures from past history and of our own contemporaries. The latter reflect the social problems of our time—this is especially true if sociology, economics, politics, urban problems, or racial problems figure in the life being recounted. Those involved in the problems of our day, or any day, are bound to be colorful characters. They lead exciting, even dangerous, lives. Adventure, conflict, struggle, all combine in their biographies. These are elements with which all students, even the poorest learners, can easily identify. History is being made by people alive today—their lives are the story of society and can bring the social studies to life.

Travel stories. Some of the travel sagas are exciting reading in the social studies, particularly when they include adventure and exploration of faraway places. They can bring geography to life and, when written in simple language, they provide the poor reader with vivid experiences of the lands and peoples of the world.

Regional novels. Stories of the West, Appalachia, the Deep South, or the inner city—even when they are fictional—give the reader a picture of life in a special culture and setting. Conversations in such stories are often written in dialect, and this adds depth to the student's understanding of cultural differences. Although dialect is sometimes difficult reading at first, it may become easy to read once the reader identifies with it.

See Chapter 7 for specific suggestions.

English. English literature is a required course in most secondary schools. Some schools still hold to rigid requirements: *Ivanhoe* for all ninth-graders— *A Tale of Two Cities* for all tenth-graders, *Silas Marner* for eleventh-graders— but fortunately, such an unrealistic and closed curriculum has now been replaced by wide freedom of choice in most schools.

In the few schools where the "classics" are still required, the English teacher has no choice but to provide abridged versions for the poorer students, In a class such as that shown on the sample profile, eight students in group 2 and four or more in the remedial group would not be able to read even the abridged classics. Simplified classics might be the answer for some of these students. It is most likely, however, that students like those in group 2 in our example will respond better to reading materials that are more relevant to their own personal lives.

When there is freedom of choice in reading, the materials are often structured around themes: adventure, mystery, stories of the sea, nature, people, horses, etc. Themes provide an opportunity for poor readers to choose books of low readability which they will enjoy and succeed in. There are hundreds of books which are appropriate for junior and senior high school students.

Short stories are another means for capturing the interest of the poor students. It may be observed that many short stories are written at a low level of readability; this has not necessarily been done with poor readers in mind: the nature of the medium seems to call for short sentences, brief conversations, and little description. The plot is not very complicated; there are only a few characters; and the length does not dismay the poor reader. Indeed, the short story is the most acceptable form of literature for the poor reader.

Poetry is another literary form that poor readers and academically disadvantaged students enjoy if the content is relevant to their own experience, and if the poem is concrete rather than abstract. Poems are for reading aloud. They are meant to be listened to. The teacher should start by reading jingles, rhymes, and humorous poems to the class. Once a poem has been successfully read to the class by the teacher, many students will want to read it again for themselves. This approach almost ensures that they will read successfully on their own.

The "real-life adventure" is another literary form that poor readers find extremely relevant. It captures the reader's imagination and provides a "significant other" with whom he can identify. Some specific books and series of great interest to young people are the following:

The "Breakthrough" series, developed by William D. Sheldon (Allyn and Bacon, 1969), consists of four books with high-interest content and elements of mature thought. *Winner's Circle*, the first book in the series, is for young people who are reading at the third- and fourth-grade levels. *Beyond the Block* consists of stories adapted to the fourth-grade level. *This Cool World* contains adventure stories rewritten at a fifth-grade reading level. *The Big Ones* consists of stories rewritten at the sixth-grade level. Most of the stories in these books are about real figures in sports, war, business, music, and exploration. All the stories were popular with young adults in their original form, and this series now makes them available in simplified form for poorer readers.

Another new series of high interest and low readability books is the "Checkered Flag" series by Henry Bamman and Robert J. Whitehead (Field Education Publications, 1969). These highly motivating books appeal to junior and senior high school boys because they are about racing cars. The titles are self-explanatory: *Scramble, Grand Prix, Wheels, Smashup, Riddler, 500, Flea,* and *Bearcat.*

Scholastic Magazine has also recently published a new series of high interest–low readability workbook-type books for the poor readers. Most of the stories are nonfictional and written at a readability level somewhere between fourth and fifth grades. The contents include mysteries, sports, rock music, fashion, heroes, and jobs.

Finally, the reader is referred to Chapter 8, and to Fader's *Hooked on Books* (Berkley Publishing Corporation, New York, 1968), which describes programs for academically disadvantaged students.

Science. The poorer student can attain considerable success in reading in science, because there are many excellent science materials written at low readability levels. Science teachers structure classroom work around units: heat, sound, growing things, insects, and machines, for example. Informational books of low readability abound on almost every subject covered in a secondary school science course: these are the books to use with academically disadvantaged students.

Elementary school science series are excellent for this purpose, and several excellent series are available from major publishers. The illustrations provide even the nonreader with considerable amounts of information; and the vocabulary load is low. There are enough such books available that there is little likelihood that many will have been read in earlier grades by the students. Several series should be obtained by the secondary school science teacher and made available in the science classroom to all students.

Trade books (that is, books for the general public) on scientific subjects may also prove interesting to poor readers. They will probably not be able to read such books well, but the illustrations may provide motivation for reading something simple on the same subject. Trade books, of course, are not written with any attempt to control vocabulary or other aspects of readability.

Many science-fiction and adventure stories provide interesting and easy reading in a scientific setting and through them the poorer student may be exposed to a scientific environment. Some, of course, are beyond the abilities of poor readers, but a search will provide quite an adequate list which most poorer students can read.

Business and vocational education. Many biographies which can be read by poor students provide business and vocational settings.

Similarly, vocational novels provide excitement and adventure within the environment of dangerous or interesting jobs. The people in such novels include policemen, special agents, lumberjacks, truckers, nurses, doctors, teachers, athletes, journalists, and construction workers. Novels of this sort are usually written in a style that is easy to read, and a good deal of motivation is created by the excitement of the job and the conflict of the situation. There is always a problem to be solved, a conflict between right and wrong, and a hero or heroine with whom the reader can identify. This is a good combination of elements for getting poor readers involved.

Short stories are equally good as portrayals of many problems, procedures, and operations pertaining to business and vocations. They should be collected by the teacher and filed under descriptive headings so that he can make them available at appropriate times. Over a period of a few years, an alert teacher can build a large collection of short stories. For future reference and use, it is helpful to note the level of difficulty of each story.

Informational books in business and the vocations are numerous. Unfortunately, however, many of these are not written with any control of reading difficulty. Some, though, are written especially for the poor reader, and these will often provide vivid illustrations that give clues to meaning. Business and vocational classrooms should have dozens of books of this type. The classroom should be full of books—especially easy ones with colorful illustrations. The presence of informational books which can be enjoyed by young people without the discouragement of reading failure provides new motivation for learning in these subject areas.

Home economics. Most of the materials in home economics are factual in nature. More vocational novels, biographies, and short stories are needed. But there are a few good short sketches and short stories of career women, and some books of job descriptions include jobs connected with home economics: dietician, textile designer, fashion designer, merchandiser, buyer, and homemaker. More will be forthcoming in the 1970s.

The home economics teacher will probably have to work harder than any other subject-matter teacher in finding suitable reading materials for the poorer students.

A number of suggestions for success in reading in the field of home economics were made in Chapter 12.

CONCLUSIONS

Generations of academically disadvantaged students have been doomed to failure by teachers who assigned reading materials which were too difficult for such students to read and were also irrelevant to them.

Materials relevant to the needs and interests of today's youth are now available. Moreover, many of them—short stories, novels, and biographies especially—are written with high interest and low readability.

Subject-matter teachers in high schools should collect novels, short stories, poems, biographies, and informational books that are easy to read, and classify them under each unit of a course. These then may become the alternatives to textbooks which a large percentage of poorer students cannot and will not read.

The first step in planning for reading success is to construct a profile of the intellectual and reading abilities of the class. Only in this way can the teacher visualize the potentials within the class. By means of this procedure, classroom teachers of social studies, English, science, business, vocations, and home economics can group students and begin to plan for alternatives in their reading assignments—alternatives commensurate with the students' actual abilities.

Questions and Activities for Discussion and Growth

1. Why are *approximations* of percentile equivalents adequate for the purpose of plotting a class profile?
2. Acquire catalogues from book publishers specializing in high interest–low readability books. Work with your librarian on this project.
3. Investigate the means by which a secondary school could acquire an adequate collection of low-readability enrichment materials.

4. Plan a two-track course in one subject, for a group of average reading ability and a group of very low reading ability. Specify the books that are included in each unit for each group.

5. After having completed the course outline for question 4 above, make plans for providing reading experiences for your gifted readers.

6. After you have planned the course outline in question 4 above, plan what reading experiences you would provide for your poorest readers.

7. Survey your poorest students to determine their *real* interests and the types of materials they would prefer to read if they had their choice. How would you word such a survey in order to obtain the "purest" responses?

8. Obtain IQ scores and reading scores from the permanent records of a class of poorer learners. Convert all scores into percentiles and make a scattergram chart comparing the two variables. What does the chart show?

9. How much would it cost to provide adequate reading materials for the poor readers in one class in one academic area of the curriculum? Specify the data that justify your answer.

10. Read *Hooked on Books* and devise a similar plan for the social studies. What would it take to get it into operation? Would the effort be worthwhile?

Selected References

Allen, Beth: "Poor and Non-Readers in the Secondary Schools: A Teacher's Dilemma," *English Journal,* vol. 57, no. 6 (September, 1968), pp. 884–888.

Crane, August: "Meeting the Reading Needs of the Non-College-Bound High School Student," *Journal of the Reading Specialist,* vol. 7 (October, 1967), pp. 26–29.

Dunn, Anita E., and Mabel E. Jackman: *Fare for the Reluctant Reader.* Capital Area School Development Association, Albany, 1964. (An annotated list in paperback for junior and senior high schools. It is well done, with titles divided into categories according to the interests of young adults. Fiction.)

Emans, Robert, and Raymond Urbas: "Emphasizing Reading Skills in an English Course for Underachievers," *Journal of Reading,* vol. 12, no. 5 (February, 1969), pp. 373–376 ff.

Emery, Raymond C., and Margaret B. Houshower: *High Interest–Easy Reading for Junior And Senior High School Reluctant Readers.* National Council of Teachers of English, Champaign, Ill., 1965.

Hardman, Lawrence: "Slow Readers—A Happy Experience," *English Journal,* vol. 57, no. 3 (March, 1968), pp. 405–408.

Spache, George D.: *Good Reading for Disadvantaged Readers,* The Garrard Press, Champaign, Ill., 1970. (Prepared especially for teachers in inner-city slum schools and for those teaching in culturally different environments.)

——: *Good Reading for Poor Readers,* The Garrard Press, Champaign, Ill., 1968. (The "classic" in the field of annotated sources of high interest-low readability reading materials.)

Sterns, Gertrude: *Help Yourself to Improve Your Reading,* Readers Digest Services, Pleasantville, New York, 1963. (Two volumes of *Readers Digest*-size paperbacks for junior and senior high school students. Excellent.)

15. UTILIZING THE TOTAL RESOURCES OF THE SCHOOL

There is no need today for any subject-matter teacher to try to work in isolation, entirely on his own. State departments of education, with funds allocated by the U. S. Office of Education, have made all sorts of services available to local schools. Moreover, book publishers and manufacturers of learning "hardware" are more than willing to demonstrate their wares and to suggest solutions, free of charge.

The teacher and his classroom are no longer an island. And no teacher should hesitate to ask for help. On the contrary, the theme of education today might well be: "Ask, and it shall be given."

In making any effort to use the total resources of the school, two questions may be helpful: Who should one ask? and, What should one ask? It is widely accepted that one must be somewhat sophisticated to know what kinds of questions to ask. Questions themselves do reveal much about the person who asks them; they indicate whether the asker has thought through the problem adequately. Naturally, one does not go about asking an indiscriminate array of questions, directed at random. Here are several suggestions which will help the classroom teacher formulate the right questions and direct them to the right people.

In bygone days, the barber often acted as a tooth extractionist and psychologist, the general store was a mini-supermarket, and the blacksmith was a general repairman. But now we live in an age of specialists, and the educational community has its share of them. Let us examine how various educational specialists can be of help to the classroom teacher.

The secondary school principal and the superintendent are both specialists in administration, public relations, budgeting, and management. Naturally, they are concerned about reading as a factor in academic achievement, but their main contribution is to encourage all reasonable efforts for improvement of learning. Ordinarily, the principal and superintendent are not sources of specific advice on reading. Indeed, they may have as many questions about reading and content area learning as does the classroom teacher. Either or both, however, may be very helpful in directing the classroom teacher to sources of help.

ASK THE PRINCIPAL

If the classroom teacher suspects that help may be available from "someone" in the state department of education, it is proper and helpful for him to start his search by asking the principal. This accomplishes four goals. First, it enlists his support for this worthwhile quest. Second, it saves much time, for the principal will have accumulated helpful knowledge at briefing sessions with specialists of the state department of education. Third, it alerts the principal to the classroom teacher's specific interest. Moreover, through the principal's contact with all his teachers, those with similar interests may be brought together to work cooperatively. Fourth, it establishes the classroom teacher as a professional who keeps the principal informed of certain classroom needs that may be met through the total resources of the school.

Another service which the principal can perform is to arrange for a group effort in solving a problem or in changing a curriculum. It is seldom good practice for one classroom teacher alone to attempt to effect change. Much is to be gained by getting the support and help of other teachers. A teacher who attempts to work entirely on his own may arouse the suspicions of his colleagues and run the risk of engendering jealousy, criticism, and opposition. On the other hand, colleagues who are part of a project cannot very well be against it. The "we" approach is far more powerful than the "I" approach. Sharing ideas, modifying expectations, and making a group effort are all benefits which can result when the principal brings several teachers together to consider a common problem.

ASK THE SUPERVISOR

The role of the supervisor in today's educational community is that of a consultant rather than an evaluator and dictator. Along with this change in image has come a change in function: the supervisor's chief function now is that of a "resource person." It would be well to consider the supervisor as the most important person to ask. The supervisor is in this special position because of several factors. First, he has been a teacher and knows the problems of the classroom from firsthand experience. Second, he travels around to many classrooms and discovers many good or promising practices. His wealth of ideas should be tapped. Third, because the supervisor's schedule is flexible, he is free to attend presentations, demonstrations, conferences, and conventions. Moreover, he must be up-to-date on methods and materials; he is the one person in the school who works under an obligation to be knowledgeable about current developments in curriculum, methods, and resources. He is the natural person to ask.

Most large school systems have special supervisors in secondary school subject areas and in reading. In smaller cities, one person may act as "curriculum director." In some places, the title "curriculum coordinator" is used to designate such a person. Regardless of title, these are "resource people": their main function is to answer questions and respond to the needs of classroom subject-matter teachers. Supervisors are there to be *asked*.

ASK THE DIRECTOR OF THE LEARNING-MATERIALS CENTER

Not many years ago, this person would have been called the "librarian"; now the title is "director (or specialist) of the learning-materials center." The change in title reflects significant changes in function, for the learning-materials center houses not only library materials but also most of the school's multisensory aids. The director is the one person in the school who has charge of its reference and enrichment resources. No program of curricular change or methodological improvement can succeed unless he is involved and helps.

The subject-matter teacher must work closely with the librarian or materials-center director (or both, if the school has both). Conversely, the librarian must work in cooperation with the classroom teacher, since the library or materials center is the resource bank for the content areas.

The reading materials in the library or materials center must be appropriate to the abilities and needs of the learners. When this is not the case, improvement of learning is almost impossible. A recent experience of the writer will emphasize this point. A visit to a large private secondary school (about 1,000 students) revealed that although 70 percent go on to college, only 20 percent of those are able to graduate from college. Selection of students at this school is based on racial origin exclusively, but the socioeconomic and ethnic background of most of the students would categorize them as "culturally disadvantaged." In seeking the cause for the huge dropout rate in college, two things were investigated: the curriculum and the curriculum materials. The library provided the key to the problem.

The library is well staffed, with three full-time graduate librarians and a number of student assistants. The shelves are full, and new books are in evidence everywhere. In fact, new books appear to be in the majority. A close examination disclosed close to four hundred books on philosophy and religion—most of them written at the college and university level. There were shelves and shelves of huge, forbidding volumes on economic theory, theory of government, political science, theory of nationalism, monetary theory, theory of history, theory of social movements and economic utopias, theory of urbanization, theory of aging, international controls and cooperation, literary criticism, theoretical physics, mathematics, oceanography, history of medicine, comparative criticism of art, analysis and criticism of music, dramatic criticism, corporate financing, corporation law, corporate structure, antitrust legislation, industrial labor theory, and so on. The biography and fiction sections showed the same preponderance of university-level reading materials.

The check-out cards provided the clue to the "new" appearance of the library's holdings. The books are not being used—and for a very good reason. The students in this school cannot possibly be able to read those books. That unfortunate situation is worsened by the fact that the school discarded all textbooks; instead, the students are expected to concentrate upon a few selected units in which they are to do intensive research of the sort done at the university level.

The library is, indeed, tailored to this method. But unfortunately the method and materials are inappropriate to the abilities, background, and objectives of the students. The method could have been adopted successfully only if the library had provided books at levels of readability appropriate for the students. It was disclosed that the academic area teachers described to the librarians the nature of the unit to be studied, and the librarians alone selected the books. The reading consultant was not consulted.

The result of this situation is a student body going through the motions of research in books which they actually cannot read. Plagiarism is almost a necessity if the type of research reports expected by the faculty are to be produced. Comprehension is at an unbelievably low level; commitment to reading and growth in reading skills are almost negative—all this in a school that is endowed with almost unlimited financial resources.

This description should serve to illustrate the fact that the various resources of the school must be coordinated and realistically oriented to the actual abilities and objectives of the learners.

The task of the classroom teachers, working together, is to develop units of learning that are based on a textbook and on the use of a resource center that contains reading materials appropriate to the reading abilities of the students.

ASK THE DEPARTMENT CHAIRMAN

One who accepts the position of chairman or "head" of an academic department in a secondary school does so with the understanding that he must function at least part of the time as a "resource person," and part of the time as a member of the school's management team. It is, therefore, appropriate to expect that a department chairman will have some answers, or at least will be able to get some answers.

Often the department chairman will have available secretarial help, catalogs, reference files, and names and addresses of people who can help, as well as a departmental collection of sample textbooks and enrichment materials from publishers' representatives. The departmental office is the common property of all members of the department, and each department member has a right to expect help from the chairman.

Because the chairman's teaching load usually is reduced, he is frequently able to attend demonstrations and conferences where new methods and materials are discussed; he sees publishers' representatives at conventions; he hears of new ideas that are being tried elsewhere. He also works closely with the director of the learning-materials center in selecting new additions to the center. The department chairman is, truly, the basic "resource person." He is the most easily available specialist and the logical person to consult first.

ASK THE COUNSELOR

The counselor is a part of the educational team and can be of service to the teacher just as much as to the student. He is the specialist on students, for his office collects a wealth of data on each student and stores it for use in helping the student.

The data in the counselor's office can provide the basis for improvement in the content areas.

The permanent records provide a cumulative profile of the demonstrated abilities and limitations of each learner. Among other data are records of performance on intelligence tests, reading and vocabulary tests, and interest inventories. These are all basic, essential measures which every classroom teacher must have for making up lesson plans and assignments for learning.

The counselor may also provide many personal insights that can make the critical difference between blind mass education and education according to individual differences. He is, then, a vital resource for the classroom teacher who wants to improve learning.

ASK OTHER TEACHERS

No teacher is alone in hoping and working for improved learning in his own subject-matter area; most teachers are interested in anything that results in more success for their students. The problems which one teacher has are likely to be problems common to all teachers.

Most teachers are faced with the problem of teaching students whose reading abilities and intellectual potential range from very low to extraordinarily high. A few teachers try to underplay the difficulties of this situation. They have no problems—at least, so they say. Other teachers tend to overemphasize their problems; they are often chronic complainers, admitting defeat and predicting doom. Between those extremes are the great majority of teachers, who are attempting to do something constructive to increase learning in their classrooms.

Ask other teachers to join you in a team effort—sharing experiences, methods, materials, ideas, skills, and talents. Working together, the entire team can make real progress.

Ask other teachers: "How many students in your tenth-grade classes have reading abilities below the 20th percentile?" "Do you have a list of good books on electrical magnetism that students with fourth-grade reading ability can read?" "How does your low-ability group like the text we are using this year?" These and many other specific questions are such that they not only elicit specific answers but also reveal your own concern over a problem and open avenues of communication that will result in worthwhile dialogue with your colleagues.

Don't try to work alone. Ask your colleagues.

ASK THE READING SPECIALIST

The reading specialist should never be thought of as a remedial instructor, since he is trained in curricular methods and materials as well as in reading methods and materials. The reading specialist can help in three ways:

First, he should be enlisted to work as a member of any team committed to improving learning in the academic classroom. He will contribute valuable suggestions about the readability of books and the reading abilities of students. He will be the leader in the discussion of individual differences.

Second, the reading specialist will act as the liaison between the classroom teacher, who has certain needs, and the learning-materials center, which makes acquisitions. The help of the reading specialist is an absolute necessity for the efficient selection of materials at various levels of difficulty for each unit in each academic area. Without his help, this enormous task falls upon the classroom teachers alone.

Third, the reading specialist is trained and competent to administer diagnostic reading tests to students suspected of having severe reading handicaps, and interpret the results. He has the know-how, the place, the materials, and the diagnostic skill for such testing, and he alone is trained to do it. Seldom has a classroom teacher the ability or time to administer individual diagnostic reading surveys. Once the reading specialist has identified an individual with a severe reading disability, he is then committed to do something about it—an impossible undertaking for the classroom teacher.

The reading specialist is by far the most valuable person with whom the academic classroom teacher should work. The reading specialist, the director of the learning-materials center, and the classroom teacher form a most logical team.

ASK THE ACADEMICIANS

College and university professors who spend the greater part of their time studying, researching, and teaching in the field of reading are in touch with all major developments in this area. In fact, they are usually part of new projects that are on the drawing boards. Most university professors of reading methods are writing and conducting experiments or research on materials and methods. They must, therefore, know what everyone else is doing in the same field. Their knowledge should be tapped.

The college or university student is in a favored position, for he is within talking distance of these people. If he shows enough interest, he may be invited to join a group working on a project to develop new materials or methods for use in the secondary school. College students who are preparing to teach a secondary school subject should recognize this valuable resource available to them.

Professors of reading methods are also to be seen and heard at local, regional, and national reading conferences. Their thoughts are available in the state, regional, and national journals of the various reading associations. They may also be hired on a per-diem basis to conduct in-service workshops or discussion sessions at which teachers can get answers to their own classroom problems.

ASK YOURSELF

When you talk to yourself, you often find that you are in good company—for one usually talks to one's "better self." The result is that, if your better self will listen, you will begin to get some honest answers.

Here are some questions that could be asked:

Do I know the strengths and limitations of the learners in my classes?
Do I have the best textbook possible?
Do I make the best possible use of the textual materials?
Do I prepare and give the best possible assignments?
Why do I do this? Why do I do that?
Just what are my goals?
Am I providing all the help possible in reading in my content area?

Don't try to work on your own—ask your better self.

CONCLUSIONS

Most secondary schools today are multimillion-dollar learning centers with rich resources in personnel, materials, records, hardware, and students. The skillful teacher exploits them all in his effort to improve achievement in the classroom. As with many projects (the space program is an example), the greatest amount of time is consumed in delineating the objectives, calculating needs, assembling a massive support organization, and getting started. In the classroom, the project will be successful only if all tasks for producing readiness have been properly planned and executed by the teacher, and if the "ground crews" and "support centers" have been properly set up. When all this is done, the students can be launched on the way to improved learning. Don't try to undertake such a program on your own—utilize the total resources of the school.

Questions and Activities for Discussion and Growth

1. Make a list of all of the things that should be done in a secondary school to improve reading in the subject-matter classroom. Survey a specific secondary school and determine which are left undone there.
2. After accomplishing the task described in question 1 above, devise a plan for getting the various undone jobs done. What new personnel would be needed?
3. Survey a learning-materials center in a secondary school, giving special attention to the holdings in one specific academic area.
4. After having accomplished the task in question 3 above, determine how each resource should be used.
5. After having accomplished the task in question 4 above, list the major resources that need to be acquired as minimal holdings in the academic area you have been examining. How may they be obtained? At what cost?

6. Plan an in-service session for teachers in a specific academic area. What could be a provocative theme which would concentrate on the relationship of reading to the daily task of instruction and learning in that area?
7. Make a list of questions you need to have answered in order to improve learning in your subject-matter area. After each question, indicate the specific person or persons on the school staff to whom you would direct the question.
8. After you have accomplished the task in question 7 above, try out the questions on the people you have designated. Keep a careful written record or tape recording of their answers.
9. After you have accomplished the task in question 8 above, analyze the the answers to determine the following points: (a) Were your questions adequate? (b) Were the answers adequate? (c) How could questioning be improved?
10. How may book publishers' representatives be of help as part of the total resources of the school? What are the positive and negative factors to be considered in utilizing their know-how and services? Plan a professional day in which publishers' representatives are used as "resource persons."

Selected References

Berger, Allen, and Hugo Hartig: *The Reading Materials Handbook,* Academia Press, Oshkosh, Wisconsin, 1969. (An extremely valuable sourcebook of materials for the improvement of reading in secondary schools and colleges.)

Criscuolo, Nicholas: "Attacking the Reading Problem in the Secondary Schools," *Journal of Secondary Education,* vol. 43, no. 7 (November, 1968), pp. 307–308.

Dobrin, Ruth M.: "The Massapequa Story: A Pre-College Reading Program," *Journal of Developmental Reading,* vol. IV, no. 3 (Spring, 1961), pp. 159–173.

Duggins, Lydia: "Teacher-Librarian Teamwork in the Senior High School Reading Program," in International Reading Association, *Annual Proceedings,* Newark, Delaware, 1964, pp. 203–204.

Florida State Department of Education: *Reading in Florida Secondary Schools,* Tallahassee, 1966.

McCracken, Robert A.: "Supervision of Reading Instruction in the Junior High School," *Journal of Reading,* vol. II, no. 4 (January, 1969), pp. 276–284.

Newton, J. Roy: *Reading in Your School,* McGraw-Hill Book Company, New York, 1960. (Delineates the roles of the various individuals on a school staff and their relationships to each other in the development of a total-school reading program.)

Robinson, H. Alan, and Sidney J. Rauch: *Guiding the Reading Program,* Science Research Associates, Chicago, 1965. (Describes in detail the responsibilities and techniques of the reading consultant.)

Smith, Richard J., Bernice Bragstad, and Karl D. Hesse: "Teaching Reading in the Content Areas—An Inservice Model," *Journal of Reading,* vol. 13, no. 6 (March, 1970), pp. 421–428.

Stewart, L. Jane, Frieda M. Heller, and Elsie J. Alberty: *Improving Reading in the Junior High School,* Appleton-Century-Crofts, Inc., New York, 1957. (Describes the cooperation of the librarian and the core teacher in an eighth-grade program at the Ohio State University secondary school.)

Wilson Library Bulletin, Vol. 45, no. 3, (November, 1970). (This entire issue is devoted to the topic "The Librarian and the Teacher of Reading" and contains some very pertinent articles.)

16. CONCLUSIONS

Reading is quite often thought of as a "tool" that, when acquired, may be used on various occasions—just as a hammer, screwdriver, or can opener. Some educators, in fact, refer to reading as one of the "tool" subjects. Additionally, there is the common notion that a child acquires this tool—reading—in elementary school and from there onward uses it in all areas of the curriculum. At the same time, it is in the elementary school that the concept of "developmental" reading is introduced—reading as a separate subject in the curriculum, running parallel to literature, social studies, science, and so on. Developmental reading sessions in grades 4, 5, and 6 are allotted equal time with the other "content" subjects. This conveys the idea that from grade 4 upwards reading per se is a separate "subject"; and, indeed, as it is handled in many schools it is actually just that.

A more defensible position would be to consider the first three grades as the training ground in basic fundamental skills in reading and the upper grades and secondary content-area classrooms as the performance areas.

Reading, like any other skill, must be practiced if some degree of perfection is to be achieved. Moreover, practice in reading, as is true of many other skills, requires the constant attention of knowledgeable coaches who are concerned and who know the methods necessary for effective practice.

This concept of reading finds a counterpart in speaking. Everyone learns the basic skill of speaking early in life—long before he enters formal school life. After he enters school, his teachers serve as coaches; he may even have "public speaking" as a separate subject in secondary school. But the measure of his success in speaking is the use he makes of this skill in all areas of life. To become proficient, he must go beyond the mechanics of producing sounds to the "performance" areas, which in the academic life are related to the content fields. Similarly, reading will remain a marginal, mechanical "word-calling" process unless the student moves upward into the performance areas, with a good coach as a guide. It is in this frame of reference that each teacher in the content areas becomes a "coach" in reading—hence the concept that "every teacher is a teacher of reading."

EVERY TEACHER IS A TEACHER OF READING

Two or more decades ago, secondary school classroom teachers were greatly surprised and disturbed by the idea, then being proposed, that every teacher is a teacher of reading. Their reaction was quite understandable. Few, if any, had taken courses in the teaching of reading. Most assumed that children learn to read in elementary school and should come to their classes in secondary school adequately equipped with the ability to read. Moreover, they reasoned, if this is not the case, why should the secondary school content-area teacher spend time doing a job that the elementary school has failed to do? But the idea that every teacher is a teacher of reading still exists, and this persistence may be evidence that the concept has some merit. The problem is chiefly a semantic one. What is meant, of course, is that all subject-area teachers must do some teaching of specific reading-study skills to ensure optimum achievement in their classes.

Although twenty years have passed since this idea was introduced, little concern has been forthcoming by some content-area teachers. In fact, research in the relationship between reading abilities and academic achievement in the secondary school has been met with a "so what?" attitude—the response is often, "Who needs research to prove the obvious?" This attitude, however, reflects something more than the idea that the relationship between reading and achievement is too obvious to merit discussion: it reflects a certain fatalism, a feeling that those with poor reading ability are predestined to be poor achievers. And most secondary school content-area teachers feel that causes of reading failure and programs for improvement in reading are not their responsibility. Furthermore, of the few who do show concern, many feel inadequate to the task of improving reading.

Such attitudes are to be expected, for only recently have the specialists in subject areas shown any widespread interest in dialogue with leaders of the reading field. The National Council of Teachers of English has only recently awakened to the fact that this area of common interest needs the combined best thinking of both types of specialists; the Council now includes sessions in reading as part of its annual meetings.

Teacher-training institutions have all but abdicated their responsibility for the complete training of secondary teachers. It has been suggested that this is the result of a cycle through which those institutions have been moving as they developed from normal schools to colleges and parts of universities. To avoid the accusation of being "practical," some teacher-training institutions have made every effort to ignore methodology—including methods of teaching reading. In place of educational "how-to-do-it" courses, there has been a greater emphasis on the liberal arts and on courses in the future teacher's own major subject. Small wonder, then, that newly graduated subject-matter teachers are no more knowledgeable concerning reading improvement than were previous generations of secondary school teachers.

But today more people are talking about reading, speed reading, retardation in reading, remedial reading, and reading to prevent dropping out of school—a situation which tends to create greater awareness of and attention to reading ability in the classroom. Consequently, many secondary teachers—even some of those who have been in the profession for many years and have perhaps never seriously considered the problem of poor reading ability as their responsibility or, indeed, as being solvable at all—are beginning to accept the possibility that something can be done for poor readers. Thus, it is not uncommon today to find an attitude of "Maybe someone should do something about this." That much progress has been made; but the suggestion that the "someone" should be the classroom teacher still raises cries of consternation and protestations of inadequacy from many—and rightly so. For the nature of reading is not generally understood.

Basically, of course, the objective of the content-area teacher is to teach "content"; still, the fact remains that in so doing the teacher is teaching individuals. Now few content teachers would disagree with the objective of helping each individual student grow in knowledge and understanding *through* content; it follows logically from this that the content teacher must be concerned with helping students grow, and that it is his responsibility to use every means to accomplish that goal. Such an objective calls for effort in two directions: first, he must determine what materials are most appropriate to the skills of the learners; second, he must help his students learn the subject by helping them acquire the specific reading skills appropriate to the nature and demands of each lesson. Let us recapitulate these two types of effort.

In the first instance, the content teacher will be searching for materials in his subject which are written at several levels of difficulty, or readability. In many cases, materials have been produced with his specific purpose in mind; but in other cases, materials which originally were not written with any specific reading level in mind can often be "discovered." The content teacher should acquire a rather substantial collection of materials or references to materials. In this endeavor, the help of a good school librarian is crucial.

Such a project can be less burdensome if it is the cooperative effort of a group of teachers, all of whom have the same goals. As a departmental project, it can become a total effort with administrative support—in contrast to individual improvement projects, which occasionally acquire the label of a "revolt" or a "dissent" and sometimes even arouse the anger of teachers who fear that a successful project by a colleague poses a threat to their own status. Another advantage of the departmental project is that in such a project materials may be pooled so that they are available to all. Under conditions of mutual respect and trust, a department can soon build up a most useful collection of materials at many levels of reading difficulty and on many units. Before this is undertaken, however, it must be clear who will have the responsibility of maintaining the various parts of the collection and arranging for scheduling the use and return of those parts. It should not be the responsibility of one person alone.

The second task of the content teacher is helping the students develop specific reading skills which are needed for getting the most out of lessons. In performing this task, the content teacher actually does become a teacher of reading, but his effort is channeled into teaching the reading skills specifically required by, or appropriate to, each lesson. The reading assignment, consequently, becomes the critical step in teaching and learning in the secondary school content classroom.

Success in content is significantly related to the reading-study skills of the students. You are a teacher of reading because you are a content-area teacher.

READING IS THE COMMON DENOMINATOR OF ACADEMIC LEARNING

The secondary school classroom teacher must recognize several variables affecting his students' performance. Fortunately, something may be done about them if they are exerting a negative effect.

First, intelligence. The modern school accepts the concept of wide ranges in intelligence at each grade level. The task of the school is to provide reading materials appropriate for the various levels of intellectual ability in each subject.

Second, reading ability. There are also wide ranges of reading abilities; reading materials of appropriate difficulty must be matched to them.

Third, interest and motivation. Almost all children, from all kinds of backgrounds, must go to school. The secondary school inherits a student population which includes unmotivated, reluctant learners; highly motivated, gifted learners; and all degrees in between. Motivation may often be triggered by reading materials that are relevant to the interests of students from various backgrounds. It is unrealistic to expect that all students will become committed to the ordinary, often outmoded, curricular materials found in many schools.

Reading, as has been said so often throughout this book, is the common denominator of all academic learning in the secondary school. Adjustments in reading materials and methods to match the ability and capture interest of the various types of students in the secondary school population are necessary if learning in the secondary school classroom is to be improved. And the improvement of learning in the secondary school subjects is also directly related to the classroom teacher's commitment to developing in his students the reading skills discussed in this book.

17. A PROFESSIONAL LIBRARY IN READING FOR THE SECONDARY SCHOOL

Secondary school classroom teachers have had, on the whole, little or no exposure to the field of reading, either through undergraduate courses or through in-service institutes. Consequently, a collection of books on reading in a secondary school will be only as effective as the response to it. A collection of books may remain unused, or it may serve as the nucleus of many buzz sessions and structured in-service discussions.

In selecting the following list of books and suggesting them as a good basis for a professional library in reading for the secondary school, four things were kept in mind: first, the collection was to be current; second, it should not contain highly technical research reports; third, it should not contain periodical references; and, fourth, it should be a very practical, usable collection.

None of the suggested books were copyrighted before 1956, but this does not mean that all books published earlier than 1956 are obsolete. Some older works might be added to the collection later if money is available for expanding it. The collection should be open-ended, of course, since worthwhile new books should be added as they are published.

Because articles in periodicals are too numerous and diversified for a secondary school professional library, it was decided that only a few journals and yearbooks which are chiefly oriented to secondary school reading should be included. In the place of scattered periodical references, a few books of carefully selected readings are suggested as much more practical holdings.

Although reference has been made to "library" holdings, the collection should not actually be placed in the high school library. On the contrary, they should be readily available in the teachers' room. Although putting books in the teachers' room on the basis of an honor system has seldom proved very successful, it is hoped that each school staff can devise some effective method. One somewhat more effective scheme is to provide checkout sheets for each book, with a place for the name of the borrower and a place for the date of return. This system lets everyone know where a book is in case it is needed by another staff member. It also gives an idea of the extent to which the professional library is being used and can serve as a source of dialogue among teachers who have read a certain book.

An effort has been made to provide brief annotations on the following books, periodicals, monographs, and yearbooks. A school system with plenty of money should have all the references listed, to form the nucleus of its professional library. Schools with less money available (a category which includes most schools) will find some books highly recommended as "musts" for a basic collections.

Bamman, Henry A., Ursula Hogan, and Charles E. Greene: *Reading Instruction in the Secondary Schools,* David McKay Co., Inc., New York, 1961.

This is a relatively short (235 pages) and easy-to-read text with especially good chapters on adolescents' interests and preferences, how to study, and reading in the content areas of the social studies, science, English, mathematics, and industrial arts.

Appendix D provides an exhaustive listing of roots, prefixes, and suffixes.

Berger, Allen and Hugo Hartig: *The Reading Materials Handbook,* The Academia Press, Oshkosh, Wisconsin (Box 125), 1969.

An excellent 72-page resource booklet on the sources of materials, texts, periodicals, and reference materials in secondary school reading. A must for all secondary school professional libraries.

Burton, Dwight L.: *Literature Study in High Schools,* Holt, Rinehart and Winston, Inc., New York, 1959.

This is a book filled with suggestions for the improvement of teaching literature in junior high schools and senior high schools.

Carpenter, Helen M. (ed.): *Skill Development in the Social Studies,* National Council for the Social Studies, *33d Yearbook,* Washington, D.C., 1963.

This presents an edited collection of papers specifically on reading and the social studies.

Ciardi, John: *How Does a Poem Mean?* Houghton Mifflin Company, Boston, 1960.

This interesting little book by a noted literary critic provides several examples of how poetry should be taught and studied for better comprehension and deeper appreciation. This is a very practical book for the classroom teacher.

Emery, Raymond C., and Margaret B. Houshower: *High Interest–Easy Reading for Junior and Senior High School Reluctant Readers,* National Council of Teachers of English, Champaign, Illinois, 1965.

An annotated listing of 350 books of high interest and low readability. The books are categorized by themes: "Historical Adventure," "Mystery," "Science Adventure," "Sea Adventure," "Sports Adventure," "Western, Pioneer, and Indian," "Dogs," "Horses," "Biography," "Family Life," "Folk Tales," "Informational," "People," and "Careers."

The series books are listed separately.

This is a valuable monograph for every secondary school professional library.

Fader, Daniel, and Elton B. McNeil: *Hooked on Books,* Berkley Publishing Corporation, New York, 1968.

This best-selling paperback by two professors at the University of Michigan should be at the top of the list for all classroom teachers. Fader is a Renaissance scholar and McNeil is a director of graduate programs in psychology. They describe a most exciting program for getting reluctant readers and potential dropouts to *read, read, read,* and the almost unbelievable results of the program. This is a best-seller because it is true, compelling, and extremely adoptable by every subject-area teacher. Every secondary teacher, principal, librarian, and counselor should read it cover to cover.

Hafner, Lawrence E.: *Improving Reading in Secondary Schools,* The Macmillan Company, New York, 1967.

This is an extensive collection of readings selected from journals and yearbooks of professional associations concerned with reading in the secondary schools. Section 10—almost one-fourth of the book—presents an excellent collection of writings on reading in the various content areas.

Herber, Harold L.: *Teaching Reading in Content Areas,* Prentice-Hall, Inc., Englewood Cliffs, N.J., 1970.

An unconventional approach to content application. Teachers will find Chapter 8 on vocabulary development helpful. The "Reasoning Guides" in the last third of the book provide what are essentially objective tests that may be used for directed reading activities. They should be used as models of what teachers might devise.

Hook, J. N.: *The Teaching of High School English,* The Ronald Press Company, New York, 1965.

The author states that his text is "for students preparing to teach the English language and its literature in junior and senior high schools and for experienced teachers who wish to keep abreast of the current teaching practices in their profession."

Hook is one of the very few specialists in English education who also has a deep commitment to the role reading instruction plays in comprehension. Consequently, his chapter on "The Improvement of Reading" is especially relevant. In other chapters he provides practical suggestions for improving the reading of fiction, drama, poetry, and nonfiction.

International Reading Association: *Corrective Reading in the High School Program,* Perspectives in Reading no. 6 (ed. H. Alan Robinson and Sidney J. Rauch), Newark, Delaware, 1966.

The papers contained in this publication were presented at the International Reading Association's Perspectives Conference, held in conjunction with the National Council of Teachers of English in Boston, November, 1965.

International Reading Association: *Developing Study Skills in Secondary Schools,* Perspectives in Reading no. 4 (ed. Harold L. Herber), Newark, Delaware, 1965.

One of the most practical monographs on the classroom techniques of teaching reading-study skills in the secondary school.

International Reading Association: *Fusing Reading Skills and Content* (eds. H. Alan Robinson and Ellen L. Thomas). Newark, Delaware, 1969.

International Reading Association: *Reading Instruction in Secondary Schools,* Perspectives in Reading no. 2 (ed. Margaret Early), Newark, Delaware, 1964.

This is a summation of the Perspectives Conference on secondary school reading, sponsored by the International Reading Association and held in Chicago in 1963. The booklet includes the papers that were presented, each followed by the reactions of the participants.

Journal of Reading, International Reading Association, Newark, Delaware.

Currently edited by Margaret Early and Harold Herber, this is published eight times a year. It was formerly the *Journal of Developmental Reading,* which originated at Purdue University. This publication devotes its entire content to secondary school reading.

Journal of the Reading Specialist, College Reading Association, Reading Clinic, Syracuse University.

This has been published since 1960; it presents articles and research reports on both college and high school reading problems and regularly publishes unique articles of special interest to secondary school teachers.

Karlin, Robert: *Teaching Reading in High School,* The Bobbs-Merrill Company, Inc., Indianapolis, 1964.

Although this is a comprehensive text on all aspects of reading, reading programs, and reading testing in secondary schools, there are several chapters of interest to the subject-matter classroom teacher. Chapter 6, "Meanings and Reading," provides some universally applicable ideas, as does Chapter 7, "The Study Skills."
"Reading for Appreciation," Chapter 8, applies to the short stories, novels, essays, and biographies used in the English classroom. Chapter 14 describes successful reading programs in eight large high schools.

Laffey, James L., (ed.): *Reading in the Content Areas,* International Reading Association—ERIC/CRIER, Newark, Delaware, 1972.

The pairs of essays on each content field deal first with the significant research and then with the application in the classroom of the research.

Lowenstein, Morris R.: *Teaching Social Studies in Junior and Senior High Schools,* Rand McNally & Company, Chicago, 1963.

Several sections of this method book deal directly with the "reading" of charts, graphs, maps, and other visuals.

Marksheffel, Ned D.: *Better Reading in the Secondary School,* The Ronald Press Company, New York, 1966.

The chapters "Study Skills" and "Critical Reading" are of value to the classroom subject matter teacher. The remainder of the book is quite pedantic.

Massey, Will J., and Virginia D. Moore: *Helping High School Students to Read Better,* Holt, Rinehart and Winston, Inc., New York, 1965.

The most important contribution of this monograph is its step-by-step prescription of methods for developing skills in reading in the content areas.

Megaliff, Cecile: *The Junior Novel,* C. W. Post College of Long Island University, Port Washington, N.Y., 1964.

This is a very interesting and informative little book on the role of the junior novel and adolescent reading. It makes an especial contribution with chapters analyzing the patterns and themes common to the writings of specific popular writers for adolescents: Betty Cavanna, Stephen Meader, Phyllis Whitney, Mary Stolz, Rosamond duJardin, and Henry George Felsen.

This book is a must for the English teacher.

Newton, J. Roy: *Reading in Your School,* McGraw-Hill Book Company, New York, 1960.

The chief contribution of this book is its practical suggestions for school supervisors and administrators. It is one of the very few books written for them.

Olson, Arthur V., and Wilbur S. Ames (eds.): *Teaching Reading Skills in Secondary Schools: Readings,* International Textbook Company, Scranton, Pennsylvania, 1970.

This collection of readings provides an excellent sampling of some of the best recent publications on secondary school reading and the content areas.

Penty, Ruth C.: *Reading Ability and High School Dropouts,* Bureau of Publications, Teachers College, Columbia University, New York, 1956.

This small book, describing the program at Battle Creek, Michigan, was one of the first which pointed to reading failure as the chief cause of high school dropouts. It is a compelling story of the problem.

Pescosolido, John, and Charles Gervase: *Reading Expectancy and Readability*, Kendall/Hunt Publishing Company, Dubuque, Iowa, 1971.

An excellent handbook on measurement of reading expectancy and textbook readability. A must for the professional library.

Preston, Ralph C.: *Guiding the Social Studies Reading of High School Students*, National Council for the Social Studies, Bulletin no. 34, Washington, D.C., 1963.

One of the few books written especially for the secondary school social studies classroom teacher. It contains numerous suggestions for improving social studies learning through increased attention to reading.

Proceedings of the College Reading Association, Reading and Language Arts Center, Syracuse University, Syracuse, New York.

The College Reading Association is a nationwide organization of college and university people investigating reading at all levels. The *Proceedings* of the annual conferences, published annually since 1959, are valuable for the high school teacher's professional library.

Reading: Grades 7–8–9, New York City Board of Education, Brooklyn, 1959 (coordinated by Joseph C. Gainsburg).

An excellent bulletin delineating many worthwhile procedures in secondary school classrooms. The details of each approach are carefully presented in Part Two. This guide is a must for the professional library.

Reading Improvement, Oshkosh, Wisconsin, Box 125.

A quarterly journal primarily devoted to reading in the secondary school, currently edited by Hugo Hartig. It has been printed since 1964.

Reading in Florida Secondary Schools, Florida State Department of Education, Bulletin 35C, Tallahassee, 1966.

This is a state-level guide to reading in the secondary school. Part III is especially good in delineating the roles of all members of the secondary school staff. Appendix E provides almost sixty unique suggestions for giving book reports.

Reading Newsreport, Sandra M. Brown, New York (11 West 42 Street, New York, N.Y. 10036).

A magazine carrying pictures and feature articles on new and exciting programs in reading. This is a popular, up-to-date news and feature magazine, unlike a traditional professional reading journal. It is a must for the teacher's room.

Sargent, Eileen E., Helen Huus, and Oliver Andressen: *How to Read a Book*, International Reading Association, Newark, Delaware, 1970.

An IRA bulletin (44 pages) in the "Reading Aids Series." Chapter 4, "Reading Narrative Materials in the Secondary School," is especially relevant. Appendixes A, B, and C, are very helpful.

Spache, George D.: *Good Reading for Disadvantaged Readers,* Garrard Publishing Company, Champaign, Ill., 1970. *Good Reading for Poor Readers,* Garrard Publishing Company, Champaign, Ill., 1970.

The latter, now in its fifth edition, is one of the standard reference works for the classroom teacher who is seeking an annotated list of books of high interest but low readability. It should be in every professional library.

Shaw, Phillip B.: *Effective Reading and Learning,* Thomas Y. Crowell Company, New York, 1956.

Although Shaw developed this as a book to aid college students, many of his suggestions are equally applicable to high school reading and learning. The first half ("Effective Reading") may be adapted by the high school classroom teacher.

Shepherd, David L.: *Effective Reading in Science,* Harper and Row, Publishers, Incorporated, New York, 1960.

One of the first books to deal exclusively with the techniques of improving science learning through reading skills. Formerly published by Row, Peterson & Co.

Shepherd, David L.: *Effective Reading in the Social Studies,* Harper and Row, Publishers, Incorporated, New York, 1961.

Shepherd presents some useful skill-development techniques specific to the social studies. This book was formerly published by Row, Peterson & Co.

Simpson, Elizabeth A.: *Helping High School Students Read Better,* Science Research Associates, Chicago, 1954.

This contains several very practical chapters on reading improvement programs in specific secondary schools during the 1950s.

Stewart, L. Jane, Frieda M. Heller, and Elsie J. Alberty: *Improving Reading in the Junior High School,* Appleton-Century-Crofts, Inc., New York, 1957.

This is a short monograph (67 pages) describing the cooperative work of the librarian and core teacher in the junior high school at Ohio State University. It describes the reading program used with eighth-grade youth and provides a statement of the outcomes of the program as encouragement to others to try it.

Squire, James: *Responses of Adolescents While Reading Four Short Stories,* National Council of Teachers of English, Research Report no. 2, Champaign, Ill., 1964.

This provides considerable insight into the feelings of young people, whose "feedback" was recorded and analyzed by Squire.

Thurber, Walter A., and Alfred T. Collette: *Teaching Science in Today's Secondary School,* Allyn and Bacon, Inc., Boston, 1964.

Chapter 18, "Encouraging Reading through Science," is an especially good addition to the literature in that area.

Weiss, M. Jerry: *The English Teacher's Reader,* The Odyssey Press, Inc., New York, 1962.

Although this is a collection of readings in the many aspects of teaching English (communication, composition, listening, usage, etc.), Part Seven and several other selections are specific to reading in the field of literature.

Weiss, M. Jerry: *Reading in the Secondary Schools,* The Odyssey Press, Inc., New York, 1961.

This paperback collection of readings on reading in the secondary school remains at the top of the list even though it does not contain some of the more recent articles. Weiss not only has selected articles from professional journals but also has included articles especially written for his book by noted authorities. Because of this, his collection of readings is well balanced. This book should be in every teacher's library.

Willard, Charles B.: *Your Reading: A Book List For Junior High Schools* (National Council of Teachers of English), Signet Books, New American Library, Inc., New York, 1966.

Yearbooks of the National Reading Conference, College of Education, University of Georgia, Athens, Georgia.

The National Reading Conference meets once annually and publishes papers presented on both college and secondary school reading problems. The *Yearbooks* have been published annually since 1952.

INDEX